SAP PRESS e-books

Print or e-book, Kindle or iPad, workplace or airplane: Choose where and how to read your SAP PRESS books! You can now get all our titles as e-books, too:

- By download and online access
- For all popular devices
- And, of course, DRM-free

Convinced? Then go to www.sap-press.com and get your e-book today.

Materials Planning with SAP®

SAP PRESS is a joint initiative of SAP and Rheinwerk Publishing. The know-how offered by SAP specialists combined with the expertise of Rheinwerk Publishing offers the reader expert books in the field. SAP PRESS features first-hand information and expert advice, and provides useful skills for professional decision-making.

SAP PRESS offers a variety of books on technical and business-related topics for the SAP user. For further information, please visit our website: *www.sap-press.com*.

Martin Murray, Jawad Akhtar
Materials Management with SAP ERP: Functionality and Technical Configuration (4th Edition)
2016, 739 pages, hardcover and e-book
www.sap-press.com/4062

Jawad Akhtar
Production Planning and Control with SAP ERP (2nd Edition)
2016, 940 pages, hardcover and e-book
www.sap-press.com/4191

Sandeep Pradhan
Demand and Supply Planning with SAP APO (2nd Edition)
2016, 831 pages, hardcover and e-book
www.sap-press.com/4011

Jochen Balla, Frank Layer
Production Planning with SAP APO (3rd Edition)
2015, 431 pages, hardcover and e-book
www.sap-press.com/3927

Uwe Goehring

Materials Planning with SAP®

Editor Hareem Shafi
Acquisitions Editor Emily Nicholls
Copyeditor Julie McNamee
Cover Design Graham Geary
Photo Credit Shutterstock.com/214947739/© StepanPopov
Layout Design Vera Brauner
Production Graham Geary
Typesetting III-satz, Husby (Germany)
Printed and bound in the United States of America, on paper from sustainable sources

ISBN 978-1-4932-1197-5
© 2018 by Rheinwerk Publishing, Inc., Boston (MA)
1st edition 2016, 1st reprint 2018

Library of Congress Cataloging-in-Publication Data
Goehring, Uwe.
Materials planning with SAP / Uwe Goehring. -- 1st edition.
pages cm
Includes index.
ISBN 978-1-4932-1197-5 (print : alk. paper) -- ISBN 1-4932-1197-8 (print : alk. paper) -- ISBN 978-1-4932-1198-2
(ebook) -- ISBN 978-1-4932-1199-9 (print and ebook) 1. Materials management--Data processing. 2. Business logistics--
Data processing. 3. Materials. 4. SAP-ERP. I. Title.
TS161.G64 2015
658.7--dc23
2015007511

Contents at a Glance

Dear Reader,

Materials planning has been a way of life in production and inventory management for half a century. In that time it has undergone multiple evolutions, eventually giving rise to the SAP ERP version of materials planning that you probably use (or wish to use) today.

SAP's MRP functionality offers users a range of processes that come together to create the four pillars of materials planning with SAP ERP: automated portfolio management, intelligent policy setting, prioritized exception monitoring, and continuous inventory optimization.

This scope means that materials planning with SAP is a complex topic, which requires a sharp mind and deft handling to teach. Uwe Goehring has accepted that challenge and risen to the task, producing this book, *Materials Planning with SAP*. In its pages you will find the information you need to develop a standardized, effective, and automated materials planning model for your business.

What did you think about *Materials Planning with SAP*? Your comments and suggestions are the most useful tools to help us make our books the best they can be. Please feel free to contact me and share any praise or criticism you may have.

Thank you for purchasing a book from SAP PRESS!

Hareem Shafi
Editor, SAP PRESS

Rheinwerk Publishing
Boston, MA

hareems@rheinwerk-publishing.com
www.sap-press.com

Contents

PART II Materials Planning in SAP ERP

PART III Evaluating, Measuring, and Improving Materials Planning

PART IV Modeling Materials Planning

PART I

Materials Planning Basics

Being busy does not always mean real work. The object of all work is production or accomplishment and to either of these ends there must be forethought, system, planning, intelligence, and honest purpose, as well as perspiration. Seeming to do is not doing.
—*Thomas A. Edison*

1   Materials Planning Basics

Materials planning, sometimes called *material requirements planning* (MRP), is a system developed to control inventory and manage manufacturing processes, such as the planning of component or raw material availability. Before Joseph Orlicky came up with the concept of MRP in 1964, reorder point/reorder quantity (ROP/ROQ)-type methods such as Economic Order Quantity (EOQ) were used in manufacturing, procurement, and inventory management. When MRP arrived it partially replaced these policies with more flexible and (in some cases) more fitting planning modes such as deterministic planning, time-phased replenishment, and forecast based ordering.

Subsequently MRP was developed into manufacturing resource planning (MRP II), which further includes the functions of rough resource planning, master scheduling, capacity planning, and sales & operations planning. From here on, the software industry took on most of the functionality, and SAP ERP was born.

Evolving from the R/2 system of the 1980s, today's SAP functionality in this area allows you to control inventory, schedule production, forecast customer demands, procure raw materials, manage capacities and resources, and watch your fill rates and service levels. SAP's functions for materials planning therefore serve as the interface between demand and supply. As such, materials planning in SAP ERP is intended to primarily meet three objectives:

- ▸ Ensure materials are available for production and products are available for delivery to customers
- ▸ Maintain the lowest possible material and product levels in the warehouses

▸ Plan manufacturing activities, delivery schedules, and purchasing activities

These functions become more important as customers demand products faster than they can actually be manufactured.

As you'll see throughout this book, the foundation of this materials planning system has four pillars:

▸ Automated portfolio management

▸ Intelligent policy setting

▸ Prioritized exception monitoring

▸ Continuous inventory optimization

As we explore a comprehensive materials planning system like the one described, these four topics will guide us in the pursuit of a standardized, effective, automated, and agile model to plan materials with standard SAP. Before we get started with the specifics, however, let's go over the basic process of materials planning.

1.1   The Process of Materials Planning

Because materials planning is so involved in the process of flowing product efficiently through the value stream, it should be designed as a set of repeatable tasks—a sequence of steps that considers demand and resource constraints as its boundaries within which optimization takes place. Materials planning lies between the functions of sales and operations planning to the north and external and internal procurement to the south. In other words, materials planning represents the connection between demand and supply.

As information flows through this system, the planner has to respect the gates that divide the inventory, the plan, and the schedule (see Figure 1.1). This is important because there are terms and conditions which constrain the free flow of information and material. We all know that there are vendor terms and conditions, but do we also respect the conditions at the production lines? Or do we consider constraints for the materials planner when we put together a sales plan? Gate control in these areas is often forgotten or simply neglected because silos exist in which isolated planning takes place.

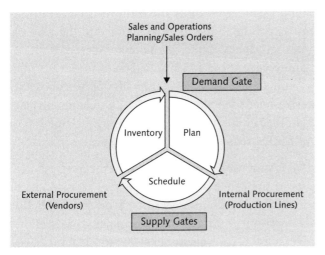

Sales and Operations
Planning/Sales Orders

Demand Gate

Inventory Plan

Schedule

External Procurement
(Vendors)

Internal Procurement
(Production Lines)

Supply Gates

Figure 1.1 Planning Cycle with Demand and Supply Gates

Materials planning, which is the central function within the planning cycle for sales and operations planning, production, and procurement, sits between the demand gate that represent the receipt of planned and actual requirements and the two gates for internal and external supply of manufactured products and purchased materials. As such, materials planning acts as an engine to fulfill the demand with the highest possible service levels and the lowest possible resource buffer (note that the resource buffer may be inventory but also capacity or time). This is quite a task to fulfill, and it becomes obvious that when things constantly change, the materials planner can't produce good results. Take sales and operations planning as an example; often a consensus plan is loaded into MRP without a feasibility check. Consequently, the numbers a sales and marketing team comes up with for the next 6 to 12 months are by no means the automatically accepted supply plan—but that is exactly what we tell the SAP system when we load the resulting requirements into Transaction MD61.

Consequently, gate control has to be executed before we transfer the demand toward the material planner, and our Sales and Operations Planning department has to perform a rough resource check and negotiate with various fractions a feasible demand plan, considering all constraints, terms, and conditions. Then, through the critical decision of make-to-stock (MTS) versus make-to-order (MTO), requirements will build the starting point for the process of materials planning.

At some point in time, the planning procedure is executed. The MRP run performs a net requirements calculation according to the rules maintained in the material master and creates supply proposals. It also explodes the bill of materials (BOM) and therewith hands down required quantities and required dates so that a further net requirements calculation—and a subsequent generation of supply proposals—can be carried out for all materials needed to meet the primary demand. The planning run does all that automatically, in the background, based on the rule set, or policy, maintained in the four MRP screens of the material master.

Now we have a supply plan that is supposed to meet demand in the most efficient way. This supply plan consists of the order proposals, purchase requisitions or planned orders, and the associated exception messages that provide information about feasibility, order status, structural problems, timely problems, or inventory availability. The MRP controller's job is to evaluate these exceptional messages, fine-tune the supply plan, keep the master data effective, and generally balance demand with supply from a pure planning perspective without any consideration of capacity constraints, supplier conditions, or forecast deviations.

So the last step in the process of materials planning is to hand over the MRP supply plan to the buyers and the production schedulers for application of constraints, terms, and conditions; for the assignment of suppliers and production lines; and for the actual execution of the plan.

And herein lies a big misconception about the job of materials planners. Expediting is *not* actually the job of the MRP controller. All too often we see materials planners being tasked with the actual procurement of raw materials or the determination of a production schedule. If one person has all of these roles, that's not necessarily a problem, but materials planning will have to be finished *before* the MRP supply plan is handed over to Procurement and Production Scheduling, who then apply their constraints, terms, and conditions to arrive at the finite, short-term supply plan. The buyer or production scheduler should negotiate with the supplier or switch the jobs on the production line.

This delegation of duties is important to note. Materials planning is the process of balancing supply to a given demand (planned or actual) under the condition of planning parameters that are part of the supply chain strategy your company has defined—and *not* under the conditions of how well your suppliers deliver or how effective your production lines operate. If we mix materials planning with expediting and exceptional situations, we won't derive a supply plan that is best on our management's strategy and direction. If lines between what we're striving for and what we're actually achieving blur, it's hard to measure the difference.

Effective materials planning will generate a supply plan that is in line with a well-thought-out and feasible supply chain strategy. Whether that plan can be executed well is an entirely different question, and partially dependent on the materials controller.

1.2 The Materials Controller

Bad decisions in the area of materials planning cause lost money and customers. More specifically, if a materials controller procures insufficient quantities of raw materials, customer demand can't be met, which reduces the company's revenue. On the other hand, if excessive material is purchased or manufactured, money is wasted, and inventories pile up.

Therefore, the position of materials planner or, even better, materials controller is a very important one and contributes considerably to the success of a manufacturing or distribution company.

In the old days—and, scarily enough, in many of today's materials planning departments—the materials controller always answered these questions:

▸ What do we need?

▸ When do we need it?

▸ How much do we need?

These are questions that when answered, only resolve *part* of the problem because they assume we know beforehand what to come and what our business can expect. But if there is even the slightest difference between the forecast and the real world—and uncertainty is certainly part of our lives—then we don't really need that material at that time in that quantity. Instead, we ultimately need a different material, or at a different time, or in a different quantity. Therefore a better question to ask is, "Given our system and environment, where should we place resources (inventory, capacity, time) to have the best protection?"

This new way of planning resources and materials is called buffer management. And you need to design and place the buffer depending on the individual conditions (predictability, expense, scarcity, newness) of your materials.

But one buffer alone can't protect your entire portfolio. What kind of buffer you need depends on the conditions and the situation the material represents. If you want to protect boats in a marina, as illustrated in Figure 1.2, you'll have to consider what types of boats and what type of marina you want to protect. If you have a marina on a glassy pond, you really don't need much, if any, protection, but if your marina is on Lake Michigan, you want to build a break wall that can withstand 5 to 10 foot waves in case of a storm. For a marina in southern Florida, you'll have to design your buffer a lot bigger if you have boats in there during hurricane season.

Figure 1.2 Different Situations Require Different Measures

And so it is with materials planning. Every material has its own, ever changing, conditions—its own story—and buffers have to be planned and designed for it.

But even if you plan and design your buffers flawlessly, there are plenty of ways MRP can go wrong in your system. Because SAP's MRP run explodes a BOM using planned or actual demand to derive at a supply suggestion, you need to ensure that the BOM is free of any errors. Data integrity is a common problem in companies that use SAP MRP. Very often, incorrect material master setups, faulty routings or BOMs, and outdated elements limit the MRP's ability to produce good results.

1.3   Strategic and Tactical Materials Planning

The importance and complexity of the material planner's job means that there cannot be just one method a materials planner uses to complete his job.

One challenge a materials planner often encounters is working with endless lists of materials. This situation arises more frequently than you might think, because companies tend to set up their MRP controller keys incorrectly.

The MRP controller key in the material master's MRP1 screen allows for the assignment of a portfolio of materials to an actual person in your organization. This way, a company's materials planning activities are usually executed by a number of MRP controllers. And so, after implementation, there are between 5 and 30 MRP controller keys in the corresponding Customizing table, depending on the size of the company. People's names are on the key, the materials are assigned, and all of a sudden a planner finds himself tasked with a list of thousands of materials when calling up Transaction MD07. Some documentation is handed out, maybe a training class on MRP, and off you go with your portfolio.

Then the entire service responsibility rests on the planner's shoulder. If material isn't available to run the production lines, everybody points to materials planning, and, as a result, human caution kicks in and safety stocks are increased. Then, when the quarterly inventory report comes out, management decides to improve on performance, and the planner is informed of an inventory reduction initiative. Because no one was ever trained in SAP inventory analysis (there was no data right after implementation), everyone resorts to spreadsheets and concludes that there is too much inventory lying around, and the planner has to come up with a way to reduce the holdings. So safety stocks are taken off, purchase orders and long-term contracts with vendors are cut, and materials with high average inventory values are targeted for reduction. In the short term, turns are going up, averages go down, and the performance report shows improvements.

However, because the planner had no particular plan or model to take important conditions such as higher consumption or slow movers into consideration, the availability for critically needed materials suddenly drops significantly, and throughput from production falls off. A throughput reduction stands in direct proportion to lost sales, so again, everybody looks at the MRP controller, who is told to do something. What's there to do? Bring more in, of course!

This never-ending cycle comes from a lack of an effective system or model for materials planning. Such a model is proposed in the following chapters throughout the book. One of its cornerstones is the introduction of the roles of strategic and tactical materials planners.

1.3.1 The Role of a Strategic Materials Planner

Strategic direction in the supply chain is more important than ever before, but yet, in many organizations, it's still lacking. Materials planners are getting confused more often than not about where to focus.

From our client visits, we can identify an overarching trend: because a missing part holding up production is considered the worst immediate problem, every person responsible for materials planning plans for more inventory than necessary to avoid the danger of lacking available material. Additionally, because the basic data isn't maintained very well, the system produces suboptimal supply proposals, and the materials planner loses trust in the outcome of the MRP run and resorts to spreadsheets and third-party bolt-ons. As a result, inventory and service levels aren't driven off of a strategy and its supporting policies, but are instead calculated manually and without regard to support from integrated SAP data.

That scenario makes good inventory planning difficult. When inventory levels higher than what was desired show up in management reports, management complains and engages in an inventory reduction project. Consultants and thought leaders are hired for a project and execute some standard methodology to reduce inventory. Often the consulting partner proposes a gain share model, and the materials planner is forced into a dangerous endeavor often disguised as an educational exercise. In the end, it's sometimes catastrophic because measures are taken in brutal pursuit of reducing cash tied up in inventory without any regard for conditions, situations, and differences in terms of predictability, consumption, value, replenishment time, or lifecycle status.

When inventories fall outside of their control limits, there is always a combination of problems. Some materials have too much stock; some too little. The key is to have the right material in the right quantity at the right place at the right time, and, therefore, an optimization or right-sizing of inventory is required.

Besides the fact that inventory optimization should never be a project but an ongoing effort, it should be clear that inventories won't come down quickly when done right. In most cases, too much inventory results from materials that don't turn fast or have slow consumption: the slow movers. Of the fast-moving materials with high consumption, it's often difficult to get enough stock to hold on to. During a right-sizing effort, the fast mover's inventory needs to be increased first, while the slow movers naturally don't get consumed fast enough. Accordingly, the inventory initially rises even more. Only over a longer period of time will we find that our surplus inventory drops while service levels stay steady, or even improve.

How can this be avoided, and how can we right-size inventory and keep service levels high? A strategic materials planner, who is equipped with the tools and competence to translate a supply chain strategy into planning and replenishment policies can make a big difference. This person's responsibility is to integrate management's targets, goals, and direction into a tactical execution to purchase materials and manufacture products. A strategic materials planner analyzes entire portfolios and sets overall policy on a periodic basis. His task isn't to tend to specific exceptions but rather to set the stage for automated replenishment on a group level. A strategic materials planner, as an example, finds all materials with predictable consumption, high consumption value, low price, low risk, and short lead time, and then gives all these materials a reorder level policy. This updates a large number of materials, and the fine-tuning can then be done in tactical planning with the exception monitor.

Example: Nature

In nature, strategic materials planning is evident in the equipping of animals with feeder policies depending on the climate zone of their habitats, their size, their capabilities to hunt, and their survival profiles. That is why a bear has a time-phased policy that shuts down the organism to make sure they can hibernate during the winter. Squirrels possess consumption-based policies, whereby they collect large amounts of inventory and safety stocks, and predators such as crocodiles go deterministic—they plan on demand (they wait until they get hungry before they hunt for fresh food). This kind of general policy for various feeder families is being set strategically. How a lioness acts when there is a shortage of zebras (maybe she then pursues other sources of meat) or how much safety stock a squirrel holds depends on many different influencing factors and is resolved with the tactical adjustment and fine-tuning of the policy.

A strategic materials planner sets the overall baseline strategy and makes sure that the tactical materials planner is handed a clean portfolio that adheres to the global supply chain strategy and has general policies in place. He also serves as the communication hub between management and execution, so that the plan is clear, concise, and supports great service levels with the least inventory investment possible.

A suggested periodicity for strategic materials planning can be taken from Figure 1.3. As quarterly strategy sessions define performance boundaries and general strategy, the strategic materials planner takes action monthly a few days after demand planning has come up with a requirements program and set buffering strategies. Strategic materials planning takes on classification or segmentation and sets overall policy for the tactical materials planner to expedite, fine-tunes policy, and reschedules from here on out.

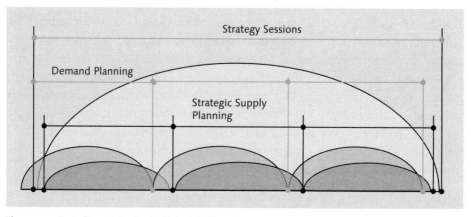

Figure 1.3 Periodic and Strategic Materials Planning

1.3.2 The Tasks of a Tactical Materials Planner

Tactical materials planning is carried out daily. It usually starts early in the morning when last night's MRP run is evaluated, and priorities are set. Because of the often-large amount of exception messages, it's important to approach tasks such as handling exceptions, expediting purchase orders, and adjusting policies in a methodical fashion. Prioritization is key, and SAP has done a great job of grouping preconfigured exceptions into the system. Of course, you're free to reshuffle these group codes and their associated messages, but we very strongly suggest you first develop a comprehensive system of prioritized portfolio management or simply take a deep dive to understand the thinking behind what those smart developers had in mind when they came up with the groupings delivered with the initial setup.

In what sequence you work these groups is often a matter of choice, but successful tactical planners mostly use a similar style. Figure 1.4 shows a suggestion we developed on a materials planning project. It depicts a typical day in the life of a tactical materials planner.

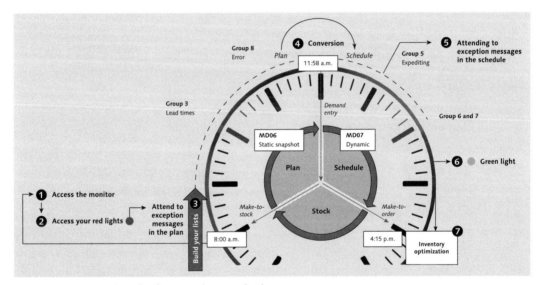

Figure 1.4 A Day in the Life of a Tactical Materials Planner

In this proposed standard operating procedure, the planner starts off in Transaction MD06 looking at MRP lists ❶. These MRP lists are still fairly close to the time they were generated, and only those materials that were planned last night are showing up in the collective display.

Then materials with red traffic lights ❷ are investigated. Those materials all have demand elements from the past and therefore need immediate attention.

Exception messages come next ❸. These usually cause a delay in starting, in conversion, in finishing or delivery. Also of importance are group 8 messages, which indicate an abnormal end of the MRP run and, by the way, only show up in Transaction MD06—you can't see them in Transaction MD07. The same is true for group 4 messages, which are of informational character. They're generated when a new demand drops in, a customer changed his mind, or anything happened with the effect that the MRP run needed to change or add to the supply plan on short notice.

At some point in time—here, at around noon—the planner needs to switch over to a more dynamic stock/requirements situation and start conversion of order proposals into fixed purchase orders ❹. Transaction MD07 provides a collective list of the actual situation of all materials in the entire portfolio, and attending to group 7 (rescheduling) messages ❺. This is the time to call vendors and check with the production floor. Very often people argue that the expediting should take place first thing in the morning; however, this is incorrect because MRP doesn't work on any more detailed level than "daily," and have you ever seen a supplier pushing the delivery to 3 p.m. when you called them at 9 a.m.? Maybe they have, but we're talking about a general model here and how a tactical materials planner could design his day in the most effective way.

Exception messages might have come up that are related to problems in the basic data structure. A recursive BOM, scheduling errors due to false basic date adjustment rules, or incorrect routing type allocation may all cause the generation of group 5 exception messages that need attention and fixing ❻.

Toward the end of the day, there should be some room to look for inventory reduction ❼. Most of the tactical planner's day is filled with the task of avoiding stock-outs. Rarely is there time to tend to the overstocked materials and apply policies to save money. In fact, most of the materials planners we know are overwhelmed with expediting shortages, which isn't a very good situation. Today's companies have to find a way to enable their MRP controllers to set policy instead of constantly putting out fires, to find ways to reduce superfluous stock instead of buffering out of convenience or lack of time, to prioritize and classify instead of looking at thousands of materials every day, and to gain control over a list of materials they're expected to manage. This can all be accomplished with the right tools, competence, and intuition.

In fact, SAP provides all the tools and functionality for exactly that. You just have to know where to look and actually leverage those tools.

1.4   Portfolio Segmentation for Decision Making

Segmentation and classification of material portfolios is one of, if not the, most powerful function in materials planning. It makes your portfolio manageable, allows for automated policy setting, and helps you evaluate and measure performance. *Segmentation* is what classifies your materials and tells their stories. Once executed, you can see if a material is predictable; valuable; bulky or easy to handle; and has high consumption, regular consumption, or slow consumption. You can see if the material is new and was created just recently or if it's obsolete, has a short or long replenishment lead time, and if it needs attention because its master data has errors.

We generally suggest that you classify in six dimensions:

▶ **ABC analysis**
The old ABC analysis looks for consumption value. Be careful, because ABC analysis isn't that useful just by itself. A cheap material that is consumed heavily every day, and therefore classified as an A item, is very different from an expensive item that's consumed rarely and also classified as A. Both have a high consumption value, but you can't apply the same policy.

▶ **UVW classification**
A UVW classification, on the other hand, can be very helpful because it separates the low-cost items from the high-cost items and therefore allows you to apply a different policy to your AU parts than your AW parts (more about that in Chapter 5).

▶ **EFG classification**
In this useful classification, E items are those that have a short replenishment lead time, F have a medium lead time, and G have a very long lead time. Replenishment lead time represents the time that it takes to fulfill a requirement when there isn't inventory—whether via purchasing or in-house production.

▶ **LMN analysis**
The LMN analysis separates bulky and big materials from the ones that are small and easy to store.

▶ **XYZ segmentation**
Everybody needs to perform an XYZ segmentation. Although a bit more complex and involved than the others, without it, good materials planning isn't possible.

Unfortunately, standard SAP ERP software doesn't provide functionality to execute an XYZ analysis. You have to resort to Excel, third-party bolt-ons, or the SAP add-on tools (see Chapter 6, Section 6.6). XYZ-classified materials tell you more about the consumption history, predictability for the future, and what policy is most fitting. In an XYZ run, the past is analyzed for its consumption postings in terms of regularity. If a material turns out to have similar consumption postings (quantities consumed) from period to period, it will be classified as an X item. The way the run determines that characteristic is through a *coefficient of variation*.

A very small coefficient means that the consumption in the past was regular from month to month and from week to week. A coefficient smaller than 0.5 usually indicates very high regularity, whereas a coefficient greater than 1.5 shows that part was consumed very irregular in the past months and therefore is classified as Z.

▸ **Lifecycle analysis**
The lifecycle analysis is indispensable for materials planning but rarely used correctly. A lifecycle analysis, as the name implies, structures your portfolio according to the material's position along its maturation and lifespan—from its inception to its deletion from the system. Although lifecycle analysis has many uses, probably its most important is the obsoleting process that follows the identification of slow movers and outdated parts.

However, identifying obsoletes isn't enough. With the lifecycle analysis, you can treat newly created parts from the ones that have a lot of historical data, you can identify slow movers and very slow movers, and you can clean your portfolios from the items marked for deletion.

These are all very useful dimensions, and you can probably think of more. Unfortunately, only one (not the most useful one) is standard in SAP ERP: the ABC analysis.

As just described, the ABC analysis goes by consumption value but isn't all that useful by itself. There are ways to perform the other segmentation methods in Excel or a database system such as Access, or you can purchase a bolt-on from a third party. You can also use the Logistics Information System (LIS) inside SAP ERP.

Dual classification allows you to do some limited analysis of all kinds. But it isn't the Holy Grail. In later chapters, we'll discuss SAP's native add-on tools that do a wonderful job with this, as well as in other areas where standard SAP exposes some white spots. Perfectly integrated and managed by standard Customizing transports, these tools provide immense optimization potential and are indispensable for the progression of the use of your SAP system. But they don't come with the standard delivery of SAP software licenses. You'll have to initiate an extra effort to use them, which you'll have to do anyway to become an organization that performs world-class materials planning, controlling, or management.

Let's first look at an example of where portfolio segmentation comes in very handy, and then we'll get into some of the strategies.

1.4.1 Portfolio Management Example

The more you fly with a specific airline, and lately the more you spend, the more perks you get through the status the airline awards you. The rewards program for United Airlines consists of Silver, Gold, 1K, and Global Services levels; if you reach predetermined milestones in mileage flown, money spent, and number of segments flown, you move up through the ranks.

Besides rewards travel and purchases perks, you get treated differently. As a 1K member, you can get upgraded to First Class if there is space available. The kicker is that when a person with 1K status books coach, he outranks the Gold and Silver members on the priority list. So unless there is another 1K with higher priority, our 1K flyer usually sits up front if a seat is available. If there were Global Services members also gearing for an upgrade, they'd outrank the 1K flyer too, but they're not generally purchasing coach tickets and hoping for an upgrade.

So who are these Global Services members and how do you become one? A mystical aura surrounds this select group of people; maybe you have to fly a gazillion miles per year, or perhaps spend large amounts of money per year on airfare. Many think that United selects its 1% or 2% top spenders every year and then rolls out the red carpet. As a Global Services member, you never miss a flight because they'd probably drive you over the tarmac if necessary or pick you up from home. You have your own little waiting section at the airport and you get some other nice treats that the lower level flyers don't know about because they've never been invited into the club.

So why does United offer such a program, if it costs the company, too? Well, there is the obvious hook for frequent flyers. Once in the program, you'd rather pay a few bucks more for United's flight and get the frequent flier miles than fly on a cheaper flight with another airline. But there is also another reason: customer relationship management. Offering a rewards program enables United to effectively manage its customer portfolio. Hundreds of thousands of customers are categorized, classified, segmented, and managed accordingly:

▶ The select few that contribute the most revenue get the most attention; for example, United can't afford to have a single exception cause a disruption for a Global Services member.

▶ Using the Pareto principle, we can say that 20% of United's flyers are in the rewards program, and together, with their frequent flying, they make up close to 80% of the yearly revenue. That's a fairly manageable amount of people that need to be kept happy. Give them upgrades once in a while, allow them to walk regally through a priority lane, treat their luggage with preference, let them wait in the lounge where you can give them drinks, and manage their rerouting automatically when their flight gets canceled. That is still a very large amount of attention United must provide, but there are standard operation procedures and policies that automate these services.

▶ And then there is the occasional flyer: vacationers, Thanksgiving travelers, and the reluctant business traveler. Besides the most basic service to get them from A to B, they don't get much more for the price of their ticket.

All of this tracking miles, rewarding loyal customers, and creating hoopla about flying as many miles as possible means United gains exceptional control over the planning process. Leadership can hand out directions and strategies for the next fiscal year. Management can then translate these strategies into policies such as, "To increase our customer base with frequent flyers, we'll hand out 20% more upgrades and increase our First Class cabins by the same margin." The planners take over from there and take appropriate steps to execute on the direction given by top management. United has total control over its CRM strategies, and everybody works toward the same goals—on a strategic as well as a tactical level. This is portfolio management at its finest!

1.4.2 Strategies in an Enterprise

A supply chain management conference speaker once asserted that "every company needs a supply chain strategy." Not many companies have one—or at least not many have clear and concise tactics that are communicated well throughout the organization.

Here's the thing: A directive from top management to "reduce inventory by 30%" isn't a well-defined strategy, and neither is the project to "increase service levels." A good strategy needs to consider all influencing factors and must be integrated so that all noses point in the same direction.

In the military, *commander's intent* is a term which indicates that the boss' direction is understood perfectly by everybody involved. Every good leader has a good strategy. And every efficient organization knows their leader's intent. For example, all employees at Southwest Airlines know and act on the CEO's intent. Herb Kelleher says to his people: "We are *the* low cost airline. Once you understand that fact, you can make any decision about this company's future as well as I can." The next time you fly on Southwest, ask your flight attendant why Southwest doesn't have first class seats, foie gras for dinner, or luggage fees. His answer will be the same as the person who checked you in because they all work toward the same goal: to be *the* low cost airline, it's not that hard to make decisions on problems such as "expensive or cheap food," "expensive seats or more seats," "expedited boarding process or first-class waiting lounge."

So it should be with your materials planning strategies. The defined strategy is your commander's intent. For some, sales and operations planning is simply forecasting; for others, it's financial budgeting. Many companies, however, integrate their financial planning with a sales forecast on the product group level, and the real good ones also roughly check whether the plant's capacity suffices and then subsequently ensure a proper transfer of demand. They also reevaluate their product strategy (MTS vs. MTO vs. finish-to-stock vs. assemble-to-order) and make the appropriate adjustments in the master data. Is all of that done inside SAP functionality without the use of external applications? Mostly, no, and here lies the crux of the matter: If you don't integrate finance with sales, if you don't connect the production department with a feasible plan, if you don't make the proper distinction between MTS and MTO, and if you work in various, different systems, you'll have a very hard time communicating the commander's intent.

A good supply chain strategy carries information about what products we stock and how much of it, what we need to invest in (resources and capital), what our profit will be, what lead times we'll promise for each product, who will make up our supplier network, and what our Plan B will be in case of variability. *This* is the strategy, policy, and general direction everybody should work toward. In short, this is the commander's intent.

So how do we implement the commander's intent into our materials planning? We need to translate the strategy into policies that drive automation, good inventory levels, and great service.

Figure 1.5 shows a hierarchical structure as to how strategies can be communicated throughout the organization. The overall company strategy is defined in each business unit and then gets broken down into financial, HR, sales, and supply chain strategies. The supply chain strategies in turn, can then be broken down into the following:

▸ **Replenishment strategies**
Focus on the MRP type on the MRP1 view (but also much more) to define the policies on how to replenish primarily raw materials.

▸ **Planning strategies**
Focus on the strategy group on the MRP3 view (but also much more) to define how the plan (sales and operations) is executed for production materials.

▸ **Scheduling strategies**
Focus on the correct production type and the associated production scheduling methods.

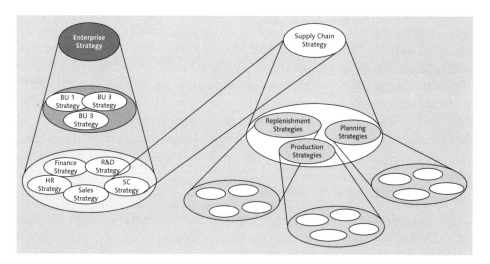

Figure 1.5 Strategies in an Enterprise

Before any definition of a strategy, the strategist will have to be aware of the conundrum faced when trying to find the perfect balance between supply and demand. And sometimes you might wonder why your continuous improvement program feels like you're moving in circles. This can be because you have to deal with conflicting goals. You can only increase profitability if a clear direction and strategy is identified and put into action. This direction requires an understanding of what's happening when a company is made up of different interest groups who try to achieve potentially differing goals.

On one hand, costs need to be reduced, and on the other, we need to increase income, revenue, or sales. To reduce costs, companies usually strive to reduce working capital (work in process [WIP], stocks, resources, etc.) and save on the cost of procurement or production. They optimize their planning processes so that they can execute more efficiently. To get the expected result, we need low inventories in raw, semi, and finished goods; high utilization of resources; and less variability in demand and supply.

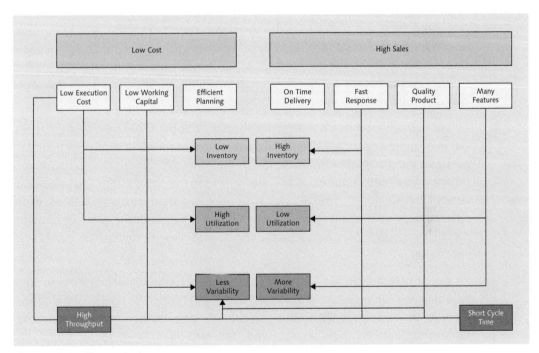

Figure 1.6 Conflicting Goals

The other side of the coin is the desired increase in sales that can be achieved by fast response to customer's wishes, on-time delivery, very high quality with less waste and scrap, and offering a wide variety of options and customized features in the finished product. Logically, this requires ample supply of all variants of the finished good and ample capacity on the production lines so rush orders can be attended to quickly, which results in a lot of variability (see Figure 1.6).

Desired low cost and high sales can't be viewed separately. Effective and lean materials planning requires a reduction in variability, and a more attractive product offering with more options and features ultimately generates more variability. Low-cost production is based on high utilization, whereas a fast response to special customer requirements needs a lot of free capacity. And cost-effective materials planning drives low inventory, whereas high availability dictates high safety stocks. There are many trade-offs that must be considered in your planning and in the definition of strategies, tactics, or policies.

1.4.3 Segmentation for Replenishment Strategies

Out of the three sets of strategies discussed, replenishment strategies are the most important for materials planning. They break down into individual policies that represent rule sets in the master data. In this book, we'll talk about policies a lot. *Policies* are the cornerstones of materials planning; most of the work that MRP controllers do revolves around policy setting.

Before you can maintain a replenishment policy in the four screens of the material master, however, you should perform a segmentation to split your materials portfolio into categories and materials that are identified by their specific characteristics: low consumption, high value, expensive, consistent consumption, newly created, bulky, or small. Each material gets a status to assign it to a specific characteristic so that eventually you're able to generate a list of materials with specific properties. Materials with the same properties can then be assigned a specific policy.

As you can see in Figure 1.7, policies are assigned to the segmentation according to which you can maintain all AX materials to a very specific policy. Should there be more than one possible policy, you enhance your segmentation with an additional analysis to get more accurate and granular.

For example, should you decide to maintain all X and C materials with a consumption-based replenishment policy, you could determine that those XC materials with a short lead time will get a reorder planning procedure, while XC materials with *long* lead times get a material forecast, which allows for the preplanning of supply elements.

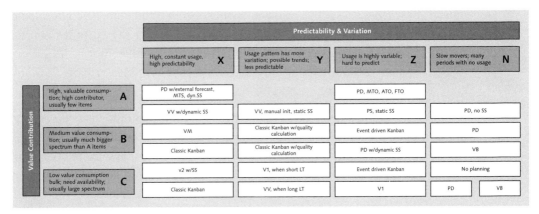

Figure 1.7 Segmentation for Replenishment Strategies

Portfolio segmentation is very powerful because it allows for the adjustment of the policy on a periodic basis and doesn't require looking up and analyzing each individual material. With segmentation, you can group materials for their likeness and properties and then update them collectively with a fitting policy. The greatest advantage of such a system is the ability to repeat the process periodically: month by month or quarter by quarter. As we all know, what's valuable and regularly consumed today might not be so tomorrow, and leaving an automated replenishment policy on an obsolete material is very inefficient and costly to the company.

1.5   Lean and Agile Supply Chains

In recent years, there has been much talk about "agile" and "lean" supply chains. They're by no means exclusive of each other, and neither are new ideas. To be flexible to your customer's requirements and to manufacture and deliver product without much extra weight (cost) has been a goal for a long time. Materials planning plays a big part in the overall effort to keep supply chains lean and agile, in that it controls replenishment to provide low inventory cost with high availability.

Many experts say that the main focus of lean is inward (to reduce waste and therefore reduce cost) and that the main focus of agile is outward toward the customer (to increase flexibility to achieve quicker response time and shorter lead times). That makes sense, but who wants only one over the other? No one should start a project with the goal of reducing cost and leaving the customer service alone. No one should increase product offerings and promise shorter lead times to the customer without making sure that the production lines support flow and don't produce much WIP.

Although you don't want to *neglect* one over the other, you may have to *emphasize* one over the other. Several factors impact the design decision regarding whether a supply chain should be more agile or lean. Nowadays, more often than not, supply chains compete, not companies. This implies that not only must companies orient themselves on the market but also on supply chains. Market orientation can be analyzed using the market winner/market qualifier concept. This also means that there is a different focus on the lean or the agile supply chain. As shown in Figure 1.8, an agile supply chain focuses on service level first, whereas the lean supply chain is oriented primarily on cost.

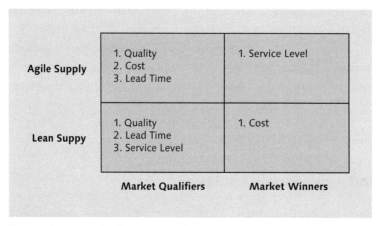

Figure 1.8 Lean and Agile Supply Chains

In terms of combining lean and agile, you can use various strategies. The following three are worth mentioning:

► **80/20 approach**
   Only a few products make most of the overall volume (20% make 80% of the volume). Therefore, for the high-volume products, choose a lean approach, while for the low-volume products, an agile strategy is better suited.

▶ **Inventory/order interface or decoupling point approach**
Strategic inventory can act as a decoupling point within a supply chain. If you select this point wisely, it's beneficial to use a lean strategy up to this point and an agile strategy after this point.

▶ **Base and surge demand**
Lean and agile strategies can also be combined if the demand pattern shows a base demand. This demand is produced using a lean strategy, while the surge is covered with a more agile approach.

Much of this book is dedicated to building a model in materials planning that allows for a flexible approach to setting the right strategy or policy, so that the lean supply chain is combined with the agile supply chain for best possible performance.

1.5.1   Pushing, Pulling, or Both?

A supply chain is like a pressure system. It has levers with which you control flow of materials, and you can either apply pressure on the upstream side of the supply chain to push materials through the system using a plan or forecast, or you can wait and see what happens and then pull with exactly the demand that occurs from your system.

The levers are procurement (where you buy components, raw materials, and maintenance, repair, operations [MRO] solution), production scheduling (where you control the flow of production quantities), and sales (where your customers dictate what happens). Materials planning generates procurement proposals with quantities and suggested delivery dates based on planned and actual demand. Procurement then opens or closes the levers to control the flow of incoming materials. If the demand comes from a forecast through the BOM, then deliveries are scheduled ahead of time, and the goods receipts are put away into inventory. The same is true for purchased parts or raw materials that are bought based on consumption-based planning policies. That inventory is issued to production when orders there are asking for it. Discrepancies between what's coming in from suppliers and what goes out to the line cause inventory to build up.

The same is true for the production scheduling lever. Materials planning may generate planned orders as a proposal for what quantities to produce for what delivery dates based on a forecast through the BOM. The receipts from these production orders are then put in inventory again, and sales picks them up for deliveries to the customer. And if the rate of sales doesn't match the rate of production based on the forecast, inventories pile up.

Even your sales can be anticipated by a forecast. What has been described so far is a pure "push" system, which has the effect that inventories develop to buffer variability. (We'll get into the three buffers that develop when variability is present—inventory, time, capacity—in Chapter 8.) You can read much more about this in *Factory Physics* (Waverly Press, 2011) by Wallace Hopp and Mark Spearman. Such a push system is depicted in Figure 1.9.

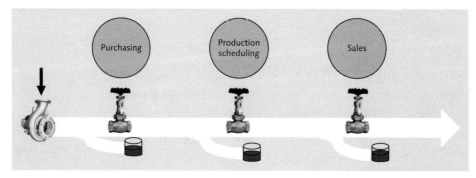

Figure 1.9 A Push System

On the other hand, we can apply suction on the downstream side of the supply chain. In that case, we don't need a plan or a forecast. Because we simply wait until demand arrives from the customer, we can purchase, produce, and deliver perfectly demand driven, which means that we procure only that what we need when we need it, we produce to a production schedule that leaves no superfluous inventory, and we deliver directly what comes from the production lines. Such a "pull" system is depicted in Figure 1.10 with the buffer time developing at each lever.

As you can see, as the inventory disappears, another buffer appears; in this case, we need time to buffer variability. Because we only start procurement and production when actual demand exists, we can't simply pick up the finished product from inventory and ship it to the customer; we have to wait until it's produced. We might also have to wait until all the needed semi-finished products are procured for the raw materials from the supplier because we waited with the order until we knew exactly what we needed. A pure pull system has a replenishment lead time for finished products that includes the entire chain from supplier lead times through the whole production cycle to the delivery time through the distribution network to the customer.

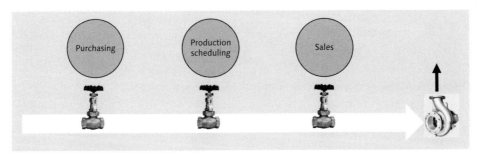

Figure 1.10 A Pull System

As you can see, there are disadvantages and advantages to both systems. Ideally, we find the happy medium, which could be a combination of push and pull, to leverage the advantages of both and reduce the disadvantages of both. That combination can be achieved with an *inventory/order interface* (this is often referred to as the *decoupling point*). The inventory/order interface sits somewhere in the middle between the upstream and the downstream ends of the supply chain. Where it sits exactly is a design issue that needs to be carefully evaluated. In any case, to the upstream side of the inventory/order interface lies a push system with inventories to buffer so that the lead time disappears, and to the downstream side of the inventory/order interface is a pull system with no inventories but a—now shortened—lead time to the customer. Figure 1.11 shows an example of the placement for the inventory/order interface.

Theoretically, you now have a lean supply chain with little waste if you can forecast the inventories in front of the inventory/order interface well, and you have an agile supply chain because you can wait until your customer tells you exactly what you need to produce and when you need to produce it. The key to this type of policy working out well is the correct placement of the inventory/order interface.

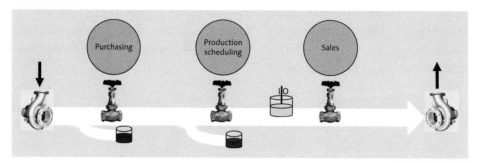

Figure 1.11 Inventory/Order Interface in a Push-Pull Combination

1.5.2   A Lean Supply Chain Flows

Lean is mostly, but not exclusively, related to the reduction of waste. The biggest problem with lean initiatives is that in that context, inventory is also considered waste. As we already discussed, inventory can also serve as a great buffer to counter variability and therefore deserves a little more respect. Very often, the ultimate goal of a lean initiative is described as "zero inventory," which, even if only set as a theoretical goal and not achievable, is almost ridiculous to strive for as well as dangerous. If you don't have inventory, you don't have anything to produce or sell. Why pursue a theoretical goal that isn't achievable?

Otherwise, a lean flow is a wonderful toolset to make a supply chain more efficient. One of the drivers of efficiency that also reduces waste is the introduction of flow. A general, better flow of orders, jobs, and materials through the supply chain is very desirable. When jobs don't flow, WIP builds up, sometimes without bounds. And when WIP builds up all kinds of negative things happen. "WIP is visible cycle time," says Spearman in *Factory Physics*. The more WIP is in the line, the longer it takes for a job to stay in the queue and the longer it takes that job to come out. WIP buildup often deceives materials planning in that it looks like we need to introduce new jobs into the line to get what we need. But very often, that job we need is already in the line, stuck in a WIP pile, waiting to be processed in front of some work center. And introducing more jobs into the line, while we don't get much out of the line, makes matters worse.

Flow is needed to remedy this, and there are many tools in SAP ERP that can be used to make things flow. First though, we need to gain some intuition about what causes disruptions and what makes things flow.

1.5.3   An Agile Supply Chain Flows, Too

In an agile supply chain, the focus lies on fast response times, a flexible fulfillment of customer requirements, and—guess what?—a steady flow of materials in the right quantity at the right time. The agile supply chain is built on the basis of a lean supply chain that allows, because of its lack of waste, for quick changeovers, is driven by small lot sizes, and supports a wide variety in the product offering. It has many variants built in its basic data. So there are many different production versions, alternative BOMs and routings, and a number of available work centers and line segments that can be chosen in scheduling. This requires a lot of work in the basic data setup; however, this is over-proportionally rewarded by utmost flexibility and efficiency in the daily process.

But agility also directly translates into more variability. Variability degrades a system's performance and needs to be buffered. As mentioned before, the three buffers that develop when variability is present are inventory, time, and capacity. That area of buffering variability effectively doesn't lie in the decision of which buffer to use, but rather in what combination of buffers are chosen. That again, is a matter of policy.

1.6   Summary

From Orlicky's early MRP concept through MRP II, SAP ERP, and SAP APO, materials planning provides the centerpiece of an integrated supply chain system. MRP ensures that the right parts will be at the right place in the right quantity when they are needed. What could be more important than that in an effective manufacturing system?

In this chapter, we laid out the basic premise on which this particular system of effective materials planning is built: a separation of strategic and tactical materials planning so that overall policy setting combines with detailed management by exception. The basis for this separation and subsequent parameter optimization is segmentation and classification. It categorizes the portfolio and describes parts into groups or segments.

Finally, we discussed the need to fulfill the quest for lean and agile supply chains. As these terms are seemingly competing with each other, we covered their dynamics so you can develop intuition that will help you work toward and anticipate future, improved results.

In the next chapter, we will explore the past and the future of materials planning with a more detailed look at typical SAP setups for SAP materials planning and how planners have used it historically.

It's like déjà vu all over again.
—Yogi Berra

2   The Past and the Future of Materials Planning

Companies have planned materials and their resulting inventory and service levels for a very long time. Base stock models defined the 1950s and 1960s inventory performances, where economic order quantities were calculated. Multilevel product structures with bills of materials (BOMs) had been used to determine dependent component requirements, based on a customer demand for finished product. However, the planner had to manually figure out how many wheels to order if the customer wanted 10 automobiles. With the dawn of information technologies and mainframe platforms such as SAP's early R/2 system, it then became possible to do a net requirements calculation throughout a deep BOM structure for very large and complex final products. Material requirements planning (MRP) was born.

In this chapter, we'll learn what materials planning was like in the "old days" and how people and SAP learned from the struggles to create a more streamlined software offering to execute it.

2.1   Past Problems with Materials Requirements Planning

While a department called Work Scheduling was tasked with planning and procurement of components and materials in the old days, a new department evolved in many companies, and the role of the MRP controller, or materials planner, was introduced. In the new world—the IT driven one—demand planning was possible, the product structure was "exploded" by the MRP run, and supply proposals were magically appearing in the material planner's work list every morning. All the planner had to do was set the basic data so that good lot sizes were generated and backward scheduling was carried out to determine start dates for orders. And those basic data parameters were greatly enhanced and improved with every new release that came up over the years.

Subsequently, MRP developed into MRP II, and the all-encompassing enterprise resource planning (ERP) systems of the 1990s became the next big thing. "Integration" was the new silver bullet, and Michael Hammer—make no mistake—pounded on the "breaking down of kingdoms." Everybody was wondering what integration was for and who needed it. So-called best-of-breed applications made their appearance (most of them were evolving from a failure to compete with the big ERPs) and were squashed by the big guys soon thereafter.

At some point SAP ERP began to see widespread implementation. With these implementations arose a new ecosystem. End users required a lot of training to use SAP ERP software, as it was comprised of a slew of transactions that needed to be customized and explained. This is when the SAP consultant was born, and quickly elevated to a status that was often beyond the value of the service they provided, simply because SAP consultants were such a rare breed. The SAP consultant became known as the voice of reason, the ultimate go-to person who had the final say when decisions needed to be made about processes or design. And yet, all that most SAP consultants knew was SAP transactions and how to execute them in standard situations. Process design fell through the cracks and SAP software (together with the functional consultant) was expected to solve all of an organization's problems through the mere installation of functionality and transactions. Integration thus became the big promise.

As it happened, the MRP run (where the BOM explosion takes place, and a net requirements calculation is performed) became the focal point of the integration. This was due to the fact that everybody hoped that the MRP run would solve all the problems in the efforts to plan for high service levels and low inventories. However, it needed a solid basic setup, clean master data, and frequent monitoring of the results. Because people involved with these activities weren't trained and educated on the process and procedural activities but rather on transactional execution, the MRP run didn't produce the expected results and with it came frustration and the exodus towards Excel and other solutions.

Implementing finance functionality was fairly straightforward and driven by legal requirements in each country as were HR and administrative functions. The situation with sales, distribution, manufacturing, inventory management, planning or purchasing functionality and processes was different. This was, and still is, the stuff that needed to work together and never did. Production orders came in late or got stuck on the line with no component availability. Purchase orders brought more than what was consumed and blew up the inventories, customers didn't buy what we thought they would, and organizations often ended up with the wrong product at the wrong place in the wrong quantity at the wrong time. Functionality was needed that could provide more information about what went wrong, where and why, so one could do something about it and get things flowing a bit better. Ah! That is what integration means and what it's good for!

It seemed that MRP, and the way the supply proposals were created, was the Holy Grail that needed to be found to fix the problems at hand. At this time, in the early nineties, SAP had already come up with its new and improved R/3 system (based on client/server technology) and the provided functionality for MRP was already very well developed with more functionality than most people understood how to use. There were many lot-sizing strategies, elaborate buffer options for safety stock planning, very automated MRP types for consumption, as well as deterministic planning, with the ability to customize these parameters with utmost flexibility, so that they can work and produce good results in any company in any industry. But the problem wasn't with the offering in functionality. The problem was the way it was implemented and the choices that were made during the implementation. It was almost always like traveling through a black hole that kept you moving toward the same old settings—the ones you knew from your last project. Very rarely would anybody ever venture into the unknown territory of creative policy setting or automated planning strategies. That kind of thing didn't fit into a project, limited by due dates and time lines, budget figures, and consultants that were specializing on modules.

Decisions were made to "live" with the bare minimum and worry about the other stuff later. Revisiting the "other stuff" never materialized, however, so everybody kept on going with MRP type PD and planning strategy 40—among many other simplified setups. What a sad result when you own the world's most advanced software system with all its beautiful functionality.

In the computer revolution that enabled the MRP run and the functionally integrated organization, IT departments were built to support the implementation, and eventually the business, with enhancements, industry-specific modifications, and—of all things—user training. For some reason, CEOs handed over the responsibility for a project to improve the business to people who had a degree in IT and didn't know much about a net requirements calculation with planned independent demand. Projects were taken over, authorizations were restricted,

Customizing became an IT task, and still to this day, the material planners at some client companies aren't allowed to change anything on the four MRP screens in the material master record. If they want to change a lot-sizing procedure from WB (weekly) to FX (fixed) to improve inventory performance, they have to submit a request ticket, so that IT can perform the needed activities and change the settings. On average, that process takes about a week (in some instances months), and, by then, the policy is outdated, and inventories are long out of sync with the service levels.

In regards to Customizing, much of its maintenance should be controlled by IT, but by far not all. If, for example, a planner wants to create a new policy, many of the tasks necessary are located in the Customizing transactions. Fine-tuning a lot-size procedure, adding a maximum coverage to a range of coverage profiles, or excluding safety stock from an availability checking rule are all to be executed within that well-protected domain of the IT department. Yes, the planner has to be kept off the Customizing ground, but often a request for a new coverage profile gets treated like a schoolboy's demand for an iPhone and gets lost in the approval process. Meanwhile, inventory is building up because the planner can't calculate a dynamic safety stock manually for every material. To be on the safe side, he would much rather order too much than run out of the part. IT should be in a supportive role here and not questioning the decision and requesting elaborate proof that a coverage profile with 3 days target, a minimum of 2 days, and a maximum ceiling of 15 days is really needed.

So the years went by, executives kept buying SAP ERP software, consultants went on implementing, and planners were forced to do their job with the newly provided functionality. Very often, the focus wasn't as much on the side of productive provision of a more effective way to plan materials for great service levels at low inventories. It was more like "...after the as-is model, we perform a gap analysis, and develop the to-be (the blueprint), and after data migration and cutover, we'll train the end user." There isn't much that can be more disappointing and frustrating than gap analysis and blueprinting. However, both are ever present in any SAP project.

Gap Analysis

We've tried to come up with a definition for gap analysis. It reads something like this: "Everything that we ever were able to do with our legacy systems, must be replicated in the new SAP system. We can't afford to move to lesser functionality. Project team members must now build a list with functionality that is essential for our business. The project members are to find out how the new system handles these functions, and the perceived gaps ought to be documented and presented to the steering committee. The same will then approve programming activities to fill the gaps."

In this way, it's guaranteed that the project replicates the exact same inefficient functionality—for which the legacy systems were to be replaced—into the new SAP system. Anything that SAP does differently (or is it better?) will now be dismissed and replaced with an ABAP-coded Z-program that, of course, the same consultancy that advised you on the perceived "enhancement," will code for you.

The gap analysis now produced a basic setup of functions that does business roughly the same way it did before. Of course, we need to get some value out of this expensive implementation. So we define improvements and benefits, and actively (or, perhaps, desperately) look for functionality that brings in advancements, efficiency, and profitability. So the SAP system is degraded to a transaction system, away from the business enabler it could be.

A good way to understand gap analysis is by considering this scenario: Charlie is moving from Minnesota to Florida. He plans to purchase a home in the new state. Charlie loves his current home, with its sophisticated heating system and basement game room, so he wants a house with similar functionality in Florida. While house hunting in Florida he finds a beautiful home, with a top-of-the-line air-conditioning system, and state-of-the-art security. Charlie performs a gap analysis and decides that the Florida home is less than satisfactory. Where is the heating system? The basement? Why would he need surveillance when the locks on his house were protection enough in Minnesota? In the end, he purchases the home, and chooses to "bridge the gap," modifying the place until it's a picture perfect replica of his old house. Unfortunately, the air conditioning that Charlie removed was exceptionally efficient, more beneficial, and much easier to maintain than the new heating system. His Florida neighborhood also has a higher crime rate than his Minnesota neighborhood, meaning that the extra security would have come in handy. Not to mention that adding a basement has weakened the foundation of his home. Charlie's gap analysis failed him because he assumed that any changes would mean a less functional home, instead of realizing that functionality must be judged based on the surrounding systems. The result is that Charlie has a home that meets all his demands, and would have been a great house in Minnesota, but fails to deliver any benefits to him in Florida.

Gap analysis for SAP often has a similar outcome, with functionality being transferred and gaps being filled, but often to the detriment of the business.

Blueprinting

After the gap analysis usually comes the blueprint. The word, taken from an architectural term, implies that after decisions are made, a plan is laid out that describes all the detail of the future functions and features. The problem with blueprinting is that the rich set of functionality that SAP offers in its initial delivery will be scaled down. Features and functions will be deemed unnecessary, useless, and not helpful. Generalization comes into play. Because the exercise is becoming a humongous "detailing" of individual features and functions, one applies general functionality to an immense scope of processes. As an example, discrete production orders are used to manage the entire production floor, even though there might be packaging lines that could be much more efficiently run with rate-based, repetitive orders. Or, the architect doesn't know how the Groff lot-size procedure works. Out that option goes. It won't be in the blueprint and therefore it will never become an option for the materials planner to have the system calculate an economical lot size. Very often, these options are even taken out of the Customizing tables.

With the blueprint document, you take your SAP system down to the bare minimum that the implementation—limited by budget, time, and what the consultant knows—can handle. Of course, the functionality we don't go live with in the first go-around can be revisited at a later stage, but the problem is that it's not so easy to change over to repetitive orders after you've created discrete production orders for many years with SAP. After the blueprint for exception monitoring is done, who will go back to the users after four years and tell them that instead of expediting the same material every week, they should set a more efficient policy, using more options that weren't available until now?

These are just a few reasons, ERP implementations often didn't produce the expected results. And interestingly enough, instead of making ERP work the way it was supposed to, thought leaders simply decided to invent something new.

Toyota found a way to reduce waste and everybody jumped on the bandwagon to get one-piece flow, zero inventories, and pull systems, which promised more efficiency. Our world became full of buzzwords. Supply chain management was probably the biggest one. People talked about the theory of constraints and drum–buffer–rope again. Heijunka, demand leveling, the agile and the lean supply chains were other popular ones. It had to sound intelligent, fashionable and—this was new to materials planning—exciting. As the new buzzwords poured in, a new software solution was needed to go along with it (you can't possibly sell demand driven manufacturing with a concept such as ERP that had its roots in the nineties).

So Advanced Planning Systems (APS; SAP called it APO) was born. These APSs did something similar to the MRP run, in that they performed calculations to generate proposals for better materials and product replenishment. As the ERP version of the planning run exploded a BOM and determined a supply plan constrained only by planning conditions, the APS planning run additionally answered the questions, "Do we have the required materials available?" and "Do we have sufficient resources in place?" However, APS works well only in less complex environments, and doesn't replace ERP. Neither does it make it better. It may improve a supply chain, but it doesn't fix the mistakes that were made during the ERP era of the nineties and beyond. APS and even SAP APO are excellent planning tools that work wonders when applied in the right way for the right situation. But let's not fall into the trap of assuming that these solutions are the silver bullet that quickly delivers all the tools and solutions we so desperately need.

The models and systems discussed in the following chapters are an attempt to find an effective way of getting the most out of standard SAP functionality for a more effective materials planning. Instead of gap analysis and blueprinting, we'll apply scientific models to derive feedback systems, which are supposed to allow us to continuously improve our operations. The idea is to raise the competence level of the planner and develop an intuition for the intelligent picking of the right option and not to degrade the planner to a job of transacting purchase and production orders or constant expediting. We won't limit the amount of policies a planner can use. No, we give them more of these options and provide them with the necessary tools to perform meaningful analysis and make good decisions on a periodic basis.

We need to move away from the transacting materials planner and take strides toward an organization that supports and provides for the analytical materials planner.

2.2   Today's Problems with Material Requirements Planning

There are still many problems with today's materials planning. One problem is that all MRP systems assume a fixed replenishment lead time. In other words, MRP uses the same amount of time it takes to replenish stock of a material every time it calculates availability and generates supply proposals. Lead times are rarely constant, and therefore the expected receipt date is often false. A possible solution to this problem is to use pull systems that replenish inventories by controlling the amount of stock that is in process (WIP) instead of releasing replenishment orders based on time-phased (by lead time) requirements.

Additionally, an MRP system isn't able to consider capacity constraints in its efforts to create a good supply plan. That is why gate control is needed to execute a number of steps to ensure that the unconstrained supply plan meets terms, constraints, and conditions required by vendors and production lines. APSs, such as SAP APO, however, deal with capacity constraints directly during the planning run.

That is why traditional MRP systems need improvement and why we need to provide our materials controllers with the tools, functionality, and competency they need to plan for great service levels and low inventories. What we need is a system that provides all these functions and is flexible enough to react to changing conditions while enabling the materials controllers to perform their tasks within their capacity. This system or model must be automated; otherwise, it would be impossible to manage the vast amount of materials to be planned correctly and efficiently. This system must also be agile because in today's world conditions change much more rapidly than only a few years ago. Product portfolios have more variations to fulfill customer demands. Product lifecycles are shorter, which means new specifications, BOMs, and material masters are added to the portfolio, while one constantly needs to obsolete materials. And due to more complex product offerings, material portfolios are increasing to a level where they become unmanageable without proper tools to automate their maintenance. It's common to see a materials planner being tasked with the maintenance, proper policy, and inventory responsibility of more than 10,000 materials. Without a proper system and the right tools, these tasks are impossible.

2.3   A Word on Customizing

As we all know, SAP ERP comes preconfigured with settings in the Customizing tables in the Enterprise Implementation Guide (IMG). Sometimes, a company makes use of SAP's efforts to provide preconfigured solutions for industries and for mid-sized companies. SAP has engaged in partnerships with system integrators, who provide a more or less advanced all-in-one solution, ready to be deployed in a very short amount of time and with a very affordable price tag.

SAP ERP in its purest delivery—without any preconfiguration—already has many settings in its Customizing tables. When you add preconfiguration for industry solutions (provided by SAP), you'll find more entries in those tables, and many of these will have a prefix "Y". So there might be an additional material type configured for the Oil and Gas Industry Solution named YOIL. As you move onto more preconfiguration, maybe as part of an all-in-one solution provided by a certified SAP reseller in your industry, you find even more settings in the Customizing tables, and most of these will start with a "Z". Lastly, your IT department and implementation consultants will add more Zs as they help you fit your requirements into the SAP system landscape.

The less your consultant understands all options, policies, strategies, and functions available in standard SAP, the more Z entries you'll have in the end. We've seen installations where almost every Customizing entry was replaced by a Z entry, but it was doing the same thing as the original entry. Some of these Zs are nestled, and after the "Z-ing" begins, it's very hard to stop it. Tables are full of Z entries, and then come the Z transactions—the endless list of reports that no one knew were already covered by the standard delivery or aren't necessary if the process would have been replicated in SAP standard properly. You're now operating in ZAP!

The problem with your ZAP system is that no one will be able to trace back what was originally intended, and the implementation consultant, who had various ideas, is long gone. As you're trying to run your business with SAP, you might run into the following problem: 12 months ago, a new product was introduced to the market, and you wanted to carefully assess the acceptance of your customers. After an initial production run, which was intended to fill your warehouse with the new product, you decided to produce more after the actual demand dropped in. Therefore, a make-to-order (MTO) strategy was set and a safety stock maintained, so that initial customer orders could be delivered right from inventory.

The availability checking rule was set up to look for stock first; if there was none available, the system was set up to switch over to promise the product to the customer by proposing a delivery date that corresponded to the total replenishment lead time. After the initial introduction phase, the product has now been accepted on the market, and you can see that there is steady, consistent demand coming through. It's time to switch the policy and make the product to stock.

As you maintain the rules in the material master record, you find strategy group Z7 and availability check Z2. Those must be MTO, you think. So you pull down on the field to see possible options for a make-to-stock (MTS) strategy. All you find is a myriad of Zx entries with vague descriptions, including "MTS with final assembly" and "MTS with comp f'cast." Short of having access to the IMG with Transaction SPRO, you can't figure out what these settings do. Now you contact your IT department and ask for help. They sit down with you, go into the IMG, and show you what a Z4 does. "It's a make to stock strategy that works with a forecast." "OK," you say, "what requirement does it generate?" "A Z4 creates a requirement type ZSF which will be consumed by a ZKS sales order requirement, if the line item category ZNOR is set in the sales screen. But if you want the ZMS to consume the ZSF, you'll have to use strategy Z5."

"All I want is to make sure that I can put forecast requirements out there to which our production scheduler can produce. I then want the sales representative to check for available stock and if there is nothing there, they tell the customer that they need to wait until the next receipt comes in," you might say.

In a "pure" SAP system, you could use strategy group 10, which creates a forecast requirement, and uses the availability checking rule 02, which checks without replenishment lead time. If it doesn't find available stock, it looks for the next production order to come in to confirm a promise date for the customer. If you consider the customer important, then you should add strategy 40 to the strategy group 10 as a substrategy, so that your sales representative can switch over to a different sales order requirement. This time, when there is no available stock, the requirement will fall right into the production schedule and tell the shop floor to do whatever they can to fulfill this important customer's request.

However, we can't recommend this type of policy if we don't know what your ZAP was set up for, and neither can anyone else who wasn't involved in the original ZAP setup.

Very often, people are too quick with the Z entry. There are, around 35 different strategies maintained in pure SAP, and we haven't come across a company or industry for which this isn't sufficient. Challenge your team to make use of what's provided. Go back to SAP standard, and, more importantly, learn about the options in the standard so you can apply them. This is easier said than done because there aren't many people around who can explain all these options, and it's very difficult to teach them to yourself. SAP documentation is sparse and sometimes hard to understand. And if you find yourself already in ZAP, it's very hard to get out. When there are 50,000 materials maintained with material type ZALL, it requires a herculean effort to do the right thing.

Strive to get back to the basics, and try to avoid workarounds, modifications, and Z settings. Of course, you can't radically change and replace everything that has been done during the implementation of your system and since, but after you understand more about all the options and settings that come with the SAP system, you might come to the conclusion that some, or maybe almost all, of your requirements can actually be actuated in the standard.

2.4   The Old Paradigm and the New

Computers were first used in the 1960s when IBM and others started exploding BOMs according to an MRP logic. A primary demand, planned or actual, was used as a basis to determine dependent requirements throughout all BOM levels, and supply proposals were generated to cover them. Advanced MRP systems included a net requirements calculation considering current stock levels and various lot-sizing procedures, and replenishment types drove more dynamic and accurate replenishment and resulting stock levels. Then MRP II came along, which included a capacity scheduling module. Whereas MRP does generate supply proposals without any consideration of available or unavailable capacity, MRP II systems promised a more realistic, more accurate production schedule.

Then in the 1990s ERP came into the picture (Figure 2.1). Integration was the great promise that everyone started to talk about. ERP systems included all functions an enterprise needs to run its business, and all these functions were promised to run in an integrated fashion. Sales, distribution, planning, manufacturing, purchasing, and even human resources were all run on one integrated platform where a goods receipt was having an impact in finance, costing, inventory management, and purchasing alike. A lot of complexity came with it and a lot of the excitement during the first successes of automation with the computer was diminished by nonfunctioning, integration issues caused by overwhelming and complicated functionality. To this day—often after decades of use—many ERP systems, including SAP, have not nearly delivered on the promise made during the implementation.

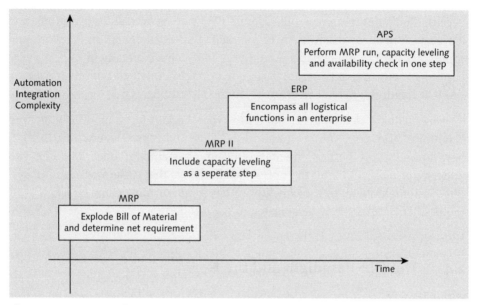

Figure 2.1 From Material Requirements Planning to Advanced Planning Systems

To make matters worse more complex systems were developed without tending to the problems at hand. As stated earlier, APSs appeared, and new promises were made to make old things (MRP, MRP II, ERP) better and to provide new inventions and management theories for a better world in supply chain management. In short, an APS promises to combine three distinct steps carried out separately and sequentially in ERP:

► BOM explosion with net requirements calculation and generation of supply proposals

► Capacity sequencing, leveling, and scheduling

► Component or material availability check and provision

APS does it all in one run. That, of course, might work very well for simple supply chains, but if you use it for complex structures and in a world of variability, uncertainty, and complexity, you'll soon run into walls.

Now all of these developments underlie one common method: they plan based on a demand entry and break through a BOM. And for years now, the Holy Grail and mantra of choice has been to improve forecast accuracy. But how can we expect certainty in the future when we can't even predict tomorrow's weather or what the price of crude oil will be in November? A forecast is an unknown outcome, and none of the planning systems and theories we just discussed will fix that problem.

However, we can work with buffers instead. As the Factory Physics™ approach points out, wherever there is variability, buffers will develop. And there are most always—and only—three buffers in the presence of variability: inventory, capacity, and time. We should use these buffers to our advantage, and instead of chasing an ever-changing demand, we can buffer variability with a combination of safety stocks, an extra shift of capacity, and some delay in the delivery. The new paradigm of cushioning variability uses the three buffers in the most effective combination. Instead of constantly adjusting a plan to an uncertain forecast and striving to be as accurate as possible, we should eliminate the need for certainty.

The mantra, visualized in Figure 2.2, revolves around a decrease in variability. This should bring on lower inventory requirements, higher service levels, and shorter cycle times.

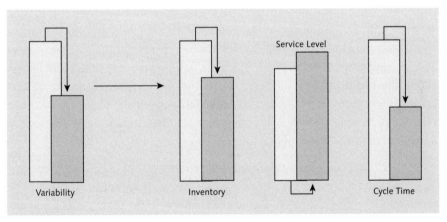

Figure 2.2 Eliminating the Need for Certainty and Improving on Major Key Performance Indicators with the Buffering of Variability

If done right, the supply chain's most important key performance indicators (KPIs) will improve drastically, and material will flow without much noise and with a shorter cycle time.

There is absolutely nothing wrong with applying the new paradigm to the systems we own. There is much discussion about when to use SAP APO over the functionality already provided in SAP ERP. When looking at the historic developments in using IT for operations management, we can see a gradual increase in automatic calculations—but not necessarily more automation with better results. There is no doubt that IT systems and the developments in computer science have enabled planning logic that is far above the level of what you could ever expect from a human being; however, sometimes it seems as if the computer with its models and heuristics fails terribly in the face of variability, or uncertainty. Computer systems work great with a perfect forecast, but a perfect forecast is as likely as the exact prediction of future price levels in the stock market.

SAP ERP has many functions, policies, and strategies to design, build, and use very effective buffering strategies. SAP APO does too, which is SAP's version of an APS. In this book, however, we want to explore ways to optimize the use of SAP ERP's standard functionality to adhere to the new paradigm of buffering variability and eliminating the need for uncertainty.

2.4.1   Using SAP ERP as a Control Mechanism

Much, if not all, basic data resides in SAP ERP. Companies that run on SAP mostly maintain their basic setup in SAP ERP. SAP ERP may hold the material master, policy, structural data, routings, work centers, and rough-cut planning profiles for sales & operations planning (SOP). Even though some of these data sets can be held in SAP APO, SAP ERP always provides the basic structures, setup, and format to operate the business. SAP ERP represents the transactional framework with which movements are posted, orders are released and closed, plans are adjusted, and missing parts are expedited. It's therefore the operational backbone of any SAP system managing the supply chain.

Often, SAP ERP had been the underlying operations system for a long time. SAP ERP is without doubt the most encompassing, versatile, functionality-rich, and sophisticated ERP system there is. But it's probably also the least understood and most misrepresented one (maybe this sort of thing comes with the territory). All too often, companies and people give up too easy and resort to third-party bolt-ons, modifications, or Z-transactions.

However, that doesn't mean that it automatically represents a good basis for an SAP APO implementation. All too often, we see organizations trying to fix their data or processing problems with the implementation of an APS such as SAP APO. Thinking along those lines almost always results in botched optimizations and doesn't deliver the expected improvements. Data cleansing and the preparation of the underlying structures inside of SAP ERP are an essential step before planning with SAP APO.

Unfortunately, the need to buy and implement SAP APO often arises from the perception that SAP ERP can't deliver the needed functionality or process performance, and companies are far too quick with the decision to jump onto an APS, hoping that their problems are solved with an implementation of new software functionality. But let's not forget that it's not the arrow; it's the hunter who shoots it that makes the kill. A competent planner can effectively balance supply and demand for a portfolio of thousands of materials without much manual effort using SAP ERP functionality alone. After the planner understands that a static safety stock is causing "bull-whipping" havoc upstream in the supply chain because the MRP run simply ignores what most people think is an effective planning buffer, he can use a coverage profile; it's resulting dynamic buffer is much more elegant and productive than any theory, model, or heuristic in an APS could ever dream of.

Much of this book will focus on a better use of standard functionality and all available options to plan material supply most effectively with SAP ERP. That said, by no stretch of the imagination do we want to hold you back from SAP APO. It's an extremely effective planning extension to SAP ERP.

2.4.2 Using SAP APO as a Planning Instrument

The SAP APO module is, as we discussed earlier, an APS. It combines the steps of exploding BOMs generating supply proposals, sequencing, leveling and scheduling orders, and checking lower level component and parts availability. So it does automate a bit more than the MRP run in SAP ERP, but it does so with the danger to produce false results when structural complexity is high.

SAP APO is primarily a planning system. It does provide functions to manage exceptions, expedite orders, and even generate purchase requisitions, but these are functions that SAP developed to allow SAP APO to run independently and with SAP ERP if so desired. If, however, you own SAP ERP, you should use SAP APO for planning only because that is what it was meant to do. As an APS, SAP APO provides many opportunities to plan for future inventory and service levels, resource requirements, and the generation of an operations plan. SAP APO gives you a more modern and effective user interface. It also improves performance and lets you execute updates without the sometimes cumbersome in and out of transactions an SAP ERP system requires.

2.4.3 Combining SAP ERP with SAP APO Successfully and Efficiently

SAP ERP and SAP APO are connected through the Core Interface (CIF) and Business Application Program Interfaces (BAPIs). It's perfectly fine to run both SAP ERP and SAP APO at the same time. The question is what tasks each one of these systems takes on. We've seen installations where the critical parts were planned in SAP APO while the noncritical materials were monitored in SAP ERP. As this is one way of doing it, to keep both in SAP ERP is a perfectly valid option too. In that case, you don't need two different methods of exception monitoring and reporting. Our recommendation is to manage the parameters for automation in SAP ERP and use these in SAP APO to plan efficiently and automated.

One combination that works well is the separation of tasks so that strategic materials planning is performed in SAP APO, and tactical and operational execution and planning takes place in SAP ERP. That way, the supply chain strategies are maintained via policy in SAP APO Demand Planning (DP) and handed over to the MRP run (in SAP ERP) so that planned orders and purchase requisitions are generated with quantities and delivery dates according to a plan developed in SAP APO.

There are many different options and possibilities on how to combine SAP APO and its excellent SAP ERP system, but they are beyond the scope of this book.

2.5 Future Potential in Operations, Supply Chain, and Materials Management

The process of planning materials for good availability with low capital investment has been given many names over the years. Operations management, for example, includes what we call materials planning, but is broader. Managing operations means more than just planning for material availability. It basically includes all the tasks necessary to run your business from sales, inventory, and resource and operations planning to the actual procurement of raw materials, including the entire value chain in between. Other than supply chain management, however, operations management is strictly limited to the operations inside only one organization. The supply chain can include many organizations, from the producer, through the manufacturer, distributor, and retail shop to the end customer. Each one of these links in the chain has materials planners trying to strike the best balance between supply and demand. And each of these materials planning departments is part of operations management and therefore eventually led by the chief of operations.

Operations management is as old as manufacturing is. Some of the functions operations management is tasked with include the following:

▸ Managing and leveling incoming demand

▸ Planning production to manufacture finish goods and intermediate products

▸ Managing inventories of finished goods, raw materials, and intermediates

▸ Planning for raw material availability

▸ Planning for MRO items

▸ Planning workers for the shop floor

▸ Reporting on actual cost and estimate planned cost

▸ Managing equipment and plant maintenance

An operations manager is usually responsible for all of these tasks and must report to shareholders and the board if the company operates as good as it should or can be. Traditionally, these operations managers have been schooled on various curriculums in universities and colleges, or they've come up through the internal ranks in a company because they demonstrated responsibility, experience, knowledge, and ethics. After being put into that position, an operations manager is usually left alone. Because no one knows what to tell him to do, he will have to figure it out himself. The spectrum of tasks is so comprehensive that it's imperative to delegate responsibility and then to focus on bringing everything together so the operations run like a well-conducted orchestra. In more recent times, there seemed to be a great solution available for the ever-larger growing problems of managing more and more complex and demanding operations: ERP and APS systems running on IT platforms, providing many, many KPIs and other measurements that the operations manager wanted to use to fulfill his task. According to Ed Pound of *Factory Physics for Managers* (McGraw-Hill Education, 2014):

Technology only provides knowledge support; predictive control depends on good scientific understanding of the natural behavior of the system being controlled. Many executives confuse the two. In reality, it's not the ERP system that has ruined performance but improper use of the ERP system. Executives and managers commonly spend vast amounts of money, invest huge amounts of time and effort, and end up with ERP systems that are merely used to track transactions ('Financial ERP') without any ability to set policy and monitor compliance to achieve predictable capacity utilization, increase cash flow and improve customer service.

To manage the operations in an organization means to apply a previously agreed upon business strategy. It's the process of selecting, implementing, and controlling an operation's logistics design that best meets the company's financial goals. And operations management refers to a framework of response time, inventory, capacity (human and machine), and variability associated with the entire manufacturing supply chain. For an operations manager to fulfill his obligation, he needs to understand the science underlying these operations and pick the best policy possible for the business. A quintessential ingredient in the understanding of manufacturing science *and* the application of the right policy is the development of good intuition. And good intuition comes from scientific exploration and understanding.

2.5.1 The Science of Operations Management

"Management is in transition from an art, based only on experience, to a profession, based on an underlying structure of principles and science..." according to Jay W. Forrester in his groundbreaking book, *Industrial Dynamics*. "...Any worthwhile human endeavor emerges first as an art. We succeed before we understand why. The development of the underlying sciences was motivated by the need to understand better the foundation on which the art rested."

Isn't it time to improve the art of operations management in SAP with some science and underlying laws and principles in order to get a foundation and common understanding that we all can reference? Most consultants and advisers still just use their experience and guide the user with poor intuition (that comes from various degrees of experience and runs the gamut from great to miserable judgment). Other disciplines, such as engineering or practicing law, wouldn't be nearly as advanced if they still rested on the same descriptive transmittal of experience. The SAP supply, for the most part, still runs without reference to its performance boundaries or a rule set based in scientific descriptions. "...but without an underlying science, advancement of an art eventually reaches a plateau," Forrester claims further, and we believe his insights still hold water. He also states, "...companies believe their problems are unique. Because of the lack of a suitable fundamental point of view, we fail to see how industrial experiences all deal with the same material, financial and human factors—all representing variations on the same underlying system." And "...to unify the separate facets of management, selected experiences have been recorded as 'cases' to provide a vehicle to discuss management as an interrelated system. This has been the best method available for integrating management knowledge, although it has been far from adequate." Far too often, people discredit ideas because they think the solution doesn't apply in their environment. Forrester talks about management (policy setting, decision making, guidance) as a discipline that needs a scientific basis and reference framework. We're here talking about managing the SAP supply chain and bringing some practical science to the table that helps us to better evaluate and fine-tune the supply chain and how it's run by SAP settings and functionality. Such a base of practical science permits experiences to be translated into a common frame of reference from which they can be transferred from the past to the present or from one place to another.

Forrester has succeeded in his vision to develop a science for the discipline of management. The topic has been evolving from Forrester through Donella Meadows with *Thinking in Systems: A Primer* (Chelsea Green Publishing, 2008) and John Sterman with his book, *Business Dynamics: Systems Thinking and Modeling for a Complex World* (McGraw-Hill Education, 2000) (both from the MIT Sloan Faculty where Forrester also lectured). Also, in *The Fifth Discipline: The Art and Practice of the Learning Organization* (Doubleday, 2006) by Peter Senge (also a senior lecturer at MIT), the premise is that the fifth discipline, system thinking, combines the other four (personal mastery, mental models, building a shared vision, and team learning) to manage and transform companies into learning organizations. Besides systems and business dynamics thinking (supported by causal loop and stock and flow diagrams), another science has been developed in the previously mentioned *Factory Physics* by Hopp and Spearman, which focuses on scientific management of manufacturing dynamics. But the principles, laws, and corollaries explained in *Factory Physics* can easily be applied to the entire supply chain. Hopp has also written a paper titled "Supply Chain Science," which translates the

Factory Physics principles to a more broad application throughout the entire supply chain.

So now it's time to use these valuable insights to build a practical science framework for the art of operations management with SAP. Systems thinking will allow us to pinpoint inefficiencies, foresee the effects of a specific policy, and support good decision making (MTS or MTO? Reduce inventory or increase availability? When to order and how much?). Through systems thinking, the bullwhip effect can be avoided, or at least reduced, and we're able to see the forest again, in spite of all the trees. Factory Physics then strives to apply practical science to help with the definition of various policies and use buffers to counter the ever-present animosity of variability. Using Little's Law, Kingman's equation (or VUT formula), and the variability of lead time demand, we can optimize the combination of buffer usage (time, inventory, capacity), fight variability, and optimize our inventory levels for lowest stock with utmost service level performance. We now know where to place WIP buffers to execute the Theory of Constraints for better flow, and we can reduce waste, for a lean supply chain, and increase flexibility, for an agile supply chain. A KPI framework can be developed that is based on meaningful and effective measures, which should move us much closer to SAP operations excellence than transactional knowledge and experience alone.

The theories and practical insights from systems thinking, Factory Physics, and our own SAP value stream mapping are an integral part of this book. They should guide us to make sense of a world of increasing complexity and help us build the confidence and intuition—based on sound science—to make good decisions as the influencing parameters are bound to constantly change. The way these principles are applied in this book should serve only as a basis to break down mental models that held us back from thinking differently about operations management than people before us have thought about it and taught as "the way to do it." As the reader, you should take those ideas much further, and standard SAP functionality certainly doesn't limit that idea.

2.6   Planning the Future with an Unconstrained Supply Plan

Often, it feels like materials planning has developed into something that doesn't have known or defined boundaries, responsibilities, or expected deliverables. The exact job description for a materials planner takes on many different shapes and forms—not only from one company to another but also internally in an organization. Sometimes the lines between materials planning and purchasing blur, and the buyer takes on many tasks that the MRP controller used to do. In some cases the materials planner is blamed for late deliveries from production. This is due to the fact that the production scheduler and materials planner were merged into one person because after the SAP implementation, many thought that the MRP run took on the task of scheduling orders on the production lines. Capacity sequencing, leveling, and scheduling were dismissed primarily because they were too complex, not really understood well, and put in that "let's do that later" box. MRP generated planned orders, and these were, without availability or capacity check, converted into production orders, and voila—there was the production program.

This is very detrimental to operations management and the outcome in the form of order fulfilment or inventory right-sizing of finished goods. Materials planning doesn't include production planning (PP). There is a gate in between. Materials planning stops at the generation of order proposals, and PP takes over from there to applies constraints. The same is true at the other supply gate: after materials planning generates proposals to buy materials, Procurement assigns vendors and considers terms and conditions.

In that sense, we can say that materials planning assumes given demand to generate an unconstrained supply plan. Therefore, the materials planner's job is to guide the system (by setting policies) toward the automatic generation of proposals for internal and external procurement that covers a given demand in the most optimal way from a planning perspective—under no consideration of production constraints or vendor conditions. It's the production scheduler's and the buyer's job to then convert those proposals into feasible and finite schedules. Of course, in an effective materials planning system, the materials planner includes some of these conditions already in the plan, that is, those that can be anticipated and don't change that much. But beware! If you assume and apply too much of those conditions already in materials planning, you're bound to step on the same spot, and you're restricted from ever grabbing opportunities to improve.

The third gate lies north of materials planning where demand flows into the system. Demand may be anticipated, planned requirements, or an actual customer order. Whatever it may be, materials planning never changes anything about it. From a materials planning perspective it's a given fixed input, and the materials planner's job is to plan the coverage of that demand with minimum inventories as close in time as possible under assumption of variability.

2.6.1 Shaping a Better Future Using the Right Side of Our Brain a Bit More Often

SAP comes with standard functions and features that need to be customized to work well for a specific company's business process and planning functions. Materials planning is no exception to this need. As it happens sometimes, materials planning isn't necessarily set up perfectly right out of the gate, and implementations with limited budgets and time lines don't always produce the perfect basis for a materials planner to use the basic model for his daily workload.

There are many reasons why SAP isn't used as intended and therefore doesn't produce the results that were expected from the acquisition of standard software tools. When this happens, we all have to think about the way we're using this excellent offering of standard functions and functionalities. Just because it isn't set up correctly and we don't know what's there doesn't mean it's bad and inefficient (the fact that we can't fly an F16 doesn't make it a bad plane).

Reading Daniel Pink's *A Whole New Mind* (Riverhead Books, 2006) about the right and left side of the brain led to the thought that our community is due for a change, and we have some mental model breakdown to do. A quick read at about 250 or so pages, this simple book in many ways is most profound and well-researched book as well. "The future belongs to a different kind of person," Pink says. "Designers, inventors, teachers, storytellers—creative and empathetic right-brain thinkers whose abilities mark the fault line between who gets ahead and who doesn't." Pink claims we're living in a different era, a different age in which those who "think different" may be valued even more than ever. He goes on to say:

> ...an age animated by a different form of thinking and a new approach to life—one that prizes aptitudes that I call 'high concept' and 'high touch.' High concept involves the capacity to detect patterns and opportunities, to create artistic and emotional beauty, to craft a satisfying narrative.... High touch involves the ability to empathize with others, to understand the subtleties of human interaction...

What was particularly valuable in Pink's book were the "six senses" or the "six R-directed aptitudes," which Pink says are necessary for successful professionals to possess in the more interdependent world we live in, a world of increased automation and out-sourcing. You can quibble over parts of his book if you like, but there is no denying that these six aptitudes are indeed more important now than they ever have been, and we need to apply them in more ways than ever before.

Whether there is a new way of running a system of materials planning is unclear, but for certain, the old way needs a lot of improvement. The following subsections provide more detail on Pink's six aptitudes—Design, Story, Symphony, Empathy, Play, and Meaning—and our take on how each one can help us improve the way we plan.

Design

To many business people, design is not mission critical. In our field, design is necessary (when we present ideas using slides, show data tables in a spreadsheet, or build a model using LEGO® bricks). But most of us decorate instead. There is a difference between design and decoration:

> *Decoration, for better or worse, is noticeable—sometimes enjoyable, sometimes irritating—but it is unmistakably there. However, sometimes the best designs are so well done that 'the design' of it is never even noticed consciously by the observer/user, such as the design of a book or signage in an airport (i.e., we take conscious note of the messages which the design helped make utterly clear, but not the color palette, typography, concept, etc.). One thing is for sure, design is not something that's merely on the surface, superficial and lacking depth. Rather it is something which goes 'soul deep'.*
> *—Garr Reynolds, author of Presentation Zen (New Riders, 2011)*

"It's easy to dismiss design—to relegate it to mere ornament, the prettifying of places and objects to disguise their banality," says Pink. "But that is a serious misunderstanding of what design is and why it matters." Pink is absolutely right. Design is fundamentally a whole-minded aptitude, or as he says, "utility enhanced by significance."

Garr Reynolds says:

> *Design starts at the beginning not at the end; it's not an afterthought. If you use slideware in your presentation, the design of those visuals begins in the preparation stage before you have even turned on your computer (if you're like me), let alone fired up the ol' slideware application. It's during the preparation stage that you slow*

down and 'stop your busy mind' so that you may consider your topic and your objectives, your key messages, and your audience. Only then will you begin to sketch out ideas—on paper or just in your head—that will soon find themselves in some digital visual form later. Too much 'PowerPoint design,' as you know very well, is nothing more than a collection of recycled bullets, corporate templates, clip art, and seemingly random charts and graphs which are often too detailed or cluttered to make effective on-screen visuals and too vague to stand alone as quality documentation.

We have to get better at designing our means of teaching, communicating, convincing and presenting of ideas.

Story

Facts and information—data—have never been more readily available, especially in our profession. But we're using it, dealing with it, and processing it in a rather boring and unemotional way. According to Pink, "What begins to matter more (than mere data) is the ability to place these facts in context and to deliver them with emotional impact." Cognitive scientist Mark Turner calls storytelling "narrative imagining," something that is a key instrument of thought. We're wired to tell and to receive stories. "Most of our experiences, our knowledge and our thinking is organized as stories," he says. Story isn't just about storytelling but about listening to stories and being a part of stories.

We always get a much better reception if we wrap our advice in a story. Merely explaining the difference between pull and push isn't nearly as effective and memorable as telling the story of how the State of California didn't allow train wagons to be pushed by the locomotive anymore. This came after an accident, where a "pushed" train crashed into a Jeep left on a crossing and had a much more devastating effect than any pulled train could have ever had.

Story can be used for good: for teaching, for sharing, for illuminating, and, of course, for honest persuasion.

Symphony

Focus, specialization, and analysis have been important in the Information Age, but in the "Conceptual Age," synthesis and the ability to take seemingly unrelated pieces and form and articulate the big picture before us is crucial, even a differentiator. Pink calls this aptitude Symphony:

Symphony... is the ability to put together the pieces. It is the capacity to synthesize rather than to analyze; to see relationships between seemingly unrelated fields; to detect broad patterns rather than to deliver specific answers; and to invent something new by combining elements nobody else thought to pair.

Doesn't this sound like integration? The best planners can illuminate the relationships that we may not have seen before. Pink says they can "see the relationships between relationships." Symphony requires that we become better at seeing, truly seeing in a new way. "The most creative among us see relationships the rest of us never notice," Pink says. Anyone can deliver chunks of information and repeat findings represented visually in spreadsheets and PowerPoints, but what's needed are those who can recognize the patterns and who are skilled at seeing nuance and the simplicity that may exist in a complex problem.

Symphony in the world of materials planning doesn't mean dumbing down information into sound bites and talking points so popular in our industry Symphony is about using our whole mind—logic, analysis, synthesis, intuition—to make sense of our world (i.e., SOP), finding the big picture, and determining what is important and what isn't. It's also about deciding what matters and letting go of the rest. A symphonic approach to our job and our ability to bring it all together will be greatly appreciated by your customers.

Empathy

Empathy is emotional. It's about putting yourself in your colleague's or customer's shoes. Empathy involves an understanding of the importance of the non-verbal cues of others and being aware of your own. Good planners have the ability to put themselves in the position of the recipient of the value-add a planner provides (your customer, the production line who asks for material). This is a talent, perhaps, more than a skill that can be taught, but everyone can get better at this. Everyone surely knows of a brilliant planner who seems incapable of understanding how anyone could possibly be confused by his explanation of how to design and apply effective replenishment policies.

We can certainly see how empathy helps a planner in the course of a cycle. Empathy allows us, even without thinking about it, to notice when the audience (or customer) is "getting it" and when they aren't. The empathetic planner can make adjustments based on his reading of this particular other person.

Play

In the Conceptual Age, says Pink, work isn't just about seriousness but about play as well. Pink quotes University of Pennsylvania professor, Brian Sutton-Smith, who says, "The opposite of play isn't work. It's depression. To play is to act out and be willful, exultant and committed as if one is assured of one's prospects."

Indian physician Madan Kataria points out in Pink's book that many people think that serious people are the best suited for business and that serious people are more responsible. "[But] that's not true," says Kataria. "That's yesterday's news. Laughing people are more creative people. They are more productive people." Somewhere along the line, we were sold the idea that a real business project must necessarily be dull, devoid of humor, and something to be endured not enjoyed.

For instance, let's employ the beer game as a way to visualize the impact of the bullwhip effect and use bathtubs to demonstrate Little's Law. It will raise interest levels but, more important, take the seriousness and dullness out and put some fun and smiles in. As Pink points out, "Laughter is a form of nonverbal communication that conveys empathy and that is even more contagious than the yawn...."

Meaning

Performing well in your daily routines and achieving a high rate of success is an opportunity to make a small difference in the world (for your customer, their managers, and your fellow employees). A planning cycle gone bad, on the other hand, can have a devastating impact on spirit and career.

Some say that we are born for meaning and live for self-expression and an opportunity to share that which we feel is important. If you're lucky, you feel passionate about your job. You look forward with excitement to the possibility of sharing your expertise—your story—with others. Few things can be more rewarding than connecting with someone, with teaching something new, or sharing that which you feel is very important with others.

Frankly, the bar is often rather low. Managers are so used to less-than-excellent performance from these planning and operating systems and how they are used, that they've seemingly learned to see it as normal even if not ideal. However, if you're different, if you exceed expectations and show them that you've thought about them, done your homework and know your material, and demonstrated through your actions how much you appreciate being there and that you're there for them, chances are you'll make an impact and a difference, even if it's just in the smallest of ways. There can be great meaning in even these small connections.

Getting the opportunity to work with SAP users and having the stage to present ideas, has been most rewarding. It's an opportunity to share knowledge and experience and to broaden our own network, and it serves as good practice. What could be better?

2.7   Summary

From the early base inventory policies, through the push MRP concepts, to today's full supply chain integration, materials planning in most organizations is still run without a framework of reference, based on no specific science, and with planners building their own way of doing things, mostly using Excel spreadsheets.

Materials planning must be adopted into a controlled and predictable science. To operate effectively and efficiently, we'll have to develop models that allow us to operate as close as possible to our upper performance boundaries. Goals and targets have to be set realistically, and we'll have to measure against them to know the actions that will have to be taken to continuously balance supply with demand for better service levels and lower capital investment.

Gap analysis and blueprinting haven't delivered the expected results. We must learn from these missteps and find better ways to run our materials planning organizations with operating procedures that provide commonality and standardization. However, it's not just the technical aspect we must improve on. Mental models, perceptions on how the real world supposedly works, must be broken down, and we must change consulting too.

In the next chapter, we'll discuss the building blocks of such a system and set the stage for a more automated, flexible, and transparent way of working.

Success is the natural consequence of consistently applying the basic fundamentals.
—*Jim Rohn*

3   Building Blocks of Materials Planning

In this chapter, we want to establish a fundamental way of thinking about how to balance supply with demand using an SAP system. As we do so, we want to break down the mental models of traditional thinking in operations management and explore alternatives for an effective planning framework that provides all the tools and functions necessary to raise the planner's competence and ability in their efforts to increase service levels and keep inventories at a minimum. We especially want to challenge the way SAP functionality was implemented, taught, and eventually used for materials planning so that new opportunities can be explored and manifested in the daily workings of an materials resource planning (MRP) controller.

Taking a different point of view often helps find a better way to do things. For example, we employ proven, scientific concepts such as Factory Physics, systems thinking, and value stream mapping to put us at a different vantage point so that we can develop good intuition and subsequently make better decisions. Modeling our materials planning system helps us gain a better understanding and see the things we need to improve or do differently. After the basic model is developed, we might rethink the organizational aspects. Maybe the introduction of a strategic materials planner role or redefining how a tactical planner does his job is required. In most cases, we need to define standard operating procedures and retrain the organization on the new system.

In this chapter, we'll explore the fundamental concepts that are required for controlled inventory sizing and predictable determination of high-service levels. These concepts include modeling the materials planning process, gate controls, demand and supply, and tactical materials planning.

3.1   Modeling

Very often, little attention is given to the subject of materials planning during an SAP implementation. MRP is considered a standard process that doesn't require much customization or elaborate design. However, an organization needs an underlying model, a framework of reference, and a system of cohesiveness to put the pieces together so that a materials planner can do his job well. With this model in place, the planner can conduct a symphony of well-takted incoming supply so that materials can flow in and out of the supply chain to cover demand in such a way that the company reaches its number one goal or fundamental objective: to make money over the long term. Simply providing the materials planner with a set of transactions and a few days of transactional training isn't going to do that.

To create a more effective model of materials planning, we can use flow charts and functional diagrams. But it's also helpful to use a more scientific approach that can provide a very structured and transparent basis for ongoing, sustainable, powerful, and long-lasting improvements.

For example, modeling the supply chain as a value stream allows you to document everything from a policy to a configuration setting or basic data. Value streams are an important guide for any SAP optimization. The information flow on top can depict inefficiencies in the transactional use of SAP. As an example, it shows where one takes flight into spreadsheets without using available, integrated functionality in standard SAP. In the materials flow part, we can use Little's Law to pinpoint physical inefficiencies such as long cycle times, suboptimized inventories, or low throughput. All of these factors are implicated by policies or the combination of basic data settings. Setting the right policy is crucial in any improvement efforts for materials planning, and therefore a value stream answers the ultimate question: How can we regularly update our policy so that it continuously optimizes planning, forecasting, and execution with throughput, inventory, and cycle time?

A generic value stream map is shown in Figure 3.1. You can see that—as in any value stream—information flows on top from right to left and material flows from left to right at the bottom through workstations, or, as in the process industry, through resources. The value stream is framed by the stream's customers and vendors. Who these are depends on the definition of the value stream. It could be an individual production line, an entire manufacturing plant, or even a supply chain. Value stream mapping isn't limited to manufacturing only. It can and should include all areas where information and materials flow through.

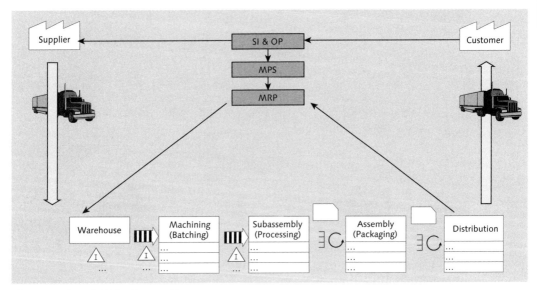

Figure 3.1 Generic Value Stream Map

During the course of this chapter, we'll discuss how you can take a generic value stream map and turn it into a comprehensive SAP value stream map with full documentation of a future, improved state. The SAP value stream map will guide you through improvement initiatives, allow for the collection of measurements and help with the creation of training documentation for the end user. It will also serve as a comprehensive framework of reference for all future improvement efforts.

3.1.1 Demand and Supply Profiles

In the generic value stream, we can depict the information flow (the top part of the value stream) as a planning hierarchy through which information cascades down through a hierarchy, to eventually end up as a production or procurement schedule (see Figure 3.2).

Such a model can be based on the concepts of *demand and supply profiles*. As some of you might know, demand and supply profiles can be viewed graphically in SAP via Transaction MD04. In the menu bar, click on List • Graphic, and the screen shown in Figure 3.3 appears.

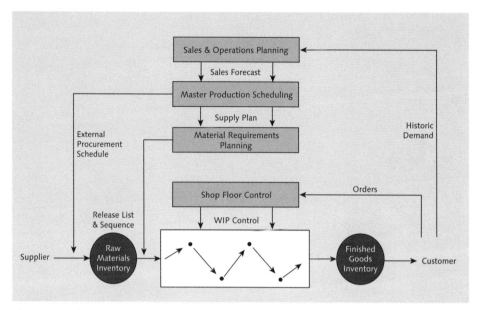

Figure 3.2 Value Stream Map Using a Planning Hierarchy

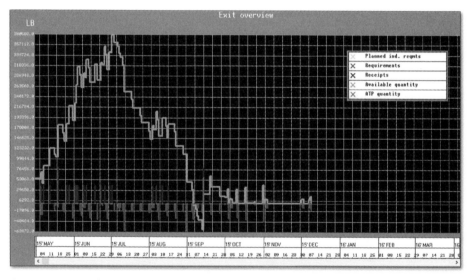

Figure 3.3 Demand and Supply Profiles in SAP ERP*

These profiles provide a forward-looking simulation of inventory development based on the policy—or master data combination—set in the material master. As you can see in Figure 3.3, supply elements (receipts) were generated to cover demand (actual and planned requirements), and inventory moves up and down over time. The way inventory moves up or down depends on the policy. As mentioned earlier, materials planning considers demand as a constant and doesn't attempt to change anything about it. Both actual and planned demand are a given, but how supply covers demand is in the hands of the materials planner. He can either figure out manually how much is needed when, or he can set a policy to automatically drive the generation of effective order proposals. The demand/supply profile shows the simulated result.

Relating this to a value stream map, the material flow shown at the bottom part of the map (see Figure 3.4), will be driven (it will flow or accumulate inventory and time buffers) by the information flow from above.

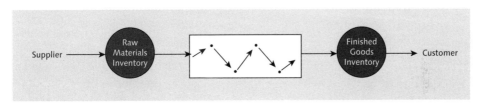

Figure 3.4 Material Flow

As information flows through the various stages of planning, demand and supply are being balanced every step of the way throughout the planning hierarchy. The circular profiles displayed in Figure 3.5, represent demand and supply balancing in different departments. Accordingly, sales & operations planning (SOP) manages the balance between anticipated/planned demand and a roughly capacity-checked long-term production program or plan. MRP typically uses the production plan as its source of demand together with actual demand from customers (which consume the planned demand). With the application of policy, supply is generated, and the planner's task is to ensure a good balance between the two. As the short-term and mid-term supply plan is handed over to procurement and production scheduling, these departments perform their own balancing act and apply terms and conditions such as capacity and delivery constraints of vendors and production lines and resources.

Eventually, purchase orders are sent to suppliers, and a production schedule is handed to the shop floor.

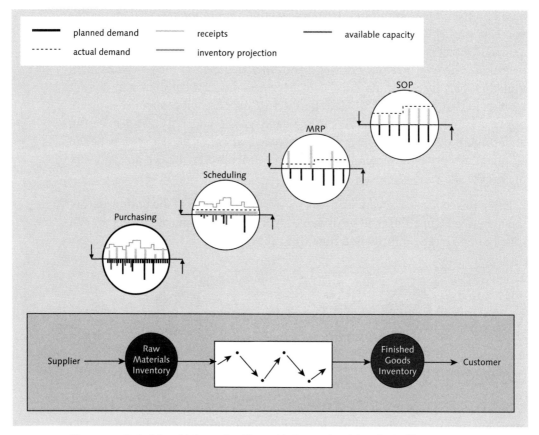

Figure 3.5 Material and Information Flow with Demand and Supply Profiles

We can now see that materials planning is constrained by incoming planned and/or actual demand and the terms, conditions, and limitations of production resources and outside vendors. It's important to recognize these "gates" because responsibility, accountability, and success for the various departments and roles in an organization need to be well defined. As often observed, a production scheduler is blamed for not delivering product on time in full. The planning department might not have performer a rough resource check on the production lines and handed over demand for a period when demand was exceeded by more than 300%! The production scheduler can't do much in this situation because in an automated system such as SAP ERP, it's very hard to see the source of the problem, especially when the hand-overs aren't carefully designed, described, and executed. It's therefore imperative that we perform some sort of gate control before and after materials planning.

3.1.2 Gate Control

In neurological science, "gate control" refers to how the brain shuts out pain under certain conditions. In other words, there is a point where signals are blocked from entering an information processing. The same should be true within a planning hierarchy, where information cascades from one area to another for it to be processed or balanced. Just like with gate control around the brain, a signal shouldn't pass through the gate until it's properly administered, so that the receiving area doesn't "feel pain."

Materials planning should be constrained by gates from the demand side as well as by gates from the supply side. Unfortunately, very often there is no gate control, and information is transferred without further examination. In that scenario, scheduling is overwhelmed with required production quantities that exceed the available capacity by more than 200, 300, or even 500%. Consequently, without proper capacity planning, component and purchased parts requirement dates are wrong, and, to add insult to injury, the resulting purchase requisitions (claiming false quantities for false dates) are converted into purchase orders and sent to suppliers without application of terms, conditions, or supply constraints.

Imagine an airline operating without gate control. A forecast of how many passengers would need to be flown to which airports at what time would directly result in a flight schedule that consists of a number of types of planes (with a certain passenger capacity) needing to fly to certain airports a number of times a day during a certain period of time. This could mean that, according to forecast, United Airlines needs to fly 700,000 passengers out of Newark Liberty International Airport every day during the month of March. Because United only has a contingency for 75 departures a day, planning without a rough capacity check and rearranging of schedules over the long term would result in chaos and probably a lot of lawsuits.

On the other hand, even if the demand gate is properly managed, and flight tickets are sold accordingly, there is still the need for short-term changes, expediting, and upgrades. When all those people arrive at the airport that day, they still need to be checked in and guided toward the right gate before they can board the plane to reach their destination. This is no different for a sports event where tickets were sold at an earlier date, and spectators need to be managed through the gates to their seats, or when jobs need to be sequenced and scheduled on a production line. Gate control is necessary to avoid chaos and it certainly helps to smooth things out for the fulfillment of ever-changing demand.

We've discussed these gates in Chapter 1, where the importance of their place in a systematized supply chain sequence of tasks was pointed out.

In between the supply and demand gates resides the policy engine, which plans, schedules, and delivers components, parts, finished goods, and material measured by service levels and inventory buffering. The key to successful and effective materials planning is in the balancing act of matching demand with a supply that needs as little as possible buffering (inventory, capacity, time) to service demand in full and on time.

The Demand Gate between Planning, Sales, and Production

When a customer orders a product, the demand is transferred into materials planning, and the sales order is asking for availability. The sales order then does or doesn't find that availability either in inventory, on a schedule, or on a plan (see Figure 3.6).

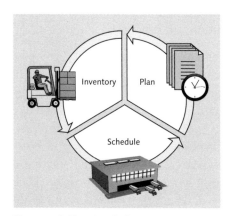

Figure 3.6 Planning Cycle

In other words, the sales order first asks, "Is there inventory to fulfill the demand right away?" If not, the availability check can then look out onto the fixed schedule and check for production orders that could fulfill the demand on the date the production order delivers it to inventory. And if that isn't happening either, we could still look if there is a planned order providing the requested quantity at an even later date out on the plan. Should the customer be happy with a delivery date that complies to this check, we can save the sales order and transfer the demand.

That process, if executed correctly, should ensure that we're not changing the plan—or schedule—every time variability has gotten the most of us and customers order a little bit more or less than what we expected. Variable demand is part of our lives, and the demand gate represents the police department that enforces policies and strategies manifested during management meetings. There the rules are laid out: "We want to hold 5 days of coverage in safety inventory." "Our service level target is 97%." "Our lead time to the customer should never exceed four weeks." These are management directives and supply chain strategies that need to be translated into materials planning and then executed accordingly.

Figure 3.7 depicts the sequence of events in a product availability check: first look for available inventory, then look for a receipt from the line, and finally look for a receipt from the plan.

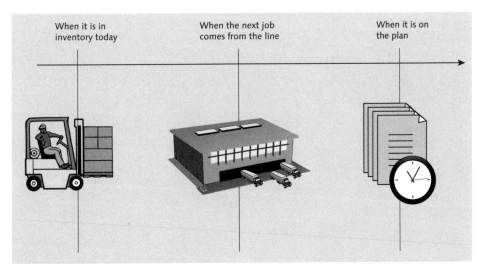

When it is in inventory today

When the next job comes from the line

When it is on the plan

Figure 3.7 Availability Check Looking for Product in the Planning Cycle

But before we work toward the execution of any given supply chain policy, we must ask the following so often forgotten questions: Do we make this product to a customer order, or do we fulfill the product demand from inventory? Do we make (product) to order or do we make (product) to stock? Are we waiting until a customer tells us exactly what she wants before we run the production lines, or do we anticipate the demand and sell to the customer from available stock in the warehouse? These are all basically asking the same question, and they have to be answered before we can execute effective materials planning. The demand gate needs to know the answer to do a good job of balancing supply and demand.

Let's look at a typical product planning cycle in which there is the entry of demand that might be customer orders, a forecast, or both. The MRP run generates planned orders to cover demand from a planning perspective. Then comes sequencing and scheduling of orders. After component availability checks, the orders are converted into a fixed and finite production program. That program is executed, and finished goods are received into inventory from where they are shipped to customers. So as described in the planning cycle, information about demand and supply moves through a plan, a schedule, and into inventory. However, there is a significant difference on whether a product moves through the cycle as an MTS or as an MTO (see Figure 3.8).

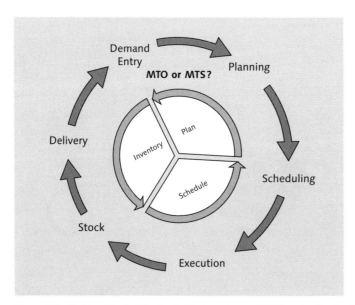

Figure 3.8 Making Product to Available Inventoy or Waiting for the Custome Order?

When MTS product moves through the cycle, it goes through all phases (see Figure 3.9). Forecast serves as the sole provider of demand, and supply is being planned, sequenced, and scheduled before it gets made and put into free available stock. Any customer orders will only look for that available inventory to be fulfilled. That is why we talk about fill rates in an MTS environment instead of service levels.

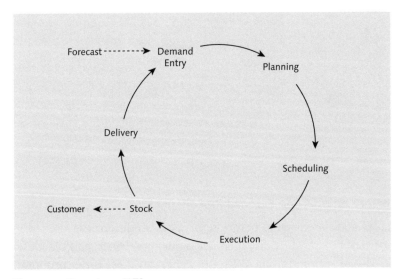

Figure 3.9 Open Loop MTS

For make-to-order (MTO) products, the process presents itself very differently. There is no forecasted demand, and we strictly wait until a customer orders the product before we spring into action (see Figure 3.10). Because there is no anticipation of demand, there is no need for planning, and the order falls directly into the schedule to be supplied. Because of this, it's important to leave some room on the production lines for MTO to drop in. If there is no capacity left open for these orders, the availability check can't promise a delivery date, and scheduling fails. MTO product isn't kept in stock and will be delivered directly to the customer.

As you can see, there are very distinct differences in the availability check, planning, scheduling, and stock keeping for MTS versus MTO products. If we don't pay attention and set up everything the same way, we'll drive noise, inaccuracy, and chaos into the supply chain. Of course there are many variations on the MTS and MTO themes that we'll discuss in more detail in the next subsection.

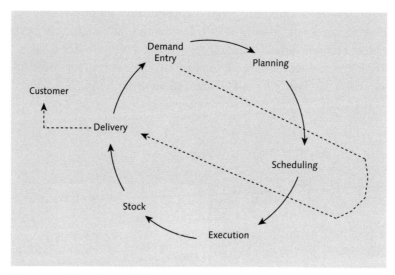

Figure 3.10 Closed Loop MTO

Supply Gates before Internal and External Procurement

The lower (supply) gates are located before terms and conditions are applied in procurement and before a production scheduler sequences, levels, and schedules planned orders. The planning run (or MRP run) generates these order proposals (requisitions and planned orders) without any consideration of resource availability or agreements negotiated with suppliers. Order proposals are simply stacked on top of each other to the latest possible delivery date so that demand can be met from a planning point of view. As can be seen in the demand and supply profile in Figure 3.11, supply is coming in just before the required dates according to a MRP policy set in the master record. There is no capacity leveling or sequencing happening during the planning run. Some action will have to take place after the MRP run so that supply is coming in according to real-world constraints. The MRP run, also called the planning run, doesn't take the real world into account—it only works in the planning world. These two gates are where the planning world result gets translated into a real-world supply plan. Planned orders are scheduled for feasibility, and purchase requisitions are adjusted so that suppliers can deliver within their own limitations and constraints. If you neglect these two gates and the associated tasks—and too many people and organizations do—your supply plan will need to be expedited and adjusted throughout its entire lifecycle.

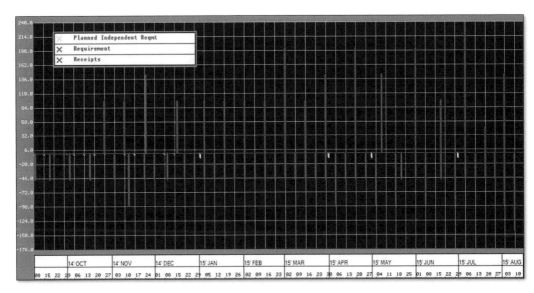

Figure 3.11 Collective Supply Covering Individual Demand*

In our personal schedules, we have to consider the planning gates too. If you want to get somewhere at a specific time, you can't just subtract the time it takes to get there from the time you want to be there—especially if you have to go through a bottleneck like the Holland Tunnel, which connects New Jersey with the island of Manhattan. If you want to enter from the Jersey side on a Friday night, you'll find yourself in a huge traffic jam. This is because lots of people want to see a Broadway show or go party in the West Village—all at the approximate same time. Ideally, somebody would anticipate this rush and sequence, level and schedule it backwards throughout the week, so that at any time of the week exactly two cars go through the toll both every 10 seconds. That would greatly enhance flow, and no one would have to wait.

Unfortunately this isn't possible because the people in the cars don't have the time to go through the tunnel on Tuesday morning and then wait in Manhattan until Friday night when the Fred Hersch Trio plays at the Village Vanguard. But in production scheduling, that is very well possible and needs to be done. As the demand—forecast and customer orders—gets collected, and the planning run generates order proposals, it does so with a delivery day that is just before the time of the demand (in MRP, that time is scheduled in calendar days)—much in the same way as if someone wants to go to Broadway and tries driving through the Holland Tunnel 10 minutes before the show starts.

We'll now have to schedule these order proposals backward in time so that they fit onto the production line and can flow through without too much work in process (WIP) piling up. For that, the planned orders in the pool need to be sequenced in a prioritized way, leveled within available resource capacity, and then backwards scheduled using the lead time from the routing.

A similar thing needs to happen with external supply where purchase requisitions must be converted into fixed supply or a purchase order. Some of the terms and conditions may already be used when the purchase requisitions are generated, and scheduling agreements might be used if there is a tight relationship with the vendor, but in its purest sense, a buyer will have to apply these conditions and go through some activities to make quantities and delivery dates feasible.

So don't forget that there are additional steps required after the planning run has generated the order proposals and the production lines and vendors get into gear to deliver on the plan. Every effective materials planning model has provisions for gate control.

Now that we've discussed the basic components of planning, let's consider the various planning strategies to achieve automation and seamless integration between the sales and production departments.

3.1.3 Strategies to Connect Sales with Production

The interface between the sales and production departments is a critical one. Very often the two departments work in silos. But in standard SAP, you can find preconfigured strategies that help you close the gap between these two departments. All strategies discussed here are at the crossroads between demand and supply, and they greatly enhance communication, transparency, and automation. The supply chain's goal is to be agile and fulfill every customer's wish on time and on quantity, but it's also important to minimize waste and enable smooth replenishment and production. Proper use of the planning strategy helps achieve both these objectives.

A big problem is that products aren't optimally set up for either one of these planning strategies. Either the wrong assignment happens, or production has a different idea than sales, about what the product assignment should be. Additionally, there is the need to periodically analyze the product portfolio and adjust the assignment if needed because what is MTO today might be MTS tomorrow. The ultimate achievement, one that both production and sales departments strive for, is to have the right product at the right place in the right quantity at the right time. Planning strategies are one of the most important drivers to achieve exactly that. So what does it mean to "make to stock"? We'll define the different strategies for managing supply and demand in the next subsections.

Overview at a Glance

All of these strategies are delivered in a SAP ERP Customizing table that includes many variations; the 35 or so strategies cover most requirements a business could have to bridge the gap between sales and production. Following is a summary of the planning strategies and the specific SAP strategies that will be discussed in Part II of this book:

- **Make-to-stock (MTS)**
  Standard product made to a forecast before any committed orders come in.

- **Make-to-order (MTO)**
  Standard products not held in inventory and made after a committed order comes in.

- **Assemble-to-order/finish-to-order (ATO/FTO)**
  Standard product where components are held in stock, and the finished product is finished after the order comes in.

- **Configure-to-order (CTO)**
  The standard product has variations; there aren't enough to justify the creation of a part number for every variation, but there are enough to make the underlying structure too complex to handle.

- **Engineer-to-order (ETO)**
  Complex structures and customer-specified projects that were never built before and make it impossible to be handled with standard variations.

Each of these strategies are explained in more detail in the following subsections.

Make-to-Stock Planning

When your product is a commodity that can be sold out of a catalog and is defined and specified through a master record, it can be planned if it's somewhat predictable. A steady consumption in the past helps predict the future; however, there may be events in the future that require a more forward-looking planning process. In any case, if you can somewhat predict what will happen, you may consider a MTS strategy. Even if it's hard to predict the future, but the customer doesn't accept long delivery times, you might be required to make some of your product to stock.

Making to stock means production without actual, customer requirements. The sales order doesn't drive the production program but the forecast does. Incoming sales orders use existing inventory for the delivery, which keeps the customer lead time to a minimum. After your product is identified as MTS, the availability check in the sales order must look for inventory and not place additional load in the production program. If there is no stock, your service level degrades, and the customer needs to wait for the next receipt from production.

A common disconnect between sales and production is the "customer is king" paradigm. It doesn't have any validity in an MTS scenario. If you want to make the customer the king, you need to make your product to that specific customer's order, which is called make-to-order.

Make-to-Order Production

This strategy still is for standard products that have a clearly defined specification. Other than MTS, there is absolutely no forecast on products that are made to an order from a customer. You start production after the customer's request comes in and not, like with MTS, beforehand. When you identify a product to be made to order, the availability check in the sales order needs a lead time — the time it takes to replenish or produce the product from soup to nuts. Therefore, when a customer requests the item, no freely available stock to fulfill the order can be found. Everything is made from scratch and takes its time.

Another typical disconnect is that you can't plan for a 100% (or more!) utilization on the production line and allow for the free flow of orders, which were set to MTO, into the production schedule. All too often, there is pressure to fully utilize the line, which can only be done with orders resulting from a forecast. If MTS fills the line, and MTO orders drop on top, they fall into backlog, and the quoted lead time to the customer is a farce.

Assemble-to-Order or Finish-to-Order with Placement of the Inventory/ Order Interface

This type of strategy allows for a placement of a stocking point, the inventory/ order interface, at the most effective spot in the product structure. What this means is that you can decide at what point material is kept in stock readily available in the bill of materials (BOM) for further processing. Therefore, upstream of the inventory/order interface, we're MTS, and downstream from it, we're MTO. This also means that downstream from the inventory/order interface, we have lead time to the customer, whereas the availability check doesn't need to consider time for the processes upstream from the inventory/order interface.

Assemble-to-order (ATO) provides flexibility, speed, and waste reduction. Some say it's agile and lean at the same time.

Assembly strategies have the capability to generate a production order to assemble the finished product right out of the sales order. As this happens, the system can also check on component availability. If there is a shortage, it can provide a reasonable date for when the finished product can be delivered. If that date isn't fixed, and we've yet to see a sales person fix a date yet, production scheduling is burdened with a demand for today, and tomorrow for tomorrow, and so on. What's happening is that a sales representative agrees on a date with the customer who would be quite happy to get the product on that date in the future. However, that same sales representative tells the production people that the product needs to be available right away. Consider how many orders there are and that this pressure pops up every day from now on until the order is delivered, and you can easily see that there is room for improvement in the communication department.

Configure-to-Order

When a standard product has variation in its specification, we need to determine whether to create a material master record number for every variation or to make use of the Variant Configurator (VC). If the VC is used, an underlying structure will have to be built, which allows you to configure a variation of one material number (configurable) based on features and options. The underlying structure has optional values and characteristics that have dependencies and limitations. Be aware that in the same way there is a line where it becomes more efficient to use options and characteristics to build a specification, there is also a line where it becomes more feasible to use a whole new project to build a complex product that has never been built before. In other words, building the underlying structure with features and options and dependencies becomes far too complex.

So there is an upper limit as well as a lower limit in complexity where configure-to-order (CTO) has its right to exist. CTO is a strategy that closely resembles MTO or ATO for the finished product, and components can be MTS using a forecast based on probability factors maintained for options and features.

Engineer-to-Order

The VC almost always fails when that fine line is crossed where engineer-to-order (ETO) should have taken over! It's not the lack of functionality and features of the VC that make it fail; it's mostly that the VC is used for a structure where projects and Work Breakdown Structures (WBSs) would much better suit the handling of the complex product or structure in question.

ETO is used when complex structures are built. In most cases, these projects organize many tasks and follow a long time line to produce large, highly customized products to specific customer specifications. The finished product and also many components and subassemblies have never been built before and receive brand new product codes. WBSs and projects are used to structure and manage the procurement of long lead-time purchased parts, the dependencies in production and procurement, and cost and timely delivery of the final product.

3.2   Strategic and Tactical Materials Planning

Strategic materials planning is concerned with the general setting of a supply chain strategy. Typically, a strategic materials planner classifies and reclassifies an entire materials portfolio once a month. He then takes materials from an entire class and sets overall policy. Strategic materials planning therefore is the act of periodically connecting a company's supply chain strategy with the way this strategy is translated into the SAP application for materials planning. This is so that the tool can take on the planning for most materials in an automated way.

The tactical materials planner is more concerned with fine-tuning, expediting, and rescheduling individual orders for materials where the overall policy didn't deliver the best results. This is usually due to variation in demand or supply and expressed by an exception message.

A strategic materials planner acts like air traffic control (ATC). Just like every airport has a set of departure and arrival patterns or policies that ATC designs and prescribes to the participating aircraft, the strategic materials planner designs and prescribes replenishment and planning policies for materials and parts.

Like ATC, a strategic materials planner reviews his standard policies on a periodic basis. Does the automatic reorder policy replenish to a maximum stock level or with a fixed lot size? Is our forecast-based planning procedure buffered with stock or a longer lead time? Is the safety stock dynamically recalculated or static? The strategic material planner answers those questions and subsequently provides the tactical materials planner with a baseline setup that he can tweak and optimize on a daily basis, depending on the exception messages that occur.

Tactical control happens in the cockpit or in the daily exception monitor (Transaction MD06). Like a pilot works within the wider boundaries of the ATC policy and fine-tunes the approach (or departure) using flap settings, landing gear, and glide slope, the tactical materials planner increases the reorder point when the supplier repeatedly delivers later than planned (or looks for a new supplier).

Let's look at some organizational considerations that might be necessary to introduce the two roles of strategic and tactical materials planning.

3.2.1 Organizational Considerations

The roles of strategic and tactical materials planning in an organization can be performed by the same person. It's not necessary to split up the job but, of course, you can institute a more strategic thinking planner role. The idea behind the model of effective materials planning is to instill a more analytically working planner (instead of one who merely executes transactions); in that sense, the strategic materials planner fulfills that requirement. The tactical planner, however, works in that direction as well. After we address exception messages, reduce superfluous inventory, and try to avoid stock-outs, we ensure that we've fixed the root source of the problem so that we aren't constantly expediting orders in and out. A tactical materials planner works with a system that has all the tools to quickly analyze and find the problem and is competent enough to know how to adjust the policy for a sustainable fix.

Many organizations implement the new role of a strategic materials planner who periodically sets policy. This person performs a segmentation on a quarterly or even monthly basis and reclassifies the entire portfolio of the plant. He then sets policy for a number of materials according to the strategies given for specific classes. For example, a company's leadership may meet to discuss supply chain strategy for the next year. In this meeting, service level goals, inventory targets, and priorities are discussed and decided on. The strategic materials planners then translate the supply chain strategy into policies and build a playbook with detailed descriptions of the policies. On a periodic basis, a strategic material planner sets and resets policy on an aggregated level to establish a general course that conforms to management's directives and the supply chain strategy for the year. The tactical materials planner takes over from here and monitors individual materials with exception messages so that the policy can be fine-tuned for better performance.

Depending on the size of the organization, there are many options on the composition of strategic versus tactical materials planners. Most commonly, there is one strategic materials planner for each manufacturing plant or distribution center, whereas there are many tactical materials planners to take care of the daily exception monitoring, expediting, and gate control. In general, no more than 5,000 materials should be assigned to a tactical materials planner, and even that may be way too much to handle. Especially when there are no supporting tools such as the MRP Monitor, and every material has to be set up with a policy manually. For that reason, it's very important to design standardized processes that can be repeated and executed by all planners in the same way

3.2.2 Designing Standard Processes for Strategic and Tactical Materials Planning

The model of effective materials planning consists of, among many other things, repeatable and sequenced tasks and processes. Automation, accuracy, transparency, and productivity occur when strategic and tactical events overlap and support each other. After the yearly management meeting that is meant to deliver a common supply chain strategy, the strategic materials planner performs a segmentation of the portfolio to classify each material in up to six dimensions. These dimensions can include an ABC analysis for consumption values, XYZ for consumption consistency, LMN for size or volume, EFG for replenishment lead time, UVW for price, and LRODI lifecycle analysis.

We'll discuss the segmentation of a portfolio in detail in Part II of this book, but without a periodic segmentation or classification, the policies maintained in the material master get quickly out of whack and drive the wrong inventory and bad service levels. Segmentation and the subsequent re-classification of materials should be done no less and no more than every three months. If you change the classification every month, you cause a lot of noise, and if you wait for six months, you might miss major changes in the behavior of individual materials and keep on using an ineffective policy.

Then there are the many tasks a tactical materials planner carries out: exception monitoring, expediting, policy tweaking, order conversion, gate control, and inventory optimization, to just name a few. In Chapter 7, we'll describe a typical day in the life of a tactical materials planner and propose a detailed model; however, in the end, every effective materials planner will use the tools at his disposal and build his own system that consists out of prioritized, sequenced, and repeatable tasks to achieve automation and control over the portfolio.

Figure 3.12 represents an example of the design and documentation of repeatable tasks in strategic and tactical materials planning. The tasks of the strategic materials planner, depicted above the line, are executed periodically either quarterly, monthly, or weekly. A tactical materials planner performs tasks as they become necessary throughout the working day.

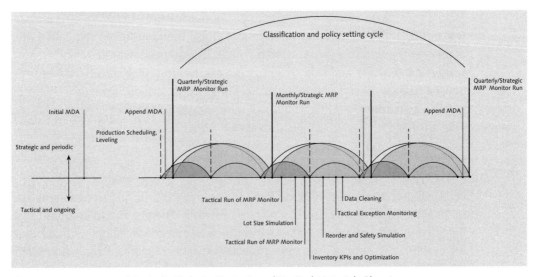

Figure 3.12 Frequent and Periodic Tasks in Strategic and Tactical Materials Planning

Because we're discussing the building blocks of an effective system of materials planning with modeling, gate control, and various roles in the organization, it's important that you understand some basic scientific principles. These principles can help greatly with the building of such a model. Let's look at some applicable theories for our materials planning model.

3.3 Scientific Theories and Global Integration

As you're very well aware, management theories and buzzwords abound in the world of supply chain management. Some are grounded in solid scientific research and evaluation; some are not. One of the paradigms of this book is to use science and predictive analysis to better manage materials planning. Especially when it comes to modeling and measuring, a framework of scientific reference comes in very handy. Without that framework, there is often confusion and downright chaos at the helm of navigating the roads of strategic direction with a destination in mind.

Materials planning with SAP takes place at the plant level. But in actuality its effects are far more global in companies that operate across continents. Most planning systems were designed and built locally and then expected to function globally. Only rarely, if ever, does this kind of thing produce the expected results; more often than not, the inefficiencies aren't visible, and no one knows where the problem is.

A scientific approach with consideration of global integration and standardization of processes might just give you what you desire and need: transparency, measurability, automation, and selective problem resolution under consideration of the holistic impact. In the following subsections, we describe our favorite theories, which might apply in a practical sense to the way you're running materials planning with SAP.

3.3.1 Systems Thinking

Let's start with systems thinking first. It's an approach to problem solving that looks at the problems as part of a system or whole. The practice of systems thinking is grounded in the fact that you can't look at one process alone without looking at the entire system. You must look at cyclical versus linear cause and effect. For example, you can't change inventory levels without affecting cost and customer service.

When working with an organizational structure, such as a supply chain or materials planning specifically, the system is the combination of the people, structures, processes, and environment that work together (or don't work together) to create a desired outcome. A healthy system delivers the desired outcome. An unhealthy system delivers unintended consequences. In most instances, we don't implement our materials planning system that way. We look at isolated processes and functions and then design standard operating procedures that are, to make it worse, almost entirely driven by gap analysis, known functionality in SAP, and a narrow point of view instead of a cause-and-effect approach that provides a holistic view of things.

Logistician David Schneider suggests, "We supply chain managers maintain and feed a conceit that we understand and employ systems thinking in the execution of our duties. That is an excessively favorable opinion of our own abilities and actions. The idea that as a class of managers we use systems thinking in the planning and execution of supply chain management is somewhat imaginary, conceived in our own minds, perhaps farfetched." And that is if managers even know about systems thinking. Schneider suggests that some people might get offended by his statement and continues, "If so, go watch the receiving dock of any large distribution center and ask yourself, how much systems thinking did the company's shipping into this operation employ? And if you still insist to use system thinking for the design of your operations management, I want to ask you: When was the last time you drew a Causal Loop or Stock and Flow diagram?"

It really is necessary to think in systems because we live in a complex world, surrounded by complex systems of people, objects, and actions. Most activities, even when they look simple on the surface, can be very complex when examined more thoroughly. Our ability to visualize the components of a system and the interaction between the components, and understand the outside impacts on the system, directly affects our ability to comprehend the complexity of that system. Visualization is key to cognitive ability; the ability to understand what is going on.

Figure 3.13 shows how causal loop diagrams (CLDs) display the causes and effects of actions taken or functions performed. CLDs are a great way to gain insight into the sometimes hidden dynamics of a system.

Schneider provides an example with a diagram from the Association for Operations Management (APICS) that focuses on new product development and illustrates the complexity of a single supply chain. He states, "As complex as it looks, this is really a basic, simple model. There are only ten nodes of influence, and only five cycles." He explains it using the reinforcing system and the balancing system, which are included here in his words:

- ▶ **The Engine — The Reinforcing System**
  The core of the model is the New Product Growth. This loop is a reinforcing loop, in which each cycle of the loop reinforces the action, like a snowball roll-

ing down a hillside. Without friction and with no end to hill or snow, the snow-ball builds in size and momentum. Demand influences the Need for Supply, influencing the Sources for Supply, influencing the Inventory, Influencing Price, which influences Demand. Without any other outside influences, Demand will drive more supply, building more inventory and lower prices, driving more demand.

▶ **Brakes and Controls—The Balancing System**

Surrounding the core engine of this supply chain system are four interdependent systems. Each of these systems influences the core from the outside, slowing it down and influencing the growth. Longer Transportation distances increase the transportation cost and the lead-time. Longer distances also increase risk of disruption. A longer lead-time can affect the inventory we need, indirectly, as supply chain vulnerability increases. As the conditions of each of these influencing factors changes, the resistance that each of the balancing systems places on the Engine changes.

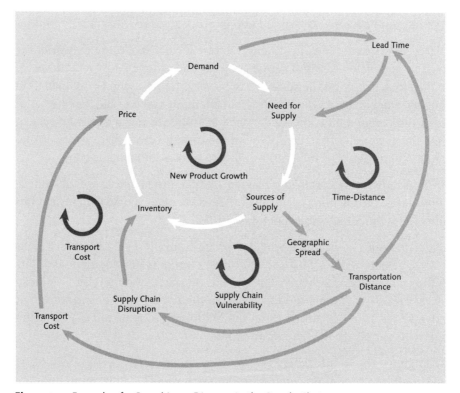

Figure 3.13 Example of a Causal Loop Diagram in the Supply Chain

3.3.2 Factory Physics and Supply Chain Science

As stated in the previous chapter, *Factory Physics* is a book written by Wallace Hopp and Mark Spearman, which introduces a framework for operations management. According to the book's preface, Factory Physics is described as "...a systematic description of the underlying behavior of manufacturing systems. Understanding it enables managers and engineers to work with the natural tendencies of manufacturing systems to.

- "Identify opportunities for improving existing systems.
- "Design effective new systems.
- "Make the tradeoffs needed to coordinate policies from disparate areas."

The book is used both in industry and in academia for reference and teaching on operations management. It describes a new approach to operations management based on the laws of Factory Physics science. The fundamental Factory Physics framework states that the essential components of all value streams or production and replenishment processes are demand and transformation which are described by structural elements of flows and stocks. There are very specific practical and mathematical relationships that enable you to describe and control the performance of flows and stocks. The book states that, in the presence of variability, there are only three buffers available to synchronize demand and transformation with lowest cost and highest service level:

- Capacity
- Inventory
- Response time

The authors of the book also say that its approach enables practical, predictive understanding of flows and stocks and how to best use the three levers to optimally synchronize demand and transformation.

As stated in the previous chapter, Hopp also authored a paper called "Supply Chain Science," which built on the laws, principles, and corollaries from Factory Physics to expand the framework to a wider area of supply chain management. In this book, we'll base much of the modeling part on the excellent work of Hopp and Spearman, which is further refined and translated into a practical science for managers by Ed Pound and his team at the company Factory Physics Inc. in Bryant, Texas.

3.3.3   SAP Value Stream Mapping and Lean Dynamics

An SAP value stream map contains the same elements as any value stream map you might use to implement in a lean manner or to gain visibility into weak spots and opportunities to improve flow and the supply chain in general. A value stream map always has an information flow running from right to left—from customer back to vendor—whereas the material flow runs into the opposite direction, downstream from vendors through production resources and lines to distribution centers and eventually to the customers. Along those ways, you can document all kinds of data. Besides the typical cycle times, throughput, demand pattern, capacity availability and so on, an SAP value stream map allows you to maintain master data settings (for material master, work center, or routing), transaction entry data (e.g., how you would use Transaction MD06), and even Customizing settings.

An SAP value stream map includes not only the material and information flow but also SAP-specific master data and Customizing settings. As shown in Figure 3.14, the SAP value stream map includes field values from the materials master record, Customizing, and document types. All this can be very useful in the decision making and design of how the SAP applications are to support a model of effective materials planning. Let's look at an example from one of the models we designed for a client using SAP to run the supply chain.

An SAP value stream map serves many purposes. First and foremost, it's meant to document the model and move the business from a current state to the new and improved future state.

Lean dynamics is a business management practice that emphasizes the same primary outcome as lean manufacturing or lean production, that is, eliminating wasteful expenditure of resources. However, lean dynamics is distinguished by the different focus of creating a structure for accommodating the dynamic business conditions that cause these wastes to accumulate in the first place. Like lean manufacturing, lean dynamics is a variation on the theme of creating efficiencies and greater value by optimizing flow rather than by maximizing economies of scale.

Lean dynamics takes a different approach. It doesn't directly target the desired outcome of waste elimination; instead, it focuses on identifying and addressing sources of "lag," or imbedded disconnects in flowing value through operations, decision making, information, and innovation that lead to workarounds and amplifies disruption when business conditions change. It promotes a different way of structuring the business that creates an inherent dynamic stability or greater responsiveness for accommodating shifting business conditions. Companies that are structured in this way show dramatically greater customer value as measured by their quality, innovation, and customer satisfaction; they also sustain greater corporate value as measured by profitability, market capitalization, and growth.

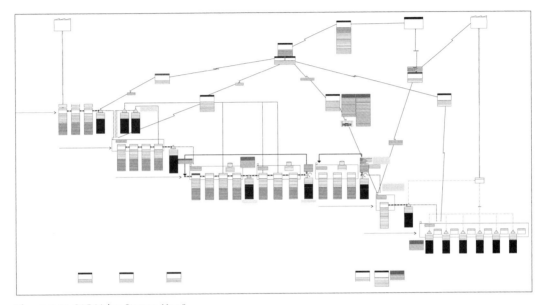

Figure 3.14 SAP Value Stream Map*

3.4 Summary

Modeling represents the first building block of a system of effective materials planning. By using demand and supply profiles, you can visualize the information flow and gain valuable insights into the dynamics of a supply chain with the intention of improving flow, automation, and transparency for better decision making.

But one must respect and deal with demand and supply gates. The demand gate, as the interface between sales and production, needs to be set up correctly so that the system can operate correctly in both a basic MTS and MTO environment. The planning strategy with its rules for availability checking, forecast consumption, and placement of the inventory/order interface is what closes the gap with that type of integration and helps make communication more efficient between the departments.

Taking a closer look at the organizational needs for effective materials planning might reveal that a separation between tactical and strategic materials planning might deliver great advantages in that it provides standardized operating procedures for handling exceptional situations but also offers an overall procedure to set general policy on a group level.

Also an important building block for the overall system of materials planning is the understanding, application, and use of proven scientific theories so that you can develop good intuition for decision making and proactively managing future results. Without a good understanding of the underlying laws and principles that make a supply chain work, you can neither plan desired results nor expect that you're getting any.

PART II
Materials Planning in SAP ERP

Change your opinions, keep to your principles; change your leaves, keep intact your roots.
—Victor Hugo

4   Principles of Effective Materials Planning

What's predictable today becomes unpredictable tomorrow, and a long lead time might be cut in half because the sourcing department signed up with a new supplier. A good materials planner adjusts his policies regularly, and a good leader provides the materials planner with a clear definition of what's expected.

In this chapter, we explore the principles to keep in mind to ensure that your materials planning is as effective as possible. A functioning system of effective materials planning includes the following three "simple" things, as you can see in Figure 4.1.

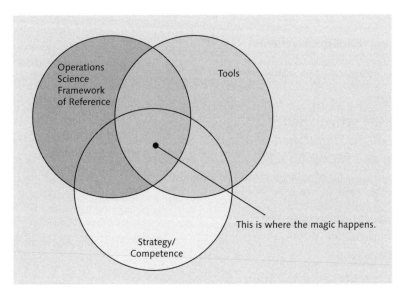

Figure 4.1 The Vital Overlapping of Three Parts of Effective Materials Planning

- ▶ Framework of reference where system boundaries are defined and performance targets are set
- ▶ Well-defined strategy by leadership that gives guidance to a competent planner
- ▶ All the tools and transactions necessary to manage policies for thousands of materials with various characteristics

Where these three areas come together is where the magic happens.

From a process point of view, we can define effective materials planning as well. Materials requirements planning (MRP) is the process of maintaining the basic data of a materials portfolio so that it supports automation to keep optimal inventories that provide great service levels at any time under changing conditions.

It's that last phrase of the statement—"under changing conditions"—that is mostly neglected or forgotten. You aren't done after MRP is implemented in SAP ERP, and all the material masters are created. What's driven by an MRP type PD and a fixed lot-size procedure today, might require a consumption-based planning strategy tomorrow to perform well. Conditions change dynamically and all the time. To combat these ever-changing conditions, we'll explore a system of effective materials planning. With it you define your performance boundaries—the limits you're forced to operate within—and execute the four pillars of our methodology:

- ▶ **Prioritized portfolio management**
  Prioritize to get your materials list in order, clean of outdated and false information, and under control in terms of managing the replenishment and exceptional situations.

- ▶ **Automated and periodic policy setting**
  Use this for the standardization, automation, and improvement of the replenishment process. This bit also solves the problem of the near impossible task of keeping the basic data of a large materials portfolio constantly clean and effective.

- ▶ **Intelligent exception monitoring**
  Use this monitoring to contain variability and to cure deviations from the plan quickly and efficiently.

- ▶ **Continuous inventory optimization**
  Use this optimization to prevent one-time reductions to stand as the only efforts to keep inventory levels low.

Using these methods, will bring about automation and standardization in your process, allow a materials planner to work intuitively and analytically (instead of constantly transacting orders and goods movements), and add transparency and understanding into the dynamics of your materials portfolio that you've never had before.

4.1   Supply Chain Strategy and Performance Boundaries

An effective system of materials planning is based on a sound supply chain strategy. With a strategy, leadership can communicate their intent and ensure that the planner goes by, and works within, the strategic direction that comes from the top. The strategy is your commander's intent. So, first of all, you better have one! Without it, planning is difficult and without bounds. To define a good strategy, it's important that the leaders understand the natural behavior of a supply chain and its influencing factors. Directions such as "reduce inventory" or "shorten the published customer lead time" are worthless and even dangerous if the full implications aren't understood.

4.1.1   Establishing a Solid Framework of Reference

A causal loop diagram (CLD) with systems thinking, as we'll discuss in Part IV of this book, is a great way to define expected results and to ensure good decision making. For example, if leadership decides to promise faster delivery to the customer to increase market share, we can see—depending on the underlying structure of the supply chain system—that variability will increase on the supply side of purchased parts (because more pressure will be imposed on the vendors), and, therefore, safety stocks will have to increase accordingly. This type of thinking ensures clear and concise communication and helps avoid the blame game when inventory levels are perceived as too high.

After the strategy is set, it can be translated into a framework of reference for the planners to use. The following questions need to be answered by a sound supply chain strategy before the planner can set up the fitting policies to adhere to management's plan:

▶ What is the expected service level and associated safety stock requirement for materials belonging to a certain segment (like AXE—high value, high predictability, short lead time)?

▶ What order frequency and lot-size procedure are fitting for an expensive part with a long lead time that is unpredictable?

▶ What level of forecast accuracy is desired?

▶ What is an acceptable variability for late deliveries from suppliers?

A concept from Factory Physics that is very useful for the definition of performance boundaries is efficient frontier curves. In accordance with the theory, there is a minimum inventory holding requirement for every service level. However, this inventory requirement grows exponentially the closer we get to a service level of 100%. There is also a third parameter—the order frequency—that defines the efficient frontier or lowest inventory holding with any given service level. The lower the order frequency in a period, the more up and left the curve goes because you need to order more if you order less frequently. So if you draft up your efficient frontiers, you can plot out how you're comparing to the optimum and whether you're in for a change of policy.

It becomes obvious that we're now using some reference from a desired state before we decide on an action to improve a situation that may or may not need improvement. Without a solid framework of reference, improvement activities often miss the desired outcome. That framework will provide the step-by-step planning procedure to set you up for success.

4.1.2 Leadership Roles

To set your planning system up for success, leadership needs to work with the planners to define a model for sales & operations planning (SOP) that delivers good results on an ongoing and sustainable basis. In Figure 4.2, you can see the necessary steps that help you find your way to translate supply chain strategy and logistics design into standard user guidelines and performance boundaries that lead into the execution of said supply chain strategy using the four pillars of effective materials planning with SAP.

As we already discussed, it's key that a strategy is defined and communicated throughout the organization, and, to that end, an annual meeting with quarterly revisions could be set up. Various standard tools such as SAP value stream mapping or CLDs can be used to define an operations and logistics design strategy. We'll discuss these tools and how to design a scientific framework of reference in more detail in Part IV of this book.

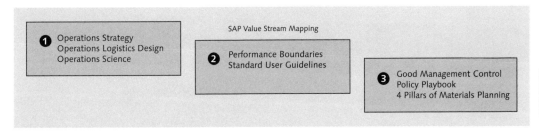

Figure 4.2 Operations Planning Design

Using efficient frontiers and other useful benchmarking tools, you can then define your performance boundaries and have them signed off by the leadership team so that everybody works toward the same goals and targets using standard user's guidelines.

4.1.3 Set Goals and Measure Results

Eventually, you can perform effective materials planning using the four pillars and measure progress and results against clearly set goals:

- Portfolio management
- Policy setting
- Exception monitoring
- Inventory optimization

Supply planning is then split into a strategic part and a tactical part, whereas overall policy is set according to a classification performed by a strategic materials planner. The tactical materials planner then manages exceptions and fine-tunes the policy on a daily basis.

As depicted in Figure 4.3, if we want to define an operations planning system, we could organize a structure of periodic meetings and ensure well-communicated targets and goals throughout the internal supply chain. First, we'll define a supply chain strategy meeting where leadership and planners explore opportunities for improvement within the boundaries of the possible performance the organization exhibits. Very often, this type of communication does not happen. But how can we define a direction, targets, and goals if we don't know or ignore the boundaries of the system?

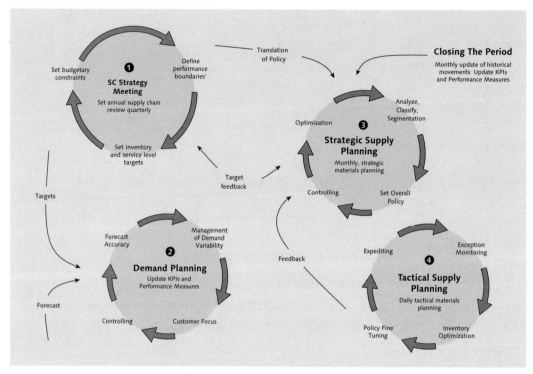

Figure 4.3 Operations Planning

What lead times will we quote to our customers? What products do we put on the shelf, and which ones do we customize to order? After these decisions are made, we'll have to be more specific about how much buffering stock we'll use to achieve a certain service level and by which order frequency raw materials ought to be supplied. We're not saying that leadership will have to define all the details around these questions; however, at the least, they will have to be informed and understand what this means to future stock holdings and customer satisfaction. And then they'll have to sign off on the decisions made in this annual meeting. Quarterly revisions of the strategy are probably a good reference and help to stay on target.

With those targets defined and well documented, another team can now execute *demand planning*. Demand planning should probably happen on a more frequent basis—perhaps quarterly. And quite consistent with the new paradigm of buffering strategies, we strive to better manage demand variability rather than trying to anticipate what, when, and how much our customers will order. Eliminate the need for certainty, and set yourself up to weather a storm of variability and changing conditions. The forecast, however, is still an important input into the demand planning process, and the more accurate the forecast, the lower the need for buffers. Forecasting is simply not the Holy Grail by which everything goes anymore. The planning of production lines and raw material purchases needs to be protected with buffers so that slight changes in demand don't amplify and constantly disturb the plan.

With that, we're moving into the supply side of things. In our system of effective materials planning, two distinct activities need to be performed to create a robust, lean, and agile supply plan: (1) strategic supply planning with classification, segmentation, and general policy setting, and (2) tactical supply planning where policy is fine-tuned and exception messages are handled and resolved. The role of a strategic supply planner or materials planner may or may not be executed by the same person that does the tactical daily planning. Some organizations choose to identify a strategic planner for the plant who doesn't own a portfolio per se but ensures a consistent and ongoing translation of the general supply chain strategy to the tactical planning process. We discuss this in more detail in Section 4.4.1.

After general policies are set, a tactical materials planner can manage his portfolio of materials and continuously optimize inventories and service levels within those performance boundaries. Here it's very important that the planner is educated on the same system of portfolio management, policy setting, exception monitoring, and inventory optimization. This guarantees that everybody knows what to do when an exception message warns of a low inventory buffer, for example. It also negates the need for endless discussions around what service level to set in the material master record or how to configure the rules for the availability check in the sales order. A clear strategy formulated well and consistently communicated through all levels of planning makes a world of a difference.

Such a system needs to be organized and documented with standard operating procedures. Figure 4.4 provides an example of defining all the steps and meetings required to accelerate and improve operations planning. We want to create a calendar of repeatable tasks, sessions, and planning activities so that continuity and success is guaranteed. Develop a standard agenda for each meeting, and provide forms for target setting and goal definition. Standard operating procedures should be provided as well as performance control charts and policy designs. Attending theses meeting avoids wasting time later. Instead of everybody guessing what might happen and what needs to be done, clearly defined rules provide guidance and direction. A structured and organized system of effective materials planning avoids confusion and endless discussions, improves on overall organizational performance, and creates a climate of productivity and contentment at work.

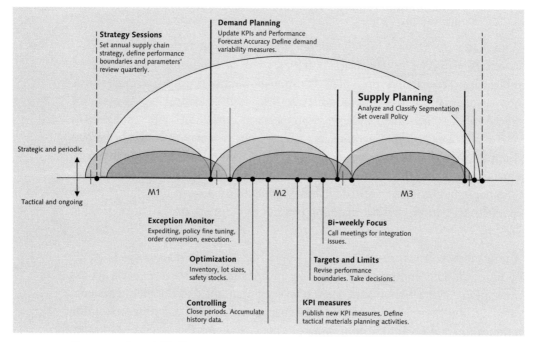

Figure 4.4 Repeatable Processes

4.1.4 Materials Portfolio Segmentation

An important prerequisite for effective materials planning is the classification and segmentation of a materials portfolio. It's like a character description for materials. To describe the character of a purchase part, finished product, or intermediate stocking unit, we must ask questions such as these: Is it small or large? Is it expensive or cheap? Is it predictable or not? Is it a valuable contributor to business success?

How many classes are used to separate the materials portfolio depends largely on the business you're in. Classifying should be done on a periodic basis because what's predictable today might become unpredictable tomorrow, what's been a high contributor for the past 10 years might become replaced next season, and what had a short replenishment lead time could be sourced from a different vendor who quotes a better price but has to send the product from China.

Segmentation is a must for effective materials planning, and we'll discuss it extensively in the next chapter, but here it's important to mention that the strategy dictates the boundaries and ranges each class adheres to.

Table 4.1 represents an example of a segmentation into six dimensions:

- ABC for consumption volume
- XYZ for predictability
- EFG for lead time
- LMN for size or volume
- UVW for price
- LRODIE for lifecycle analysis

	CLASS		RANGE
Volume	A	High consumption volume	80%
	B	Medium consumption volume	15%
	C	Low consumption volume	5%
Predictability	X	Low consumption variation in the past	>0.4
	Y	Medium consumption variation in the past	
	Z	High consumption variation in the past	<1.5
	N	Non-movers	No movements in the last 12 months
Lead Time	E	Short replenishment lead time	<30 days
	F	Medium replenishment lead time	
	G	Long replenishment lead time	>84 days
Size	L	Large footprint/size	>30 sq. ft.
	M	Medium footprint/size	
	N	Small footprint/size	<5 sq. ft.

Table 4.1 Segmentation Boundaries for Six Dimensions Analysis

	CLASS		RANGE
Price	W	$	<100
	V	$$	100-500
	U	$$$	500-1000
	T	$$$$	1000-3000
	S	$$$$$	>3000
Life Cycle	L	New material master	Creation 6 months ago or less
	R	Regular part	
	O	Obsolete	No movements in the past 365 days
	D	Dying	No movements in the past 180 days
	I	Inactive part	Marked for deletion
	E	Error	Process error

Table 4.1 Segmentation Boundaries for Six Dimensions Analysis (Cont.)

Depending on the business you're in, you might want to leave the LMN analysis out or maybe add a Make or Buy decision tree. You may also add a D to the ABC analysis as a fourth category or, as in Table 4.1, an S and a T to the UVW classes. But you must set the ranges ahead of time, before you perform the classification. And the ranges can be different from one location (e.g., a manufacturing plant) to the next, but in the end, a consensus must be reached in the strategy meeting and then adhere to throughout the planning cycle. These ranges don't have to be defined during the strategy meeting, but at the least, they should be signed off there by the leadership team, so that the planner knows exactly how to assign various policies to various classes. All must be done with the agreement and understanding of management.

4.1.5 Performance Boundaries Examples

Table 4.2 depicts a few examples for setting performance boundaries that could be used in demand management and strategic supply planning.

		Predictability/Consistency			
		X	Y	Z	N
	AU	94%	94%	94%	0%
Volume Price	AV	96%	96%	96%	0%
	AW	98%	95%	98%	0%
	B	98%	98%	80%	0%
	C	98%	90%	85%	0%

Table 4.2 Service Levels for the Calculation of Static Safety Stock

In our first example, we'll provide guidelines for service level settings in the MRP2 view of the material master record. This is to determine and calculate static safety stocks that may be used to raise a reorder level. With a service level setting of 94% for all AUX items, we're allowing the possibility of a stock-out for these items in 6% of all cases. AU items are expensive (A for lots of movements, and U for an expensive price); therefore, let's say, a 99% service level would require proportionally higher inventory holdings. On the other hand CX items, because of their low consumption variance and therefore high predictability, can be set up with a very high service level to avoid embarrassing stock-outs of an inexpensive part, which might lock down the production lines and result in lost sales.

As another example, we can define acceptable late deliveries from our suppliers. In Table 4.3, for AU items (expensive and lots of movements), we allow the suppliers to deliver three days late in only 10% of the cases, whereas we give them a little more slack for inexpensive parts. An exception should be generated when this boundary is exceeded, and the suppliers should be made aware of the limits, or you might want them to commit to those limits in a contract.

		Price		
		U	V	W
	A	10%	15%	20%
Volume	B	15%	20%	20%
	C	15%	20%	20%

Table 4.3 Acceptable Late Delivery Rate for a Three-Day Delay

If you use a policy to replenish with a material forecast driven by an MRP type VV, you can define various degrees of accuracy. In the situation shown in Table

4.4, a planner wants to make sure that replenishment for bulky, large parts that take up lots of space in the warehouse is more reliable than something that is cheap and can easily be put away on a shelf.

		Size		
		L	M	N
Price	U	95%	90%	80%
	V	90%	90%	85%
	W			70%

Table 4.4 Required Material Forecast Accuracy

Here we establish clarity around the performance of a dynamic safety stock. A range of coverage profile, which, among other things, drives dynamic safety stock levels, is a very powerful tool for optimizing inventory levels in an automated and dynamic fashion. This dynamic safety stock procedure only works when there is future demand, and it resolves the problem of a static safety stock not being considered in planning. It also allows a planner to set a maximum range of coverage so that our inventories don't explode in a forecasted, under-consumed situation.

Table 4.5 defines various coverage profiles with minimums, targets and maximums to fully leverage the dynamic coverage calculation for various segments of our materials portfolio.

		Predictability/Consistency		
		X	Y	Z
Price	U	1/3/5	1/5/10	1/7/15
	V	1/4/10	1/6/15	1/7/15
	W	1/5/10	1/7/15	1/7/15

Table 4.5 Dynamic Safety Stock/Range of Coverage

Another valuable performance boundary setting is the identification of various lot-size procedures (Table 4.6)—and therefore the determination of order frequencies—according to lengths of the replenishment lead time and storage space requirement of the part. Note that the order frequency is equally important for purchased parts as it is for internally produced products, in which case, a run rate or lot size is used.

The tables in the preceding figures are just examples for a system of defined performance boundaries. By no means do they represent a full list of the boundaries you may define in your environment. Go through the effort to design these boundaries at least once a year and have them signed off by your management, your suppliers, and your production lines. You'll be pleased about the clarity this will bring to your organization, the increase in effectiveness, and the reduction of confusion and finger-pointing in your planning process.

		Size		
		L	M	N
Lead Time	E	Static	Static	Periodic
	F	Static	Optimizing	Periodic
	G	Optimizing	Optimizing	Periodic

Table 4.6 Lot Sizing Procedure/Order Frequency

4.2   Developing User Guidelines and a Policy Playbook

Every football coach provides his team members with a playbook, in which pre-defined strategies are described so that the coach, or quarterback, can call an audible when the situation requires a quick adjustment. That kind of preparedness, standardization, and communality comes in handy in materials planning too. After the performance boundaries and control limits are set out of the strategy meeting at the beginning of the year, we must translate the strategy into detailed policies that the planner can use as the situation affords it.

We recommend detailing the boundaries on paper and summarizing the strategy in a document that we call the Planner's or User's Guidelines. In these guidelines, you can also assemble a policy playbook that each plant can customize and then hand out to the planners so that everybody uses the same strategy—or policy—to counter long lead times and inconsistent consumption, set a service level depending on the importance of the part, and employ a buffering strategy that ensures utmost availability with minimum inventory holdings dependent on a multitude of influencing factors.

The important thing is that everybody uses the same policy for the same situation: service level of 98% if the item is AX, optimize lot size procedure for items that are taking up a lot of space, and have a long lead time and a material forecast for predictable items with a long lead time. No more discussions or guesswork are called for because the strategy is clear, well documented, and the guiding light for every planner.

Creating visuals in the form of cards for the policy can be very helpful. On the card, which looks like an approach plate for an Instrument Flight Rules (IFR) pilot, you can document all kinds of information as shown in Figure 4.5.

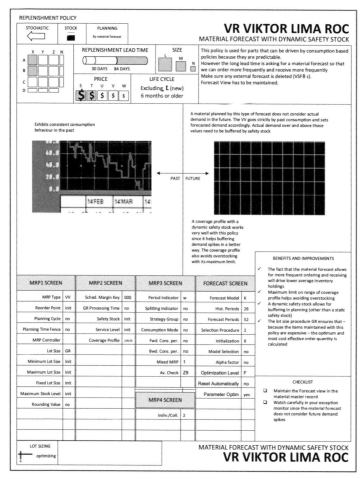

Figure 4.5 Consumption-Based Replenishment Policy Card

Create your own system, but create it with the team. Publish it and see that every-one is using it. Otherwise, planners will develop their own way of doing things that isn't always aligned with the supply chain strategy in the minds of leadership.

4.3   Setting Control Limits

Control limits and control charts are terms from Six Sigma literature. Control limits are horizontal lines drawn on a statistical process control chart, sometimes at a distance of ±3 standard deviations of the plotted statistic from the mean. They can be used in materials planning as well. When you display the inventory graphs from the Logistics Information System (LIS), you can overlay the control limits to compare planned inventory levels with actuals.

Control limits should not be confused with tolerance limits or specifications, which are completely independent of the distribution of the plotted sample statistic. Control limits describe what a process is capable of producing (sometimes referred to as the "voice of the process"), while tolerances and specifications describe how the product should perform to meet the customer's expectations (referred to as the "voice of the customer"). In materials planning we can therefore define desired inventory level ranges and depict violations of the boundaries when inventory gets too high or too low.

We don't have to necessarily use the control limits here exactly as they are described in Six Sigma, but we can make use of the concept in, let's say, inventory management. As an example, we could define upper- and lower ranges for acceptable stock holdings. The range of coverage key performance indicator (KPI) lends itself perfectly to this, and with the setting of a range of coverage profile, you can even drive the MRP run to the desired results.

Figure 4.6 shows minimum and maximum control limits for upper and lower inventory coverages. The figure was designed according to the performance boundaries identified earlier and aligned with traffic light colors in Transaction MD07. Thus we can see that AX parts ideally have an inventory coverage of between 4 and 10 days. If the inventory coverage actually moves between those limits, the Transaction MD07 collective view displays a yellow light for that part. Anything less than 4 days of coverage alerts you with a red light, and inventory coverage of more than 12 days results in a green light in this example. At a glance, you can now see in Transaction MD07 where you have too much inventory, where you're spot on, and where you start getting into dangerous territory for stock-outs.

	A	B	C
X	12 days	10 days	10 days
	10 days	8 days	8 days
	4 days	3 days	2 days
	2 days	1 day	1 day
Y	15 days	16 days	16 days
	10 days	15 days	15 days
	5 days	6 days	7 days
	4 days	3 days	3 days
Z	20 days	18 days	18 days
	15 days	13 days	13 days
	7 days	6 days	5 days
	6 days	5 days	4 days

Figure 4.6 Minimum and Maximum Upper and Lower Control Limits for Inventory Coverage*

Full-Color Figures

The asterisk denotes that a full-color version of this figure can be viewed in the supplemental downloads that came with this book. The full-color version shows a clearer representation of the traffic light colors. The figure in the e-book is full-color as well.

To gain even more control, you can now set a minimum and a maximum coverage in your range of coverage profile. Those minimum and maximum settings correspond to the minimum lower control limit and the maximum upper control limit, respectively. They also drive automation into the inventory management process because they generate additional replenishment on the low side of inventory and cut the replenishment (or generate an exception message to alert you that the maximum inventory level is exceeded) on the high side of your inventory holding.

The control limits, of course, can be vastly different for expensive, unpredictable items than they are for cheap items that feature consistent past consumption from period to period.

You can also visualize the control limits on the inventory graph as shown in Figure 4.7. The line shows past inventory levels over time, and, in this example, the perfect inventory levels were only reached twice over the past 13 months. This type of bad performance usually occurs when the planner doesn't use a manual planning process and has to watch every item. To reduce monitoring workload, inventories are inflated so that stock-outs don't ever occur. Management then usually reacts with a directive to reduce inventory on an aggregated level. Because of a lack of a fitting policy (most materials are planned on demand even though they could be automated with the consistent consumption patterns), stock-outs will occur and production lines can't run. The result is bad service levels and unhappy customers. And the cycle continues.

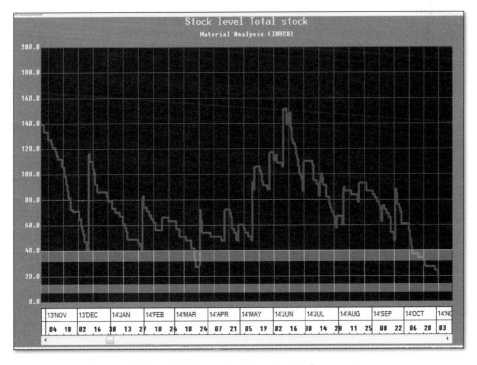

Figure 4.7 Visualization of Control Limits on Past Inventory Performance*

To better this situation, implement performance boundaries, have these signed off by management, communicate the boundaries, and then set policies according to the classes the materials are segmented into to automatically drive the desired inventory levels. We'll discuss these and other programs in much more details in future chapters.

4.4   The Competent Materials Controller

As we've discussed, the magic happens when a scientific framework of reference (performance boundaries and user guidelines) is combined with the right tools and a competent materials planner. It's imperative that all three components are fully available. SAP standard software, as we'll explore in detail in this book, can provide all the right tools. However, the lack of a framework of reference and the fact that the materials planner wasn't trained and educated on all the functionality and how to best apply policy sometimes totally incapacitates the standard SAP and makes it impossible to run effective materials planning. All too often, standard SAP was implemented poorly, meaning that a vast amount of functionality is untapped or enhanced (in a bad sense of the word) by workarounds and additional third-party functionality to do all kinds of things already available within the integrated and standardized SAP system.

This causes the SAP materials planning system to be degraded to transactional SAP ERP, and any automation and optimization that can be performed by the system becomes impossible to do. Users distrust the data coming out of the system and start exporting every list and every piece of data into Excel spreadsheets. Then, the materials planner forms his own system of materials planning, and any standardization, automation, and performance goes out the window. The materials planner is eventually overwhelmed with the sheer amount of manual activity to monitor the critical parts, so that the noncritical parts are filled up to the max, resulting in a "sea of inventory" that covers up all the problems. The workday is filled with expediting orders and manually adjusting inventory levels because the plan doesn't work, and the number one priority—avoid stock-outs at all costs—makes it impossible to find any time in the day to tend to planning, policy setting, or sustainable inventory optimization.

To combat this scenario, you must establish a system of materials planning so that you can set policy periodically and avoid your basic data getting out of whack because you don't have the time in the day to worry about each and every material master record. Separating the materials planner's tasks to set overall policy from the expediting and exception handling of the tactical materials planner is a step in the right direction.

4.4.1 Overall Setting of Strategy and Periodic Fine-Tuning of Policy

One of the solutions to the problem just described is to separate strategic materials planning and tactical materials planning. A strategic materials planner manages the portfolio, or a number of portfolios, on a periodic basis and from a generic point of view. Strategic materials planning means to set and update general policy for entire classes of materials. This type of planning usually happens once a month, and a reclassification of materials is performed to ensure proper segmentation of the individual portfolios. This way, no materials should remain on an outdated policy that might drive the generation of suboptimized replenishment.

For example, a material that was previously sourced from a vendor with a short lead time might have to be purchased from a vendor overseas, extending the lead time significantly. If the material is procured with a reorder point policy, the next reorder point calculations, using the new longer lead time, might now determine a much higher reorder point that renders the policy ineffective. However, if a classification by lead time is carried out, the strategic materials planner can rectify the situation, and the material will now be set up with a material forecast and a range of coverage profile. That policy ensures adequate replenishment and drives lower average inventory holdings.

The tactical materials planner then manages exception messages on a daily basis, expedites fixed orders, and fine-tunes the policy. A tactical materials planner uses Transaction MD06 on a daily basis and monitors the replenishment process for each individual material—of course, this only happens when an exception message occurs. So as part of an overall effective materials planning system, the strategic materials planner and the tactical materials planners both have their place and set of tasks to contribute to good planning and execution.

4.4.2 Tools for Decision Making

A competent and effective materials planner makes good policy decisions. Following are some of the questions that need to be answered while we maintain the policy for our materials:

▶ Are we replenishing based on historic consumption, or do we wait for what the future holds and buffer uncertainty with a safety stock?

▶ Do we use dynamic or static safety stock?

▶ Should we manually set reorder points or have them calculated automatically?

▶ Do we replenish to stock or to an order?

There are a number of tools that can help in the decision-making process: flowcharts to find the MRP type or planning strategy, a (SAP) value stream map to find an inventory/order interface or a Kanban-fit stock point, CLD to better understand the big picture and what dynamics the physical system setup holds in store for us, and decision trees (see Figure 4.8) for a more standardized approach to ensure consistency across the board.

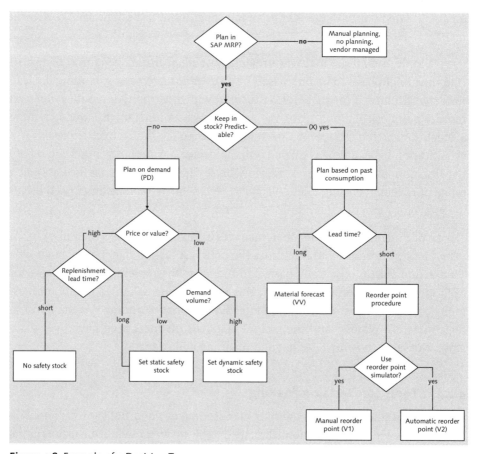

Figure 4.8 Example of a Decision Tree

We'll be discussing quite a number of these tools and how you can integrate them into your system of effective materials planning in this book. The most important thing is that everybody uses the same framework of reference and operates within the performance boundaries of the physical model.

4.4.3   The SAP Add-On Tools

You might find that the transactional nature of the SAP system makes it difficult to stay on top of materials planning. If, for example, you want to perform inventory analysis with the LIS, you need to get in and out of a multitude of transactions. Even though most people don't even use the LIS, after you get the gist of it, you soon become frustrated because the effort to get good reports is too time-consuming. Another problem is that there are undisputable white spots in the current offering of standard SAP software. Besides a very rudimentary ABC analysis, you can't do much segmentation in SAP ERP. Most planners resort to Excel spreadsheets when calculating a coefficient of variation for an XYZ classification or when separating long lead time items from the shorter ones. And policy setting, the act of maintaining an efficient combination of master data settings in the fours MRP screens, becomes an insurmountable task and effort, especially when you want to keep the policy periodically up to date.

So, while involved with various clients running their supply chain on SAP ERP, SAP Consulting in Germany has developed a whole suite of monitors, cockpits, and simulators that allow you to analyze, monitor, and plan inventory, service levels, lead times, and safety stocks.

Figure 4.9 depicts the entire suite of SAP add-on tools for SAP ERP. There is an additional suite for SAP Advanced Planning & Optimization (SAP APO), and all functionality is seamlessly integrated into the standard suite of software because all development is native to SAP and resides in the SAP namespace. The same tables are used as in the standard transactions, and no interfaces are required. Some of these tools help you clean (and keep clean) your master data, some do controlling for you, and others perform planning tasks.

During the course of this book, we'll focus on standard SAP functionality that you already own and ensure that you can implement a system of effective materials planning using just that. However, at the end of each chapter, we'll suggest an even more effective methodology and functionality by giving you a glimpse of how your materials planning world could look like if you enhance your SAP with some of these add-on tools.

SAP SCM Consulting Solutions					
MRP Monitor (1333018)	Simulation ROP & Safety Stock (1363890)	Simulation Lot Size (1363889)	Replenishment Lead Time Monitor (1341571)	Master Data Check Monitor (1653328)	Change Log Monitor (2057957)
Inventory Controlling Cockpit (1363888)	Service Level Monitor (1341710)	Forecasting Monitor (1341755)	Production Controlling Cockpit (1653327)	MRP Simulation Cockpit (1911251)	Supply Chain Performance Indicator (2154259)
MRP Exception Monitor (1341705)	Purchasing Monitor (1832851)	Supplier Preview (1783469)	Transport Planner (2059000)	Transport Scheduling (in development)	BOM Analysis (1745268)
SD Order Monitor (1832777)	Discontinuation Monitor (1560053)	Customer-Specific ATP Check (2203492)	Inbound Monitor (1541340)	Capacity Requirements Planning Cockpit (1907791)	Capacity Data Monitor (1907823)
MRP Extension: EX-Works Supplier (2011149)	MRP Extension: EX-Works Stock Transfer (2011149)	MRP Extension: Multi Planning Calendar (1783924)	MRP Extension: (Scrap) (1962072)	MRP Extension: Cross-Plant Planning (1649107)	Kanban Monitor (1653329)

Source: http://scn.sap.com/docs/DOC-53389

Figure 4.9 The Suite of SAP Add-On Tools

4.5 Summary

Basic principles of effective materials planning include the task of communicating a supply chain strategy throughout an organization so that everyone works toward the same goals. This also helps define standard principles and control limits.

To know the performance boundaries of the system and being able to bring inventories within a range of control limits is then an achievable feat. Therefore, with the documentation of standard user guidelines containing the current performance boundaries and control limits, we can provide and make available all the tools necessary for a competent planner to use and be successful.

In that sense, we'll now delve into the inner workings of the four pillars of effective materials planning: prioritizing and managing your materials portfolio, performing a segmentation and setting policy that automates replenishment process, the subsequent monitoring of exception messages, and, last but certainly not least, continuously optimizing your inventory holdings.

He uses information as a drunken man uses lamp posts—for support rather than for illumination.
—Andrew Lang

5   Prioritized Portfolio Management

Portfolio management is the first of the four pillars of an effective materials planning model. It allows for controlled parameterization and policy setting with predictable results for groups of materials. Inventory analysis, exception monitoring, policy setting, and cleaning basic data are all carried out for portfolios of materials. Good materials planning starts by breaking down materials and grouping them into portfolios.

The planner must find a way to group, sort, and prioritize the materials he is responsible for. This person is most often responsible for a large number of parts, some of which are sometimes ignored in favor of more critical activities. This represents a somewhat inefficient way to deal with all the materials that have to be kept available in stock and/or replenished on a regular basis. There are critical parts and expensive parts; there are items that take a long time from the point of the order to the time it's received. But each and every one of these materials "deserves" a policy that not only drives the correct replenishment strategy but also automates the process—instead of just filling up inventory to the max.

On the following pages, we'll explore possibilities in SAP to build and manage effective portfolios of materials for all the functions in materials planning. Good portfolio management saves time, keeps basic data clean, and provides a good basis for segmentation and periodic policy setting.

5.1   Portfolio Basics in SAP

The MRP CONTROLLER key field on the MRP 1 screen of the material master record represents the materials portfolio. Typically, every materials planner is assigned a three-digit, alphanumeric MRP controller key with a description and a telephone number. The field itself resides on the plant level of the hierarchy and therefore the same materials planner can have the same MRP controller key in various plants.

As shown in Figure 5.1, most MRP controller keys refer to a specific person in your organization. However, this isn't something that needs to be strictly adhered to. There is absolutely nothing wrong with keeping your MRP controllers generic or creating more than one key for every person. Let's be a bit creative and have management efficiency in mind.

Warning

After you've assigned the material to an MRP controller key, the lists you produce with that key include all the materials you've maintained the key in. The only way to change that is to manually update all those materials with a different MRP controller key manually, material by material (unless you use mass updates with Transaction MM17 or the MRP Monitor add-on, which we'll cover later in Chapter 6).

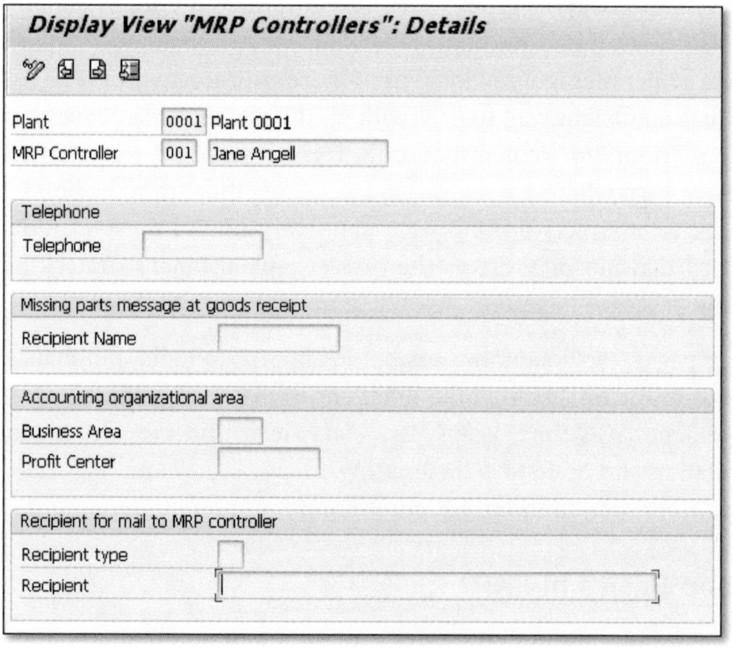

Display View "MRP Controllers": Details

Plant	0001 Plant 0001
MRP Controller	001 Jane Angell

Telephone
| Telephone | |

Missing parts message at goods receipt
| Recipient Name | |

Accounting organizational area
| Business Area | |
| Profit Center | |

Recipient for mail to MRP controller
| Recipient type | |
| Recipient | |

Figure 5.1 Customizing MRP Controller Keys

There is another key available in the material master that you may use for portfolio management: the ABC indicator. It was actually meant to hold the result from an ABC analysis and can be executed in the Logistics Information System (LIS). If you have another means of performing an ABC analysis, you could use this key to separate strategic materials from generic ones, for example.

ABC analysis, and with it the ABC indicator that we're talking about here, is a traditional way to perform segmentation and classify materials into three to four buckets for separating high consumption value from low consumption value, or big contributors from small contributors. But as described in the previous note, the ABC classification by itself isn't very useful and needs to be supplemented with at least a UVW analysis for price to be beneficial.

5.1.1   ABC Analysis

It's a very good idea to classify your value contributors. Even though nobody wants to admit it, everybody pays more attention to the customers that contribute the lion's share to the success of a company. Manufacturing companies depend, at least to a great part, on customers who buy their products. Undoubtedly there are customers that buy more product more frequently than others. Why wouldn't you treat those customers that produce more revenue differently from those that buy your product once in while... if even that?

And to separate the valuable customer from the others, you can use an ABC analysis. For example, you can use ABC analysis to classify those customers that generate 80% of your sales volume as A customers, the next 15% as B customers, and the rest as C customers. In the same manner, you can classify your materials portfolio by aggregating the consumption value (or sales volume) of materials until you reach 80% (or whatever boundaries you define) of your total value and then designating all these materials as A items.

Based on this scenario, you might think you've identified and separated your critical parts from the rest and can set policy or otherwise treat these items in a special way. However, some of these A parts could exhibit a high consumption value because they are cheap but have many movements in each period, or they could be expensive and have only few movements. Those are fundamentally different characteristics, so you should make a clear policy distinction for either group in your materials planning. Even if you add a UVW analysis (for valuation price), it's only telling part of the story. Short or long lead time, newly created material, slow mover or fast mover, or large or small volume are all characteristics that need to be taken into account when performing a segmentation of your materials portfolio.

ABC analysis by itself is better than no classification at all, but for effective materials planning with automated policy setting you need more than that. Performing an extensive segmentation without using the ABC indicator in the MRP 1 screen of the material master record (you can build your own segmentation outside of SAP or use the MRP Monitor add-on) allows you to use the MRP indicator for priority.

In Customizing, you can configure the ABC indicator to identify a priority. For example, you can set the priorities A = Critical, B = Strategic, and C = Slow Mover to call up the exception monitor for a portfolio and still distinguish according to a priority you define with the ABC Indicator. Figure 5.2 shows the Customizing transaction to define the ABC IND. for various priorities.

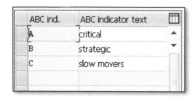

Figure 5.2 Customizing ABC Indicators

With that, we can see that the MRP 1 screen contains two important fields for portfolio management: MRP CONTROLLER and ABC INDICATOR (see Figure 5.3).

Maintaining these two fields effectively sets up your materials portfolio, and you can now use groupings and priorities in a multitude of transactions.

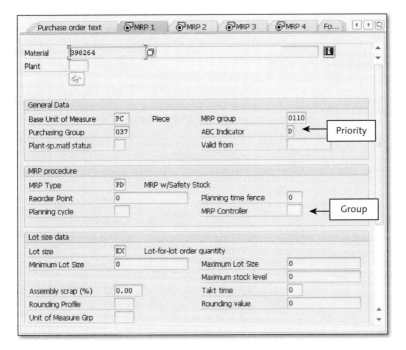

Figure 5.3 Using a Grouping and a Priority in the Material Master Record

5.1.2 Groupings and Priorities

To group and prioritize your portfolio, you can call up Transaction MD07 (the collective stock/requirements list) with your MRP controller key to get a list of all the materials in your portfolio (see Figure 5.4). Additionally, you can identify an ABC IND. (that was configured as a priority) and further limit the list to only show your slow movers.

In a similar way, this type of listing is available in many LIS transactions, and you're now able to selectively list, sort, and manage items by portfolio, group, and priority throughout a multitude of applications. Exception monitoring, inventory analysis, data cleaning, and policy setting are all applications that depend on good portfolio management. Using the MRP controller and ABC indicator fields effectively means better manageability of your materials planning as a whole.

Figure 5.4, Figure 5.5, and Figure 5.6 provide some examples of how the MRP controller and ABC indicator fields can be used effectively to prioritize, list, and sort a materials portfolio.

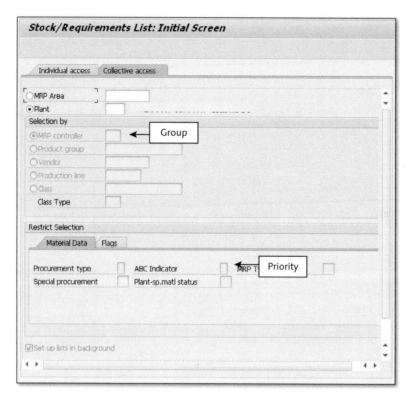

Figure 5.4 Grouping and Priority Selection in Transaction MD07

Figure 5.5 shows the selection options for the dead stock report, while Figure 5.6 shows the selection options for the average stock report. As in most of these reports, you can select and filter on the ABC IND. and the MRP CONTROLLER fields. This gives you better control over your portfolio and allows for standardization of your reporting and information.

As with anything else, a manageable number of items in your portfolio ensures good results. No materials planner in the world can manage a portfolio of thousands of materials well, if they have neither the tools nor the system to group and prioritize. All too often planners have to deal with thousands of materials when they call up Transaction MD07 or Transaction MD06 (Figure 5.7).

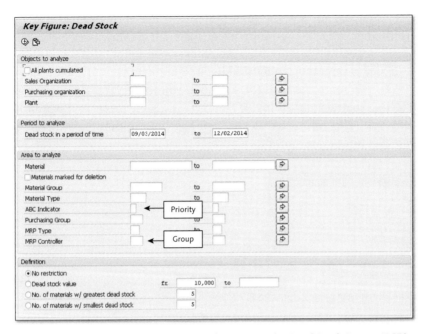

Figure 5.5 Selection Options for Group and Priority in the Dead Stock Report MC50

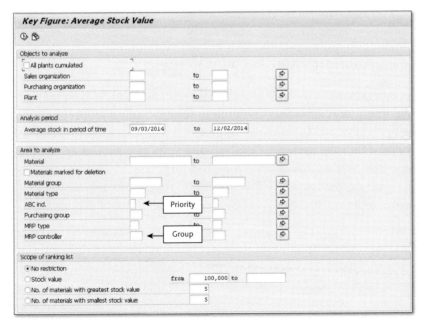

Figure 5.6 Selection Options for Group and Priority in the Average Stock Report MC49

Because every material deserves a good policy and needs to be managed for utmost performance, a very large number of materials as shown in Figure 5.7 makes it almost impossible to work with the exception monitor, let alone manage the replenishment of critical or noncritical items. Setting up your SAP portfolio is important because it builds the basis for all subsequent functions and processes to perform effective materials planning. If you get this right from the beginning, you're setting yourself up for success and avoiding time-consuming reassigning of MRP controller keys.

Figure 5.7 Difficulty in Managing Very Large Portfolios in Transaction MD07

Note that the LIS is collecting data with reference to the MRP controller key, so when you shuffle your MRP controller assignments too often, you'll lose valuable historical data for analysis and reporting.

5.2 Responsibilities and Accountability

Materials planners need to be held accountable for their portfolio, and they usually are. The question is how they're being measured and what direction they were given by the leadership team. Without strategy or direction, the materials planner develops his own system of conduct and primarily tries to avoid stockouts (because that is what makes them look bad on first glance). The occasional (mostly year-end) decree to reduce inventories is woven into a sometimes chaotic—and more or less creative—necessary evil of replenishment planning.

There are no inventory targets, control limits, or desired ranges of inventory holdings, and the planner is left with the tool ("...we bought you this expensive SAP system to do your job") and no performance boundaries to manage the replenishment, inventories, and good availability for thousands of parts. Because there are no targets to work toward or directions to follow, there is no accountability or responsibility.

Be accountable for your materials portfolio. Find out what your company's supply chain strategy is, set targets, and help your superiors think about what they expect you to achieve. Even though it might not be your job to figure out and enforce a supply chain strategy, it makes your day-to-day workings easier and brings about satisfaction and success, which leads to a richer and more interesting workday.

5.2.1   Outdated Elements

Another point of contention is the responsibility for outdated elements: purchase orders that still show that they delivered days or weeks ago, material reservations in the past, unconsumed forecast, late sales orders, and fixed order proposals that promise delivery of quantities on dates long gone. Many of these outdated documents can't be set right by the material planner because he can't change sales or production orders. But they're still the planner's responsibility because they're messing with his portfolio and the way MRP generates supply. Get all involved parties to the table (or at least on the phone), and escalate the problem until it's resolved. Daily, bi-weekly, or ad hoc meetings where the materials planner meets with a production scheduler, a buyer, and a sales representative can clear up a lot of old data and help communicate and rectify issues up and down the supply chain.

Figure 5.8 illustrates how an outdated element can falsify the stock/requirements situation and drive the MRP run to order the wrong quantity at the wrong time. You might think the stock/requirements situation shows the correct result in the first line, but that isn't true (the first line only shows the current stock holding and not the situation). What actually matters to planning is the last line; imagine that today is 12/02/2014 and wrongfully states that we're all good (it displays available stock of 0, or even 20 pieces if you consider the safety stock). The MRP run doesn't think of any further action—other than an exception message 10 to bring it in earlier than the past, which is meaningless at this point.

E..	Date	MRP element	A..	MRP element d...	St...	Receipt/Reqmt	Available Qty	Stc...
96	12/02/2014	Stock					0	0
	12/02/2014	SafeSt		Safety Stock		20–	20–	0
10	11/25/2014	PchOrd		0004123614/00..	1000	100	80	100
	12/02/2014	CusOrd		0500600311/00..		7–	73	0

Figure 5.8 Outdated Puirchase Order Falsifying the Stock/Requirements List and Keeping the MRP Run from Planning

This leads us to our next topic: housecleaning. We'll show you some ways to clean outdated elements (and other data). But be sure that after you clean the overdue elements, you have a process in place that keeps old elements from creeping in.

5.2.2 Housecleaning Materials Portfolios

You have to clean out your portfolio every now and then as objects become outdated with time that passes by. A materials portfolio that was set up years ago and never underwent a housecleaning is something that SAP MRP can't handle. If there is a consumption-based replenishment strategy on a nonmoving part or a purchase order that has a planned delivery date from six months ago, MRP then simply produces the wrong result. It works with inventory that isn't available or tries to replenish where we don't need anything. All too often, judgment is imposed on SAP functionality, and managers are too quick to replace it with spreadsheets and workarounds when, in fact, all that's needed is some housecleaning and better portfolio management.

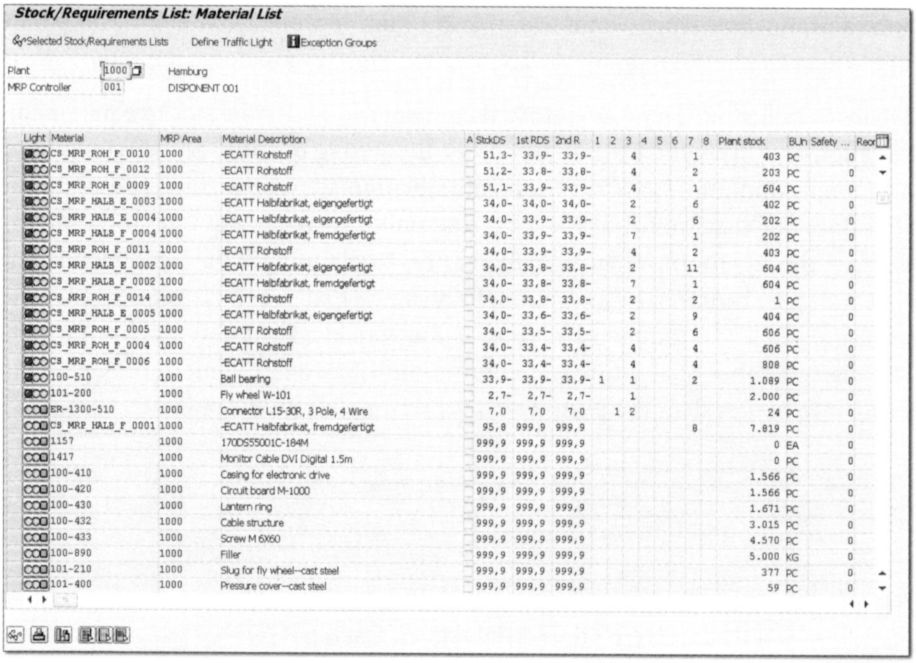

Figure 5.9 List Screen in Transaction MD07 for Housecleaning

Housecleaning is best performed in Transaction MD07 (see Figure 5.9). It lists all items that are assigned to a materials planner and is useful when the planner is responsible for his own portfolio of materials.

> **Portfolio Management across Multiple MRP Controller Keys**
>
> Transactions MD07 and Transaction MD06 are called up using a specific MRP controller key, which means you can't view a bigger list than the one that lists the items assigned to that MRP controller key. However, sometimes there is a need to build a list that contains items assigned to more than one MRP controller. In housecleaning, for example, you may want to check for outdated elements throughout the entire plant or across all materials planners. In that case, you can use SAP standard Report RMMD0700 (also available as Report RMMD0600), which allows you to use a range of MRP controller keys (and other fields).
>
> Many of our clients made transactions—Transaction ZMD07 and Transaction ZMD06, respectively—out of the report, which their users may now apply.

Because Transaction MD07 lists assigned materials without any date or other restrictions, you can be sure not to miss any part or outdated element. To manage and clean the portfolio, proceed as follows:

1. In Transaction MD07, identify your MRP CONTROLLER key and PLANT code. Press Enter.

2. When a window appears asking whether you want to set up the list beforehand, click YES.

3. Click the binoculars icon at the top of the screen, and a window pops up.

4. Select the FIND MRP ELEMENTS tab, which will allow you to find the elements that are outdated.

5. In the To field, fill in yesterday's date. Click the FIND MRP ELEMENTS button, and the system will return the list with all materials selected that have at least one MRP element that is older than yesterday's date.

6. As shown in Figure 5.10, select the elements you want to investigate, and click on the FIND MRP ELEMENTS button, and the system will take you to the stock/requirements list of the first material with an outdated element.

7. In the STOCK/REQUIREMENTS LIST, click on SHOW OVERVIEW TREE, and a window opens on the left (or on top, depending on configuration) with all the materials that have at least one outdated element.

135

8. You can now double-click on any one material and see the stock/requirements list with its outdated elements marked in blue font.

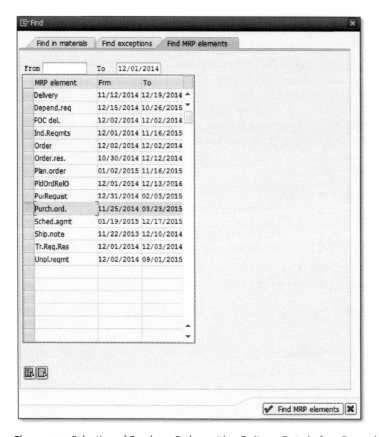

Figure 5.10 Selection of Purchase Orders with a Delivery Date before December 1, 2014

What you'll do with the outdated elements depends on the specific situation. For example, a purchase order with a delivery date in the past must be updated to a future, estimated delivery date. A production or process order with a receipt date in the past must be updated in the same way; however, note that other than a purchase order or a requisition, an internal order most likely has a bill of material (BOM) and therefore demotes the past, overdue date down to its components. For that reason, if you see an outdated dependent requirement or reservation, solve the problem at the source, and follow the requirement through its pegging to the top.

Sales order requirements might be outdated too. People can be very reluctant to bring the delivery date forward; they often fear that we cover up a late delivery that didn't meet the customer's requested delivery date. But as with purchase orders where the new date doesn't change the statistical, original date, the sales order will keep a history and trace of moving dates and keep the original customer requested delivery date safe. It's just that you have to set that date right because no one will ever be able to deliver three days ago, and MRP needs to know the right date to function properly.

5.3   Using Buckets

As we discussed earlier, you can use the ABC INDICATOR field on the MRP 1 screen of the material master record to prioritize your portfolio. With this field, you can separate the critical parts from the strategic, the nonmovers, and so on. On the other hand, you could bucketize your portfolio using the MRP controller key. Bucketizing is the process of organizing your materials portfolio according to the degree of automation in exception monitoring (see Figure 5.11). Note that you should break down your portfolios by assigning MRP controller keys to a person rather than product categories or groups. There should never be multiple persons assigned to a MRP controller key, but you may have multiple MRP controller keys to a person. In that way, you may assign three buckets (MRP controller keys) to a materials planner so that he can manage his portfolio in order that materials needing a lot of attention may be called up for exception monitoring more frequently than materials that might not have had a movement in over a year. In the same manner, the buckets can be used to separate materials with an automated policy from the ones that need parameterization work.

Example

You can use three different MRP controller keys for any one materials planner. That way, you can take your portfolio and move all items that had only few or no movements over the past 12 months into your number 3 bucket (use the MRP controller key UG3). All other items are assigned to MRP controller bucket number 2 (UG2). Now you start applying policy, and as you do so, you move each item from number 2 to number 1. In the end, you'll find all your nonmovers and slow movers in an MRP controller key that you check with Transaction MD07 infrequently. None of the materials in that bucket should have a consumption-based replenishment strategy or safety stock. Bucket number 1 then contains all parts that are critical to business success and set up with a fitting

---

policy. You must watch these very closely and call up Transaction MD06 every day. Policy fine-tuning, expediting, and monitoring are crucial. When your policy doesn't work anymore, move the item back to bucket number 2, which contains your workload, that is, all the items that need a new policy or that need to be planned manually.

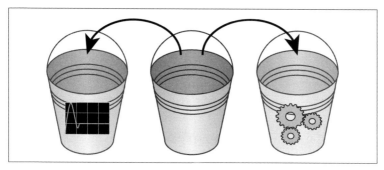

Figure 5.11 Bucketizing

As your working through these suggestions, remember that every business is different (although not that much different at their core). You need to develop your own system of effective materials planning that works best for you. Try something new, communicate with your peers, and find out what works well and what doesn't. Somebody once said, "It's not guaranteed that things get better when you change. But things certainly don't get better if you don't change."

5.4 Monitoring Your Portfolio

As you bucketize and house clean your materials portfolios, you need to constantly manage and monitor them so that you don't fall back into a contaminated list with outdated elements and obsolete materials. You should have processes in place to keep elements such as purchase orders or production orders from becoming outdated or obsolete. Materials can become obsolete as well when they aren't needed anymore and are being replaced by a new part. You must then ensure that there is also a process in place to mark that material as being obsolete and take it out of your portfolio.

To periodically monitor and look for possible problems so your portfolio stays clean, manageable, and up-to-date, you need a tool. In standard SAP, that tool is Transaction MD07, but there's also an SAP add-on tool—the MRP Monitor—that provides excellent functionality for not only monitoring your portfolio but also performing a segmentation and setting policy.

5.4.1 Transaction MD07 Setup

Most likely, you're using Transaction MD07 (Collective Display of Stock/Requirements Lists) to monitor your portfolio. This transaction lets you work with traffic lights to gain a quick view of which items are in trouble and which items are balanced in terms of supply and demand. The traffic lights correspond to a number of days of supply of current inventory, and you can set up the ranges for red, yellow, or green lights per user individually. In the standard delivery of SAP, the traffic light setup simply assigns a red light to any item that has an unfulfilled demand in the past, and it assigns a green light to any item that has more inventory (if only one piece) than is needed today. If you have exactly that much inventory as you need today, and there is no demand in the future, you'll get a yellow light for that item.

This isn't a very useful setup because you're working with lot sizes, and you have future demand. Other than the red light indicating that you fell behind (past tense, it's already too late), there isn't much useful information here.

> **Note**
>
> A green light doesn't mean everything is good and well. A green light can point to a potential (sometimes significant) overstocking situation.

So here is a possible setup for your traffic lights. In Transaction MD07, the list screen displays all materials in your portfolio with a traffic light as shown in Figure 5.12. A red light (circle) indicates that the inventory the material holds currently will run out in less than 5 days, considering the future demand situation. Any material with inventory lasting between 5 and 20 days will get a yellow light (triangle), and materials with more than 20 days of supply (up to 200 days) will get a green (overstocking) light (square). Note that in row 1, we'll set the traffic lights for the STOCK DAYS' SUPPLY, which calculates how long the current inventory will last until it's used up by the demand in the future.

The second row calculates how long the current inventory will last under consideration of receipts from fixed orders (e.g., purchase order), and the third row even considers the receipts from order proposals.

Note

Row 1—STOCK DAYS' SUPPLY doesn't consider any receipt elements, meaning that if a purchase order would deliver enough material tomorrow to get you through the end of time, you would still see the number of days to the demand elements that takes out your current stock holding.

Additionally we want a red light in case a material bears an exception message out of group 3 (those are "late" messages), group 6 (missing stock), or group 8 (termination of the MRP run).

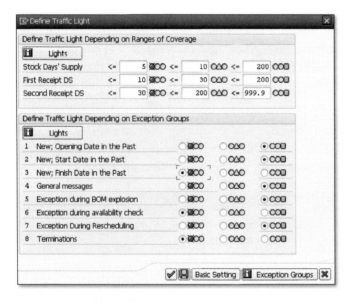

Figure 5.12 Possible Traffic Light Setup

Again, this is just a proposed setup, and you'll have to find your own best way to set up the lights, but there is a lot of flexibility and a good setup can make a world of difference in your portfolio management.

Figure 5.13 shows an example of the collective display in Transaction MD07.

The display is also influenced by the sort sequence, which you can customize after you right-click on Transaction MD07. In the window that pops up (Figure 5.14), you can change the sort sequence by which Transaction MD07 lists the materials, by choosing an ascending or descending sort after right-clicking and selecting SORT.

Light	Mat...	M.	Material Description	A	StckDS	1st R...	2nd R	1	2	3	4	5	6	7	8	Pla...	B...	M...	P..	S..	A..	M.	Cde	C
⬤⬤⬤	69971	3..	SWITCH, SEAT		0.2	0.4	0.4			1				1		12	PC	HALB	F		C	V1	006	✓
⬤⬤⬤	82526	3..	HOSE, FUEL, 0.31ID, 03.0L		0.6	0.6	0.6							1		22	PC	HALB	F		C	PD	006	✓
⬤⬤⬤	3835..	3..	CABLE, .13D, 13.5L, .2CLEV..		2.7	2.7	2.7									74	PC	HALB	F		C	V2	006	✓
⬤⬤⬤	3694..	3..	BEARING, NEEDLE, 0.25B 0..		3.0	999.9	999.9									22	PC	HALB	F	U	B	V1	006	✓
⬤⬤⬤	65665	3..	SWITCH, CONTACT, 12VDC ..		4.7	4.7	4.7								1		10	PC	HALB	F		B	V2	007	✓
⬤⬤⬤	1208..	3..	CONTROLLER, STEERING, 3..		5.0	5.0	5.0	1						1		4	PC	HALB	F		B	V2	003	✓
⬤⬤⬤	1208..	3..	BEARING, BALL, 0.67B, 1.85..		5.1	32.1	32.1									5	PC	HALB	F	U	C	PD	005	✓
⬤⬤⬤	2232..	3..	LEVER, BRAKE, 102MML		5.3	5.3	5.3						1			1	PC	HALB	F		C	V2	006	✓
⬤⬤⬤	58590	3..	STRAP, MTG, TANK, LPG		5.6	42.9	42.9									6	PC	HALB	F	U	C	PD	005	✓
⬤⬤⬤	1207..	3..	MESH ASSY, CLOTH [T17]		5.8	5.8	5.8									28	PC	HALB	F	U	B	PD	004	✓
⬤⬤⬤	1459..	3..	CLEVIS, ADJ, 0.25PIN, 0.25-..		5.8	5.8	5.8									415	PC	HALB	F		C	V1	008	✓
⬤⬤⬤	3820..	3..	ROD-END, 0.50-20LH FEM 0..		6.0	6.0	6.0							1		49	PC	HALB	F		C	V2	005	✓
⬤⬤⬤	3680..	3..	CORD, PYES, 0.188D, BULK		9.9	9.9	9.9									.20	FT	ROH	F		C	V2	006	✓
⬤⬤⬤	1019..	3..	RESERVOIR, HYD, 10.0GAL		10.0	10.0	10.0							3		16	PC	HALB	F		A	PD	005	✓
⬤⬤⬤	3840..	3..	BUSHING, SNAP-IN, 0.31B 0..		10.1	10.1	10.1									7	PC	HALB	F	U	C	PD	005	✓
⬤⬤⬤	3608..	3..	ARM, LEVER, BRAKE, 4.1 [K..		10.1	52.7	52.7									64	PC	HALB	F		C	V2	004	✓
⬤⬤⬤	1201..	3..	SHAFT ASSY, STEERING		10.2	52.2	52.2							1		29	PC	HALB	F		B	V2	004	✓

Figure 5.13 Example of a List Result in Transaction MD07

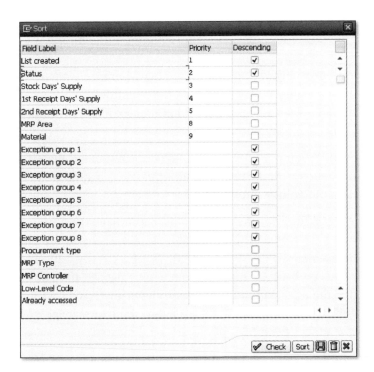

Figure 5.14 Sort Sequence for the Collective Display of Stock/Requirements Lists in Transaction MD07

As you can see, there are lots of possibilities for a structured list display and much to think about regarding how you monitor your portfolio on a daily basis. We'll discuss much more on this subject in Chapter 7 when we cover exception monitoring.

5.4.2 Portfolio Management with the MRP Monitor

As pointed out in a previous chapter, the SAP add-on tools are a product of SAP Consulting in Germany. These tools were developed to cover needs arising from consulting gigs at countless customer sites. Whenever standard SAP functionality leaves a gap, clients like to ask SAP to develop a new transaction or report to make life better. Often, it's not possible for SAP to quickly develop or eventually integrate the new solution into its standard suite of software. It is possible however, for SAP Consulting, an SAP company, to make use of the standard SAP namespace and use the same development resources that are meant to develop the standard package. Therefore, these add-on tools don't represent a third-party tool that must be integrated into the standard software. The tools are already integrated using the standard tables and links, so they look and feel exactly like SAP... because they are SAP!

One of the central tools for materials planning is the MRP Monitor. Its main features are segmentation and policy update, but the MRP Monitor also allows for sorting, filtering, listing, and prioritizing, which makes it an excellent instrument for portfolio management.

You'll typically run the MRP Monitor once a month to perform strategic materials planning—much more about that in the next chapter—but you can also run it any time to clean up and sort out your portfolio.

When you call up the transaction for the MRP Monitor, you have the option to select various features on six tabs. On the first tab—DATA BASIS—you can first identify the period for the analysis (see Figure 5.15). This isn't really critical for portfolio management, so go back 12 months from a start date in the current month. This means that the MRP Monitor will classify your materials based on movements during the past 12 months. You'll probably want to manage your portfolio on the plant level, but the other options are valid too.

Next comes choosing the data source. Again, we're looking at how the MRP Monitor classifies your materials and what historic data is used to do so. Table MVER (MATERIAL CONSUMPTION TABLE radio button) contains all movements that are flagged as relevant for consumption in Customizing. Usually controllers decide what is consumption relevant and what isn't, so if you want a logistics point of view, you're probably better off building your own history. Building your own history can be done by using the Materials Document Analysis (MDA) tool, which comes with the MRP Monitor. However, you can also access a portfolio that's based on INFO STRUCTUR S031, SALES ORDERS, FINANCIAL DOCUMENTS, or PLANNED REQUIREMENTS, as shown in Figure 5.16.

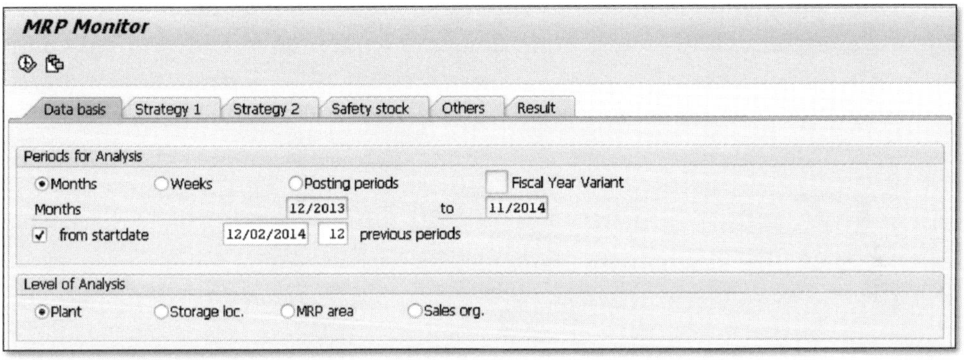

Figure 5.15 Period and Level of Analysis Selections in the MRP Monitor

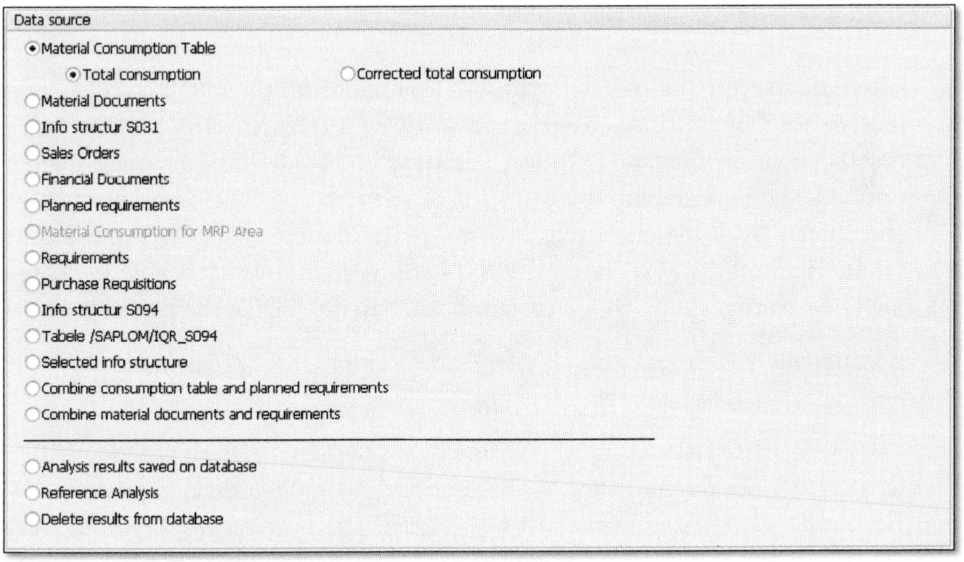

Figure 5.16 Picking a Data Source for the MRP Monitor Classification

In the Area of Analysis part of the screen, you can limit the scope of the selected materials by PLANT, MATERIAL GROUP, MRP CONTROLLER, MRP TYPE, and so on (see Figure 5.17).

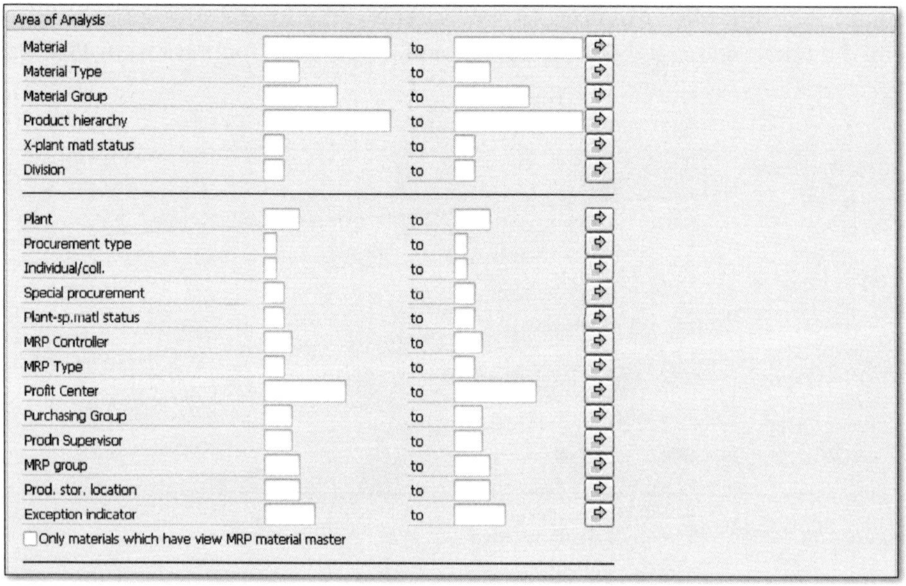

Figure 5.17 Limiting the Displayed Portfolio

After you execute the monitor with the limitations on the initial screens, you'll receive a list of classified materials to work with (Figure 5.18). For the task of portfolio management, you can use this list to build subsets of materials that you can update en masse with the correct data settings. For example, you could sort and filter out all materials that had no, or few, movements over the past 12 months and set the MRP TYPE to "PD" to ensure that no stock is held in case the materials were planned with a consumption-based policy in the past.

Additionally you can take off all safety stocks and reorder points that might have been left because of a previous change.

To execute these tasks, you sort, list, and then select all materials with fewer than, let's say, 12 movements over the past 12 months, and then click on the MAT.MAS-TER button as indicated by the arrow in Figure 5.18. The screen shown in Figure 5.19 appears, which allows you to maintain data in the four MRP tabs and much more.

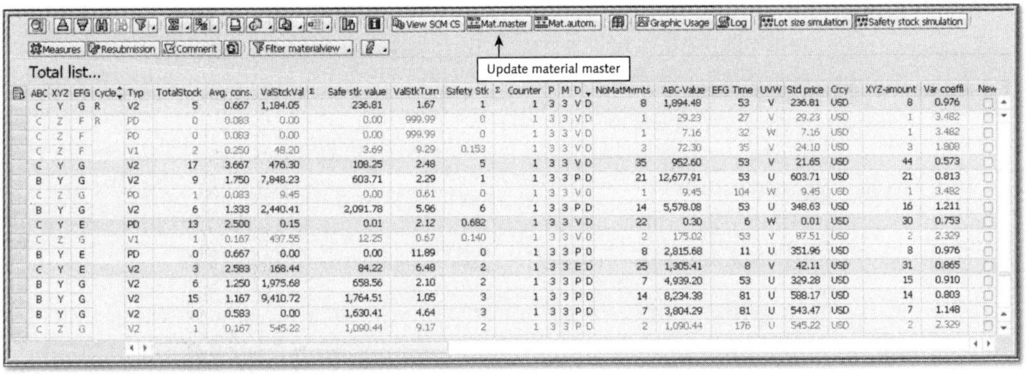

Figure 5.18 List Window in the MRP Monitor with Classification and Inventory Key Performance Indicators

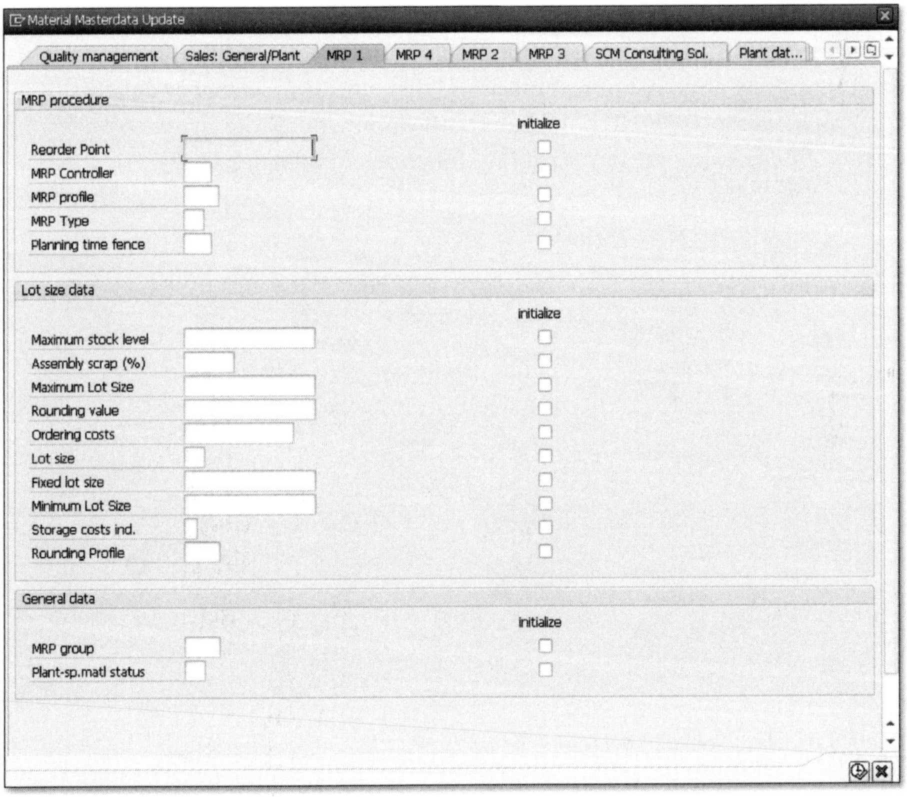

Figure 5.19 MRP Monitor: Material Master Record Update Tabs

This is a powerful feature that gives you total control over your materials portfolio. It's main purpose is to set policy for entire segments of your portfolio—and we'll discuss this in detail in the next chapter—but it's also an outstanding tool to keep your portfolio clean, to take away any safety stocks on nonmoving materials (by initializing the safety stock fields in MRP 2), to ensure that reorder point controlled materials don't have a periodic lot-size procedure, to move blocks of materials from one MRP controller bucket into another, and to find and rectify master data inconsistencies according to the rules previously agreed to.

All these activities—and more—are absolutely essential to a working model of effective materials planning and need to be performed on a periodic basis. Of course, you can do all this with out-of-the-box SAP functionality, but it's a lot more manual labor than using the SAP add-on tools.

Let's dig a bit deeper into the MRP Monitor by looking at the result screen. This screen has four windows: ❶ a tree structure to select specific classifications, deleted materials, slow movers, nonmovers, and so on; ❷ the classification grid that can display any class and some associated key performance indicators (KPIs); ❸ a graphical representation of the classification; and ❹ the list view with all its sorting, filtering, updating, and layout functions (see Figure 5.20).

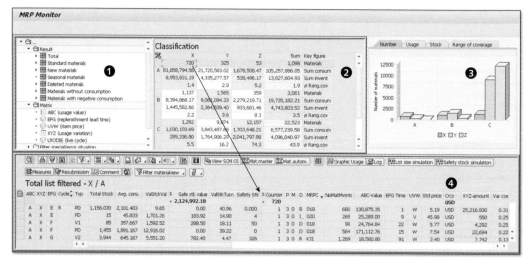

Figure 5.20 Result Screen of the MRP Monitor

For example, you can change the layout of the list screen by clicking on INSERT and selecting CHANGE LAYOUT (see the resulting screen in Figure 5.21).

Figure 5.21 Options to Change the Layout in the MRP Monitor

Here you can access the list layout and how you display your data. There are many KPIs and master record fields that you can use in your list. After you put your layout together, you can determine a sort order, filter, different views, and show column totals and ranges.

You can also use the history function (see Figure 5.22) to select all materials for which the classification has changed or a deletion indicator has been set and to update the policy accordingly.

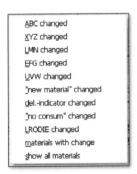

Figure 5.22 Accessing Historic Changes in the MRP Monitor

You may even store a policy and use it automatically as a material fulfills the conditions that are agreed to meet the policy. For example, if you decided and agree to run the inventory down on nonmoving items (which is a very good idea), you could store a policy that sets the MRP TYPE to "PD" and initializes (sets to zero) all safety stocks and reorder points for nonmoving items. Therefore, as soon as your pre-defined conditions for a nonmover are met during the analysis, the policy kicks in automatically and updates the items' master record with the policy (see Figure 5.23).

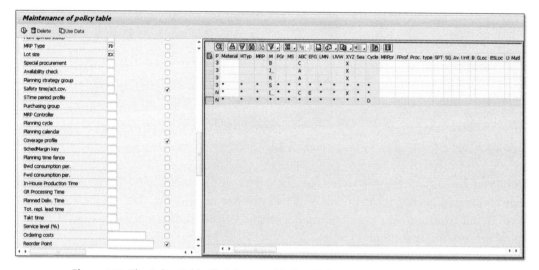

Figure 5.23 The Policy Table That Comes with the MRP Monitor

As you can probably see now, the MRP Monitor is a powerful tool and should be used with care. Remember our fool, who is still a fool with a tool? Well now he's a dangerous fool if you give him that tool. The idea is to provide these tools to an empowered, knowledgeable, and responsible materials planner who needs to perform a difficult and challenging task of balancing demand with supply in the most optimum way. For that to be successful, you need not only the right strategy and competence but also the tools to get the job done.

5.5   Summary

Prioritized portfolio management represents a more practical approach to the task of managing and replenishing a number of materials that a materials planner is responsible for. Outdated elements, obsolete materials, and too many materials in a portfolio make it nearly impossible to do a good job in managing inventories for utmost availability and low stock holding cost at the same time.

To get started with prioritized portfolio management as a basis for the other three pillars in effective materials planning, start managing your materials in buckets, clean up outdated elements (and make sure the stay clean), and get obsolete items out of the way. This will provide automation and provide a set-up for policy setting and exception monitoring.

Using the right tools for portfolio management is important, but don't forget that a well-defined process and an empowered user are indispensable for it to work well. Getting into the sweet spot of bringing together people, strategy, processes, and tools will lead us into the second pillar of a system of effective materials planning: automated and periodic policy setting.

Everything should be made as simple as possible, but not simpler.
—*Albert Einstein*

6   Automated and Periodic Policy Setting

Many companies teach their planners how to expedite orders and convert proposals from the MRP run. In that sense, a planner's job becomes reactive and manual-intensive. These organizations could profit greatly from a transition to a more controlled and automated management of desired results by use of policy. A more analytical approach to materials planning, where items and products are maintained with a fitting master data setup, will generate a plan that is less of a coincidence but more of a skillful and measured system that automatically balances demand with supply.

Policy setting is at the heart and soul of materials planning. Without policy, the planner is degraded to an expeditor who must manage thousands of, often meaningless, exceptions, ineffective order quantities, and suboptimal delivery dates. In this chapter, we develop a guide to successful and periodic policy setting for entire groups of materials. We describe how an organization can develop, design, and implement a portfolio of tactics and policies that produces the desired improvement in inventory holdings and service levels on a continuous basis and in a sustainable fashion with a competent and analytical materials planner. A policy is primarily, but not exclusively, maintained in the four MRP screens of the material master record. That is why this chapter will focuses on all the field values within those four screens and explores all the possible combinations and impacts that are so hard to figure out otherwise.

Finally, we explore implications and results coming from the simulation of various policies so that a feasible plan can be developed and results can be measured against predefined targets.

6.1 Employing Strategies and Policies in an Enterprise

As policy setting takes the main stage in our system of effective materials planning, we first need to discuss how policy comes about. A policy is a predefined combination of settings and field values to drive a certain type of replenishment within the performance boundaries of a company. The policy should be documented so that a planner can use it for a group of parts that all exhibit the same or similar characteristics. Therefore, buffers and safety stocks must be designed based on agreed-upon service levels, lot sizes need to be negotiated with suppliers, and inventory targets must be set for the year. All of this should come from the company's supply chain strategy. The strategy therefore builds the basis for policy setting on a more detailed level. Strategy is what needs to be signed off by leadership and communicated clearly and precisely. Most important, strategy must be followed by all and can't be a moving target.

So a strategy represents the overall guidelines, and policy describes the rule set by which the strategy is executed on a more detailed level.

But beware, using MRP TYPE "PD" by itself doesn't constitute a policy! All too often, we can see that during a typical SAP implementation the MRP type PD (plan on demand) is used for every finished or semi-finished product and raw materials. With this type, a primary demand can be handed through the bill of material (BOM) structure all the way down to the lowest level material. When the MRP run does its magic, it looks at the MRP type and acts accordingly, but not exclusively based on that MRP type. Because the primary or secondary demand causes the creation of an order proposal to fulfill the requirement, the lot size of the replenishment depends on the LOT SIZE PROCEDURE field in the MRP 1 screen. The replenishment quantity also depends on the safety stock settings on the MRP 2 screen, and the type of the order proposal (external or internal replenishment) is controlled by the procurement indicator and possibly a special procurement type, also maintained on the MRP 2 screen. There are many more field settings in the MRP screens of the material master that impact the generation of an order proposal, and together they make up a strategy or policy that tells the MRP run and other functions how to balance supply with demand.

In that sense, it's not the MRP type alone that makes up the policy, and it's certainly not just PD. PD simply is one possible MRP type, which, in conjunction with various lot-size procedures, safety stock settings, strategy groups, or special procurement types, can make up many policies for various material types. A policy, therefore, is a combination of many different settings in the material master record and a few other areas.

> **Note**
>
> Policy isn't an SAP term, so you won't find any SAP documentation on how to set up a policy. Neither will you get an error or warning message when you combine field settings that don't make any sense, as in the example of using a periodic lot-sizing procedure with a reorder point method. A message won't pop up in that instance hinting to a fixed or maximum stock replenishment procedure.

A policy is something that is quite complex and setting it up and using it effectively requires a good understanding of the planning and replenishment process. A policy may be expressed in words, for example: "…replenish based on an automatically determined forecast model on past consumption, ordering weekly demand with a minimum of five pallets, rounding to a pallet size, keeping safety stock in line with growing demand and at three days, receiving only Tuesdays and Thursdays, sourcing with quantity contracts and quota arrangements." The same policy can now be translated into the material master record with the following settings:

▶ MRP Type: VV

▶ Lot Size: WB

▶ Forecast model: J

▶ Min Lot Size: 2,500

▶ Rounding: 500

▶ Range of Coverage Profile: 003

▶ Planning Calendar: TT

▶ Source List: YES

Of course, we'll get a lot more elaborate and detailed throughout this chapter, but the point here is that every business should develop a set of standard policies that may be used throughout and gives the material planner a bit of a wiggle room for creativity and fine-tuning.

The development of policy is a creative process that can provide you with a lot of standardization, guidance, and automation. Without a policy playbook, the planners will develop their own system with varying degrees of success. It will be very hard to determine and to see what works and what doesn't. Trying out a reorder procedure on a predictable item with a short lead time might work very well, but would you know if it works on that other part too? You can only see what's going on and how performance improves if you classify and segment your portfolio into telling characteristics and then apply a common policy for all similar parts. That brings us to the other prerequisite for effective policy setting: classification and segmentation.

6.2   Segmenting a Materials Portfolio

To organize your materials portfolio into groups of similar characteristic values, you should perform a segmentation. A *segmentation*, as the word implies, is the act of building segments of items, parts, or materials that have similar features for the purpose of policy setting.

If you take a look at the airline industry, you must wonder how they can manage millions of people and reservations every day with utmost safety, reliability, and accuracy. Airlines put extreme focus on standardized routines—so that customers can balance service and cost—on data accuracy and availability of resources and structured sales and planning processes. In the end, you can go on a website, pick a destination, and choose from a multitude of options, sorted by price, convenience, or timely arrival.

How do they categorize all this data and ensure proper decision making in the process of flight and seat assignments? Segmentation is a big part of it (and policy setting another). With segmentation, an airline can sort, filter, prioritize, and create smaller chunks of manageable data and information. Frequent flyers are given priority on seat selections, lower fares are handed to people that commit to flights earlier, and a higher price is paid by business travelers who need more flexibility (see Figure 6.1).

There is much more, but as you can see, each segment receives a different policy: high flexibility = higher fare; frequent flyer = better seat; early commitment *and* frequent flyer = good seat at low price. In the latter case, two dimensions are used for the setting of a policy.

It's the same way in materials planning. A materials portfolio can be segmented into various dimensions such as consumption value, lead time, variability, price, lifecycle, or size. After the segmentation is done, you can create multidimensional grids and assign policies to the individual segments of materials. The most common grid is the two-dimensional ABC over XYZ, which classifies consumption value over consumption variability. With this grid, you can assign policy to materials with high consumption value and low variability in consumption as observed from period to period in the past. An example of an ABC/XYZ grid is shown in Figure 6.2.

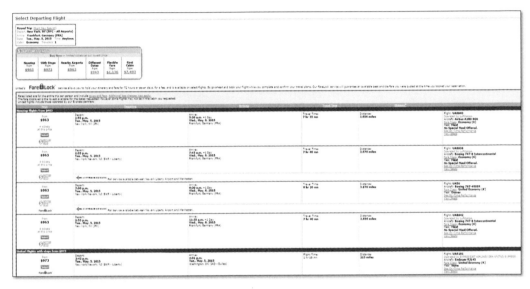

Figure 6.1 Flexible Option for a Flight Reservation Example

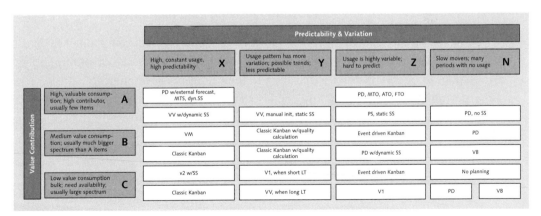

Value Contribution	Predictability & Variation			
	High, constant usage, high predictability **X**	Usage pattern has more variation; possible trends; less predictable **Y**	Usage is highly variable; hard to predict **Z**	Slow movers; many periods with no usage **N**
High, valuable consumption; high contributor, usually few items **A**	PD w/external forecast, MTS, dyn.SS		PD, MTO, ATO, FTO	
	VV w/dynamic SS	VV, manual init, static SS	PS, static SS	PD, no SS
Medium value consumption; usually much bigger spectrum than A items **B**	VM	Classic Kanban w/quality calculation	Event driven Kanban	PD
	Classic Kanban	Classic Kanban w/quality calculation	PD w/dynamic SS	VB
Low value consumption bulk; need availability; usually large spectrum **C**	v2 w/SS	V1, when short LT	Event driven Kanban	No planning
	Classic Kanban	VV, when long LT	V1	PD / VB

Figure 6.2 ABC/XYZ Segmentation

Before you can use a grid like the one shown in Figure 6.2 for policy setting, you have to perform an analysis for each one of the dimensions you want to explore and segment, which we examine in the following section.

6.2.1 Performing an ABC Analysis

ABC (or sometimes called Pareto) analysis, is a procedure that allows you to classify large volumes of data and processes. For materials planning, we're concerned with data such as material consumption, volumes, and movements. After the data is evaluated, it's usually separated into three classes: A, B, and C.

An ABC analysis is easy to use because its basic premise is to separate items that deserve a lot of attention from the rest. According to the Pareto principle—or the 80/20 rule—a small number of items (about 20% of all items) make up a very large portion (maybe 80%) of the total revenue, consumption, or some other quantifiable unit of measure that contributes to the success of the company.

The SAP analysis can be carried out using SAP ERP's Logistics Information System (LIS), and its result can be stored in the material master's MRP 1 screen (Figure 6.3).

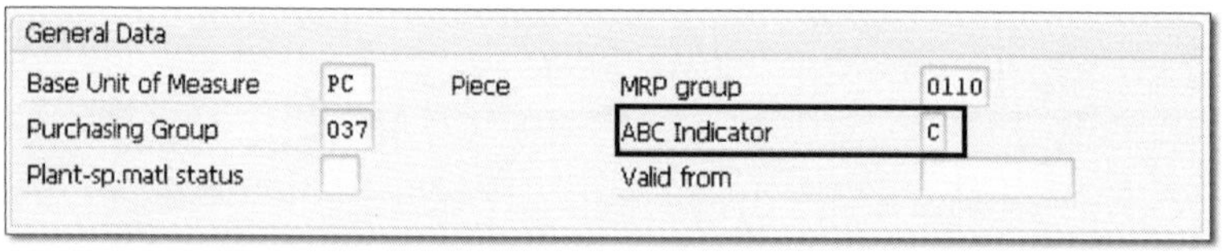

General Data				
Base Unit of Measure	PC	Piece	MRP group	0110
Purchasing Group	037		ABC Indicator	C
Plant-sp.matl status			Valid from	

Figure 6.3 ABC Indicator in the General Data Section of the MRP 1 Screen in the Material Master Record

Using Transaction MC40, you can start an ABC analysis for your plant. As you can see in Figure 6.4, Transaction MC40 allows you to select one or multiple plant codes to classify materials according to their usage values in percent, absolute, or per number of materials. You can also store the result in the individual material master's ABC Indicator by checking UPDATE ABC IND. IN BACKGROUND PROCESSING MODE.

Figure 6.5 shows the result of the analysis.

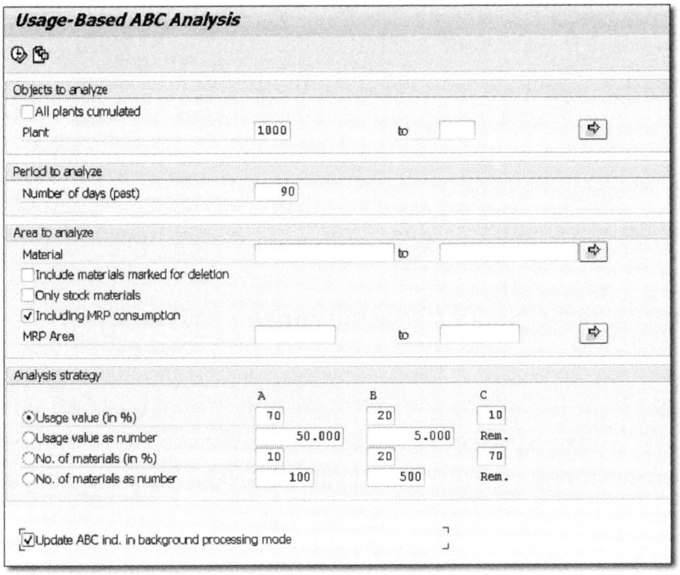

Figure 6.4 Initial Screen of Transaction MC40

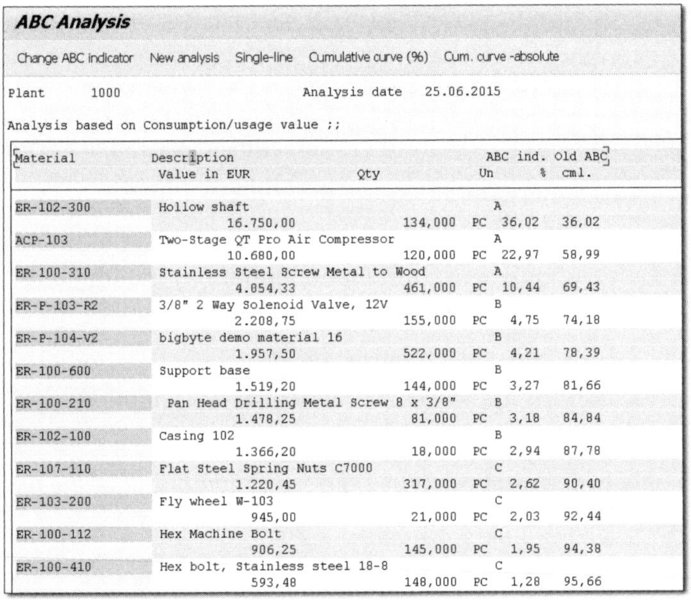

Figure 6.5 Result of the ABC Analysis with Transaction MC40

You can also start an ABC classification based on requirements in the future. Although the ABC analysis is the only one offered in the standard SAP ERP delivery, the other five that we'll discuss in the next sections are essential for an effective system of materials planning. One option is to use spreadsheets or third-party programs to perform a complete segmentation of your portfolio. Another, much better option is to acquire the MRP Monitor (an SAP add-on tool), which we'll discuss at the end of this chapter.

6.2.2 Determining a Coefficient of Variation for the XYZ Analysis

A very important analysis and one that works very well together with the results of an ABC analysis is the XYZ analysis. XYZ separates your portfolio for consumption consistency by calculating a coefficient of variation (CV). The CV is an indication about the past consumption pattern of a material. The essential question the XYZ analysis will answer is whether consumption was regular from period to period.

The CV is defined as the ratio of the standard deviation (σ) to the mean (μ). In that sense, a spreadsheet macro could analyze the consumption of, let's say, the past 12 months and then use this formula to calculate a CV for each part. Then you set the boundaries—for example <0.5 = X and >2.0 = Z—and each material is being put into the respective X, Y, or Z bucket.

The classifications that result from XYZ analysis are sometimes referred to as runners, repeaters, and strangers, and they can be categorized as follows:

▸ **X items (runners)**
Products that have had very consistent consumption month by month.

▸ **Y items (repeaters)**
Products that have had somewhat consistent consumption in most months, but the pattern shows irregularities and sometimes very little consumption.

▸ **Z items (strangers)**
Products that have only had consumption in 3 or fewer months out of the past 12 months.

After you've assigned XYZ codes, you can then apply varying inventory expectations and planning rules to the high-velocity runners, intermittent-selling repeaters, and the very sporadic strangers. This objective and relatively simple approach will help optimize inventory levels to support superior customer service performance. Most importantly, however, the XYZ analysis is an indispensable criterion for policy setting as we'll see soon.

6.2.3   Combining ABC with XYZ

In many enterprises in which the classification of stocks is divided on the basis of ABC analysis, it turns out that the articles aren't differentiated enough. It only assesses the products according to their share in the company's sales or consumption volume. However, the Inventory Management and the turnover rate are also relevant aspects. Combining an ABC with an XYZ analysis delivers a number of great insights and sets a very good basis for initial decisions in regards to policy setting. Following are a few recommendation regarding ABC/XYZ combination:

▸ AX, BX, CX, AY, BY, and CY are suitable for fully automatic computerized processing. Fully automated computerized processing is easily done with consumption-based planning methods or policies.

▸ AZ, BZ, and CZ should be scheduled manually. Manual planning needs to be done with MRP type PD (plan on demand). Many companies implementing SAP software don't (or can't) perform an ABC/XYZ analysis and therefore set all or most items up with a MRP type PD. The consequence then is that everything is planned manually, and all the automatism that SAP provides is lost. That is why every optimization effort should include an ABC/XYZ analysis so that opportunities for automation are being leveraged to their fullest extent.

▸ AX, BX, AY, BY, and AZ are in general suitable for Just-In-Time (JIT) deliveries.

▸ AZ and BZ products have a large share in revenue. However, they are difficult to control and they need special attention.

6.2.4   Adding an EFG Classification for Long and Short Lead Times

EFG are the letters of choice to separate long lead time items from those that can be procured quickly—and the ones in between. Often the dilemma with a reorder point procedure is that if the lead time is long, you will have to keep too much in stock so that the procedure gets you through the long lead time. In such cases, you need a different policy, and there are plenty of choices. The point is that if you want to set the perfect policy for each item, you'll have to include a lead time analysis as well.

6.2.5   UVW Classification for Purchase Price Segmentation

A drawback with the ABC analysis is that you won't know if an item was classified as an A because it had few movements with high price or because it had many movements with low price. There is just no way of telling unless you perform a UVW analysis by valuation price. This way you're able to set a different policy for A items with a low price than what you set for an A item with a high price.

6.2.6   LMN Classification for Volume or Size

The LMN classification isn't an essential part of portfolio segmentation for policy setting but it's nevertheless useful. It separates items by volume or size and allows you to set rules for replenishment of large parts differently than for parts that use up only a little space in your warehouse. For example, a certain company buys very large tanks as a component for gas-insulated switchgear. The tanks, obviously, take up a lot of space and often need to be stored outside. So it was necessary to make a differentiation in the replenishment policy for these tanks. The customer decided that the material forecast accuracy in the MRP type VV must be much higher for these components than usual.

The LMN classification is often forgotten; however, if you use it, you might come across the fact that you're consuming lots of very small parts, which, combined with a low price, are much better planned in bulk and with plenty of inventory. This is in stark contrast to stock-outs and production orders getting stuck in front of the line because cheap, small parts are missing.

6.2.7   Lifecycle Analysis

Finally, the lifecycle analysis separates new materials from slow movers, really slow movers, and obsolete items. Categories may vary, but in its essence a lifecycle analysis sorts and filters items according to their degree of maturity throughout their useful lifecycle.

Typically, an items grows through the stages of being new, maturing to be regularly consumed, slowing down in usage, and eventually becoming replaced and obsolete. So why do we need to worry about these stages in our efforts to assign replenishment policy to parts? If, for example, you want to assign a consumption-based replenishment policy to a group of materials, you should definitely exclude items that are too new to have consumption history. Failing to do so will result in an inefficient plan, and the danger of stock-outs of high inventory levels will be too great.

On the other hand, using a lifecycle analysis, you can easily filter out your slow movers, eliminate safety stocks, and make sure they're all planned on demand.

6.2.8 Putting It All Together for Policy Setting

As we've discussed a number of times, classification and segmentation are essential parts of an effective system of materials planning that enable you to set the stage for policy setting. The result of an elaborate classification is a segmented portfolio of parts, items, and materials into multiple dimensions. The result might be displayed in the form of a grid. But because a grid is two-dimensional, you can't put all the classes on there. There are techniques and tools to manage this kind of thing very well, but, unfortunately, standard SAP ERP doesn't provide a good way to do that.

Third parties and consulting companies have been taking on this problem with more or less useful successful outcomes. The preferred solution, however, comes from SAP itself. As we've mentioned in previous chapters, a group out of Germany, SAP Consulting, has developed the SAP add-on tools, including the MRP Monitor. This tools not only allows for classification and segmentation into six dimensions, it also allows for automated policy setting on a periodic basis. As an added incentive, the software is entirely written within the SAP namespace and therefore is actual SAP software, which is easy to install and integrate into the standard offering.

There will be a more detailed description of the functionality of the MRP Monitor and some other SAP add-on tools at the end of this chapter.

6.3 Replenishment Policies

A policy is mainly a combination of settings, but not exclusively, found in the four MRP screens of the SAP material master record. To design and use an effective policy, you must understand each and every possibility you have in putting any one of these combinations together. If done right, a policy not only optimizes inventory holdings and availability but also drives automation, takes over the "heavy lifting" from the planner, and provides transparency and information for better monitoring of the replenishment and consumption process.

Replenishment policies are used for materials to be procured from outside the company or by way of a stock transport order from another internal plant or warehouse. They revolve mainly around the MRP type that is being used, and they can be split into those policies that go by the past (consumption-based replenishment strategies or stochastic) and those that look into the future (deterministic replenishment policies). All replenishment policies fall into either one of those categories with the exception of Kanban-based policies. But we'll talk more about that later.

In the upcoming sections, we're going to deep dive into the components that make up a policy. Thorough understanding of how these components work within SAP is helpful and essential in the design of an intelligent policy for effective materials planning.

6.3.1 MRP Types

The MRP type is the main driver of any replenishment policy. The MRP TYPE field is on the MRP 1 screen, which you can access by using Transaction MM02. Many predesigned MRP types are already available in the dropdown list (see Figure 6.6).

Very often, companies add their own "Z" MRP types, but make sure to understand all the options available with the standard delivery first, before going off and designing a new one. With that said, there is definitely the need for adding new MRP types to suit the individual business processes and requirements. Mostly these additional MRP types are variations of an existing concept.

> **Example**
>
> You might want to add an automated reorder procedure that considers external demand out over the entire planning horizon. The existing standard MRP type V2 only considers external demand within the replenishment lead time.
>
> Most people would now go off and add a "Z something" MRP type because they were told to do that when configuring or customizing anything in SAP. I recommend against this practice. There is absolutely no need to call an additional MRP type—especially when it's just a variation of a standard procedure—"Z something." This method leaves you with only one digit to use to name your indicator. Instead, call it V3 and put something in the description so everybody understands its workings and when to use it. This way, you're building a vast array of options and combinations that your planners can use as the need arises.

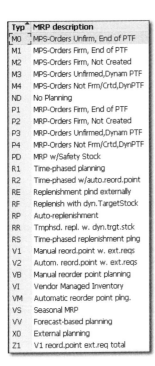

Typ	MRP description
MO	MPS-Orders Unfirm, End of PTF
M1	MPS-Orders Firm, End of PTF
M2	MPS-Orders Firm, Not Created
M3	MPS-Orders Unfirmed,Dynam PTF
M4	MPS-Orders Not Frm/Crtd,DynPTF
ND	No Planning
P1	MRP-Orders Firm, End of PTF
P2	MRP-Orders Firm, Not Created
P3	MRP-Orders Unfirmed,Dynam PTF
P4	MRP-Orders Not Frm/Crtd,DynPTF
PD	MRP w/Safety Stock
R1	Time-phased planning
R2	Time-phased w/auto.reord.point
RE	Replenishment plnd externally
RF	Replenish with dyn.TargetStock
RP	Auto-replenishment
RR	Tmphsd. repl. w. dyn.trgt.stck
RS	Time-phased replenishment plng
V1	Manual reord.point w. ext.reqs
V2	Autom. reord.point w. ext.reqs
VB	Manual reorder point planning
VI	Vendor Managed Inventory
VM	Automatic reorder point plng.
VS	Seasonal MRP
VV	Forecast-based planning
X0	External planning
Z1	V1 reord.point ext.req total

Figure 6.6 *MRP Types Provided in Standard SAP*

A really bad practice (and one that we've seen on multiple occasions) that some planners fall into is deleting the standard delivered options that they think they may not use. In that case, your options, and with it possibilities to continuously improve your planning procedures, diminishes. To take out functionality that isn't understood, means that you have no intention to ever understand it, which limits your ability to advance. The big goal isn't to scale down SAP-provided functionality and degrade planning to a few simple and easy-to-understand procedures, but rather to strive to understand as much as possible about the options and procedures at hand and use the full functionality for an automated, effective, and sophisticated planning process. This might take a long time, but considering the very high investment in SAP software and the implementation, it's well worth the wait.

In the following sections, we'll discuss the different types of procedures and reference specific MRP types that SAP provides to meet these needs. Over the next few pages, we'll talk about some of the most commonly used forms of replenishment. These lay out the groundwork we must provide for the design of an effective automated policy. We'll go over the two major categories of replenishment—

deterministic and stochastic (or consumption-based). All of the following procedures can be expressed with a standard MRP type out of the list shown previously in Figure 6.6. After you understand these basic procedures, you can develop policy for many different situations using variations around the common theme.

Deterministic Replenishment Procedures and MRP Types

Deterministic planning means to plan from the future. BusinessDictionary.com describes deterministic as:

> *Algorithm, model, procedure, process, etc., whose resulting behavior is entirely determined by its initial state and inputs, and which is not random or stochastic. Processes or projects having only one outcome are said to be deterministic... their outcome is 'pre-determined.' A deterministic algorithm, for example, if given the same input information will always produce the same output information.*

For our purposes, this simply means that if we employ a deterministic MRP type, the MRP run will create order proposals in a quantity, and for a time, exactly as we can expect without any probability or randomness, as stochastic planning does. In other words, a material set up with MRP type PD will always be covered with the exact quantity that is needed at the exact time when the material is needed (if we don't maintain any fixed or minimum order quantity, rounding values, or safety stock settings). PD is the most commonly used MRP type in SAP systems. It's also the one that is easiest to use and understand and has the least degree of automation.

A typical implementation of an SAP planning system starts with using PD for everything from a washer to the most expensive thrust reverser on an aircraft. Whether the material is predictable or not, large or small, has high consumption value or not, the use of PD is relentlessly applied across the board. It's easy to teach, quick to set up, and fast to understand. But it doesn't necessarily fit, and if applied throughout the portfolio, it certainly doesn't go with a concept of effective materials planning where planners act analytically, and the system does all the heavy lifting. It degrades your planners to transaction laborers and forces them to develop their own system of planning the replenishment of their materials portfolio.

First, there come the creative policies; instead of using a reorder point procedure, a safety stock is maintained on the PD driven material, so that it somehow acts like a reorder point driven material. For long lead time items, the planner must then apply a very high safety stock, and the inventory blows up. Desperate, the planner then plays around with safety time and other settings, and nothing works. Executives then demand inventory reports and direct the planner to do an inventory reduction. After the safety stocks are reduced, the stock-outs occur, and the only way out of the vicious circle is—you got it—Microsoft Excel!

SAP then gets a bad rap for not providing the functionality that is needed, and all those beautiful features and functions are dismissed and never even looked at.

All of this doesn't mean that the PD type doesn't have the right to exist. When used appropriately, it plans all those materials that can't be automated and require a bit more attention because they're important to business success, difficult to predict, and high in value.

Figure 6.7 shows the Customizing screen for MRP TYPE PD with its standard settings. Here is where you can fine-tune and change how deterministic planning with the PD works or acts.

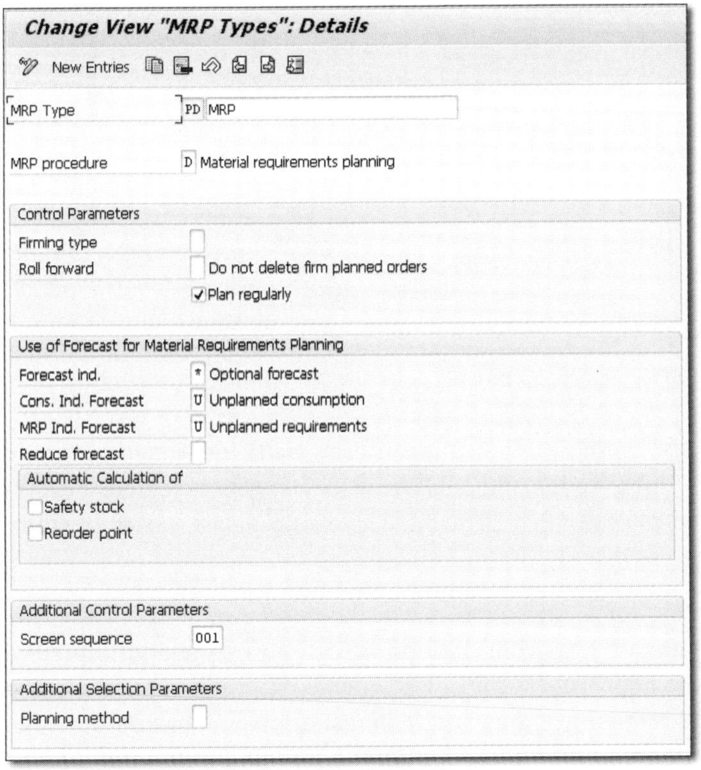

Figure 6.7 Configuration Settings for PD

The MRP type PD is planning deterministically (SAP calls that MRP). In its initial configuration, the PD may also include a forecast on unplanned consumption (see the FORECAST IND. and CONS. IND. FORECAST fields). When you enter a FORECAST MODEL in the FORECASTING screen, the PD will forecast unplanned consumption (you can see the unplanned consumption in the consumption history) and display additional requirements (UNPLD. CONS.) in the STOCK REQUIREMENTS LIST.

PD simply looks at demand in the future and covers it with a procurement proposal that has a delivery date just before the demand occurs, as shown in Figure 6.8.

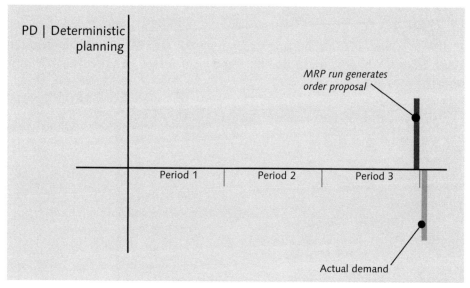

Figure 6.8 MRP Type PD Procurement Proposal

PD is deterministic and therefore, in its purest form, waits for demand before it springs into action. If there is demand, and the MRP run gets executed, a supply proposal is generated to cover that demand. There's no magic, no automation, nothing. It's as simple as that.

No demand/no supply works really well when the purchased part is expensive and therefore costly to store, its consumption is highly variable and unpredictable, and the lead time to procure is short. But when your production lines starve because a component is missing, , then you're in real trouble. Your PDs should be worth the constant attention they need. It's okay to carefully watch and monitor how much of Johnnie Walker's Blue Label you hold behind the bar, but to tell a patron that you ran out of salt because you were waiting to buy a sack until they asked for it, is flat out ridiculous. (Now's the time to check to see if any one of your highest consumable standard parts is set to PD).

There are ways to make a PD work for the situations we just described. You can set a safety stock, create a parts forecast, or work with lot-sizing procedures. That way, you cover up the disadvantages of a PD with stochastic (consumption-driven) methods that help you somewhat to automate. However if the part calls for such methods, why not employ a standard consumption-based planning method altogether? They work beautifully if combined with the right lot sizing, safety stock, or availability checking rule.

Other deterministic MRP types are P1, P2, P3, and P4. They require a planning time fence to be set, and they help you by keeping planned orders that are generated by the MRP run out of that period of time. These MRP types can also protect a short-term production program and are being fixed automatically when they fall within the frozen zone. The difference between these four MRP types lies in the firming or not firming of the procurement proposals and what requirements in which period are considered.

The MRP type M0 is used to plan your important finished (or unfinished) products separately from the rest. It has its own Master Production Scheduling (MPS) planning run and is meant to cut down on processing time before the plan is released to the BOM structure. As in the P series, the M1, M2, M3, and M4 types allow for the protection of a planning time fence and automatic fixing of procurement proposals.

Consumption-Based Replenishment Procedures and MRP Types

Consumption-based procedures are also called stochastic or random. A definition of stochastic can be found on *www.BusinessDictionary.com*:

Situations or models containing a random element, hence unpredictable and without a stable pattern or order. All natural events are stochastic phenomenon. And businesses and open economies are stochastic systems because their internal environments are affected by random events in the external environment. Stochastic is often taken to be synonymous with probabilistic but, strictly speaking, stochastic conveys the idea of (actual or apparent) randomness whereas probabilistic is directly related to probabilities and is therefore only indirectly associated with randomness.

This can be interpreted as planning by past patterns as opposed to future events. Stochastic processes always involve probability, such as trying to predict the water level in a reservoir at a certain time based on random distribution of rainfall and water usage. In contrast, deterministic processes never involve probability; outcomes occur (or fail to occur) based on predictable and exact input values.

In stochastic planning procedures, we try to cover future requirements by providing stock levels that fulfill these future requirements with the least amount of inventory investment. There is a probability and randomness to this process that can be buffered with safety stocks, capacity, or time. That is why consumption-based, or stochastic, replenishment policies underlie an estimating process.

And before we go into the details of stochastic procedures, we'll briefly discuss the role of safety stock settings for these procedures. Because future stock holdings are predicted to the best of the procedures capabilities and because there is some level of randomness and variability in demand, a buffer is helpful and in most cases indispensable to avoid stock-outs. How much that buffer needs to be depends on the lengths of the replenishment lead time, the variability of that lead time, the variability in demand, and a desired, stipulated service level that communicates the planner's percentage of acceptable stock-outs to the system. Using these parameters, the system—or in case of manual procedures, the planner—can calculate a safety buffer that should deliver the expected results in terms of availability and stock holding.

The first class of consumption-based replenishment procedures are the *reorder point types*. Reorder level planning is a consumption-based method because it requires inventory to be available at all times and doesn't wait until there is demand before replenishment is triggered.

> **Example**
>
> Imagine the way your metabolism works. Its inventory is energy and when that energy level drops, you get hungry, and a desire to fill it back up is triggered. You get some food and eat. Now, you don't wait until you're completely depleted of all energy; there is an acceptable level—or range—from where you trigger replenishment. When you trigger energy replenishment, you usually have some lead time to deal with until you get that food, eat it, and metabolize it so it becomes energy. You instinctively know that you have to have enough energy left at the trigger point so that you don't run out completely within the replenishment lead time. This is no different with the raw materials you need to keep your lines going.

This kind of replenishment, like all other ones too, only works well in certain situations. Because you can predict really well what your rate of loss of energy is over time, you intuitively know how to set your trigger point. If your energy loss rate were completely unpredictable, the trigger point would have to be set very high because you really don't want to risk losing your life when you have a very sudden drop in energy.

Also, if you're very far away from food—let's say on a marathon run where you can't stop and sit down for lunch—you may eat some extra carbohydrates beforehand so that your energy level is very high and gets you through a long lead time. And last, but certainly not least, you want to think about your service level. What is the percentage of time that would be acceptable for you to wither away? (Now this metaphor doesn't work that well anymore).

These three variables determine where you set your reorder level. The more predictable the consumption, the lower the reorder level needs to be. The longer the lead time, the higher the reorder level needs to be. And the higher your expectation to never run out (e.g., a 99% service level), the higher the reorder level for safety. In the latter case, the reorder level moves up exponentially. This kind of thinking will also help you determine at what situation reorder level planning doesn't make sense anymore. Obviously, if you have unpredictable consumption in combination with a long lead time and high expectations to never run out, you should look for another strategy. Your reorder level, and therefore your inventory holding, is too high.

Don't forget about the other dimensions: value and size. Salt, something that is cheap and doesn't take up much room, is assumed to be in inventory at all times. Even if the use is unpredictable, it takes a long time to get it, or you never want to run out, it still makes sense to bring it back in after it breaks through an even very high reorder level because it's cheap to hold and easy to store.

There are four (actually five if you consider the time-phased R1) preinstalled reorder point procedures in SAP ERP:

- **VB**
  A manual reorder point procedure.

- **VM**
  An automatic reorder point procedure that calculates reorder point and safety stock using the FORECASTING screen in the material master.

- **V1**
  A manual reorder point procedure that considers demand within the replenishment lead time.

- ▸ **V2**

  An automatic reorder point procedure that considers demand within the replenishment lead time.

- ▸ **R1**

  An automatic reorder point procedure that takes into account the added replenishment lead time resulting from limited MRP runs only on the day of the planning calendar.

With the reorder point procedure, a planner or system can determine a stock level that is as high. When reordering at the time that level is reached, the anticipated future consumption doesn't exhaust the inventory holding before the end of the replenishment lead time. And at that time, a receipt to bring the inventory holding back up to a maximum stock can be expected. Any variability of that demand can be buffered with a safety stock, which is shifted underneath the previously calculated reorder point to lift the ordering trigger further up (i.e., to trigger the ordering process at an earlier time).

As shown in Figure 6.9, a reorder point procedure drives inventory holdings between a maximum and minimum level. It's important to use the appropriate lot sizing in combination with this procedure so that the ordering isn't triggered too frequently, and the averages aren't too high. Obviously, there must be some degree of predictability for this procedure to be useful, and too long of a replenishment lead time will produce bad results.

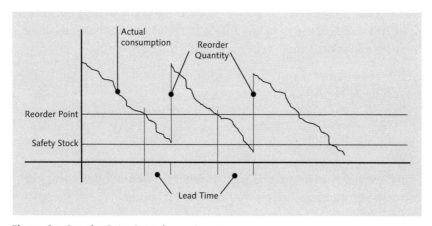

Figure 6.9 Reorder Point Procedure – Generic

Next, let's discuss the preinstalled reorder point procedures listed previously and some other MRP types in more detail.

VB

VB is the simplest and most manual of the reorder point MRP types. When using MRP type VB, you'll have to calculate and set the reorder point and the safety stock manually (see Figure 6.10).

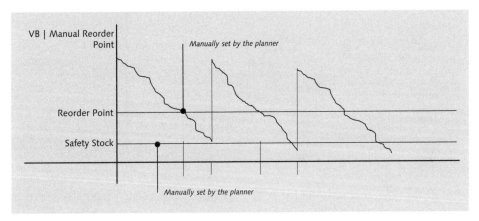

Figure 6.10 Manual Reorder Point MRP Type VB

When using this MRP type, you'll have to maintain the REORDER POINT field manually with your best guess. Look at the past consumption of the material in question and derive an estimated, future daily consumption quantity from that amount. You can then multiply this quantity with the number of working days (those days where your company consumes the material) within the total replenishment lead time (TRLT). That lead time should be maintained in the MRP 2 screen of your material master record (PLANNED DELIVERY TIME + GR PROC. TIME + PURCHASING TIME fields), and you may imagine that you'll get really bad results if that time is maintained correctly. The product of future daily consumption with the lead time gives you an inventory point that, if reached, you'll have to reorder so that you don't run out before the next receipt comes in. Depending on the variability you have in your estimated consumption or lead time, you should raise the reorder point by a safety stock you shift underneath.

That SAFETY STOCK is maintained on the MRP 2 screen of the material master record (see Figure 6.11).

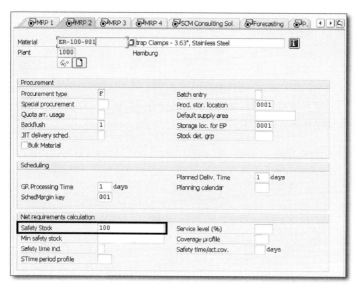

Figure 6.11 Safety Stock Field in the Material Master Record

The MRP Type VB is customized in the standard SAP ERP delivery as shown in
Figure 6.12.

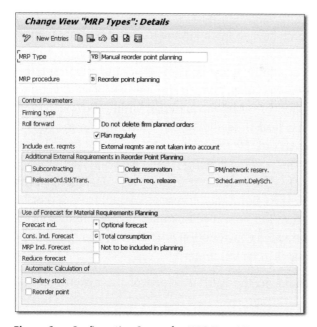

Figure 6.12 Configuration Screen for MRP Type VB

In the configuration for the manual reorder point procedure VB, the AUTOMATIC CALCULATION OF REORDER POINT and SAFETY STOCK checkboxes are unchecked.

There are many ways to calculate and guess the future daily consumption. One way is to look at the LIS and find the past consumption. Transaction MC.9 for example, gives you that history. However, when looking at the table with key figures and characteristics, you can only see monthly totals, and even though you might want to divide the monthly total by the number of working days in that month, you can't ensure that there was somewhat consistent consumption day by day. But if you display the consumption graphic in the LIS (see Chapter 8, Section 8.1), you can apply a number of helpful tools to get all the information you need.

Figure 6.13 shows a graphic with historic inventory behavior from which you can derive insights you may use to set reorder points. After you know the replenishment lead time, you can see how much you're usually consuming within it. Adding a safety stock adjusted to the visible variability in the downward slopes provides a needed buffer.

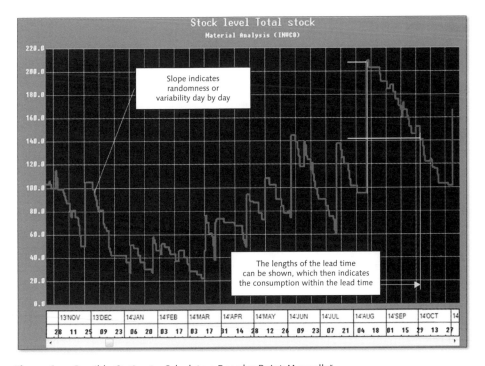

Figure 6.13 Possible Option to Calculate a Reorder Point Manually*

This way, you can see if there's consistency in the consumption over time and figure out how much inventory you need to get you through the lead time without any stock-outs. Then add a safety stock and put it into the material master's MRP 2 screen. Subsequently you maintain the MRP TYPE VB and fill in the REORDER POINT in the MRP 1 screen. The reorder point quantity is your estimated consumption within the TRLT plus the safety stock quantity. You actually aren't required to maintain a safety stock setting at all in MRP 2, but it's nice to have that kind of information readily available. As an added incentive, you'll get an exception message 96 every time you dip into that range, so you'll be able to tell over time whether your reorder point is too low or you have an opportunity to lower it (and with it the average stock holding of this material). The more often you get exception message 96, the more likely your reorder point is too low. But if you get exception message 96 only on rare occasions, it's time to look into lowering that reorder point.

VM

To achieve more automation and maybe more accuracy in the reorder point procedure, you can use MRP TYPE VM (see Figure 6.14).

Figure 6.14 MRP Type VM in the Material Master Record

VM takes the human guesswork out of the equation and lets the machine do the figuring (see an example in Figure 6.15). But beware, the machine can only figure and calculate good values if the underlying basic data and specifically the historic consumption are accurate. This procedure requires timely and accurate goods receipts and goods issues postings because it's using that data to figure mean absolute deviation and therefore consistency in consumption, lead time deviation, and various setting such as planned delivery time and service level to come up with a reorder point. If any of this information isn't maintained correctly, the VM will produce reorder points that either cause stock-outs or drive the inventory to potentially very high levels.

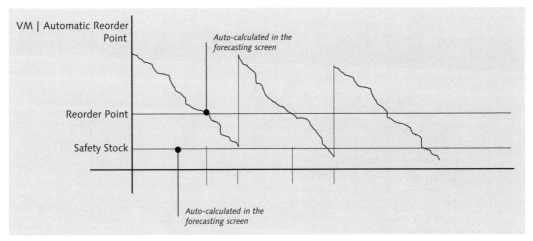

Figure 6.15 Automatic Reorder Point Procedure VM

In any case, the VM uses the material master's FORECASTING screen to automatically calculate the reorder point and a safety stock quantity via the following procedure:

1. In the FORECASTING screen, use its settings and historical consumption to calculate a past, mean absolute deviation (MAD). It does so by comparing a so-called ex-post forecast to the actual past consumption.

2. Use the service level being maintained in MRP 2 and a standard formula to calculate a safety stock quantity.

3. Calculate the future anticipated daily consumption by running a forecast in the material master record.

4. Multiply the working days in the TRLT with the future anticipated daily consumption. This is the basic value.

5. Add the safety stock quantity to the basic value. This is the calculated reorder point.

During this procedure the FORECASTING screen (Figure 6.16) is used for simulation purposes only. The forecasted quantities will not become MRP relevant. The forecast is simply used to perform an ex-post forecast, which allows for the determination of an MAD. The MAD is then used to determine the degree of variability for the calculation of reorder point and safety stock.

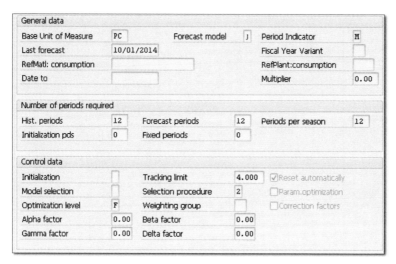

Figure 6.16 Forecasting Screen in the Material Master Record

Regarding this procedure, consider the following:

▸ The higher the degree of variation (MAD), the higher the safety stock requirement and the higher the reorder point will be.

▸ The longer the replenishment lead time, the higher the reorder point needs to be to get through the replenishment lead time.

▸ The longer the replenishment lead time, the greater the chance of an unforeseen consumption. This is increasing variability and with it safety stock requirements and the reorder point.

▸ The higher the service level percent maintained in MRP 2, the higher the safety stock requirement and with it the reorder point.

▸ The higher the daily consumption, the higher the reorder point.

Be careful using this procedure when you're not sure about all these conditions. All related settings must be fully understood, and the basic data has to be set correctly because otherwise you can end up with an automated disaster. It's also imperative that you design a reorder policy with the fitting lot-sizing strategy. All too often, reorder point procedures are in place where the inventory is so low that over two years, it never touched the reorder point. This was caused by the use of a lot-size procedure EX, or the fixed lot size was simply too low so when the receipt came in, that received quantity couldn't push the inventory above the reorder point.

As shown in Figure 6.17, the automatic reorder point procedure VM has the automatic calculation of safety stock and reorder point checked on. At the same time, the forecast is obligatory and uses total consumption.

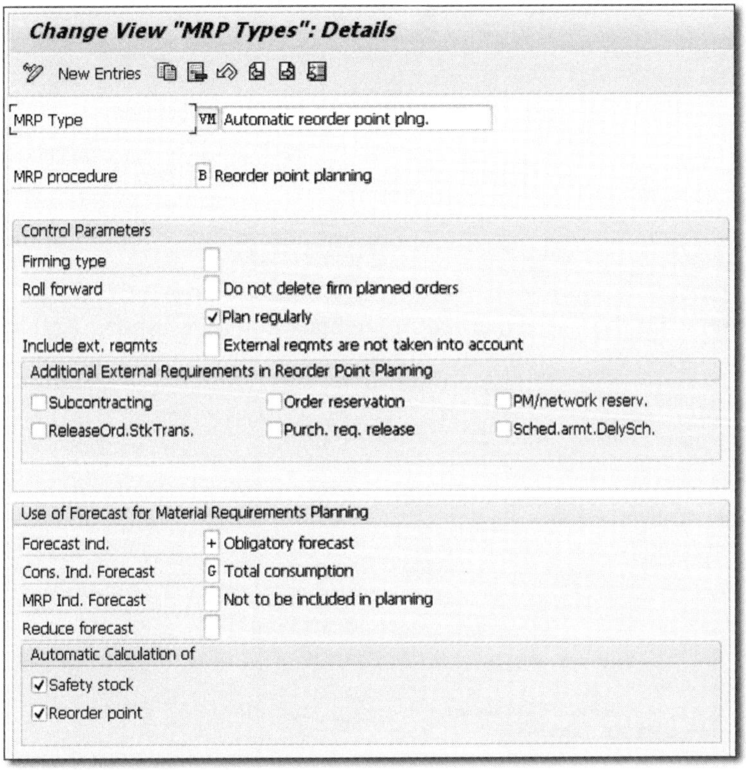

Figure 6.17 Configuration of MRP Type VM

V1

MRP type V1 acts exactly like VB, except that it takes external requirements into consideration. The safety stock and reorder point have to be set and calculated manually for this procedure, as shown in Figure 6.18.

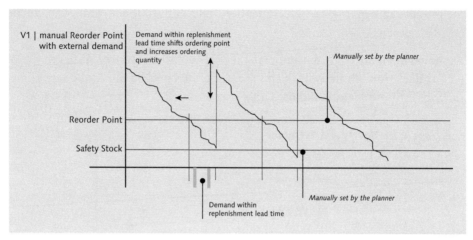

Figure 6.18 MRP Type V1

You can determine what those external requirements are in a Customizing table, as shown in Figure 6.19.

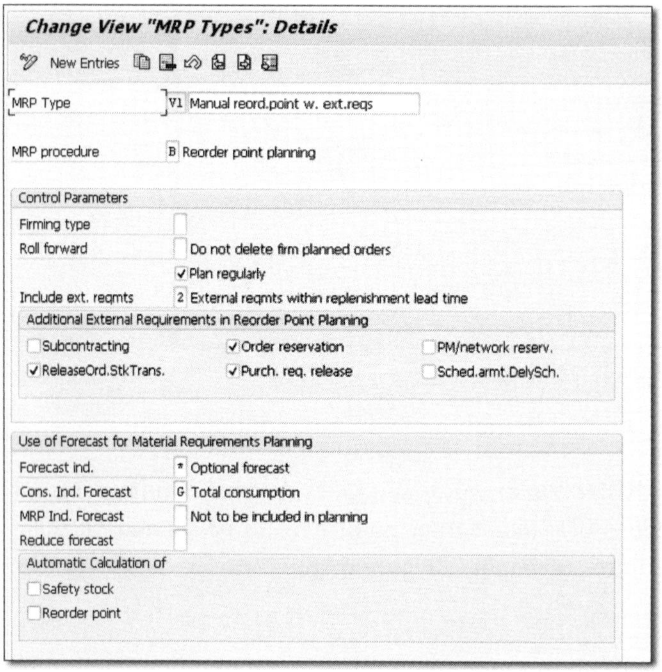

Figure 6.19 Configuration Screen for MRP Type V1

Here, the V1 type uses order reservations, released stock transport orders, and released purchase requisitions for external demand. If there is a sales order reservation within the replenishment lead time (INCLUDE EXT. REQMTS "2"), then the order is triggered early because the amount of demand from the reservation is taken into account for the determination of when the reorder point is broken.

This is a procedure where it's helpful to use a lot-size procedure that adds those external requirements within the lead time to the ordering quantity. Because these demands are already known, why not add it to the order size, so that at the time of receipt, the consumption can be replenished in full?

Therefore, the V1 type poses an advantage over both the VB and the VM types in that it's not purely driven by the past but a little more pro-active and includes future requirements in the planning process.

V2

In that spirit, the MRP type V2 provides the *most* sophisticated reorder point procedure so far (see Figure 6.20). Not only does it include external requirements, but it also calculates safety stock and reorder point automatically using the FORE-CASTING screen in the material master record.

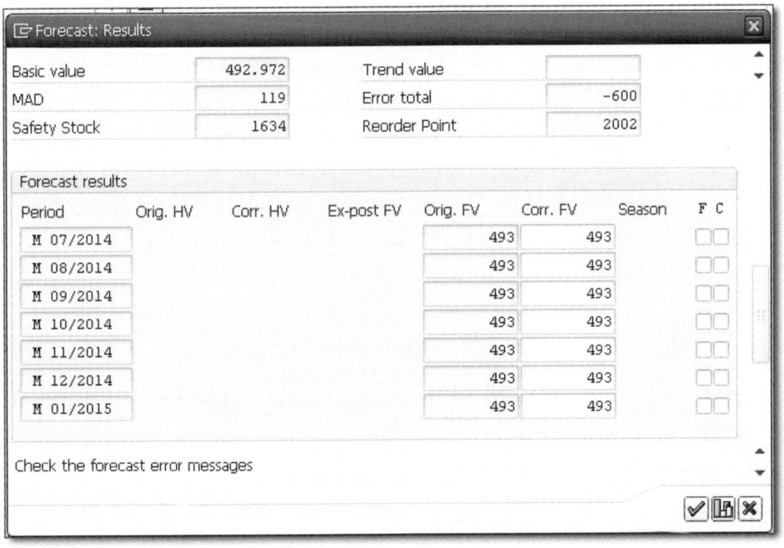

Forecast: Results								
Basic value		492.972		Trend value				
MAD		119		Error total			-600	
Safety Stock		1634		Reorder Point			2002	

Forecast results

Period	Orig. HV	Corr. HV	Ex-post FV	Orig. FV	Corr. FV	Season	F C
M 07/2014				493	493		
M 08/2014				493	493		
M 09/2014				493	493		
M 10/2014				493	493		
M 11/2014				493	493		
M 12/2014				493	493		
M 01/2015				493	493		

Check the forecast error messages

Figure 6.20 Results Screen for a V2 with Calculated MAD, Reorder Point, and Safety Stock

> **Caution**
>
> Again, just as in the case of VM, beware of too much automation, unless the procedure is fully understood, or the basic data has flaws.

Figure 6.21 illustrates MRP type V2, which automatically calculates a reorder point based on length of lead time, variability in the consumption, and the service level you set.

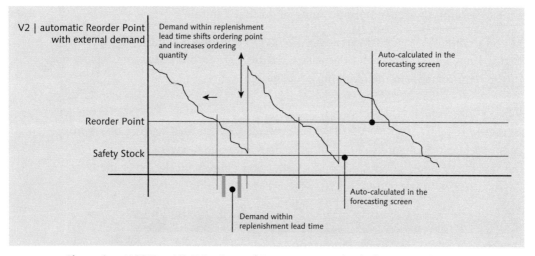

Figure 6.21 MRP Type V2 Using External Requirements and Calculating Reorder Point and Safety Stock automatically

So the V2 type combines the automatic calculation of the planning parameters with the consideration of external demand. This procedure is grounded on a simple reorder point philosophy that is sophisticated enough to automate the planning process and optimize your inventory holdings. Figure 6.22 illustrates the Customizing settings as delivered by SAP ERP.

There are a number of options for fine-tuning your preferred MRP type for reorder point planning. You could, for example, create a V3 that includes external demand not only within the replenishment lead time but over the entire planning horizon. You could also create a V4 that considers dependent requirements as external demand, or you could use a VU that calculates safety stock and reorder point automatically but only uses unplanned consumption for the calculation.

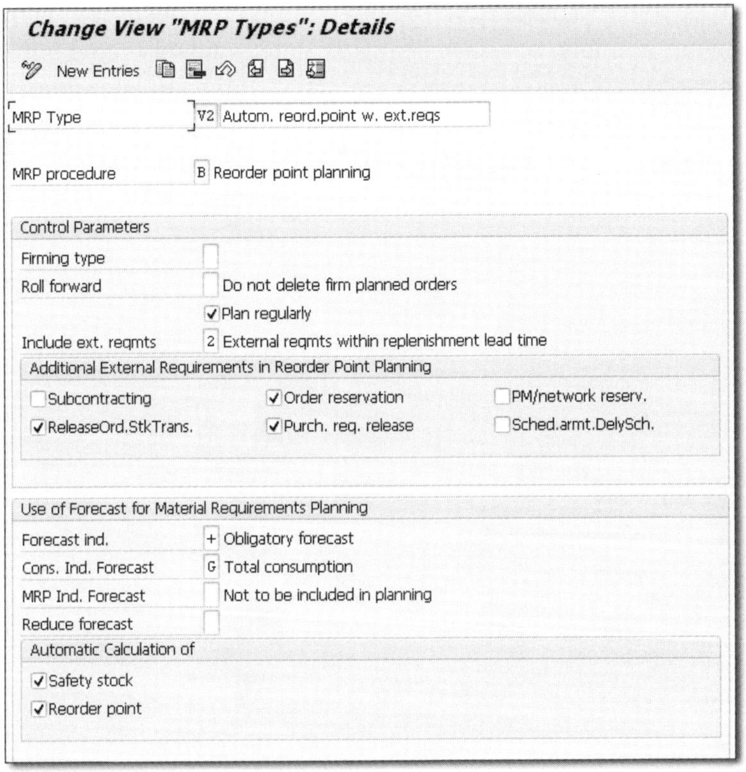

Figure 6.22 Configuration for MRP Type V2

As you better understanding how these things work together, the many different options mean the possibilities are endless. The key lies in understanding all the settings and picking the right options to put together a playbook of policies that works just right for your company. We'll talk more about that later, but for now, know that it's clearly not the lack of options that is to blame for all those inefficiencies people blame the SAP system for.

Kanban

Before we get to other consumption-based replenishment strategies, let's explore the Kanban method, which is very often confused with a reorder level procedure and isn't controlled by the MRP type on the MRP 1 screen. However, it's a consumption-based replenishment strategy nonetheless

In its original, simple sense, Kanban uses two bins with a certain quantity of parts in each, and when one is empty, replenishment is executed while the other bin— or its content—is used up. You just have to design the quantity available in each bin, so as to have enough in one bin to not run out while the other is filled back up. Figure 6.23 illustrates the Kanban replenishment procedure. When the demand source uses up a container, a signal is sent to the supply source, and the container is replenished.

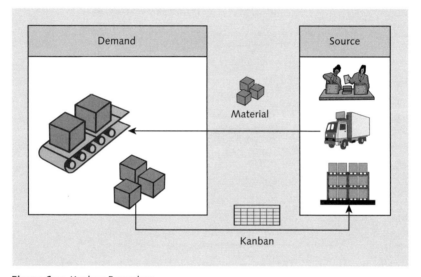

Figure 6.23 Kanban Procedure

So if you're wondering if you can use that instead of a reorder level procedure, the answer is no. There are situations where you can't simply trade a reorder level procedure for Kanban. When you fill rum into bottles from a tank over the bottling line, you don't want to switch back and forth between two tanks but rather start the replenishment process for the blending at some point when that one available tank gets to a level where the replenishment lead time fills it back up to where it needs to be, before you run out.

Kanban is great for parts needed on an assembly line. You put two bins of screws on there, and the worker takes what he needs. When the bin is empty, he takes screws from the second bin and sends the empty one to the warehouse for replenishment.

VV — Forecast-Based Planning

Forecast-based planning, also part of consumption-based replenishment, is a procedure where you actually run a material-based forecast to generate planned demand to which you can order and plan future inventory. This procedure isn't to be confused with what SAP calls the external forecast. The material forecast we're talking about here is driven off MRP type VV, and its forecast is carried out material by material. In fact, each material can have its own forecasting screen activated in the material master. We've used that screen already for the MRP types V2 and VM, but the FORECASTING screen with all its parameters and functions is much more powerful and useful than most people know.

First, a VV type can also be used for finished goods. There are many situations that call for setting up a finished product to VV. For example, you can create a forecast in the material rather than in sales & operations planning (SOP) and then copy the VV forecast as an external forecast into demand planning (DP). This gives you perfect, individual control over the product's forecast and the added advantage that sales orders consume that forecast.

So what does the VV do? It's a consumption-based replenishment strategy, in that it maintains inventory in anticipation of actual demand. The inventory is replenished to a forecast, which is based on the material's own consumption history, hence the name material forecast. This is a good strategy when you have predictable demand, but the lead time to replenish is long. Because you put "artificial" demand out there by way of a forecast, MRP can generate all supply elements way ahead of time. All you have to do is turn the requisition into an order at the date the system tells you to do so.

> **Warning**
>
> VV doesn't take demand spikes into consideration. Any changes in demand will flow into the consumption pattern and eventually be picked up by the forecast module. The system might increase or decrease the forecast or tell you that the current underlying model doesn't hold water anymore. So, like all the other strategies, you can only use VV when it fits the bill. Don't blame SAP when you use VV for a finished product, and it doesn't pick up immediately on a demand spike. It simply won't.

Forecasting means to anticipate consumption. When a squirrel accumulates nuts to help it survive through the winter, it does so by anticipating how many nuts are likely to be consumed, without too much variation. There will be safety stock, but a squirrel will not plan for a possible spike of three to four times the consumption it had in the previous year. Yet, in materials planning, we are always concerned about that possibility. Planners always ask, "What if we experience a huge spike in demand?" If it happens once, we would resort to a time buffer or expedite orders manually. If it happens constantly, the material doesn't qualify for VV replenishment anyway. More often than not, as we analyze a material's history, we see that the much feared spike in consumption hasn't occurred even once in the past five years.

You can cover variability in demand, but with VV, you do this with safety stock that is static, forecast adjusted, or dynamic with a range of coverage profile. After the safety stock is depleted, you run out, and the service level degrades.

VV provides a high degree of automation, but it needs to be monitored, and SAP provides various options to do so. To determine how good the forecast was, you can look at the ERROR TOTAL parameter shown in Figure 6.24. It looks at each period where there was a forecast and subtracts the forecast values from what was actually consumed. As the consumption most likely differs from the forecast, the question is how much does it differ. If the underlying model (constant, trend, season, or seasonal trend) is correct, then the error should sometimes exceed and sometimes fall short of what was forecasted, and over the long run average out and approximate zero.

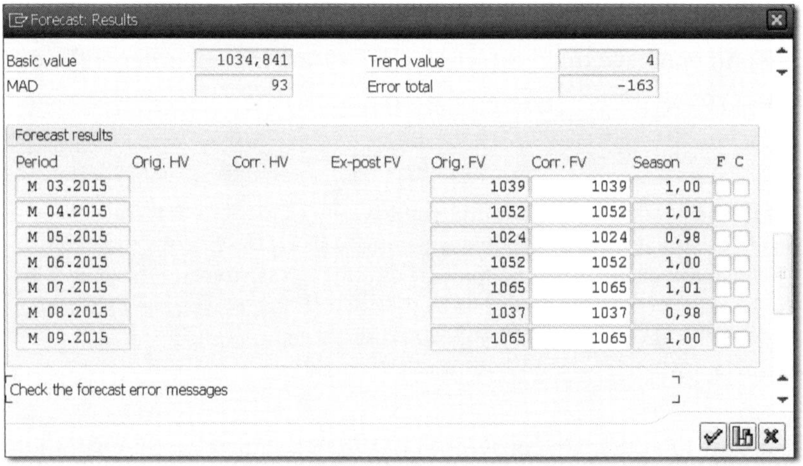

Forecast: Results							
Basic value	1034,841		Trend value			4	
MAD	93		Error total			-163	
Forecast results							
Period	Orig. HV	Corr. HV	Ex-post FV	Orig. FV	Corr. FV	Season	F C
M 03.2015				1039	1039	1,00	
M 04.2015				1052	1052	1,01	
M 05.2015				1024	1024	0,98	
M 06.2015				1052	1052	1,00	
M 07.2015				1065	1065	1,01	
M 08.2015				1037	1037	0,98	
M 09.2015				1065	1065	1,00	
Check the forecast error messages							

Figure 6.24 Error Total in the Forecast Results Screen

For MRP Type VV to function, you need to maintain all the parameters in the FORECASTING screen as shown in Figure 6.25.

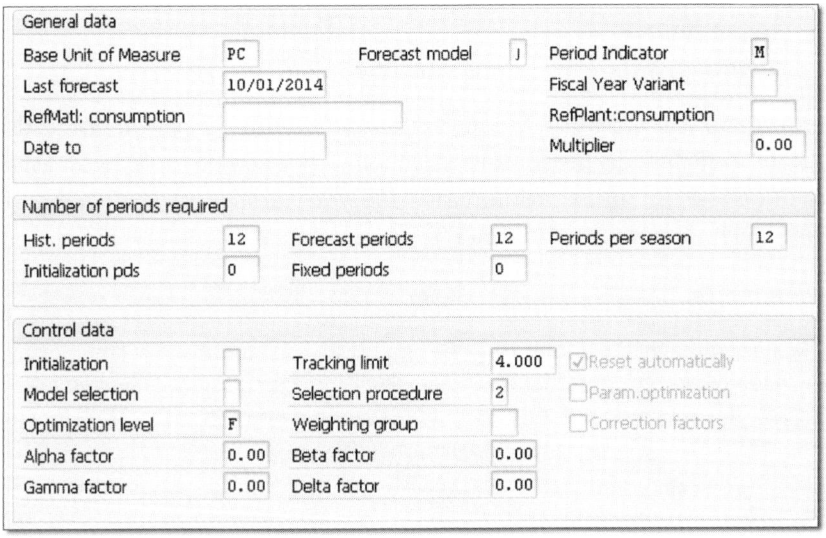

Figure 6.25 Forecasting Screen in the Material Master Record

Identify the periodicity by which you want to run the forecast to create demand with the PERIOD INDICATOR. This setting will eventually determine with what frequency the forecast is run automatically for the material in question. The options are listed here:

▸ **Daily (D)**
Results in daily demand records for every working day visible in Transaction MD04 and relevant to the MRP run. We haven't yet come across a good reason for a daily demand forecast, but the option is there if you need it, and it will allow you to keep your average inventories at a minimum if you can fairly accurately predict your consumption. Be aware, however, that a daily forecast will also result in daily replenishment unless you're using a periodic lot-size procedure (but if so, why forecast daily in the first place?).

▸ **Weekly (W)**
The most often used periodicity allows for relatively low average inventory holding because you're bringing in less than in a monthly periodicity, and it's flexible and quick to detect spikes and periods of low consumption.

▶ **Monthly (M)**

Used for less important or less expensive items because you can bring in large quantities with few orders.

▶ **Posting period (P)**

Freely definable according to a period you've set up in financial accounting (FI).

After the PERIOD INDICATOR is set, you can decide how many periods from the past you want to include in the forecast calculation. It's also possible to set aside a number of periods for an ex-post forecast, and you can identify the amount of periods for which the forecast run generates demand.

The Ex-Post Forecast

A useful feature of the material forecast is the ex-post forecast for the calculation of an MAD. The underlying concept is that the system compares the just now generated forecast to the actual consumption of the past and can therefore determine how close (or far away) the forecast would have been, if it have been used in the past.

You can see the deviation of the actual past consumption to the forecast in Figure 6.26 if it would have been applied to the past. SAP's forecasting run can now calculate an average deviation from that forecast and display an MAD in the FORECAST RESULTS screen. The MAD then helps the planner identify the degree of variability and a subsequent decision on buffering strategies to avoid stock-outs.

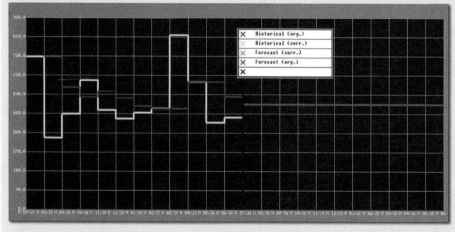

Figure 6.26 Ex-Post Forecast*

The FORECAST MODEL is another important parameter (refer to Figure 6.25) because it tells the system what to look for: a trend pattern, constant consumption from period to period, or seasonality. You can also choose to let the system perform a number of tests so that it can automatically identify the pattern and set it after the run is being executed. Therefore, you'll end up with the respective model in this field, and the next forecast run can — using the TRACKING LIMIT field — detect whether the previously detected model is still valid for the new period. The system does so by dividing the total forecast error by the MAD. If the result exceeds the values set in the TRACKING LIMIT field (default value is 4.00), then the forecast run initializes the forecast model and performs a new pattern test.

In the CONTROL DATA section of the FORECASTING screen, you can also set the INITIALIZATION field to "X" to rerun the forecast in a period where it was already executed, with a different set of parameters for simulation purposes.

Also in the CONTROL DATA section of the FORECASTING screen, you'll find the smoothing factors fields: ALPHA FACTOR for the constant model, BETA FACTOR for a trend model, and GAMMA FACTOR for seasonality. The DELTA FACTOR controls seasonal trending. You can control how far the system looks back to smooth past consumption for the calculation of future forecast values. If, for example, you use a low alpha value of maybe 0.1, then the system smooths and averages out the entire time line in question. If, however, you use an alpha factor of 0.9, the calculation weighs the more recent periods of consumption much higher than the ones further in the past. It's also possible to have the system perform a parameter optimization. After the field is checked on, the forecast run performs a step-by-step simulation (that can be controlled by the OPTIMIZATION LEVEL field by choosing either fine or granular steps) to find the best alpha value and sets it automatically in the FORECASTING screen. The best alpha factor, in this case, is the one that produces the lowest MAD.

The MRP type VV is, as we pointed out before, a consumption-based planning method. It figures out how much is needed in the future based on what happened in the past. For purposes of generating replenishment proposals — as illustrated in Figure 6.27 — VV puts forecasted demands into future periods and replenishes accordingly. This, of course, requires somewhat consistent consumption in the past and a safety buffer.

A VV type replenishment procedure goes strictly by forecast. Actual demand, whether reservations from production orders or sales orders, doesn't reduce the available quantity as can be seen in Transaction MD04 (see Figure 6.28).

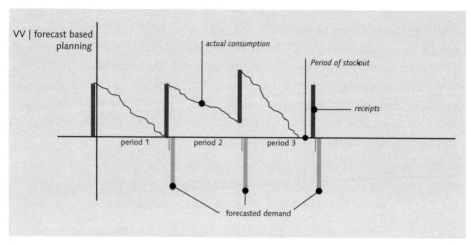

Figure 6.27 MRP Type VV Material Forecast

E..	Date	MRP ...	A..	MRP element data	Receipt/Reqmt	Available Qty
	01/17/2015	Stock				1,112
20	07/25/2014	PchOrd		0004071918/00020	600	1,712
	08/28/2014	TrRes.		4257819617/SDeb	100-	
20	10/16/2014	PchOrd		0004085476/00010	200	1,912
	11/03/2014	TrRes.		4257833422/SDeb	147-	
	11/18/2014	TrRes.		4259688877/SDeb	200-	
	11/26/2014	TrRes.		4255824687/SDeb	6-	
	01/19/2015	ForReq		M 01/2015	139-	1,773
	02/02/2015	ForReq		M 02/2015	139-	1,634
	02/20/2015	TrRes.		4255869860/SDeb	4-	
	03/02/2015	ForReq		M 03/2015	139-	1,495
	03/18/2015	TrRes.		4255816674/SDeb	100-	
	04/01/2015	ForReq		M 04/2015	139-	1,356
	04/02/2015	TrRes.		4255824472/SDeb	34-	
	05/01/2015	ForReq		M 05/2015	139-	1,217

Figure 6.28 Available Quantity Not Reduced by Actual Demand with Type VV

The planner often fails to use this procedure either because it was never taught or well explained, or when it doesn't produce the expected results during testing (often based on false expectations), it's quickly dismissed. It's probably the hardest MRP type to set up because you not only need to make sure all parameters in the FORECASTING screen are correct and optimal, but its success depends to a very large degree on how the overall policy is designed. This means that the right lot-size procedure is used, the buffering strategy is correct (using a range of coverage profile with VV is recommended, which makes the policy even more complex), and it's applied in the right situation (if demand is spotty and a large spike occurs in consumption, VV can quickly fail). The fact that actual demand isn't considered at all in the replenishment process of VV holds back a lot of planners from using it because they fear stock-outs without warning and explosion of inventory holdings when consumption drops off.

The appropriate use of minimums and maximums in the coverage profile used with VV can alleviate these fears and steer the replenishment clear from stock-outs and excess inventory, but all control parameters need to be fully understood and setup correctly, and the process needs to be monitored by the system so the appropriate exception messages are generated and tended to. Then, VV will become a very powerful tool in your box.

Time-Phased Planning Procedures and MRP Types

Materials that are replenished using a time-phased planning method are scheduled so that the MRP run considers them for planning only at specific dates in the week. This is determined by the planning cycle as shown in Figure 6.29. There you can see that the MRP run is only triggered on a Tuesday or on a Friday.

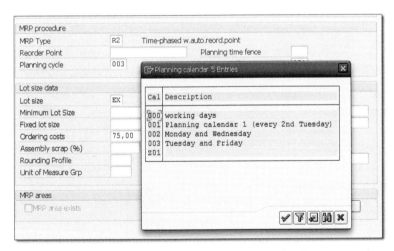

Figure 6.29 Time-Phased Planning Type R2 with a Cycle for Planning Tuesdays and Fridays

Time-phased planning can be carried out with consumption-based—stochastic—procedures or with deterministic ones. If you use time-phased planning with deterministic methods, you must set the TIME-PHASED WITH REQUIREMENTS indicator in MRP type Px. Here it makes sense to create a new MRP type PT for deterministic, time-phased planning with MRP.

MRP type R1 simply plans for an MRP run on the days scheduled by the planning cycle, which might lead to stock-outs when large consumption happens on a day not included in the planning cycle. This is where MRP type R2 is the better choice because it calculates a reorder point automatically and triggers the planning run whenever the reorder point is broken.

Summary—MRP Types

Table 6.1 summarizes the MRP types discussed in the preceding sections. Note that the MRP type doesn't constitute the policy but is only part of it.

MRP Type	Description	When to Use
VB	Sets the reorder point manually	When consumption is regular (X items) and lead time is short
VM	Calculates reorder point automatically	When you must update many materials on a periodic basis, and the consumption is less regular (Y items)
V1	Considers external requirements	When you want to include external requirements that consume inventory within the replenishment lead time
V2	Considers external requirements and calculates reorder point	For items that need to be updated frequently
VV	Material forecast	When consumption is regular, and lead time to replenish is long
PD	Plan on demand	When there is irregular demand and valuable materials
P1, P2, P3	Plan on demand with a time fence	When you need to protect a frozen zone from too much "noise"
M0	Master planning	When you have A items that have a large value contribution
R1	Time-phased planning	When you want to limit the amount of planning runs
R2	Time-phased planning with automatic reorder point	When you want to minimize stock outs occurring with MRP type R1

Table 6.1 Summary of MRP Types

6.3.2   Lot-Sizing Procedures

Determining good lot sizes is critical to optimum inventories and good service levels. Minimum order quantities, demanded by suppliers, often blow up inventory levels especially for slow-moving items. All too often, a materials planner is told to maintain the minimum lot size of a certain supplier and then is questioned by leadership about why there is too much inventory. Don't forget that there are gates that need to be managed. Between procurement or purchasing and materials planning there is a gate, which means that materials planning should generate the most economical lot size, generate an order proposal with that optimal lot size, and push it through the gate to purchasing. Purchasing then needs to deal with outside restrictions, pick a vendor that is best suited to fulfill the order proposal (considering many criteria), and then apply the terms and conditions that were negotiated at the beginning of the year by the sourcing department.

Figure 6.30 depicts the gate between purchasing and planning in that a materials planner could require 18 pieces to perfectly match demand, but the buyer is restricted by a minimum lot size and must bring in 20 pieces.

Figure 6.30 Control Gate between Materials Planning and Purchasing

The advantage of having these kinds of gates is that you can build a basis for nego-tiations with the supplier. If the materials planner applies the conditions in the MINIMUM LOT SIZE field in the material master, then the MRP run will always generate order proposals using the minimum quantity. But what if the supplier can be challenged? What if there is more than one supplier? What if the supplier with that specific minimum isn't around anymore? Don't limit the material plan-ner's ability to order the best possible quantity from an internal point of view. It's the buyer's job to find the best supplier that delivers the goods under the best conditions.

Lot-size procedures in SAP help the planner find the most optimal quantities to order. As they are part of a policy, the MRP run not only automatically generates the order proposal but also suggests the perfect lot size to bring in, so that avail-ability is assured without holding too much inventory. There are many lot-size procedures already preconfigured and available in the initial delivery of the stan-dard SAP software (much in the same way as the MRP types). To gain a better overview of what is available, SAP has broken down the lot-size procedures into three categories:

- Static lot-size procedures
- Periodic lot-size procedures
- Optimizing lot-size procedures

Each one of the individual lot-size procedures can then be combined with a min-imum order quantity, a rounding value, or a maximum stock level. But beware— not every combination makes sense.

In the material master's MRP 1 screen, there is a whole section that's dedicated to the determination of a good lot size for the generated order proposal. The most important indicator is the lot-size procedure, and the available choices are depicted in Figure 6.31. Again, we're presented with choices that SAP provided preconfigured with the initial delivery of the software. By no means does this rep-resent a complete list, but it's a very good start. As with MRP types, sometimes a consultant, IT representative, or other team member wants to keep things simple and throw out the lot-size procedures we don't immediately have use for. That is a bad idea. Taking options out of the system because we don't know how they work is like telling the quarterback to only use three offensive plays—no matter what the defense is up to.

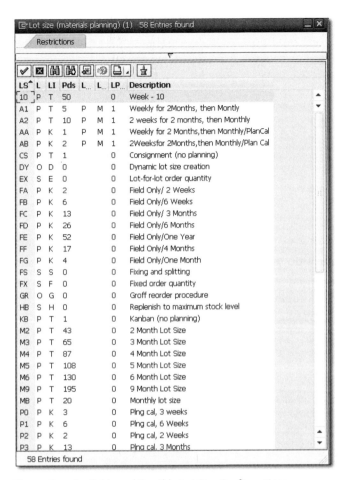

Figure 6.31 Available and Possible Lot Size Configurations

Keep your options open, and add more to the list. Remember, however, there's no need for "Z" stuff. Make it mean something. You have only two digits to work with.

Static Lot-Sizing

Static lot-size procedures generate order quantities that correspond to either a fixed or an exact (as in exactly what's needed) quantity to cover demand. A fixed lot-size procedure (FX) requires maintaining the fixed lot-size quantity that is to be used (see Figure 6.32).

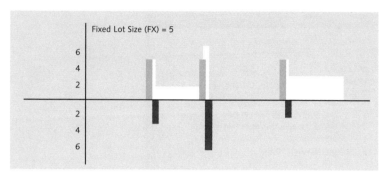

Figure 6.32 Fixed Lot-Size Procedure FX

Fixing and Splitting

A variation to the fixed lot-size procedure is the fixing and splitting procedure (FS), with which you can use the TAKT TIME field to space out the split, fixed quantities. For example, if you want to replenish inventory consumption with a fixed order quantity of 1000 pieces, you could split the order into 10 equal quantities of 100 pieces and space these out by the number of days in the TAKT TIME.

Change View "MRP Lot-Sizing Procedures": Details

 New Entries

Lot size	FS Fixing and splitting
☐ Last lot exact	

Horizon lot-for-lot ord qty ☐

Lot Size in Short-Term Horizon

Lot-sizing procedure	S Static lot-sizing procedure	No. of periods ☐
Lot-size indicator	S Stat.lot size: fixed w. splitting/dyn.lo	
Max. Stock Level	☐	
Scheduling	Requirements date := delivery date	
Date Interpretation	☐	
Overlapping	+	☐ Splitting quota

End of Short-Term/Start of Long-Term Horizon

PerInd: LT Lot Size	Initial value	Number of periods ☐

Lot Size in Long-Term Horizon

Long-Term LSP	☐	No. of periods ☐
Lot-Size Indicator	☐	
Scheduling	Requirements date := delivery date	☐ Check Min. Loz Size
Date Interpretation	☐	☐ Check Max. Lot Size
Overlapping	☐	☐ Splitting quota

Lot Size: MtO	☐ Lot-for-lot order quantity

Figure 6.33 Configuring a Lot-Size Procedure with Fixing and Splitting

This is particularly useful when you want to distribute planned orders throughout the week in internal production. There you could generate a fixed production run that you split into five equal portions and space them out from Monday through Friday with a TAKT TIME of 1 day. Whether the split works backwards or forwards is determined by a + or a – in the OVERLAPPING field in configuration of the FS lot-size procedure as shown in Figure 6.33.

As you can see in Figure 6.34, the lot sizing with FS splits the lot sizes in a forward mode using the TAKT TIME maintained in the material master record.

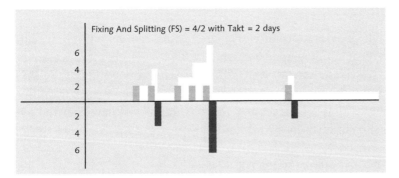

Figure 6.34 FS Fixing and Splitting

Lot-for-Lot
Another static lot-size procedure is the EX or lot-for-lot procedure (Figure 6.35). It generally brings in exactly the same quantity that's needed. Of course, you can use it in combination with a minimum or rounding value, but it's meant for valuable parts so that no excess inventory is left over after coverage of the demand.

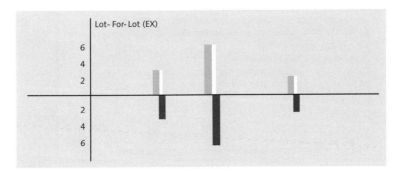

Figure 6.35 Lot-for-Lot Calculation Using an EX Procedure

Reorder Point Strategy

A fixed lot-size procedure is often used together with a reorder point strategy. Fixed lot sizes work with a reorder point, but you have to be careful to design the fixed quantity so that the received lot pushes the inventory far enough above the reorder point. An EX, for example, would generate a reorder quantity that would only fill up the inventory to exactly the reorder point. That would result in a "hang-from-the-ceiling" dilemma where MRP creates order proposals every time right after the receipt of an order. Many of you may combine it with a minimum order quantity, but that's like opening up a small wound so you can put a bigger bandage on to dress it.

A much better static lot-size procedure to be used with a reorder point procedure is the HB, which means "filling up to a maximum stock level." For it to work, you must maintain a MAXIMUM STOCK LEVEL in the LOT SIZE DATA section of the MRP 1 screen. Then, when the reorder point is broken, the MRP run figures the difference between the current sock level and the maximum stock level desired and creates a replenishment quantity correspondingly.

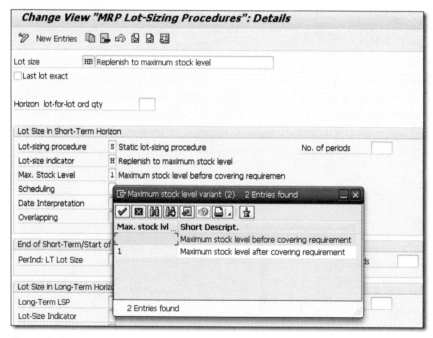

Figure 6.36 Lot-Size Procedure HB Configured to Include Requirements in the Building of the Lot Size

The problem with this procedure is that consumption occurs during the replenishment lead time, and when the replenishment quantity is received, the stock level might be considerably lower than at the time the replenishment quantity was calculated. A quasi fix to this problem is the inclusion of demand within the replenishment lead time. This can be configured in the Customizing of the lot-size procedure HB.

In Figure 6.36, you can see that it's possible to include any demand that is visible at the time when the reorder point is broken and to add those quantities on top of the difference between the current stock level and the maximum stock level. If you want to add this option to the planner's toolbox, copy the HB to an HM and customize it as shown.

Periodic Lot-Sizing

When many demands ought to be covered with a single supply element, the periodic lot-size procedures come in handy. These procedures all collect demand in a specified period and create exactly one supply element to cover the total demand quantities in that period. You may use a daily, weekly, monthly, or any other freely definable period within which you want to collect your demand.

Be aware, however, that the longer the period, the more inventory you have to carry. This is because the MRP run generates an order proposal that brings in the entire quantity needed in that period to the date of the first demand. In other words, if you're using a three-month period, and you have a demand of one piece on the first date of the first month, the order proposal would bring in the entire quantity needed for three months' worth of demand on the first day. In that case, you would have lots of inventory carrying cost to deal with if the item in question is of high value.

Periodic lot-size procedures are effective when used with cheap items when inventory cost is low.

Optimizing Lot-Sizing

Optimizing lot-size procedures strive to strike a balance between ordering cost and stock holding cost. They are therefore optimizing the total cost of inventory. For example, let's look at the lot-size procedure EX, which brings in—in its simplest version—exactly as much as you need at exactly the time when you need it.

In other words, you don't have to carry inventory forward to meet any other demand, but what is coming in is being consumed immediately. Therefore, with EX, you have no cost to hold stock. What you have, however, is the ordering cost, which you have every time there is a demand. So if you have five demands in one month, you'll end up paying for five orders.

This is different with a monthly lot-size procedure where you have only one order per month. But if you take the same situation with five demands, the order will bring in the total quantity to meet all demands throughout the months to the first demand, and you'll have to carry forward the stock that isn't consumed by the first demand. On the other hand, you have the cost of only one order.

When you use an optimizing lot-size procedure instead, the system (the MRP run) will figure out automatically—for any given demand situation—what the optimum order quantity and order frequency is to arrive at the minimum between ordering cost and stock holding cost. It does so by using various formulas such as the least unit cost formula, the Groff formula, or the part period balancing formula (see Figure 6.37). They all intend to do the same thing: strike the optimum balance between ordering and stock holding cost.

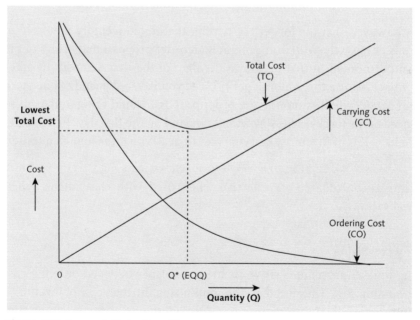

Figure 6.37 Economic Order Quantity

The question often arises of what to use as ordering cost, and there is no easy answer. Some people include the cost of carrier and transportation; others simply make up a fixed fee. You can also take the cost of the purchase department and divide it by the number of orders being processed per month. Remember, it's only an approximation so that the system has something to work with.

Minimum, Maximum, and Rounding

To form a policy, each of the previously described lot-size procedures can then be combined with a MINIMUM LOT SIZE, a ROUNDING PROFILE, a MAXIMUM STOCK LEVEL, and other indicators in the LOT SIZE DATA section of the MRP 1 screen (Figure 6.38).

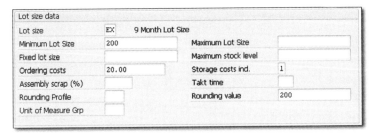

Figure 6.38 Lot Size Data Section in the MRP 1 Screen of the Material Master

The possibilities are many, but be aware that not every combination makes sense, and the SAP system doesn't give you an error or warning message if you design a senseless combination. Lack of understanding of these options is one of the sources of bad master data quality. Put in the effort to have all planners understand the lot-size procedures and combination options. It will pay off later.

Lot-size procedures have a major impact on inventory holdings. They represent a very important part of the policy. Arguably, safety stock or buffering provides maybe an even more important part of the policy as we'll see in the next section.

6.3.3 Safety Stock Strategies

Another important part of policy is the use of safety stocks to buffer variability in supply and demand. On the MRP 2 screen of the material master record, you'll find the NET REQUIREMENTS CALCULATION section dedicated to buffering strategies (see Figure 6.39).

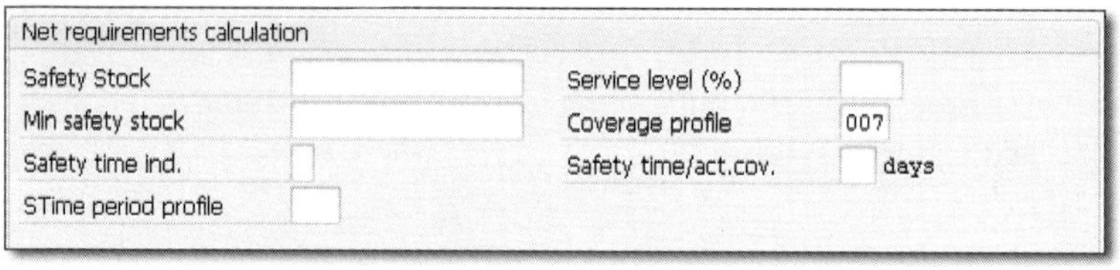

Figure 6.39 Section in the MRP 2 Screen of the Material Master Containing Buffering Strategies

We'll discuss some of the most used strategies from this screen in the following subsection.

Static Safety Stock

The simplest buffering strategy of all is the use of a static safety stock that can be maintained manually in the SAFETY STOCK field. All you have to do is enter a quantity, and the MRP run will ignore that quantity for planning purposes and set it aside for bad times. In fact, the STOCK/REQUIREMENTS LIST in Transaction MD04 subtracts that safety stock in the first line and then works without it for everything it does and looks at. As you can see in Figure 6.40, the safety stock quantity is immediately subtracted from free available stock and simply ignored for all future planning.

E..	Date	MRP element	A..	MRP element d...	St...	Receipt/Reqmt	Available Qty
	01/17/2015	Stock					60
	01/17/2015	SafeSt		Safety Stock		10-	50
	01/13/2015	OrdRes		378932	1215	4-	46
	01/14/2015	OrdRes		378932	1215	4-	42
	01/15/2015	OrdRes		378932	1215	4-	38
	01/16/2015	DepReq		383887	1000	1-	37
	01/19/2015	OrdRes		378932	1215	4-	33
	01/19/2015	DepReq		378932	1000	4-	29
	01/19/2015	DepReq		378932	1000	4-	25
	01/19/2015	DepReq		378932	1000	4-	21
	01/19/2015	DepReq		378932	1000	4-	17
	01/19/2015	DepReq		378932	1000	4-	13
	01/19/2015	DepReq		378932	1000	4-	9
	01/19/2015	DepReq		378932	1000	4-	5
	01/19/2015	DepReq		378932	1000	4-	1

Figure 6.40 Static Safety Stock Excluded from MRP and Not Counted toward Available Quantity

Even when you call up the graphic by choosing LIST • GRAPHIC Transaction MD04, you can't see the safety stock quantity in the stock line (green) included (*see* Figure 6.41). Even though there are 60 pieces in stock, the graphic shows only 50 pieces available for planning today (all the way to the left).

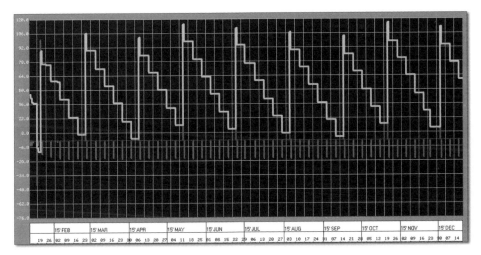

Figure 6.41 Static Safety Stock Excluded from the Graphic*

This type of situation helps place more items into inventory, but it's not really effective if you're told to buffer variability for high service levels with the minimum possible stock holding. And yet, in most companies using SAP, this is the number one strategy employed when there is uncertainty in supply and/or demand. The static safety stock certainly has its uses, especially when your objective is to guarantee 100% availability on a cheap part, but for most situations, the system will drive up dead stock.

Let's get into the problem first and then discuss some better alternatives.

Assume that the planner has maintained a safety stock of 30 pieces in the MRP 2 screen. The MRP run picks up on the safety stock as soon as it's set and brings in 30 pieces to cover it. So we can safely assume that the current stock level on hand is 30 pieces. Now a planned demand through the BOM drops in for 50 pieces. The demand is due on August 15 and MRP runs to generate a supply proposal for 50 pieces to cover the future planned demand. So far, it's all very good. We'll have 80 pieces on hand on August 15 to cover the demand and have 30 pieces put aside in case the demand increases.

As the date draws near, we get a better idea of what is actually demanded (customer orders for finished goods drop in and consume the forecast), as illustrated in Figure 6.42. Then it turns out that the demand is actually not 50 pieces as planned, but 60 pieces. Because the MRP run ignores the static safety stock of 30 pieces, it detects a perceived void of 10 pieces and generates a new order proposal. If we have a minimum order quantity of 40 pieces maintained, the new order proposal brings in 40 more pieces to raise the inventory up to 120 pieces (50 for the planned demand, 30 for the safety stock, and another 40 because we're not using the safety stock). Of that, 60 pieces will be consumed by the actual demand, and 60 pieces will end up in dead stock. Yes, that is what static safety stock does—it raises dead stock!

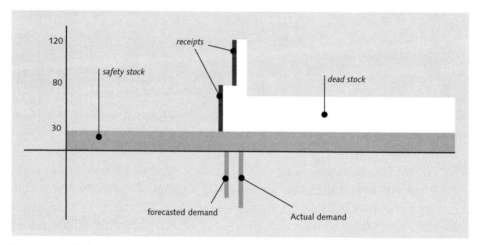

Figure 6.42 Static Safety Stock – No Buffer Demand Variability in Planning

To make matters worse, if the item has a long lead time, and changes to demand occur close to consumption, you'll end up with a super nervous system that lives by "reschedule in, reschedule out."

The static safety stock certainly has a right to exist but not for effective buffering strategies. There's something better for that in standard SAP, which we'll discuss next.

Dynamic Safety Stock

A dynamic safety stock in SAP can be employed by use of the RANGE OF COVERAGE profile in the BUFFERING section of the material master's MRP 2 screen. With the profile, you can set a target dynamic safety stock, a minimum level, and a maximum level. If done right, the MRP run will always try to keep the target dynamic safety stock available for planning. But other than with the static safety stock, no additional quantities are brought in unless the safety stock falls below the minimum. Therefore, if you set the minimum low in planning, all safety stock is used as a buffer. Additionally, if the actual demand turns out to be less than what was planned, the maximum level in the coverage profile keeps the stock from blowing up in case of under-consumption of the planned demand.

So how does it work in practice? First off, in a coverage profile, the levels (minimum, target, and maximum) aren't set in quantities but managed in days of cover. That fact provides the dynamic part of the safety stock because we can say that we want to hold three days of future demand in safety to buffer demand *and* supply variability. That means, if the demand goes up, you'll have more stock in safety, and if the demand goes down, it'll be less.

Figure 6.43 shows that the coverage profile takes action when either the minimum is breached or the maximum is about to be exceeded. The MRP run will always try to cover demand. If there is a coverage profile maintained for the material, the MRP run also generates a new supply proposal when inventory drops below the minimum coverage—even though there might not be any demand to cover—and fills the inventory up to the target coverage or dynamic safety stock. It does so if the lot-size procedure is EX.

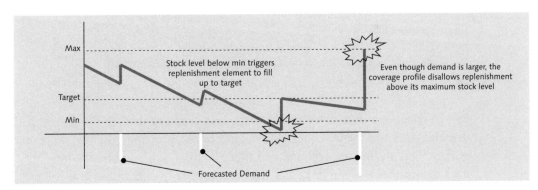

Figure 6.43 Dynamic Safety Stock with a Range of Coverage Profile

Of course, with a fixed lot size or a minimum order quantity, the target coverage may be exceeded. But the coverage profile also has a maximum coverage, and if for some reason—maybe because of a fixed lot size, a rounding value, or a minimum order quantity—the maximum is exceeded, the coverage profile takes action and tries to avoid the inventory going above the maximum. This is a great feature for when actual consumption is lower than the forecast, and a VV type replenishment keeps on bringing more in according to the forecast. In that case, inventory goes up without bounds—except when the coverage profile puts a lid on it.

For all these reasons, you should maintain all three parameters—min, max, and target—in the coverage profile. It can be a very powerful automated tool when applied in the right way.

The coverage profile is maintained in Customizing and has two sections, as shown in Figure 6.44.

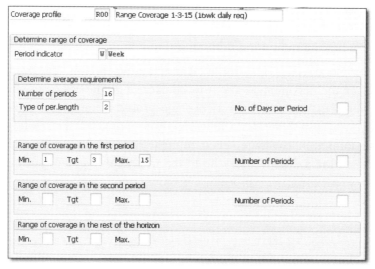

Figure 6.44 Configuration Screen of a Range of Coverage Profile

The DETERMINE RANGE OF COVERAGE section is used to calculate the future daily demand. This is done by collecting demand over a horizon (you have to set the horizon here in the first section), and then the total is divided by the number of days within that horizon (whether working days or calendar days also has to be identified in this section) to arrive at a future average daily demand. This future average daily demand is then multiplied with the levels you set in the DETERMINE AVERAGE REQUIREMENTS section. Therefore, when calculated, you end up with a quantity for minimum target and maximum. For example, if the levels are MIN. = 1, TGT = 5, and MAX. = 20, and the future average daily demand was 10 pieces for the next three months, then the levels will be 10 pieces minimum, 50 pieces target dynamic safety stock, and a maximum desired stock level of 200 pieces. Remember, those numbers are only valid for the period where the future average daily demand is 10 pieces. If that changes, the levels change also.

You can see all this—and more—in Transaction MD04 after you click on the period total (see Figure 6.45).

	Days	Weeks	Months	Plng Calendar	Indiv. Split										
A...	Period/se...	Requir...	Receipts	Avail. qua...	Actual cove...	Stat. c...	Target ...	Daily req...	Max...	Min....	Target ...	Minimu...	Maximu...	
	Stock			120	4.7	0.0		0 0	0	0	0	0	0	
W	03/2015	31-	0	89	4.7	6.7		0 13.229	0	0	0	0	0	
W	04/2015	102-	42	29	4.1	2.4		3 12.275	7	3	36.825	36.825	85.925	
W	05/2015	59-	42	12	1.0	1.1		3 10.900	7	3	32.700	32.700	76.300	
W	06/2015	47-	84	49	5.2	4.5		3 10.900	7	3	32.700	32.700	76.300	
W	07/2015	47-	84	86	9.1	7.9		3 10.900	7	3	32.700	32.700	76.300	
W	08/2015	59-	42	69	8.4	6.0		3 11.500	7	3	34.500	34.500	80.500	
W	09/2015	59-	42	52	4.8	4.6		3 11.200	7	3	33.600	33.600	78.400	
W	10/2015	59-	84	77	9.2	7.1		3 10.900	7	3	32.700	32.700	76.300	
W	11/2015	59-	42	60	8.1	5.5		3 10.900	7	3	32.700	32.700	76.300	
W	12/2015	47-	42	55	4.9	4.8		3 11.500	7	3	34.500	34.500	80.500	
W	13/2015	59-	42	38	4.8	3.3		3 11.500	7	3	34.500	34.500	80.500	

Figure 6.45 Dynamic Safety Stock Information in the Period Totals Display in the Stock/Requirements List

Now here is another trick: instead of creating a coverage profile for a target of three days, another one for four days, and another one for five days, you can possibly create a coverage profile for AX parts and another one for CX parts. The levels you set then in the coverage profile depends on the current strategy set force by management. For example, your management might demand that you maintain a dynamic safety stock of four days for all your AX parts during the holiday season, but in the new year, they want to drop that down to only two days. Because you assigned the AX coverage profile to hundreds or thousands of AX parts, all you have to do is change the target level in the coverage profile from four days to two days on January 1st, and the strategy will apply across the board.

Coverage profiles are very powerful features of a replenishment policy. Not only do they provide utmost flexibility and automation, they also facilitate master data maintenance, and, most importantly, they feature a true buffering strategy that allows for optimized inventory holdings for great service levels.

The Difference between Safety Stock and Safety Time

In the material master's MRP 2 screen, you'll also find the SAFETY TIME/ACT.COV. field. As depicted in Figure 6.46, the system uses the number of days you fill in this field to simulate the requirements to an earlier date, displaced exactly by those number of dates. In fact, by using this field, you pull your requirements in so that the MRP run creates the receipts for replenishment order proposals to an earlier date. In that sense, the safety time is nothing more than a time buffer and doesn't increase any quantities. Because the actual requirement doesn't change, the only difference is that the receipt comes in earlier and provides an additional coverage for the time it was pulled forward.

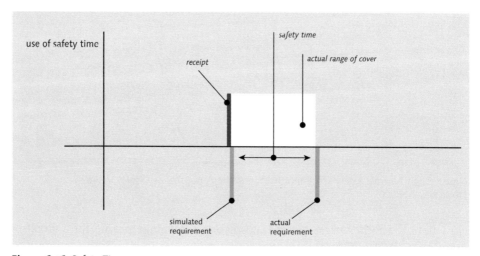

Figure 6.46 Safety Time

The fact that the safety time brings the receipts in earlier as actually needed serves the purpose that when the supplier delivers late, we're not immediately in trouble. It therefore provides a time float and thus works alongside the safety stock, which acts as a quantity float.

6.3.4 Developing a Playbook for Replenishment Policies

Like a football team, your materials planning department should standardize and prepare their moves according to a playbook. If no such standard exists, a diligent planner is forced to develop his own system of decision making and policy setting. What that system looks like and how effective it will be depends almost exclusively on the competence, motivation, and ability of the planner.

In a system of effective materials planning, standardization and the required tool set are provided, and the planners are given the general performance guidelines and operating boundaries set force in the supply chain strategy. In a yearly meeting (possibly with quarterly revisions), a team comprised of leadership and planners should determine performance guidelines such as expected service levels; agreed-upon buffers to counter variability with minimal cost; clearly defined planning horizons for the long-, mid-, short-term; and the frozen zone and upper- and lower control limits for inventory holdings according to a segmentation by ABC and XYZ.

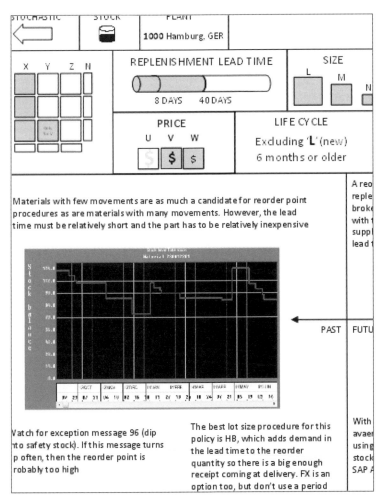

Figure 6.47 Example of a Replenishment Policy in the Policy Playbook*

Only then is the planner fully equipped to put together a policy playbook that clearly documents which replenishment method is used for which item. The following example describes one such policy. If a planner think about how to set up an AX item with a short lead time and a low price, there is no question about what to do.

Figure 6.47 shows a sample policy documented on one page. All information necessary to select the group of materials that should be updated with that policy can be found in the upper part of the policy. The lower part then details the settings to be maintained in the material master record to automate the policy. Otherwise, there are general descriptions, special instructions, benefits, and a checklist that can help the planner make the best use of the policy.

As you're building your library of replenishment policies, you're in effect extending your toolbox for replenishment planning, and you'll find yourself using a standard approach with predictable results in your efforts to optimize inventory levels for utmost availability. As we've seen, replenishment policies will drive the planning for purchased parts primarily. In the next section, we'll discuss planning policies, which are assigned to finished goods and other sellable products.

6.4   Planning Policies

As discussed in previous chapters, to buffer variable demand with good tactics is much more effective than trying to chase a forecast that's always wrong. Policies provide the opportunity to manage these buffers and therefore counter variability in demand and supply. You might be wary of automation because you think it brings with it the risk of a hidden mistake, but isn't there an even bigger risk in dealing with each material separately? If a portfolio that is assigned to a planner exceeds 200 materials—and most portfolios contain thousands of materials—it's almost impossible to manage effectively if you decide to set up each material individually. This is especially true because you have to perform that task on a periodic and repeated basis.

Planning policies are meant to automate the planning and distribution for sellable products. These may be finished goods, spare parts, or anything that moves out of the plant. They revolve primarily—but not exclusively—around the STRATEGY GROUP field and its setting in the MRP 3 screen of the material master record. Just as MRP type PD isn't a policy, the statement that strategy 40 isn't a policy is equally true. Therefore, strategy group 40 isn't a policy, but with a consumption procedure and an availability checking rule, it becomes one. Of course, the MRP type, lot sizing, and buffering strategies are also part of a planning policy, but to distinguish from the replenishment policy, we'll focus heavily on the settings in the MRP 3 screen. These settings harbor the main differences between individual planning policies.

In the next sections, we'll discuss some of the most-used practices and policies.

6.4.1 Forecast and Order-Based Fulfillment Practices

When analyzing the setup and use of the functionality in existing SAP customers who have been using the system for many years, we often come across the problem of order-based planning and fulfillment practices in a make-to-stock (MTS) environment. What this means is that the client has developed a habit of chasing a customer order throughout the entire organization with the noble intention of making the customer happy at any price.

This is all good when you have less than 20 customers, but most—if not all—organizations don't have the resources to do that with all orders. Let's revisit MTS versus MTO (make-to-order) (or finish-to-order [FTO], which for our purposes here and on the finished goods level is the same as MTO). In an MTS situation, there shouldn't be any customer order that gets special attention. The customer order is entered independent of any resource restrictions, special exception situations, or outages in production. That is why we do planning, so we can put the product on the shelf for the customer to pick up. And if there is no product on the shelf, then the customer will have to wait until the next receipt comes from the production line—no matter who he is—first come, first serve. The availability check is simply looking for available stock.

If you want to put preference on a certain customer's order over the others, you'll have to make that to the order—either ahead of time with a customer independent requirement or by following the MTO process, in which case, the customer will have to wait until you get his products on the production line. But you can't take it from the planned forecasted requirement because that is neutral product and is for everyone who wants to buy it. Neither can you follow an MTS product for a special customer through the production cycle. Intermediate components and raw materials are procured independently of any special customer order and should not disturb the process.

For example, a maker of bulk products that are sold out of a distribution center in very large quantities to hundreds of customers triggered production with an orange slip. There was a forecast coming from the distribution center but because of distrust in the accuracy of the data, production was only kicked off when a real customer order was present. As you may imagine, the orders were always late, and to fix that problem, somebody though of running an orange slip with the order through the entire process. The end result was manual work without planning that never delivered on time, constant firefighting, and moving of orders and extreme confusion on the shop floor (all slips were orange; there wasn't a green one that could have been ignored). The whole organization was so obsessed with the orange slips that after we implemented a better process and threw away the orange paper the slips were printed on, all of a sudden a slip on white paper turned up that had a headline in big, fat font that read, "Orange Slip."

The problems just described may be grounded in a misunderstanding on how the SAP planning strategies work or a misunderstanding of how general planning principles work—or both. Either one is essential to effective business planning. A good setup in the SAP master data is important, or even indispensable, but without understanding the basic workings of MTS, MTO, and all the variations, making the customer and shareholders happy is almost impossible—unless, of course, you plan product by product every day. But that's really not what one should call planning.

As in the case of replenishment, you'll have to get to a point where the organization understands planning policy and its detailed workings, before you can expect happy customers and rising revenues. SAP is certainly equipped with everything that's needed to achieve just that. Let's try to lay out all the options and provide you with enough detail to develop your own planning policy playbook.

6.4.2 Strategy Groups and Strategy

Strategy groups and strategy are the central parameter in a planning policy. They'll identify the difference between MTS, MTO, and FTS, which we mentioned in the previous section, as well as assemble-to-order (ATO), engineer-to-order (ETO), configure-to-order (CTO), and all their variations. Be aware that what you enter in the STRATEGY GROUP field in MRP 3 isn't the strategy itself. It can be a grouping of strategies where there is a main strategy that is employed automatically if there is no "audible,"—that is, spot change in process—and then there can be several substrategies, which can be chosen as the need arises. For example, when you create a sales order for a product, the main strategy might be 10, which means the product was MTO for a forecast on a certain customer segment. Imagine that all of a sudden a customer from another segment (maybe another region that wasn't part of the forecast) wants to buy the product. In that case, the order entry clerk can switch over the requirement to a strategy that transfers a demand to make the product in the quantity to the customer that requests it, so that the forecast for the first segment isn't exploited by orders from outside the planning region.

With that kind of option, you can have total control over the planning of your operations and retain utmost flexibility in the ordering process. But you must know your strategy, and you must set up the products with the right group.

You can find STRATEGY GROUP field in the PLANNING section of the MRP 3 screen (see Figure 6.48). In standard SAP, there are only a few true groups. Most groups have exactly one strategy maintained, which means that if you pick strategy group 40, you're in fact selecting strategy 40. There are a few exceptions, as in strategy group 31, where the main strategy is 30, and you can switch over to strategy 20 when needed. We recommend that you focus your Customizing efforts around the configuration of your specific strategy groups, rather than the strategies themselves. There are 30 preconfigured strategies that come with the initial delivery, give or take a few with industry solutions (the Y types). Before you start "Z'ing" your way into the complex world of planning strategies, you should explore and understand the standard ones in detail.

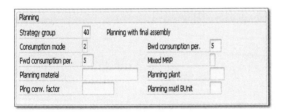

Figure 6.48 Strategy Group Field in the Screen of the Material Master

Strategies are maintained in a Customizing table. As you can see in Figure 6.49, strategies may have a requirements type used in planning and a requirements type used for actual orders. These two different types of requirements—each identified by the requirements type—can consume each other, so you can, as an example, use strategies that let you compare planning against actual consumption or sales. This is a very interesting aspect of planning strategies because you can report on the effectiveness of your plan and continuously fine-tune and improve your operations planning.

Strategy	Planning strategy description	Reqs-DM	Reqs-Cu.
00	No planning / no requirements transfer		
10	Make-to-stock production	LSF	KSL
11	Make-to-stock prod./gross reqmts plng	BSF	KSL
20	Make-to-order production		KE
21	Make-to-order prod./ project settlement		KP
25	Make-to-order for configurable material		KEK
26	Make-to-order for material variant		KEL
30	Production by lot size	LSF	KL
40	Planning with final assembly	VSF	KSV
50	Planning without final assembly	VSE	KEV
51	Plng w/o final assembly / project settl.	VSE	KPV
52	Plng w/o final assem. w/o make-to.order	VSE	KSVS
54	Planning variants	VSE	KEKT
55	Planning variants w/o final assembly	VSE	KELV
56	Characteristics planning	VSE	KEKS
59	Planning at phantom assembly level	VSEB	
60	Planning with planning material	VSEV	KEVV
61	Plng with plng material / project settl.	VSEV	KPVV
63	Planning w.plng material w/o mke-to-ord.	VSEV	KSVV
65	Planning variants with planning material	VSEV	ELVV
70	Planning at assembly level	VSFB	
74	Plng at assembly lvl w/o final assembly	VSEM	
80	Project settlement for non-stock items		KPX
81	Assembly processing with planned orders		KMSE
82	Assembly processing w. production orders		KMFA
83	Assembly processing with networks		KMNP
84	Service orders		SERA
85	Assembly processing with network/project		KMPN
86	Filling with process orders "Assembly"		KMPA
89	Assembly proc. w. characteristics plng	VSE	KMSE
Y0	Automotive planning strategy	Y90	Y50
Y7	automotive MTO/repetitive production	YA1	YA69

Figure 6.49 Standard List of Strategies Available in SAP, Including Two Industry-Specific Y Strategies

By clicking the drop-down on the STRATEGY GROUP field in MRP 3, you'll get an overview of some of the strategies you can employ (Figure 6.49). It's not a complete list of strategies you'll see there, so you'll have to know your strategies, and you'll have to know what they do and when to use them. It's part of the planning policy. Strategy groups are maintained in yet another Customizing table as shown in Figure 6.50.

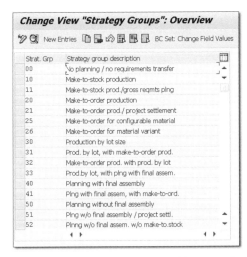

Figure 6.50 Strategy Groups Available in Standard SAP

As mentioned before, some of these strategy groups refer directly to the corresponding strategy. Strategy group 40, for example, has only a main strategy — strategy 40. However, strategy groups 31, 32, and 33 all have a main strategy and a substrategy that can be used if the specific situation calls for it. We go over each here:

▶ **Strategy 31**
Allows you to select the MAKE-TO-ORDER PRODUCTION (20) or PRODUCTION BY LOT-SIZE (30) strategies by selecting the KE or KL requirements types (strategy 20 [KE] is the default or main strategy).

▶ **Strategy 32**
Allows you to select the PRODUCTION BY LOT-SIZE (30) or MAKE-TO-ORDER PRODUCTION (20) strategies by selecting the KL or KE requirements types (strategy 30 [KL] is the default or main strategy).

▶ **Strategy 33**
Allows you to select the PRODUCTION BY LOT-SIZE (30) or PLANNING WITH FINAL ASSEMBLY (40) strategies by selecting the KL or KSV requirements types (strategy 30 [KL] is the default or main strategy).

These are therefore true strategy groups, and you'll have to know what you're dealing with, while you're assigning a strategy group to a specific material master record in MRP 3. Then there are the requirements types for planned, independent requirements such as a forecast type (e.g., LSF or VSF), and there are customer requirements types (e.g., KE or a KEV) that are specific to actual, confirmed requirements (see Figure 6.51). As mentioned before, a strategy can be assigned to one of each, and then those two types can be allocated to and consumed against each other.

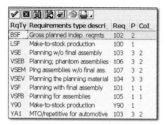

Figure 6.51 List of Requirements Types for Planned, Independent Requirements

Each one of the planned, independent requirements types refers to a requirements class (see Figure 6.52).

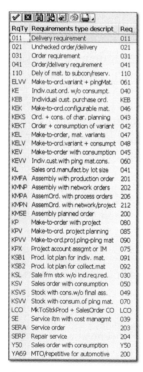

Figure 6.52 List of Requirements Types with Associated Requirements Classes for Customer Requirements

Strategy 10—Classic Make-to-Stock

When using an MTO strategy, procurement (or production) takes place before an actual customer order is placed in the system. In the German language, MTS is identified as *anonyme Lagerfertigung*, which directly translated means "anonymous production to the warehouse." *Anonymous* is the key term here because it clearly describes the state the planning process is in: with absolutely no regard to any actual demand or customer order. So don't try to chase the order for an MTS designated material through the system. You shouldn't be able to find any order-related information anywhere but in the sales order itself. If you do, you're doing something wrong. MTS materials are exclusively procured or produced anonymously to the inventory from which the customer order can pick—from anonymous inventory!

Therefore, there must be some planned individual requirement that serves as demand and a trigger for the procurement of a certain lot size to fill up the inventory. For strategy 10, that planned independent requirement is an LSF, as shown in the configuration screen in Figure 6.53.

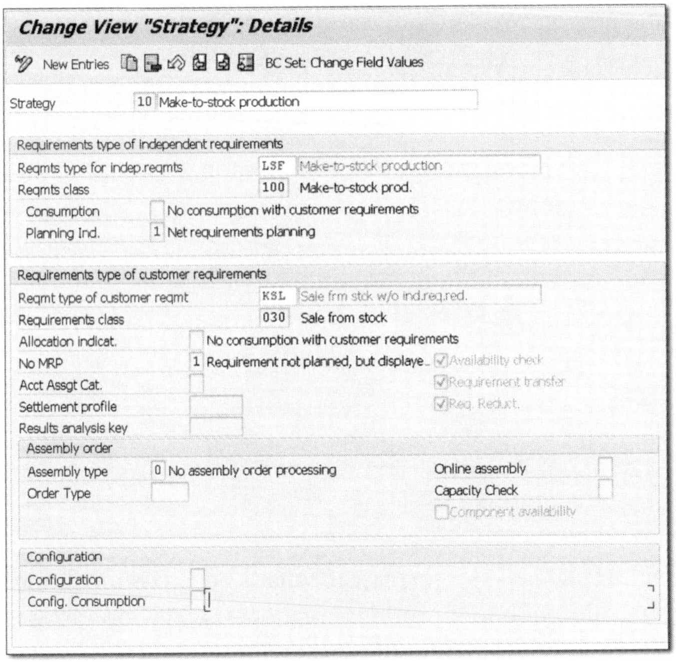

Figure 6.53 Standard Configuration Settings for Strategy 10

Note that the only configuration you can maintain for the strategy is the requirements type. Because the selected requirements type is directly associated to a requirements class, all other settings are taken over from the configuration for the requirements class.

The corresponding actual customer requirements type for strategy 10 is KSL. A KSL type requirement is aligned with requirements class 030. Sales are fulfilled directly (and only) from stock. Strategy 10—through requirements type 030 and its ALLOCATION INDICAT.—is configured so that sales orders do *not* consume the forecast LSF. For strategy 10, the consumption of forecast happens at the time of the goods issue.

Figure 6.54 illustrates the detailed workings of the classic MTS strategy 10.

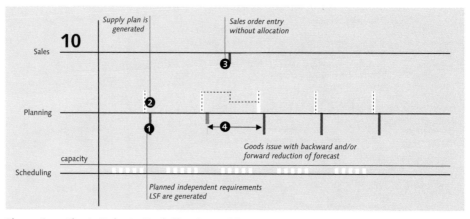

Figure 6.54 Classic Make-to-Stock Planning and Execution

With strategy 10, demand is planned as a forecast to what's being assumed to be sold. However, there is no allocation to incoming actual orders. The forecast will be reduced when a goods issue from inventory is posted. First the forecast is generated ❶. This can happen through manual input into Transaction MD61, an upload from an Excel or Access datasheet, or using SAP ERP's forecasting module in the LIS with a subsequent transfer of demand.

After the forecast has been generated and is relevant to MRP, the MRP run will generate order proposals to meet the forecast at the respective periods ❷. The order proposals are now turned into a supply program, and inventory is built up accordingly. Incoming sales orders have absolutely no impact on that supply (or production) program and are fulfilled from available inventory ❸. This is where strategy 10 differs from other MTS strategies: it protects the production schedule and allows for the smooth flow of the replenishment process. To make sure the process works in its entirety, you'll have to ensure that the sales availability checking rule does *not* use the total replenishment lead time (TRLT). After a goods issue is posted (to a sales order or not), the planned independent requirement is reduced (unallocated) ❹.

Strategy 10 is like the old central planning systems of the socialist, former German Democratic Republic or Soviet Union. Plans were created by the central committee, and resources were deployed to produce and distribute to plan without any consideration to what was eventually and actually happening. When riding the bullet train that runs from Beijing to Shanghai, you can see entire cities with no one living there. These ghost cities were planned (and built!) according to a plan established by the central committee, and the project was stubbornly finished before any demand (or lack thereof) for the apartments was considered. The fact that in some cases a relocation to another place was ordered didn't put a dent into the construction efforts, and the project was finished without disturbing "production."

Whether that situation is right or wrong, productive or not, it's still a planning strategy that has its right to exist. If your primary goal is to protect the production schedule, this might be just the right strategy for you. We're not suggesting that you put expensive products such as entire cities in your inventory for customers to pick up, but maybe washing detergent? It's something you're producing in large run quantities and don't want your customers to wait for because they wouldn't wait anyway. If the detergent isn't on the shelf, they will buy another brand, so you better make sure there is enough to sell.

That is very different for expensive products such as cleaning machines where you want a close tie between what was planned and what is actually happening. But we'll cover more about that when we talk about strategy 40.

Strategy 11—Make-to-Stock without Inventory Consideration

Strategy 11 is a gross requirements strategy because it doesn't perform a netting against already available inventory. The difference from strategy 10 lies in the requirements class 102 (as opposed to 100 for strategy 10), which comes to play through the requirements type BSF. As you can see in Figure 6.55, requirements class 102 asks for gross requirements planning, meaning that it doesn't look at available inventory to determine the quantity to replenish. In other words, if your planned demand is 100 pieces, and you have 50 pieces in inventory, the MRP run will generate an order proposal for 100 pieces, ignoring the 50 that are already available.

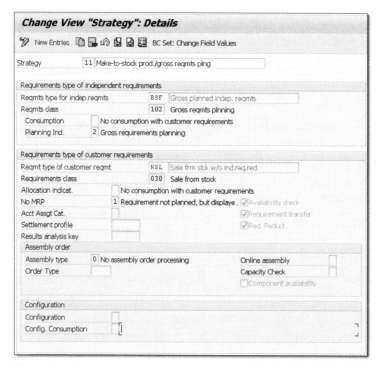

Figure 6.55 Strategy 11

You might think that this isn't a very good strategy because it blows up inventory, but again, there is a lid for every pot. In many production facilities, the lines need to be running on. If you're pulling fiberglass strands to make insulation, you can't stop the lines because your net requirements calculation says you'll end up with too much inventory.

Other than the gross requirements planning, it acts exactly as the classic MTS planning strategy and doesn't get allocated to customer orders

Strategy 20—Classic Make-to-Order

In an MTO process, there is no plan, and therefore there are no planned independent requirements. Classic MTO assumes no inventory and everything, from raw material through semi-finished parts to final product, is procured solely to the customer order. Out of the three buffers—inventory, capacity, and time—only the latter two are available to the MTO process. After a rush order comes in, you can only either increase the resources you need for production or ask the customer to wait.

As you can see in Figure 6.56, a sales order is entered first ❶. If the customer requests the delivery within the TRLT, the availability check in the sales order allows confirmation only for the first date after the lead time counting from today ❷. That date—after being fixed in the delivery proposal of the sale order—then drives the MRP availability date, and the MRP run can generate the replenishment or order proposal ❸. Only then, the production scheduler can find time on the schedule to fit production in ❹.

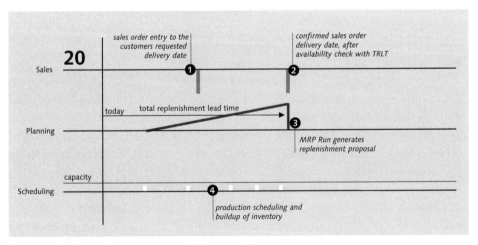

Figure 6.56 Classic Make-to-Order with Strategy 20

A special aspect to consider is the indicator "E" entry in the Acct Assgt Cat. field in the Requirements type of customer requests section (see Figure 6.57). It drives the posting of any value add during the replenishment process to the customer-specific account—throughout all levels of the BOMs! This is an MTO strategy, so everything isn't only made to order but also accounted for to the order.

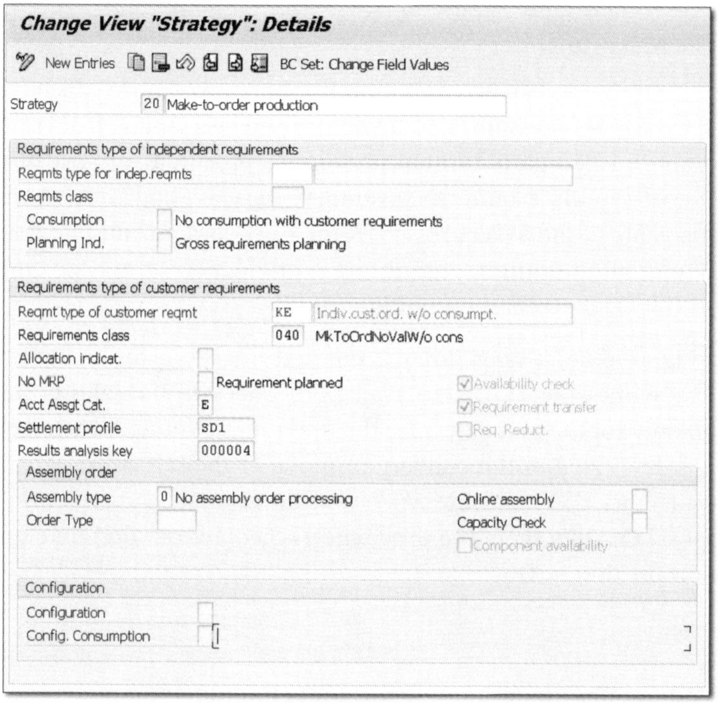

Figure 6.57 Strategy 20

Strategy 20 ensures that inventory, production quantities, incurred costs, and resources are all managed specifically for the customer order itself. It's therefore not a planning process but rather an execution process where all focus is geared toward a fast and effective fulfillment process of a customized, hardly predictable wish from an important customer. Don't mix this strategy with a CTO or ETO, which are very similar but yet different. A part setup for MTO is still in the product catalog and has a material master record. We know exactly what it looks like and what it is, we just don't know ahead of time when and how much we're going to sell. And it's too expensive to put in inventory by anticipation.

Strategy 30—Make Lot Size to Order and Fulfill General Demand from Stock

In most—if not all—SAP literature, strategy 30 is described as a process to plan relatively small quantities but allow for the procurement of large quantities for select customers. To that end, the planned independent requirements type LSF is used to fill inventory for the general public. If a large order from a select customer comes in, the extra production quantity is put on the line with a fixed lot size, and superfluous quantities are put in inventory so they can be used for the general public and netted against future forecasts (LSF).

There's absolutely nothing wrong with that, but it's better to use strategy 30 as making lot sizes for large orders and fulfilling smaller demand from leftover stock. In that case, there is no planned independent requirement and therefore only inventory if something is left over from a large lot size. In fact, you're not holding any stock before a customer orders the product. Then you'll make more than what the customer requires and put the rest in inventory. Later customer orders can then simply pull from free available stock until you're out.

In Figure 6.58, nothing happens unless a sales order is entered ❶, and the availability check determines a feasible delivery date for confirmation. The MRP run will then create an order proposal with a larger lot size (rounding or minimum) ❷, and the lot size is produced into inventory. The sales order will then take the requested quantity from inventory ❸, and the rest remains in inventory for future orders to consume ❹ until the inventory runs out. As soon as a new sales order demands more product than what remains in inventory, the cycle will repeat itself.

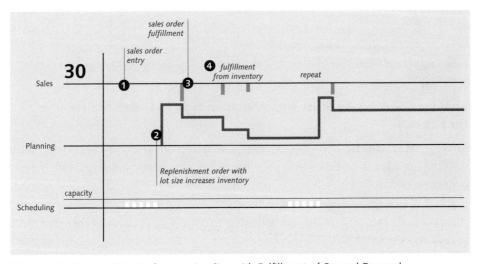

Figure 6.58 Strategy 30—Producing a Lot Size with Fulfillment of General Demand

Figure 6.59 shows the configuration of strategy 30 as it comes with the standard SAP-delivered system. According to the process we just described, you won't need a planned independent requirement; however, don't take it out of the configuration because it may be used if the situation calls for it.

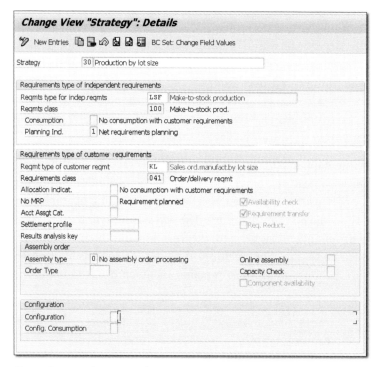

Figure 6.59 Configuration of Strategy 30 with Planned Independent Requirement Type LSF

Strategy 40—Make-to-Stock with Allocation of Sales Orders to Consume the Forecast

Strategy 40 is configured so that the plan gets consumed by incoming sales orders. The idea is to provide a plan for future inventory holdings, but if sales orders exceed that plan, additional production will be requested by sales. Accordingly, this strategy introduces some noise into the replenishment process to meet important customer demand for valuable products. This is probably the most widely used planning strategy in the SAP supply chain world because it supposedly provides peace of mind for organizations that want to produce as close as possible to fulfill their customer's requests.

As shown in Figure 6.60, a VSF, through the requirements class 101, is consumed when a quantity is demanded through a KSV. The entire setup seems complex but it's very logical. However, as soon as people start introducing Z strategies with associated Z requirements types and Z requirements classes, all logic may be lost, and it will get very difficult to re-create the scenario the original design team had in mind.

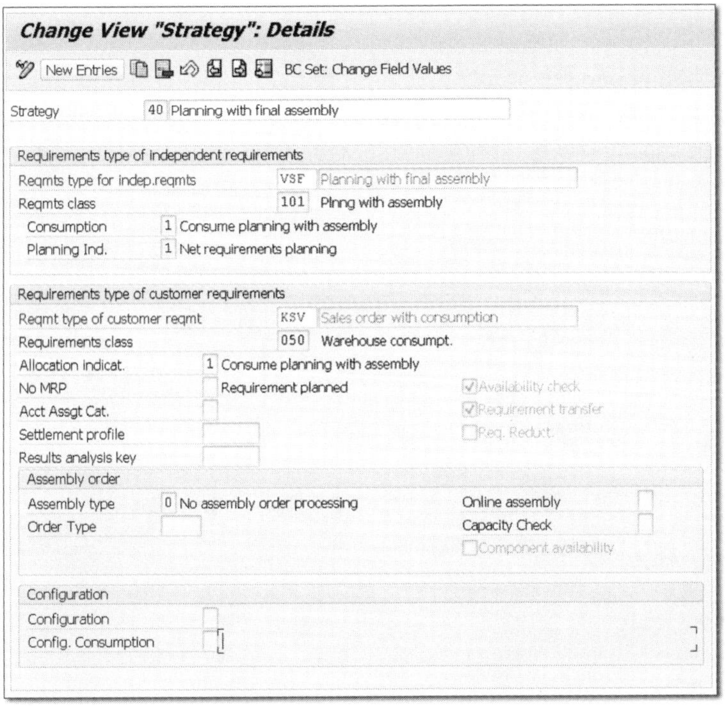

Figure 6.60 Strategy 40 Configured to Have Requirements Type VSF Consumed by Incoming Sales Requirements of Type KSV

Tip

Stick with the standard strategies and only change the requirements class if absolutely necessary when no fitting strategy can be found in the standard delivery.

Strategy 40 is very powerful if connected with the fitting availability checking rules and the correct consumption rules. It's no coincidence that all of these control fields are in the MRP 3 screen of the material master. If you have inconsistencies in the policy and how these fields work together, strategy 40 can work very badly against you. We'll talk more about that in the next section when discussing building a policy playbook.

The MTS strategy 40 starts with the entry of the forecast ❶ in Figure 6.61. This can be done manually via Transaction MD61, through upload from a spreadsheet, or via transfer out of SOP in SAP ERP by use of infostructures, product groups, or a flexible planning hierarchy. You can also employ the Long-Term Planning (LTP) component in SAP ERP to simulate various version and activate a specific one into DP. The MRP run then generates supply proposals ❷ that can be sequenced, leveled, and scheduled within available capacity ❸, and then collectively checked for missing parts. The resulting production schedule will fill up the inventory before the sales orders drop in.

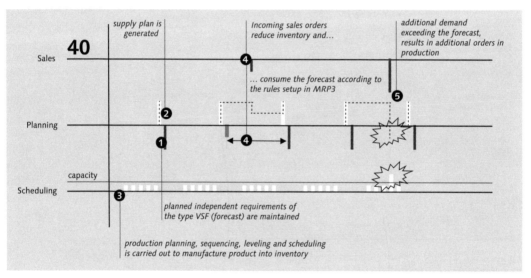

Figure 6.61 Consumption of a Forecast with Strategy 40

Any customer's request for product can now be directly fulfilled from free available, neutral inventory ❹, and as the orders come in, they find the remaining quantities of the forecast (looking backwards, forwards, or both according to the rules set in MRP 3) and consume it with the respective quantities of the orders ❺. This allows for comparing and monitoring of forecasted quantities with the actual order quantities.

With strategy 40, when the forecast is exceeded (more actual orders than what we anticipated), additional orders will be dropped right into the production program. On one hand, the production scheduler scrambles with the added noise and resulting increased variability, while on the other hand, the sales department can flexibly maintain high service levels with relatively low inventories.

Here we need to tend to the trade-offs with the three buffers time, inventory, and capacity and make good decisions. Safety stock, capacity profiles in shift schedules, and good availability checking rules in combination with the right consumption strategy all build up to good policy and better decision making, which are the keys to effective materials planning. We'll go into more about that when we start building the planning policy playbook.

Strategy 50—Segregated Make-to-Order for Finished Products

Strategy 50 is a segregated make to order planning for finished products with final assembly, only after the sales order entry with an inventory order interface and procurement of intermediates and purchased parts are completed.

This strategy is very often used for MTO processes because the lead time to the customer is shortened by the fact that only the top level of the BOM structure is procured to order instead of the entire BOM. An inventory/order interface is introduced just below the level of the finished product. This means that intermediates are procured into stock so that they are available after the sales order comes in, and the only time it takes to finish is the time for final assembly.

This is achieved by way of statistical orders of the type VP. Regular planned orders are of the type LA or PE in repetitive manufacturing, and they can be converted into executable orders such as production orders. This isn't possible with planned orders of the type VP (statistical). The VP type orders still contain the BOM, however, and are therefore able to transfer demand to the next level so that production for intermediates and procurement of purchased parts can be executed to the plan.

Therefore, if you set up the finished product with strategy 50 and maintain a forecast, the multilevel MRP run will create statistical orders to cover the demand on the finished products level so that secondary demand can be placed on the levels below. After a sales order comes in, its required quantities replace the statistical order with a regular planned order that can be converted, and the final assembly can begin. Figure 6.62 shows the standard Customizing settings for strategy 50.

Note that with MTO strategy 50, the customer orders are segregated in Transaction MD04, and separate planning segments are generated for every customer order.

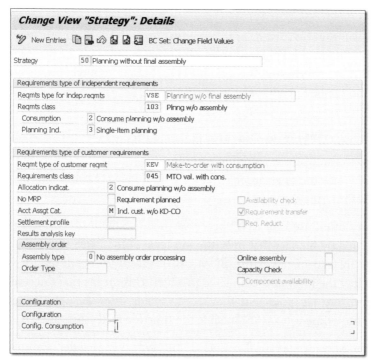

Figure 6.62 Strategy 50—Consumption of Forecast without Final Assembly and Individual Customer Segments according to Make-to-Order

Strategy 52—Anonymous Make-to-Stock with Final Assembly

This strategy is an anonymous make to stock planning with final assembly, only after the sales order entry with an inventory order interface, and procurement of intermediates and purchased parts has been completed.

Strategy 52 is very similar to the previously discussed MTO strategy 50, except that the actual sales orders aren't segregated in individual segments in Transaction MD04 but rather are listed in the NET REQUIREMENTS section (see Figure 6.63).

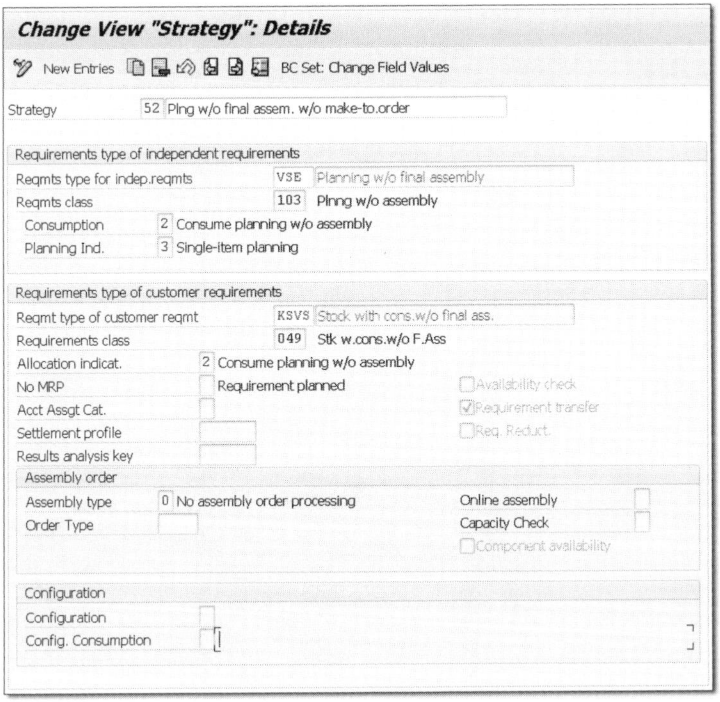

Figure 6.63 Strategy 52—Consumption without Final Assembly in a Make-to-Stock Environment

Planning at Intermediate Levels with Strategies 70, 59, and 74

You don't have to always plan at the finished products level. You can also plan the components with a forecast and therefore improve the availability of intermediate products for the final assembly process.

To that end, strategy 70 allows for the placement of the forecast on the intermediate level with consumption of the forecast is happening at the time of the goods issue to the production order of the final assembly.

Strategy 59 then allows you to work with a forecast for components that have been grouped together into an assembly.

And strategy 74 acts very similar to strategies 50 and 52 in that it creates statistical orders that are only executed after the actual demand flows in. The Customizing screen in Figure 6.64 controls this behavior by using CONSUMPTION 2 – CONSUME PLANNING W/O ASSEMBLY.

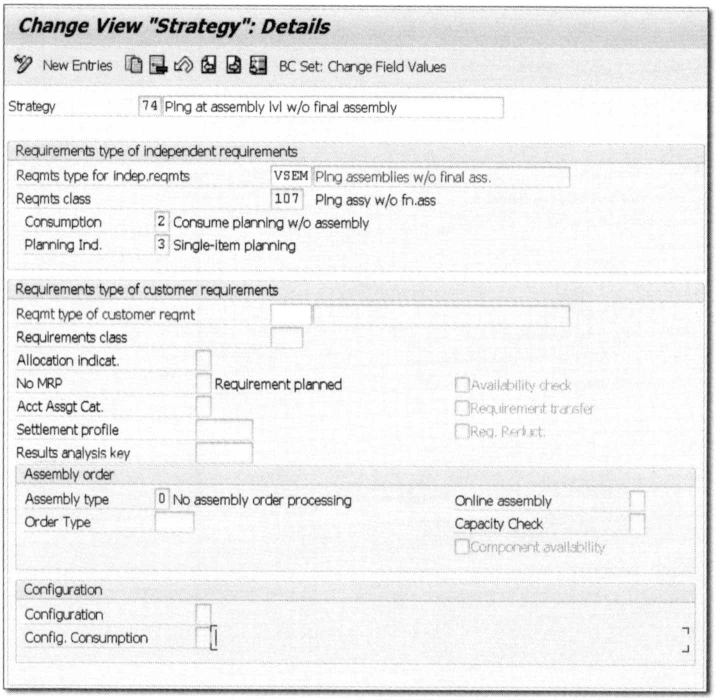

Figure 6.64 Strategy 74 with Requirements Class 107 Which Consumes Planning without Actually Triggering Procurement on that Level

Strategies 81, 82, and 86—Assembly-to-Order

An ATO environment is one in which the product is assembled on receipt of the sales order. But key components can be planned ahead of time and stocked so that they are available on receipt of the order. This procedure is useful where a large number of finished products can be assembled from common components. It's a special kind of MTO planning strategy.

In an ATO strategy, you can check material and resource availability at the moment when the sales order is created. You can quote reliable delivery dates to your customers because you know whether the desired quantity will be available on the desired date. If the complete quantity can't be committed, the system tells you when the total quantity will be available and whether you can commit a partial quantity. Because the finished product isn't usually kept in stock, an availability check is carried out at the component level when the sales order, quotation, or inquiry is created.

Another important factor for ensuring that customers are provided with reliable due dates is continuous feedback between sales and production as we discussed before. The ATO process allows for changes to quantities or dates for production or procurement of components synchronized with the sales order. Changes are passed back to the sales order of the finished product where the committed quantity or confirmation date is also changed. Similarly, changes to quantities or dates in the sales order are passed on to production and/or procurement.

Figure 6.65 shows the Customizing screen for strategy 81, an ATO strategy that generates planned orders to finish assembly directly out of the sales order. The ASSEMBLY TYPE 4 PLANNED ORDER (DYNAMIC PROCESSING) ensures that an incoming sales order triggers the generation of a planned order.

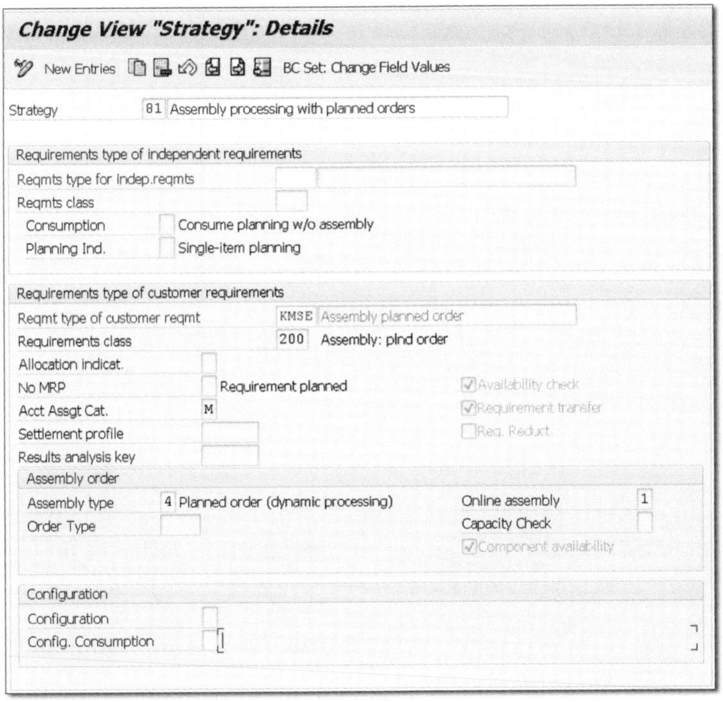

Figure 6.65 Strategy 81

Strategy 81 is specifically useful in repetitive manufacturing because the newly created repetitive order can be placed directly in a takt-based, heijunka schedule as a make to order requirement.

Strategy 82 also triggers the direct generation of an order out of the sales order. However, it's configured to generate a production order. In Figure 6.66, you can see that this time, a production order with the ORDER TYPE PP04 is created.

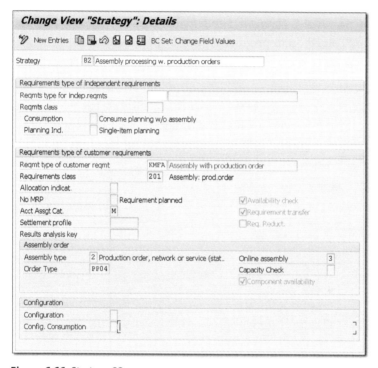

Figure 6.66 Strategy 82

A further variation to the ATO process is strategy 86 which is used in the Project System (PS) component. Instead of a planned or a production order, a project order is generated with the ORDER TYPE PI04 (see Figure 6.67)

You can also use strategy 89 when you're working with the Variant Configurator (VC). In this case, you can configure the final product in the sales order, and, once done, a configured production order is placed on the production schedule.

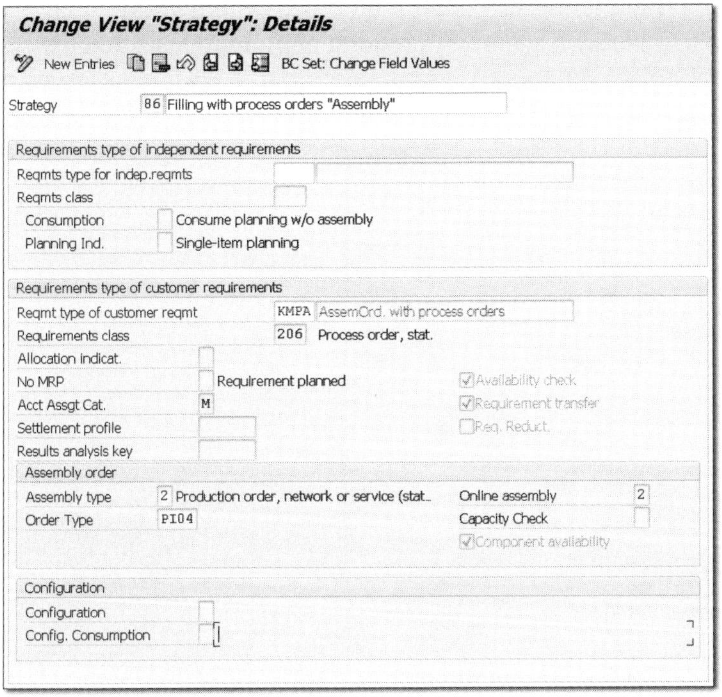

Figure 6.67 Strategy 86

6.4.3 Availability Check and Transfer of Demand

A crucial element of an effective planning policy is the way availability is checked in the sales order and how the demand is transferred from the delivery proposal to the production schedule. To set up this process, you have to maintain an availability check and a TRLT (or not) on the MRP 3 screen (which happens to house the strategy group and the consumption rules as well (see Figure 6.68).

Figure 6.68 Availability Check Section in the MRP 3 Screen of the Material Master

The availability check with its associated rule and scope of check will drive what happens when a sales order is entered. Typically a sales representatives takes a customer request and enters the line item into an order using Transaction VA01.

Then the availability check is triggered, and if the customer's requested delivery date can't be met, a screen with a delivery proposal pops up (see Figure 6.69).

Standard Order: Availability Control

Complete dlv. Delivery proposal Continue ATP quantities Scope of check Other plants

Item   10   Schd. Line   1
Material   2451122
              WHISTLEBLOWER 20 INCHES / 3 LBS
Plant   PROD
Req.delv.date 20.08.2012   Open Quantity   840.000 LB
Fix qty/date   Max.Part.Deliveries 0

One-time del. on req. del. dte : not possible
Dely/Conf.Date 20.08.2012 / 02.01.2013 Confirmed Quantity   0.000

Complete delivery
Dely/Conf.Date 07.01.2013 / 03.01.2013   ✔

Dely proposal
Dely/Conf.Date 03.01.2013 / 03.01.2013 Confirmed qty   240.000 ✔
                07.01.2013   600.000

Figure 6.69 Delivery Proposal in the Sales Availability Check

The delivery proposal screen answers three questions:

1. Is a one-time delivery in full on the customer-requested delivery date possible?

2. When is the complete delivery of all requested items possible?

3. At what times and dates can partial deliveries be shipped?

If you look closer, you can see two dates separated by a forward slash (/). The first date indicates the ship date, and the second is the material availability date that is relevant for MRP and will show in Transaction MD04—if some other conditions are met and the dates and quantities are fixed. So depending on what proposal you choose and agree to with the customer, you click the checkbox next to the delivery proposal and so confirm the dates. Those dates will then be relevant for MRP and everything in planning works toward meeting these dates. How these dates were determined depends on the scope of check.

Figure 6.70 shows the scope of check. It's parameterized by the combination of AVAILABILITY CHECK (from the MRP 3 screen of the material master) and the CHECKING RULE (according to the transaction you carry out with the availability check). In it, you define the objects, parameters, and elements that participate (or not) in the procedure to check for availability.

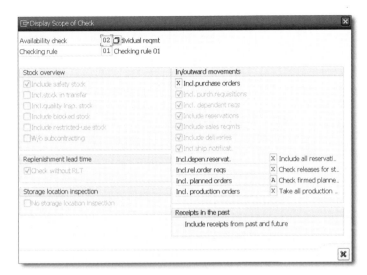

Figure 6.70 Scope of Check

One of the most relevant settings in the scope of check is the decision regarding whether you check with or without TRLT. Naturally, the TRLT is a measure primarily used in MTO because it's the time it takes to replenish the product in question if there is nothing readily available in stock. Let's see what happens when you select the CHECK WITHOUT RLT checkbox and what happens if you don't. Figure 6.71 depicts a typical situation for a sales availability check. A customer order was placed with a requested delivery inside the lead time.

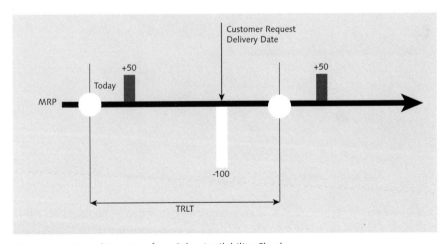

Figure 6.71 Typical Situation for a Sales Availability Check

Let's assume that a customer orders product in the quantity of 100 pieces. The requested delivery date according to the wishes of the customer lies before the end of the replenishment lead time. There is a receipt coming in for 50 pieces at a time before the customer-requested delivery date, so the availability check will find inventory of 50 pieces freely available for the customer to pick at the date requested.

However, the order of 100 pieces can't be delivered in full to the customer's requested date for delivery because there are 50 pieces missing. So there are two possible things that can happen, depending on whether we're checking with or without TRLT.

If the system checks with TRLT as in Figure 6.72 (the field SCOPE OF CHECK is unchecked), the availability check only looks out to the end of the lead time. If it doesn't find enough quantity to fulfill the demand in that period, it confirms *any* quantity just after the TRLT. Subsequently, the next MRP run will generate an additional order proposal to fulfill the demand.

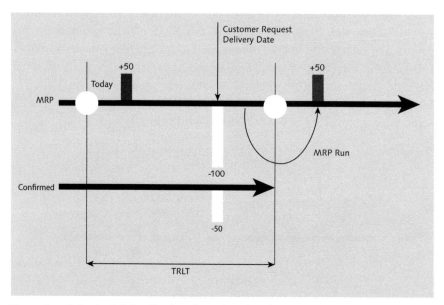

Figure 6.72 Sales Availability Check with Total Replenishment Lead Time

That is a good solution when you don't have any inventory planned to fulfill demand, as in a MTO situation. However, if you planned for inventory, and there is a future receipt on the horizon (maybe only a few days away) as in MTS, the additional order not only disturbs your production planning but most likely causes the production of too much inventory. Also, beware that this type of check confirms *any* requested quantity after the replenishment lead time (Figure 6.73).

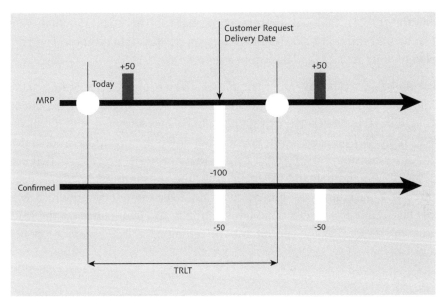

Figure 6.73 Sales Availability Check without Total Replenishment Lead Time

When you check without TRLT, the system looks for receipts throughout the entire planning horizon and confirms to the date when the order can be fulfilled with enough available quantity. Here, the delivery proposal can suggest partial deliveries or a complete delivery to the latest date. This case should mostly be used in MTS scenarios where you want a smooth production program and not to produce over and above the plan when you miss the forecast just by a few days.

In this case, you must ensure that your consumption rules are set up correctly and ensure a smooth transition from the buffer inventory to the buffer time, which is the subject of our next topic.

6.4.4 Consumption Procedures

Another important aspect in the design of a planning policy are the consumption parameters. What's being consumed are planned independent requirements or forecasted quantities. These forecasts are allocated to customer requirements (e.g., a sales order), reservations, or dependent requirements, and then they are consumed according to the configuration in the planning strategy (through requirements type and requirements class). The purpose of consumption is to compare the plan to what is actually happening. A sales order, as an example, will consume the forecast because the forecast brought in the quantities that were meant to be sold through the sales orders. If you do this right, you can compare your plan to your actual sales later on in a report.

It's all about balance. The inventory (supply) that you brought in according to the plan is in balance with the forecast (demand)—you forecasted 10 for March, so you brought in 10 to March 1st, and supply is in balance with demand. If you sell 2 with a sales order on March 5th, you'll bring down the inventory to 8, and if the sales order consumes the forecast by 2 at the same time, you'll have that balance of supply (8) and demand (8) again. After the consumption itself has been configured and picked into the policy, you'll still have to understand which way and how far in time it happens. That information is also maintained on the MRP 3 screen, which serves as the central hub for setting up a useful planning policy (Figure 6.74).

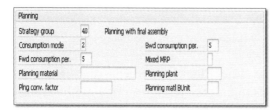

Figure 6.74 Planning Section in the MRP 3 Screen of the Material Master with Relevant Fields for Consumption

In the PLANNING section of the MRP 3 screen, you'll find the following fields: STRATEGY GROUP, the CONSUMPTION MODE, BWD CONSUMPTION PER. (backward consumption period), and FWD CONSUMPTION PER. (forward consumption period. Whatever you maintain in these three fields will determine which way and how far out a sales order will look and search for a forecast to consume. If, for example you're using the settings in Figure 6.74, an incoming confirmed sales order will first look back for five working days to consume a planned independent requirement. If there are still quantities left, it will switch to look forward for five days to look for another one to consume.

This procedure, and the way it's set up in the MRP 3 screen, has many consequences in the manner that exceptions are generated (reschedule in, reschedule out), order proposals are pushed in and out, and the nervousness or smoothness of your plan over a specific horizon. You'll have to fully understand all these consequences and build the logic into your policy; otherwise, you'll end up with chaos and bad inventory levels.

There are many things that can go wrong with a faulty setup of the consumption modes. For example, as we discussed, you have the option to consume a forecast (through incoming actual sales orders) going forward, going backward, or doing both. Let's assume there is a monthly forecast, which means there is a VSF with a negative quantity (a demand element) standing at the first working day of every month. The planning run covers the demand by creating a supply element (usually a planned order) to bring in the quantity just before the first working day of the month. This ensures that there is enough inventory available at the first day of the month, so that you can sell (with actual sales orders) the forecasted and produced quantity throughout the months.

Naturally, every sales order coming in during these months is reducing the inventory and should consume the forecast—but only the forecast that was created for it, right? You achieve that by maintaining a consumption strategy that consumes in a backward direction of no more than 22 working days. If your consumption strategy consumes backward and then forward, you will, after you sell more than what you forecasted, not dip into safety stock alone but also start consuming the forecast from the next month. That will result in putting less into inventory for the next month and essentially telling the system that because your sales went up this month, they will be less next month. That is most likely not true and makes the forecast planner look bad!

6.4.5 Developing a Playbook for Planning Policies

To develop a planning policy, you have to combine the individual elements we just discussed. So you have to combine a strategy (group) with an availability checking rule, consumption logic, a lot-size procedure, and buffering strategies. The best way to do this is to think in stories—little tales that are good to remember and visualize the sometimes complex combinations and relationships. But before we do that, let's summarize some of the options we have for building an effective planning policy.

Planning Strategies

Table 6.2 shows the important planning strategies.

Strategy	Usage	Short Description
10	MTS strategy	The production program is undisturbed. Demand above the forecast isn't causing any additional demand. Consumption occurs during goods issue.
11	MTS strategy with gross requirements	This strategy is used when a production line must keep on running.
20	MTO strategy	Stocks and requirements are managed for each customer order separately in its own segment.
30	MTO/MTS strategy	Production occurs by lot size. If lot size exceeds demand, the additional quantities are available for the next order.
40	MTS strategy	Forecast is consumed by incoming customer orders. Additional demand over and above the forecast can drop into the frozen zone. Strategy is used when customer orders are important.
50	FTO strategy	Forecast triggers procurement of intermediate parts or raw materials with long lead times. Final assembly is only triggered when an actual demand is present. Stocks and requirements are managed for each customer order separately in its own segment.
52	FTS strategy	This strategy acts the same as strategy 50, only that all demands are managed and planned in the NET REQUIREMENTS section.
74	Component planning	Planned independent requirements are placed on components and not on finished goods.
81, 82, 86, 89	ATO strategy	At the time of a sales order entry, the supply element (planned order, production order, network, or configured production order) is generated immediately out of the line item. There is a tight connection between the sales order and the supply element so that changes on either side can be communicated effectively.

Table 6.2 Overview of Some Important Planning Strategies

Availability Checks

There are basically two main availability checks: the MTS and the MTO check. You can define many more availability checking rules, which you can use for many different type of checks. It is, however, noteworthy to point out the major difference between an MTO and an MTS availability check for sellable products in a sales order (see Table 6.3).

Checking Rule	Demand Type	Check with RLT?	Check for Stock?	Check for Future Receipts
MTO	Sales order	Yes	No	No
MTS	Sales order	No	Yes	Yes

Table 6.3 Availability Checks

Consumption Logic

Consumption logic determines the synchronization of actual customer orders with a forecast (see Table 6.4). Of course, consumption logic is only relevant for materials using a forecast strategy.

Consumption Logic	Description
1	Backwards consumption only
2	First backwards, then forwards (be careful with the forward consumption as it reduces future forecast)

Table 6.4 Consumption Logic

Lot-Sizing Procedures

Some commonly used lot-size procedures for finished goods planning are listed in Table 6.5.

Lot-sizing Procedure	Description
EX	The lot-for-lot procedure can be combined with min/max and rounding values.
FX	Fixed lot size provides advantages if you produce according to a sequenced production program in an MTS environment.

Table 6.5 Lot-Sizing Procedures

Lot-sizing Procedure	Description
MB	Periodic lot-size procedures aren't very effective for production scheduling, especially if you're using a monthly lot size, because it's not very useful when there is a weekly forecast.
WB	If you're using a weekly lot size, you have no means of distributing production over the days of the week.

Table 6.5 Lot-Sizing Procedures (Cont.)

MRP Types

Table 6.6 describes some common MRP types.

MRP Type	Description
PD	Most often used MRP type for finished goods
Vx	Not very effective for finished goods planning
Mx	May be useful when you need to look at important products separately

Table 6.6 MRP Types

Buffering Strategies

Policy development is a custom procedure. Every business is different, you might say, but are businesses really so different? There must be a way to generalize for the purpose of policy setting and coming up with a playbook full of standard policy. Although there are discrete manufacturers and process manufacturers, you can have standard policies in each category; even across industries, the way we manufacture to stock or build to order is fundamentally the same.

Following are two examples, one representing an MTO environment and the other representing an MTS environment.

Planning Policy #205 – Make-to-Stock with Consumption of Forecast

In an MTS environment, product is always produced to a planned requirement—not an actual one. Actual requirements are looking for stock on hand to be fulfilled. The policy we've developed here is used for AX, AY, and BX products with a short or medium length lead time. Predictable items can, obviously, be forecasted, and if they have a short TRLT, we can use a method that allows for rush orders to be placed on a production schedule, even into the frozen zone. However, that is very difficult when the replenishment lead time is long; therefore, those products will get a different policy (most likely strategy 10 instead of 40, and requirements type LSF instead of VSF).

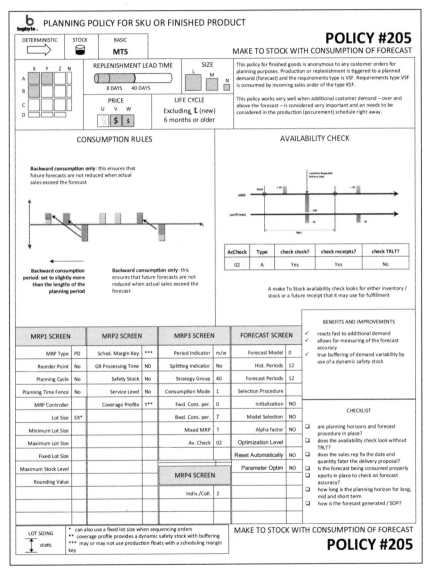

Figure 6.75 Planning Policy for Make-to-Stock with Consumption of Forecast

The policy in Figure 6.75 also suggests to consume the forecast with incoming sales orders—but only looking backwards for seven working days. This is because we assume that incoming sales orders of this week were planned to come in this week, and any additional demand wasn't meant to reduce the forecast of the next period. There might be situations where this type of consumption doesn't work very well, but that's for another policy.

The availability checking rule is an MTS check. Therefore, when a sales order comes in, the check looks for available inventory. If no quantities are found, it looks out in the future for incoming receipts from the production lines.

Policy #205 (Figure 6.75) puts a lot of focus on customer service with its ability to place immediate demand on a production line when there is no available inventory to fulfill the customer order. The disadvantage of this procedure is that it introduces a lot of noise. Therefore, this policy should only be used for products where we do want to put a lot of focus on individual customers. Keeping the noise out of the production program is an objective for another policy and with it for another group of products.

Planning Policy #211 — Make-to-Order with Preplanning for Components

Another example is policy #211 as shown in Figure 6.76. Policy #211 is a variation of an MTO policy. The final product is finished to a customer order, and important components or raw materials can be procured ahead of time through a forecast on the finished product.

The main piece of the policy is strategy 50. Using this strategy, Transaction MD04 for the finished product will show a section for preplanning and a section for execution. A forecast is maintained for the product, and planned orders will be generated during the MRP run to cover the forecast. However, planned orders to cover the forecast are of a statistical nature in that they can't be converted into production orders. Only when an actual customer demand appears, will a convertible planned order be moved from the preplanning section into the execution section, allowing final assembly to begin.

Components and raw materials may be procured based on the forecast through a BOM explosion.

In that sense policy #211 acts like an FTO strategy and has the benefits of a shorter lead time to customer combined with very low, if any, inventory holdings for the finished product.

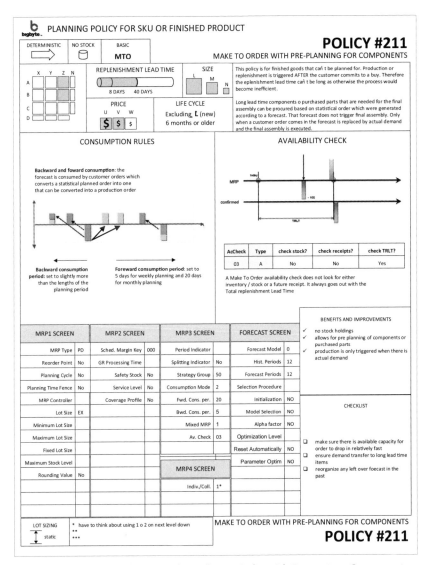

Figure 6.76 Planning Policy #211 for Make–to-Order with Forecast on Components or Purchased Parts

6.5 Setting Policy

So when you translate the policy into your SAP ERP system, you'll have to—like with replenishment policies—update your material master record with the respective settings from the policy playbook. When setting up planning policies, most fields for this type of policy are housed in the MRP 3 screen in the material master record.

In Figure 6.77, you can see the Strategy group field, which identifies a main strategy and several optional strategies; the fields to set up the rules for consumption; the Availability check field; and the Tot. repl. lead time (TRLT), which is used in an MTO availability check. Some more fields to make up a planning policy can be found in the MRP 1 and MRP 2 screens.

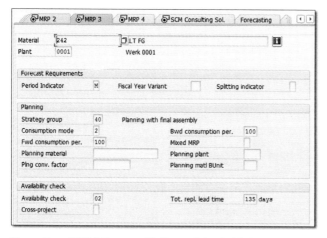

Figure 6.77 MRP 3 Screen with Most of the Fields Necessary to Set Up a Planning Policy

Setting the policy, therefore, can be a very involved process because you must update every material master record individually—on a periodic basis. Standard SAP ERP does offer the MRP group to maintain something like a policy, but there is only a limited amount of field settings you can maintain in there. And then there is Transaction MM17 to do mass updates, but that is really not a transaction the planner or buyer should execute on a frequent basis.

When implementing a system of effective materials planning, the SAP add-on tools are very useful, as mentioned previously in this book. Developed by SAP in the SAP namespace, these tools offer an excellent extension to your standard SAP functionality and provide everything you'll ever need to run your materials planning in a standardized, automated, and efficient manner.

6.6 Using the SAP Add-On Tools for Segmentation and Policy Setting

As shown in Figure 6.78, there is a whole set of these additional modules available for a one-time purchase price. The SAP add-on tools perform functions primarily in the supply chain.

There are monitors, cockpits, operational tools, and controlling tools, as well as an ongoing effort to extend and improve on the functionality in SAP ERP. In fact these add-on tools might represent the only further development of the SAP ERP system.

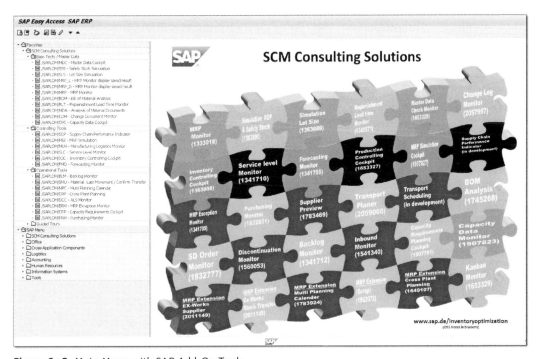

Figure 6.78 Main Menu with SAP Add-On Tools

6.6.1 MRP Monitor

The MRP Monitor is one of the main components of the SAP add-on tool set. It can be used for portfolio management, segmentation, and classification, and it's an excellent automatism for policy setting.

After you segment your portfolio into ABC, XYZ, EFG, and so on, you can pick a segment (e.g., all XCE items) and update all materials in this segment with the same policy. This is done by opening up a window with master data fields that you can maintain from within the monitor. In Figure 6.79 you can see the result of the portfolio segmentation. The grid in the upper-middle window allows you to select a segment of materials and then, through the click of a button, open up the master data screens to maintain policy as shown in Figure 6.80.

It's also possible to set policy automatically. In Figure 6.81, you can see the policy table where you can store your policy playbook. Each of the stored policies has a key for selection and an argument for settings. Using this table, you can automatically update your entire portfolio periodically. After the segmentation is done, the system can look for materials that match the selection criteria in the key and update all the materials with the policy maintained in the argument. That way, your materials are always up to date with a fitting policy.

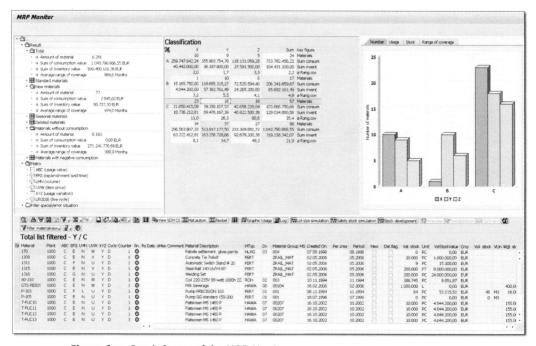

Figure 6.79 Result Screen of the MRP Monitor

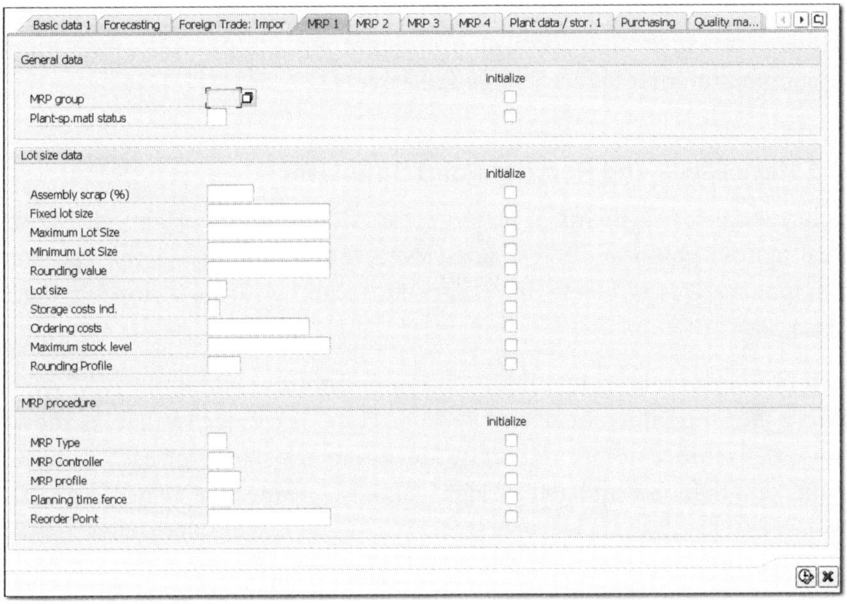

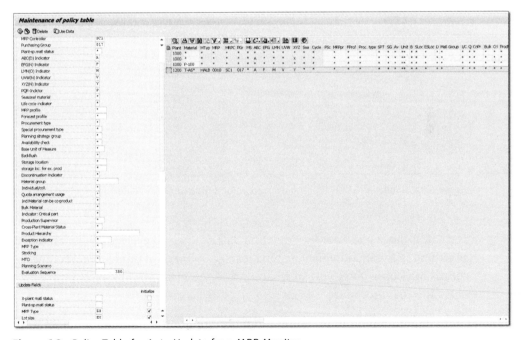

Figure 6.80 Popup Window to Update Policy in Material Master Records

Figure 6.81 Policy Table for Auto Update from MRP Monitor

Be careful, however, because the setup and policy assignment must be near perfect for this automatism to work well. You might want to ease into the various levels of automation first before you go full force.

6.6.2 Safety Stock and Reorder Point Simulator

After policy is set for segments of material classifications, you might have to set individual reorder points and safety stock levels for those materials that received a reorder policy. This is where the Safety Stock and Reorder Point Simulator comes into play.

You can pull all materials set up with a reorder policy from within the MRP Monitor straight into the Safety Stock and Reorder Point Simulator so that, as shown in Figure 6.82, reorder points and safety stocks are calculated for each material. The result can then be updated straight into the respective material master records.

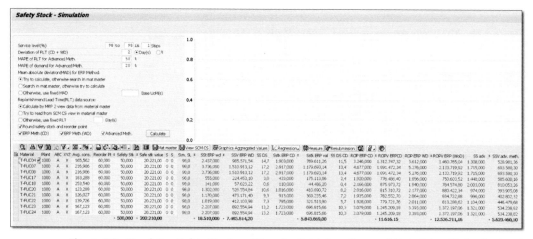

Figure 6.82 Simulating Safety Stock and Reorder Point for a Group of Materials with Service Level of 98%

The Safety Stock and Reorder Point Simulator can also be used to simulate safety stock setting for an individual material using a number of service level settings. A correlation curve gives you an indication of the ideal service level. Figure 6.83 illustrates that procedure.

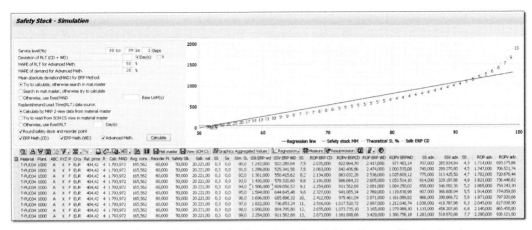

Figure 6.83 Simulating Safety Stock and Reorder Point for a Material in a Range of Service Levels

As demonstrated in Figure 6.84, safety stock reorder point and service level can be updated from within the simulator for a number of material master records. Safety stocks and reorder points may be calculated according to various methods.

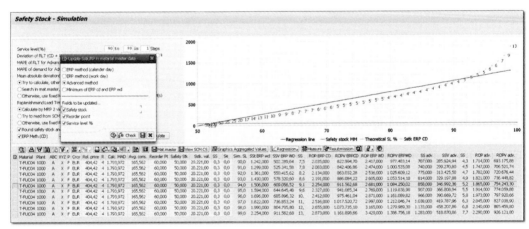

Figure 6.84 Using the Advanced Method to Update the Material Master with Service Level, Safety Stock, and Reorder Point

6.6.3 Lot Size Simulator

Another SAP add-on tool is the Lot Size Simulator and, as its name suggests, it allows for the simulation and subsequent updating of the most optimal reorder point for any given demand situation.

Lot size simulation can compare ordering cost and stock keeping cost for a given actual demand situation and simulate this using many different lot-size procedures. The result can then be shown in the result screen, and you can choose the least cost procedure and update the material master record with it. Figure 6.85 shows the result of such a lot size simulation.

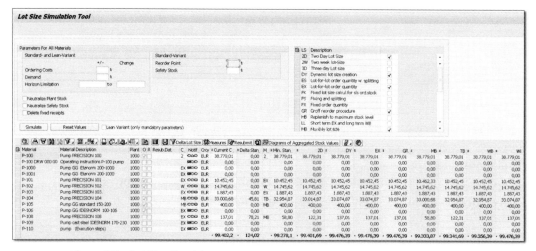

Figure 6.85 Lot Size Simulator

In that way, you can simulate the least cost procedure for each material during each period as the demand situation changes (Figure 6.86).

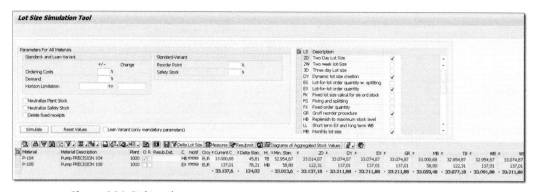

Figure 6.86 Picking the Least Cost Lot-Size Procedure

6.7   Summary

Policy setting is the heart and soul of a system of effective materials planning. Policy allows for automation and efficiency as it provides a standardized approach to translate supply chain strategy into execution.

There are replenishment policies, primarily used for raw, packaging, and purchased parts, and planning policies, primarily used for finished products or sellable products. A policy playbook should be developed so that policy can be set and updated on a periodic basic to attribute to changing conditions.

Replenishment policies revolve mainly around the MRP type, which we discussed in detail, whereas planning policies are mostly driven by the strategy held in the STRATEGY GROUP field. However, it's not one select field setting that makes up a policy. It's rather the combination of the various settings in the four MRP screens and forecasting that make up effective policy.

The art of policy setting must be practiced over and over, and without a functioning tool set, it's hard to execute for a large portfolio of materials. This is where the SAP add-on tools can be of benefit. MRP Monitor, Lot Size Simulator, and Safety Stock and Reorder Point Simulator tools provide an excellent toolset to round out the system of effective materials planning.

There is no exception to the rule that every rule has an exception.
—James Thurber

7 Intelligent Exception Monitoring

Exception monitoring provides immense opportunities to move companies toward becoming "exception-minded organizations." Within its rich set of exception messages and alerts, you can gain deep insight into your company's dedication to the plan. With its automatic generation of exception messages, rescheduling proposals, and functions to proactively manage and cure exception situations, SAP's exception monitoring module provides all functions, processes, and tools to take a huge workload off the planner, buyer, or production scheduler. Intelligent exception monitoring improves performance; avoids disruptions in the process, material, and information flow; and narrows the gap between the plan and what actually happens.

Exception monitoring, in that sense, serves lots of purposes in an organization, but primarily facilitates the planning process and negates the need to look at everything every day, moving your organization toward coming an exception-minded business.

Example

An airline operation with scheduled, commercial flights is an excellent example of an exception-minded business. Everything from flight planning to the safe delivery of passengers to their requested destination is routine and being managed using standard policies. Ground personnel checks passengers into their purchased flights according to standard operation procedures, Air Traffic Control handles all the taxi procedures, routing options, and flight handovers according to a well-designed protocol, and the pilot puts the airplane on auto-pilot after ATC has assigned departure and arrival procedures. Routine operations from A to Z are performed by very well-trained personnel who know every procedure and policy by heart. Only when something out of the ordinary happens—an exceptional situation—will the staff take an action that strays from the general rule. Maybe a passenger doesn't show up for the flight even though his luggage was checked in. Or a weather system pops up on the planned route. As the pilot goes through the checklist, he finds a faulty part in the aircraft's hydraulic system. The crew got delayed from another flight. These are all exceptional situations that require action off the regular routine activities. And for every exceptional situation, there is a standard plan of action, a standard procedure to cure the exception.

This type of operation should be part of every effective materials planning system. There should be general policies for classes of materials that automate the replenishment process to constantly balance supply with demand according to our goals and guidelines. But if there is a deviation from the plan—and only then—we should be alerted to take action and bring everything back to plan and toward the desired results. This is why it's so important to build the rule set—the policies—first and communicate to everybody in the system what we're striving for. Only then can the system determine what is and isn't an exception. Without such thinking and acting, you're shooting blanks into the dark and managing by chaos. Exception messages become meaningless, and the materials planner gets overwhelmed and frustrated with senseless calls for action.

In this chapter, we want to further explore the process of exception monitoring, detail the prerequisites that make such a system effective, and provide a framework of reference for building a method to observe and react to meaningful exceptions.

7.1 Exception Monitoring in SAP ERP

Monitoring the exception messages present in the SAP ERP system is an important part of an effective system of materials planning. A well-organized monitoring procedure doesn't only provide valuable insight into what works and what doesn't, but it also reduces workload and frees up time for inventory reduction activities, planning, and expediting. Prioritized exception monitoring pinpoints inefficiencies and leads us to problems otherwise hidden and undetected in the process.

Exception messages are generated during the MRP run, which performs a net requirements calculation, generates order proposals, and then attaches messages to supply elements when an exceptional situation occurs. Exception messages relate to many things such as start dates, end dates, inventory levels, structural issues, or lead times. To introduce more structure into the process, SAP has provided exception groups into which exception messages can be collected. When exception messages are grouped, it's possible to monitor exceptions in a prioritized way. As you'll see, you can develop a customized system of prioritized exception monitoring using these groups. This is "a day in the life of a tactical materials planner," system that includes step-by-step instructions and guidance as to what exception messages, groups of messages, or exceptional situations to monitor and what actions to take to cure these messages in a specific and customizable order of priority.

We use such a system instead of simply work these messages as they come up because these exception messages lead us to more insight into the workings of our processes. When an exception message appears, it tells us something is broken in the following:

- ▶ Process
- ▶ Behavior
- ▶ Policy
- ▶ System setup

Taking a closer look, it becomes apparent the a materials planner has the biggest leverage point with setting the policy by performing master data adjustments for more optimized and automated replenishment. But this fact isn't always understood very well and therefore not used efficiently. Sometimes the materials planner tries many other things first before thinking about policy. But often, and especially after materials planners are trained on policy setting, they choose another suboptimal way of dealing with exception messages: the relentless adjustment of basic data settings.

As we know, order-based replenishment is a big inhibitor of productivity and automation, because it introduces nervousness and variability into the process. Fiddling around with policy is another one. We're referring here to the often seen urge to change parts (and its policy) on a very frequent basis. Especially for expensive and important parts, it seems like there is no limit as to what some planners think is necessary to persistently update and modify basic data manually on parts, in the hope that sometime and somehow it will work out to their advantage. To change a lot-size procedure or an MRP type six times a month doesn't mean things will get better. It just means that things get blurry and confusing.

In the following sections, we'll outline all of the exception groupings and their associated messages. We'll then discuss the order of preference and priority to work and cure those exceptions.

7.1.1 Exception Groups and Exception Messages

As discussed already, exception messages in SAP ERP are generated by the MRP run. Once created, these messages are categorized into eight groups. SAP has done a great job of sorting and grouping these various messages in the standard delivery. Yet there are many installations where people (consultants and customers, users, and IT personnel) reconfigured the assignment of exception messages to their preconfigured groupings. This might very well serve its purpose and sometimes regroupings make a lot of sense.

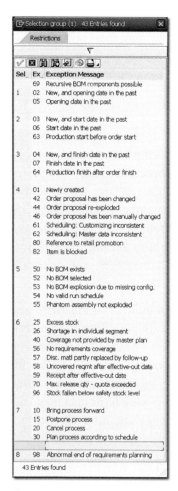

Figure 7.1 Exception Groups and Their Exception Messages as Delivered in Standard SAP

More often than not, however, these new groupings aren't based on a good understanding of how SAP ERP exception monitoring works, and then it interferes greatly with an effort to introduce sense, automation, and effectiveness into the exception management process. Next, we'll explain the groupings as they are delivered by SAP. Use Transaction MD06 or Transaction MD07 to open the screen that lists the groups as shown in Figure 7.1.

First of all, the 69 RECURSIVE BOM COMPONENTS POSSIBLE. exception message isn't assigned to any group. A recursive bill of material (BOM) is a BOM that contains the same material (number) in the header as in a line item and therefore can circulate and "dead-spiral" demand. There are rare instances where a recursive BOM might make sense; however, when getting this message, it's a good idea to check on your master data and see if a mistake might have crawled into your BOM setup.

To take action to cure exception 69, investigate the BOM and take out recursive items.

In the following subsections, we'll discuss each of the eight group exceptions in detail.

Group 1 Exceptions – You Missed a Warning to Convert Proposals

Exception messages in group 1 are generated when the date that was determined using the opening period was falling into the past.

As you can see in Figure 7.2, the scheduling margin key (SMK column) is using an opening period of 10 days (in the OP.PD field). The opening date is calculated by subtracting the number of working days in the opening period from the start date of the order. For example the start date of a purchasing requisition might be March 12th. That is the date when the requisition must be converted to a purchase order so that the goods are received on time to fulfill a demand. From that date, the system then subtracts the 10 working days from the opening period (as shown in Figure 7.2) and with it arrives at the opening date of the requisition. So what's the meaning and purpose of the opening date? It simply serves as an extra time buffer to be alerted to the need to convert an order proposal into a fixed supply element. With the opening period, you can define a buffer with which to remind you of an upcoming conversion or start date.

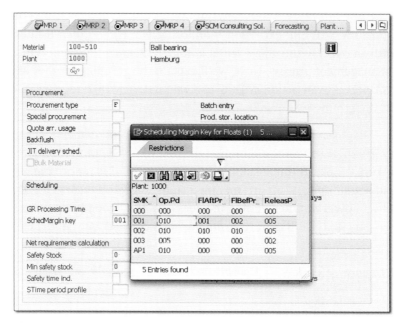

Figure 7.2 Opening Period Defined by the Scheduling Margin Key in the Material Master Record

These are exception messages that don't necessarily have to be included in the daily exception monitor. Look at group 1 messages only once in a while depending on how large of a buffer you've set in the scheduling margin key. Obviously, you don't need to react right away after this message pops up—you still have the time buffer you've chosen through the opening horizon.

So if you're getting exception message 02 New, and opening date in the past, you're dealing with an alert telling you that a new order proposal was generated. The requirement is so close that after backward scheduling the replenishment lead time and the opening period, the opening date falls into the past. This doesn't necessarily mean that you're late; you might still have time to convert the proposal on time to meet the requirement. But you're within the time buffer you configured through the opening period.

The other exception message in group 1, 05 Opening date in the past, simply means that enough time has passed on an existing order proposal, so that the opening date was finally falling into the past.

Group 2 Exceptions – You Missed the Release or Conversion Date of the Order Proposal

This group contains exception messages that inform about missing the release date to convert a purchase requisition or planned order into a purchase order or production order. You can see the release date in Transaction MD04. There are actually two hidden columns—one for the opening date and the other one for the release date as shown in Figure 7.3. If you can't see the START/RELEASE DATE and OPENING DATE columns in Transaction MD04, be sure to make them visible. Move the cursor so that you can see two lines, and then drag the columns open. These columns provide valuable information about opening and conversion dates of your order proposals.

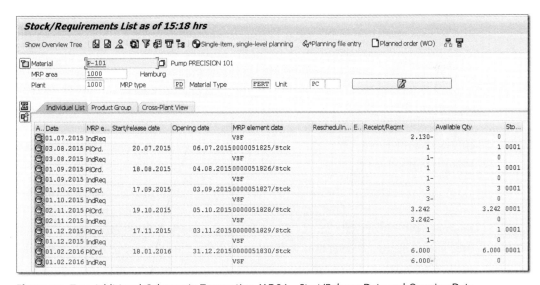

Figure 7.3 Two Additional Columns in Transaction MD04 – Start/Release Date and Opening Date

The release date was calculated by subtracting the lead time from the requirements date (backward scheduling); therefore, it represents the latest date an order proposal has to be started (fixed, converted, a purchase order sent out, a production order send to the shop floor) so that the material can be received at the required date (see Figure 7.4). If you miss that date, your material might not be received on time, causing your service level to degrade.

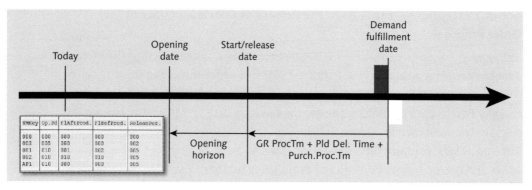

Figure 7.4 Start/Release Date of an Order Proposal

As in group 1, we have an exception that informs us of a new order proposal, 03, and an exception that informs us of an existing order proposal. Only this time, it's the start (or release) date that is relevant. To cure message 03 New, and start date in the past, investigate possible lead time errors in the master data, or look at the availability checking rule, which might have allowed a requirement to drop in within the replenishment lead time. Maybe it was a rush order that was entered manually, ignoring the general rule. You can also use a Customizing setting with which you can tell the system to switch onto forward scheduling from today's date onward, in case the start date falls into the past.

With 06 Start date in the past, you deal with an existing order proposal that has missed its conversion date. Maybe your release procedure isn't thought out well, or some order proposals simply fall through the cracks in the selection for a periodic and collective conversion. Whatever may be the case, try to get all these elements up to date and release them on time with the correct lead time, which will determine the correct start/release date. If you feel that the order proposal should be rescheduled instead of released, then your basic data setup is probably faulty and doesn't generate the correct dates automatically.

As for exception 63 Production start before order start, we have a problem in Customizing if you're using lead time scheduling with the MRP run. It tells you that the system has suggested a production start that lies before the order start in lead time scheduling (see Figure 7.5). This happens when you don't select the option to adjust the basic dates in the scheduling parameters for the order proposals (Customizing Transaction OPU5).

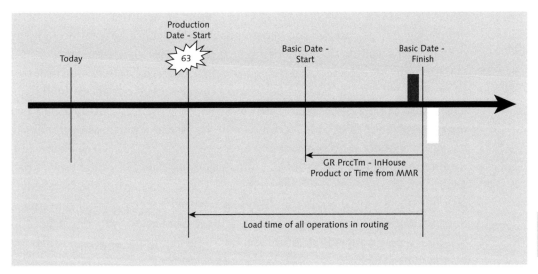

Figure 7.5 Production Starts Earlier Than the Basic Date Start

Think about it this way: if the in-house production time in the material master is shorter than the processing time in the routing, and you perform lead time scheduling where the routing is used for backward scheduling, your production start date will break through the basic start date determined by the in-house production time. That represents an inconsistency in scheduling and needs to be cured. Either customize scheduling to adjust the basic dates, or set the lead times in the master data correctly.

Group 3 Exceptions – Delivery Date Has Passed

Group 3 messages constitute a more serious problem. When it occurs, we know that not only did we miss the start/release date of the order, but we've already passed the finish date as well. With message 04 NEW, AND FINISH DATE IN THE PAST, we're still on the proposal side of things, and the planning run keeps on trying to adjust the proposals to match supply with demand. Dates are being adjusted with the creation of new order proposals, which generates a lot of noise in the planning process. You should prioritize your exception monitoring in a way that running finish dates into the past is kept at an absolute minimum, or better yet, doesn't occur at all.

07 FINISH DATE IN THE PAST is a very critical message because it alerts you of an impending outage, unless you have enough safety stock to get through the demand that's waiting for that order to be received. Message 07 can come from a purchase requisition, a planned order, a purchase order, or a production order. In all cases, you'll have to take action to cure. Under no circumstances should you have orders in the system where the finish date has passed. It actually means that the finish date (or the goods receipt date in the case of a purchase order) lies in the past, and there is no way that you'll receive goods yesterday (see Figure 7.6). Go find those orders and estimate a future delivery date. This might mean that you're curing one exception only to replace it with another (maybe "reschedule in"), but that is why there is a multistep, prioritized system of intelligent exception monitoring. If a passenger missed a flight connection, you might have to place them on a waitlist first before you can route him to the desired destination; it's the same concept.

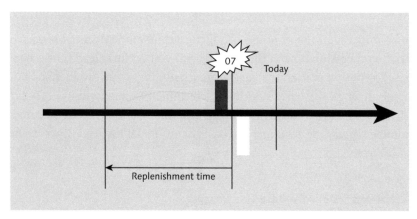

Figure 7.6 Finish Date Fell into the Past

Also part of group 3 for late finishing, is exception message 64 PRODUCTION FINISH AFTER ORDER FINISH, which tells you, again, that there is an inconsistency in scheduling (see Figure 7.7). The production finish, which was calculated using the routings lead time, lies after the basic date (calculated from the material master's lead time). Again, this is because the basic dates aren't adjusted—a setting in Customizing Transaction OPU5. You might also want to check on the correctness of the lead times in routing and the material master record.

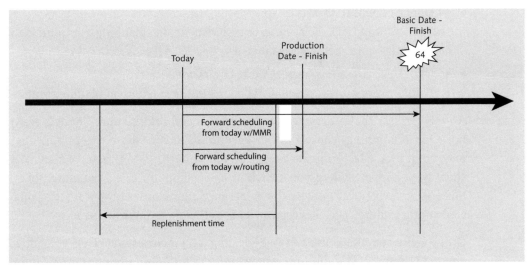

Figure 7.7 Basic Date Finish after Production Finish

Group 4 Exceptions – Information about Changes and Inconsistencies in Customizing and Master Data

Exceptions from group 4 are general messages. These messages don't pose a problem and are of the informative kind. It's important to know that you can only view the exceptions named above in Transaction MD06 (Collective MRP Lists) — not in Transaction MD07 (Collective Stock/Requirements Situation)! This is because the system can't tell when the last planning run was, as the dynamically created stock/requirements situation (in Transaction MD07) has no time stamp and therefore doesn't know what's new. Make sure these messages are part of your Transaction MD06 procedure in the morning. Following is a bit more detail about exception messages in group 4:

▶ 01 NEWLY CREATED ORDER PROPOSAL
  An order proposal was newly created in the last planning run. This message is generated if there is new demand in the system or when MRP runs using planning mode 3 – delete planning dates.

▶ 42 ORDER PROPOSAL HAS BEEN CHANGED
  The order proposal was changed in the planning run, either because of a changing demand situation or because of a change in policy that was maintained after the last planning run.

- 44 ORDER PROPOSAL RE-EXPLODED

  The order proposal's BOM was reexploded in the planning run, and new dependent requirements were created.

- 46 ORDER PROPOSAL HAS BEEN MANUALLY CHANGED

  The order proposal was manually changed in the single-item planning run.

As you can see, these messages are just for general information. There is really not a lot, if anything, you should or have to do to cure these exceptions. They may point to a sales order that was entered yesterday afternoon, or they may show what happens when you switch to a consumption-based planning policy, but they're not critical—unless the creation of a new order proposal also generated another, more critical exception such as 07 FINISH DATE IN THE PAST.

Group 4 also contains some messages dealing with inconsistencies. As you know, your SAP system had to be customized, and master data had to be set up (and is still being adjusted). These settings aren't always done correctly, and sometimes a change in one area causes an inconsistency in another. That is where exception 61 and 62 will help you pinpoint and cure such inconsistencies:

- 61 SCHEDULING: CUSTOMIZING INCONSISTENT

  Customizing Transaction OPU5 includes all settings for scheduling order proposals (see Figure 7.8).

  You can define scheduling levels, a routing type selection through the selection ID, and parameters for detailed, rate-based, or rough-cut scheduling. If any of these selections conflict with the way the MRP run tries to schedule order proposals, you'll get this exception message, and you'll have to investigate the root cause and get it fixed.

- 62 SCHEDULING: MASTER DATA INCONSISTENT

  The system couldn't find a valid routing when scheduling via the routing, or the routing is incorrect. To cure, check the routing for all the scheduling levels, detailed, rate based, or rough cut, set in Customizing in Transaction OPU5.

- 82 ITEM IS BLOCKED

  An item could be blocked by quality control.

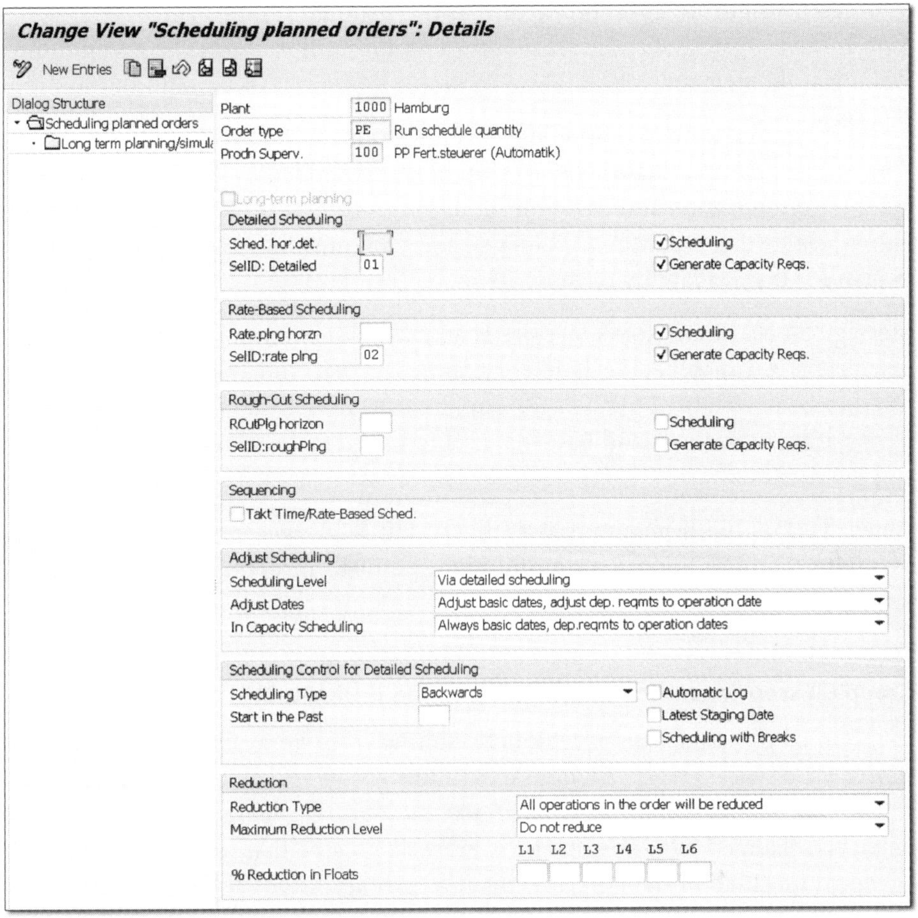

Figure 7.8 Scheduling Parameters in Customizing

Group 5 Exceptions – Errors when Exploding the BOM during the MRP Run

Group 5 exceptions point to messages resulting from errors in the BOM explosion during the MRP run. When getting message 50 NO BOM EXISTS, there is most likely no BOM existing for the material in question, or, in sales order processing, a sales order BOM could be missing.

And if the MRP run generates a planned order to cover demand, but it can't find a BOM that's fitting for the order, you'll get message 52 NO BOM SELECTED. It could be that there are BOMs assigned to the material, however, the selection criteria can't assign the appropriate one to the planned order. In that case, you'll have to investigate selection procedures and the root cause of the exception by looking at the demand.

If you're running into exception message 53 No BOM EXPLOSION DUE TO MISSING CONFIG., you'll know that the BOM couldn't be exploded by the MRP run due to missing configuration and customization. This means that line items in the BOM didn't receive dependent requirements, and you must find and cure the problem to plan for the availability of those items.

Message 54 No VALID RUN SCHEDULE is an exception when using repetitive manufacturing. A run schedule is like a planned order, and the correct quantities couldn't be determined by the MRP run. Investigate selection procedures, scheduling parameterization, and basic data setup in the material master, rate routing, and BOM.

When working with phantom assemblies, you might get message 55 PHANTOM ASSEMBLY NOT EXPLODED. This again might point to incorrect basic data or Customizing settings.

Group 6 Exceptions – Too Much Stock or Too Little Stock

In group 6, you deal with exceptions resulting from an availability check, stock shortages, or excess stock. All messages in this group are related to quantities and stock levels. For example, message 25 EXCESS STOCK is generated by the MRP run when the planned available stock coverage is greater than the maximum stock coverage specified in the range of coverage profile. As you tell the system to not exceed the maximum coverage defined in the range of coverage profile, the MRP run is tasked to keep inventory below that ceiling. However, if there is a rounding value, fixed lot size, or minimum order quantity maintained in the policy, this maximum will be exceeded. That is when exception message 25 can alert you to look further into your stock levels and maybe adjust the policy to produce more effective inventory levels.

If you're using customer individual stock segments to manage individual customer stock, exception 26 SHORTAGE IN INDIVIDUAL SEGMENT will alert you to higher stock levels than what you planned for in a range of coverage profile.

Message 40 COVERAGE NOT PROVIDED BY MASTER PLAN lets you investigate a possible "miss" in planning. The availability check (according to Available-to-Promise [ATP] logic) determined that this requirement isn't covered by the master plan.

When using a planning time fence with fixing types (P2 or P4 in deterministic planning), message 56 No requirements coverage can alert you of a shortage within the planning time fence.

Message 57 Disc. matl partly replaced by follow-up is used in the discontinuation process. As you can replace a part with a follow-up material in the discontinuation process, you might want to receive an alert if the discontinued part was only partially replaced by the substitute material.

Another exception in discontinuation is message 58 Uncovered reqmt after effective-out date. This message is generated if a requirement exists after the effective-out date for a part that is to be discontinued and therefore can't be covered by planned stock. And if there is a receipt—maybe from a previously generated purchase order, that brings in stock after the effective-out date of a discontinued part, you'll receive exception 59 Receipt after effective-out date. Obviously, these are very helpful alerts to manage discontinuation of parts without interruptions, stock-outs, or leftover, unconsumed stock.

When using quota arrangements, you'll source parts or materials from various vendors with an equal or unequal distribution of required quantities called a quota. For example, you could order a quantity of 100 pieces for the same part from three different vendors with quotas of 50%, 30%, and 20% of the required total quantity. Should the MRP run, for whatever reason, exceed the maximum release quantity of the quote, then you'll be alerted of that fact by exception 70 Max. release qty – quota exceeded.

An exception message that you probably see often is 96 Stock fallen below safety stock level, which informs you that you've dipped into your static safety stock that was set in the MRP 2 screen of the material master record. Looking at Transaction MD04, we can see that the safety stock quantity is subtracted from available stock (Figure 7.9).

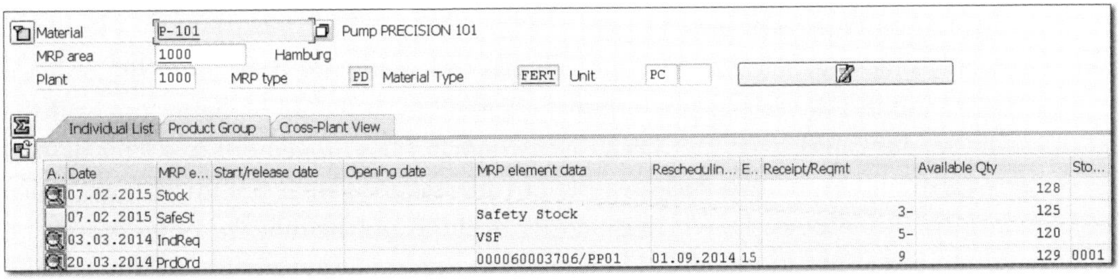
Material
P-101
Pump PRECISION 101
MRP area
1000
Hamburg
Plant
1000
MRP type
PD
Material Type
FERT
Unit
PC
Individual List
Product Group
Cross-Plant View
A..
Date
MRP e...
Start/release date
Opening date
MRP element data
Reschedulin...
E..
Receipt/Reqmt
Available Qty
Sto...
07.02.2015 Stock
128
07.02.2015 SafeSt
Safety Stock
3-
125
03.03.2014 IndReq
VSF
5-
120
20.03.2014 PrdOrd
000060003706/PP01
01.09.2014 15
9
129 0001

Figure 7.9 The Use of Safety Stock in Material Requirements Planning

There are a number of things to note here. First, if you never receive this message, then your inventory level is probably too high, and all of the safety stock turns into unused dead stock. So it's a good thing to receive the occasional message 96 because it means that you're making good use of your buffer without binding too much cash in inventory holdings. Also, when a material has exception message 96, its traffic light turns to red, and its DAYS OF SUPPLY turn to -999.9, which means that you can see all materials whose safety stocks are breached on top of your list in Transaction MD07. This might help a great deal in the prioritized management and curing of exception messages. We'll talk more about that in the next chapter.

Group 7 Exceptions – Manual Rescheduling Required

Four exception messages are contained in this group. One is for nonfixed order proposals (30), and the other three are for fixed replenishment elements such as purchase orders and production orders. The latter three are telling you that you must reschedule the orders manually (because they are fixed, and the MRP run doesn't change them anymore), and you'll also receive a suggested date to reschedule to. The four messages are explained in more detail here:

▸ 10 BRING PROCESS FORWARD
The system suggests bringing the quantities on order in at an earlier time—reschedule in to the rescheduling proposal. This is because a demand date or quantity has changed, and a certain quantity of goods is needed at an earlier time. Instead of creating another order proposal at an earlier time, the MRP run suggests bringing the already-ordered quantities in to an earlier delivery date so they can be used to fulfill the changed demand. The rescheduling has to happen manually, and the process is often called expediting because a vendor will have to be called and asked if they can expedite the delivery to an earlier date, faster than the originally agreed lead time.

▸ 15 POSTPONE PROCESS
This message tells you the opposite has to happen: we don't need the ordered quantities as early as was originally agreed to. It would be better for us if the vendor can deliver later because the demand has moved out to a later date. If we don't expedite out as suggested by message 15, we'll end up with too much inventory too early, which is bad for business. At the time the order was fixed, it looked like we needed that much, but things have changed and the demand

was moving out, or, as indicated by exception message 20 CANCEL PROCESS, fell off altogether. In that case, you need to ask the vendor to cancel the order altogether. But don't do that before you thoroughly investigate the demand and supply situation and make sure you really don't need those quantities. Following these expediting messages blindly can anger your suppliers and introduce a lot of noise into the replenishment process. That is why you can set tolerances in Customizing for your MRP group as to how many days your MRP run can operate "expediting message free."

▶ 20 CANCEL PROCESS
This message occurs when a demand is reduced or disappears altogether. This message only appears on fixed supply elements such as a purchase order or a production/process order. At an earlier time, there must have been a demand causing the creation of an order proposal that must have been converted to a fixed supply order. Subsequently, the demand disappeared or was reduced, but because the supply was fixed, the MRP run can't delete the order. However, it can then attach a note (exception message 20) to inform the planner that this receipt isn't needed anymore.

▶ 30 PLAN PROCESS ACCORDING TO SCHEDULE
The MRP run isn't able to fulfill the demand because, according to master data or routing settings, the lead time is too long for it to bring it in on time.

As you can see in Figure 7.10, the demand date lies within the replenishment lead time, and it's therefore not possible to bring the part in early enough to meet the demand. Expediting is necessary.

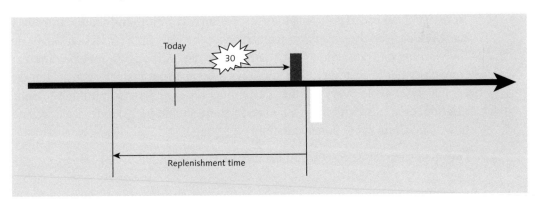

Figure 7.10 Exception 30 Plan Process according to Schedule

Group 8 Exceptions – The MRP Run Ended Because Master Data Settings Do Not Allow for Planning

As with group 4, messages out of group 8 can't be seen in Transaction MD07 but only in Transaction MD06 (see Figure 7.11). If the planning run was terminated for a material, message 98 ABNORMAL END OF REQUIREMENTS PLANNING pops up.

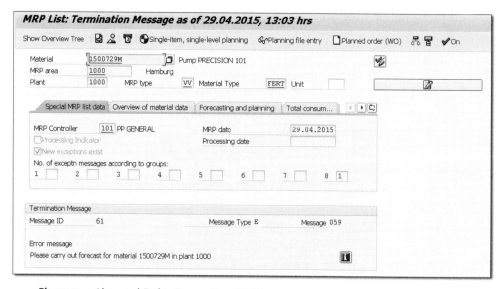

Figure 7.11 Abnormal End in Transaction MD06

7.1.2 Prioritization of Exception Groups and Exception Messages

So what's the sense in grouping these exceptions? The grouping simply prioritizes the workload for the exception handler when he calls up Transaction MD06 in the morning or Transaction MD07 later in the day. Although it may be different from customer to customer, find your own system and adjust it as you go and see fit, but try to avoid every planner developing his own system. Within one organization, or at least within one plant code, there should be a standardized way on how to go about exceptional situations.

Let's first summarize the exceptions discussed in Section 7.1.1 in Table 7.1.

No.	Message Description	Remedies and Actions to Take	Importance
03	NEW, AND START DATE IN THE PAST	The requisition is scheduled to start in the past. High potential that this order will need to be expedited or that the demand can't be supplied!	Critical
04	NEW, AND FINISH DATE IN THE PAST	The requisition is scheduled to finish in the past. High potential that this order will need to be expedited or that the demand can't be supplied!	Critical
06	START DATE IN THE PAST	The order or requisition is scheduled to start in the past. High potential that this order will need to be expedited or that the demand can't be supplied!	Critical
07	FINISH DATE IN THE PAST	The order is scheduled to finish in the past. High potential that this order will need to be expedited or that the demand can't be supplied!	Critical
10	BRING PROCESS FORWARD	Order or requisition is too late to cover requirements. Review and reschedule appropriately.	Important
15	POSTPONE PROCESS	Order or requisition is too early based on requirements. Review and reschedule appropriately.	Important
20	CANCEL PROCESS	Supply is beyond total demand in the system. Stock not required! Review and replan appropriately.	Critical
26	SHORTAGE IN INDIVIDUAL SEGMENT	There is material in the "Provided to vendor" bucket in SAP. Remove the material using Transaction MB1B, and run MRP manually.	Critical
52	NO BOM SELECTED	SAP was unable to find a valid BOM for the item. Check the BOM, production version, and selection method.	Error
53	NO BOM EXPLOSION DUE TO MISSING CONFIG.	Plant set up incorrect. Contact the helpdesk to report this error.	Error

Table 7.1 Exceptions Summary

No.	Message Description	Remedies and Actions to Take	Importance
58	UNCOVERED REQMT AFTER EFFECTIVE-OUT DATE	System unable to find replacement material. Review the run-out strategy, and adjust master data appropriately. Run MRP manually once resolved.	Critical
59	RECEIPT AFTER EFFECTIVE-OUT DATE	Receipt of discontinued material planned. Review the run-out strategy, and adjust orders appropriately. Run MRP manually once resolved.	Critical
62	SCHEDULING: MASTER DATA INCONSISTENT	Check master data! Remove IN HOUSE PROCESSING TIME from the material master MRP 2 view. Ensure that the PRODUCTION VERSION and ROUTING are correct. Run MPS/MRP manually once corrected.	Error
82	ITEM IS BLOCKED	The requisition has been manually blocked and therefore can't be converted. Remove the block from the requisition, or delete the requisition and run Transaction MD02 for the material to regenerate.	Critical
96	STOCK FALLEN BELOW SAFETY STOCK LEVEL	Supply plan insufficient to cover safety stock requirement. Review and adjust if appropriate.	Informative

Table 7.1 Exceptions Summary (Cont.)

When dealing with exception messages, prioritize in the following way:

1. Group 8 is the most important of all the groups, so look at the abnormal ends first. You don't want to have any materials in your portfolio where the planning run aborts. Clean those out first.

2. Next, look at group 5. These are concerning structural problems, and the planning run can't even come up with a date or quantity because the demand doesn't get exploded down to the lower level.

3. Then check out group 3. Not only did you miss a date to firm a receipt, you're so far behind that you missed the date when the receipt was supposed to come in to fulfill a demand.

4. After that, you'll have to deal with the group 2 problems where you missed the date when a proposal needed to be firmed, so that you can receive the quantity

after the regular lead time. If you miss that date, rescheduling and manual expediting is your only option.

5. Group 1 exceptions are only relevant when you use an opening horizon and if you want to have an additional check where your external procurement is triggered first by a planned order and then by a purchase requisition. Therefore group 7 messages ought to be tackled next. These require expediting and may take much more time to get through, but in the least, create a list at this point. The list can be worked off later in the day (call vendors, check with purchasing, look at the warehouse for inventories, etc.).

6. Next deal with group 6. Inventory excess or shortages usually require a change in strategy and that can't be done on the fly or in the morning during an exception-handling session. Again, make a list and see if you can reduce these exceptions over time, applying a different MRP type, changing the lot-size procedure, looking at safety stock levels, and a lot more.

7. Last but not least, you have to look at the general messages in group 4. Why is there a new proposal? Why have these been changed? These messages are information only and don't necessarily require action.

As you reduce your exceptions (you'll never be able to rid yourself of all of them), you'll find all kinds of problems in the process, the master data setup, the system setup, or with human behavior. You'll get yourself into a more analytical mode of operandi and proactively solve issues rather than work transactionally and constantly try to put out fires. It's a very worthwhile exercise to learn about all exception messages and their purposes. Don't waste your time trying to regroup and reinterpret what SAP has already figured out for you.

7.1.3 Fixing the Root Cause Instead of Expediting the Problem

If we think about an airline to describe a superior system of intelligent exception monitoring, we can clearly see that if they operate any less than outstanding and near perfect, world travel would be much worse and downright scary. The question is, then, why do we allow less than perfect dealings with exceptional situations in our business. Maybe we do so because it's not life threatening. Although that's a good point, our motivation to get better shouldn't be driven off life or death decisions only. Of course, there is the aspect of cost. Airlines spend a lot of money on security procedures and operations science research. That research, not only from airlines, is freely available for your perusal. Have a look at it and take from it what works for you. It doesn't cost anything but is time well spent if your materials planning system is profiting from it. And who wants to be anything but great in their job, right?

Along those lines of thinking, there isn't enough training, coaching, and support that today's materials planners can fall back on. Usually, after an SAP implementation, the user is trained on how to use transaction A and how to use transaction B, and then they are left to their own devices and expected to develop their own system of how to plan for materials availability. The only input they will receive from management is, "Don't hold too much inventory, "Don't starve the production lines," and "Our customers will make or break our business, so do whatever they need to have done."

There you have it, materials planner, go on and be excellent. Now, as we all come from different backgrounds, different education, and different mindsets, we'll all design different systems to deal with the various situations that come at us. Of course, there will be discussion, bouncing off of ideas, brainstorming, and probably a lot of Excel spreadsheets.

The basic idea behind this book, however, is to standardize the approach to materials planning and, because exception monitoring is part of it, to build a standard model on how to monitor and handle exceptional situations. The next section details an example of such a system with its individual components.

7.2 Building a Monitoring System for Exceptional Situations

To build an effective system to manage exceptional situations, you first have to define what the expected, standard result is. Only then can you know what an exception to the rule is. If the pilot has never seen an approach chart for Newark (EWR), how would he know that strong winds from the southeast would pose an exception and require landing on the short runway? There need to be basic procedures in place, guidelines to adhere to, and, most importantly, good policies in place to generate meaningful exceptions.

The second part of a system of exception monitoring deals with a set of standardized actions to be taken to cure the exceptions and get everything back on track. It's here where some experience, creativity, and common sense are needed.

Exception monitoring isn't part of planning. Planning has ended before we get to do exception monitoring. Now we're in a phase of the replenishment process where the exception message indicates a deviation from the plan that requires action from the materials planner. This is where a good materials planner separates himself from the rest.

Finally, we need to periodically evaluate whether the exceptions occur so regularly that at one point in time, they represent the rule. In that sense, exception monitoring is a circle of continuous optimization of the materials planning process and needs to get the attention it deserves.

One of the more important points to consider is how, when, and in which mode you run MRP. We discuss these points in the next section.

7.2.1 How to Initiate the MRP Run

What the engine is for a sports car, the MRP run is for materials planning. It usually runs during the night, delivering a vast amount of information, order proposals, adjustments, and exception messages for us to use in the morning. It balances supply and demand, detects shortages and surplus, makes suggestions, and warns us of impeding problems. It's undoubtedly the heart and soul of any MRP and supports automation, provides transparency, and takes over the heavy lifting from the materials planner. The MRP run needs to be set up and coordinated in a joint effort between the planning department and IT. There are many options on how the MRP run can be run. Periodicity, run type, and run parameters have to be discussed, understood, and decided upon for the MRP run to deliver good results.

Periodicity of the MRP Run

In terms of periodicity, most companies decide to run MRP just once every 24 hours, usually overnight. As MRP operates with daily increments (its shortest time unit is "date"), and generally speaking, it doesn't make much sense to run it more than once a day. Very often people argue that a sales order that is entered at 2 p.m. in the afternoon needs an MRP run to have a planned order generated so that the sales requirement can be fulfilled right away. Nothing could be further from a sense-making business procedure. If a sales order that doesn't find available inventory at 2 p.m. can make a customer happy when the MRP run generates an order proposal at 2:30 p.m., then your organization is also capable of delivering finished product from that production order—maybe by traveling through a wormhole and fixing the supplier lead time.

No, it doesn't work this way. If the product is made-to-stock (MTS), the MRP run doesn't need to create an order proposal, unless there's a shortage, but then the MRP run has time to adjust the plan because the customer is told to wait. If the product is made-to-order (MTO), then the customer will have to wait anyway... as long as the total replenishment lead time (TRLT). In that case, there's no need to create an order proposal at 2:30 p.m., but it can wait until the next day (unless your TRLT is less than a day, in which case, you should use assemble-to-order [ATO]). In assembly processing, the MRP run isn't needed to generate an order proposal. The sales order will do it directly and automatically as part of the process. When the product is promised and manufactured as ATO, any required quantities in a sales order item will immediately generate a planned order, production order, or repetitive order that can be checked for capacity availability and be directly placed in the production program.

The other question is the following: Should you run MRP in longer intervals than 24 hours? That choice greatly depends on your business environment. Naturally, if the smallest planning unit in MRP is one day, and you run MRP once a week, you might miss an adjustment, an exception message, or a necessary order proposal by six days. Most companies run MRP at night when it doesn't occupy processing resources and provides new results readily available first thing in the morning. That, of course, isn't the case if you're operating globally. If you're headquarters in Tennessee start the run at midnight, then the China plant is planned after 1 p.m.

If you're concerned about runtime, you can always get the Business Suite on SAP HANA, which can make your MRP run ten thousand times faster than before. All these concerns about speed, frequency, and runtime are valid, but far more important is a good setup based on solid understanding of the process and what it can do for you.

Don't apply more technology, buy more tools, or run the MRP run more frequently in the hopes of fixing your problems. Include the MRP in the overall system and make it work the way it's supposed to run.

The Type of MRP Run

You can start the planning run in two different ways. Depending on which of the following you choose, the system selects the materials that ought to be planned:

▸ **Regenerative run (NEUPL mode)**
All materials in the planning file are planned.

▸ **Net change run (NETCH or NETPL mode)**
Only materials that have received MRP-relevant changes since the last MRP run are planned.

To understand these modes of planning, think of a reservation agent with United Airlines. As ticket reservations are received, flights are being filled with passenger reservations on a predetermined flight operations plan. If everything goes well and the weather holds, these flights will take off and land with all those passengers at the planned departure and arrival times. When, however, variability happens and a storm comes in, there will be a lot of rerouting, reshuffling, and cancellations.

There must be some sort of program that airlines use to help them automatically find and book tickets on alternate planes to get the passengers to their destination through an alternate route. They likely don't run that program for every passenger on every flight but only when there is a need for it. In the same way, you can think about net change planning. You only run it on those materials that need planning, and you leave the others alone. The real advantage with net change planning is that the planning run creates MRP lists only for those materials it plans. When you call up the collective list of MRP lists (Transaction MD06) with the date of last night's run, then you'll get a list of only those materials that are of interest to the planner who manages exceptions.

Like the reservation agent, you don't want to look at every ticket every day.

Setting Up the MRP Run

The MRP run, as discussed before, usually runs at night using a batch job so it starts automatically with predefined settings. That batch run can be executed for the entire company using a sequence with which it runs plant by plant in the mode we discussed before. In Figure 7.12, you can see a customized sequence depicting the order in which to run the individual plants.

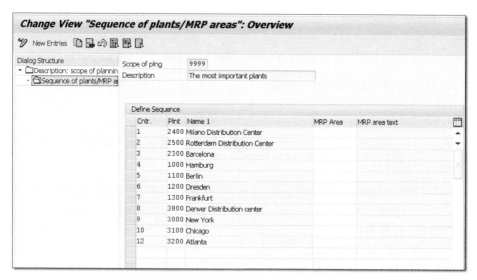

Figure 7.12 Customizing the Sequence of the MRP Run

In the sequence, you might find it necessary to run certain plants multiple times because stock transport orders request and deliver product and parts from other plants in the same network of operations. In that case, a plant might place a demand on another plant, and the first plant might have to be planned again after it receives yet another demand within the network. The effective setup of the sequence of MRP planning runs requires some thinking and needs to be set up carefully.

But the automated, nightly batch run isn't the only way to start the planning run. You might also use one of the online transactions to start it manually:

▸ Transaction MD01 runs across the entire plant—but only one, specific plant— and explodes any BOMs if there is a demand for the product. SAP calls this multilevel planning.

▸ Transaction MD03 runs MRP for one specific product and explodes its BOM (multilevel planning), or you use Transaction MD03 to plan for exactly one material with the explosion of the BOM (single-level planning).

In either one of these transactions, you'll have to set parameters in the initial screen to control how the run is being carried out.

You can use these transactions by calling up the respective transaction code, or you can configure a transaction call from, let's say, Transaction MD04. This is very helpful when you analyze a material, change its policy, and then like to see the results it will produce. Figure 7.13 is an example screenshot from Transaction MD02.

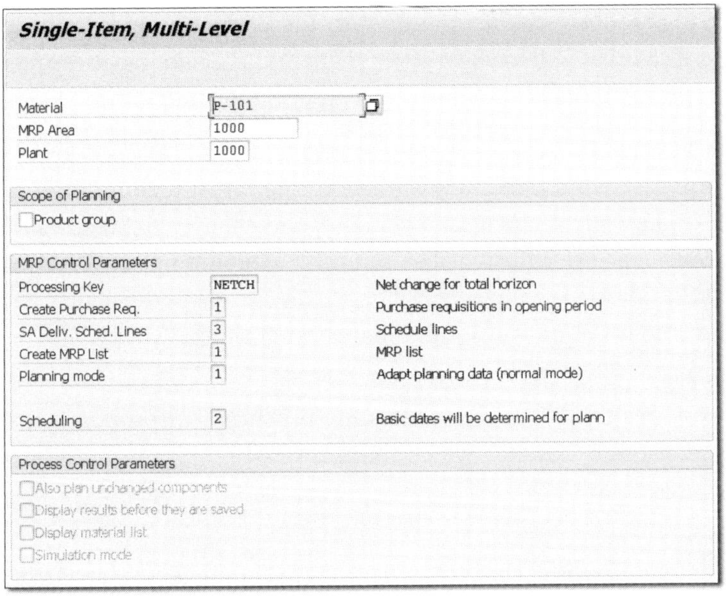

Figure 7.13 Starting the MRP Run Manually with Transaction MD02

The parameters you need to set are in the MRP CONTROL PARAMETERS section. We already discussed the first one, PROCESSING KEY, which is set to NETCH for netchange mode. The second parameter CREATE PURCHASE REQ. determines in which planning horizons the run is generating purchase requisitions. You can limit this to an opening period, and outside of the opening period the MRP run creates planned orders.

The parameter SA DELIV. SCHED. LINES handles the automatic generation of schedule line items for a scheduling agreement if one exists for an item being planned.

Whether to create an MRP List or not is defined in the parameter setting for CREATE MRP LIST. The MRP list is a snapshot in time of the stock requirements list and can be generated by the MRP run right after its done planning for each item. MRP lists can be viewed with Transaction MD05 and Transaction MD06.

The PLANNING MODE setting controls how the system deals with procurement proposals (planned orders, purchase requisitions, scheduling agreement lines) from the last planning run, which aren't yet firmed, during the next planning run. Usually, the master plan is adjusted in the planning run to adapt it to either new dates or new quantities. If a requirements quantity is increased, the system automatically adjusts the quantity of the corresponding procurement proposal. If changes are made in the BOM or material master, the planning mode controls whether or not these changes will have an effect in planning. There are three possible settings for planning mode in the initial screen of the planning run:

▶ **Planning mode 1**
The run doesn't re-create but rather adjust the existing procurement proposal. Changes in date and quantity, changes in demand, and changes to lot-size procedure and/or MRP type are adjusted. The run only explodes BOMs for order proposals that were adjusted, which greatly improves system performance and helps reduce the amount of new order numbers.

▶ **Planning mode 2**
The system reexplodes the BOMs for all existing procurement proposals that aren't firmed and also for those for which the dates and quantities don't have to be adjusted.

▶ **Planning mode 3**
Existing procurement proposals that aren't firmed are completely deleted from the database and re-created. The system then reexplodes the BOMs. We use this mode when testing a new policy to make sure that everything that was changed is considered during the planning run. However, it isn't recommended to use this planning mode in mass planning because it will soon exhaust your order number range.

The last parameter Scheduling has two settings. Either the MRP run schedules using the basic dates, or it performs lead time scheduling. In the latter, the routing is used for scheduling, and besides a more detailed scheduling result, the MRP run can also generate capacity requirements for the planned orders. That has the added advantage of you being able to perform capacity planning, sequencing, leveling, and scheduling with planned orders.

7.2.2 Exception Cards

Within our system of effective materials planning, you can use standardized action sheets to document specific exception messages and suggest procedures to fix the situation. We call these notes exception cards, on which you can describe the conditions that cause the generation of the specific exception such as a missed conversion date, failed delivery, or a dip into safety stock. You can also list the actions that can be taken to take care of the situation and provide a graphic that gives deeper insight into the problem to avoid the exception in the future.

In Figure 7.14, you can see an example of an exception card for exception message 10 (reschedule in), which is assigned to group 7.

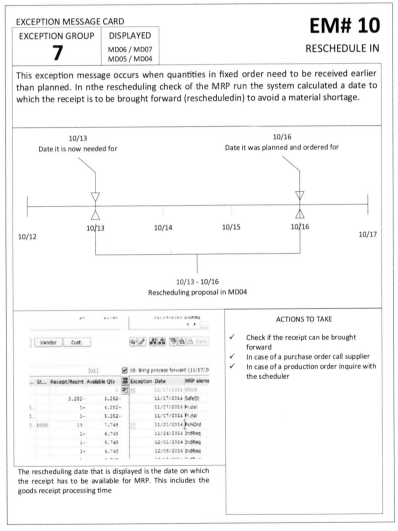

Figure 7.14 Example of an Exception Message Card for Exception Number 10

Different companies require different procedures on how to deal with certain exceptions. That is why it might be advantageous to develop a set of exception cards and distribute them among planners. It helps to standardize the system, keep the portfolios clean, and lower the amount of exceptions you're dealing with.

7.2.3 Monitoring Exception Messages

Exception messages are displayed primarily in four transactions:

▶ Transaction MD04 to display the dynamically created stock requirements situations for an individual material

▶ Transaction MD05 to display the MRP list, a snapshot from the time when the MRP run last planned the material

▶ Transaction MD06 to display a collective list of materials with their respective MRP lists

▶ Transaction MD07 to display a collective list of materials with their respective stock/requirements situations

These four transactions make up the monitoring system you have available in standard SAP ERP. Using them correctly and knowing what information each of these can provide is essential for a good monitoring system. In the following subsections, you'll learn how to use and apply stock/requirements situations, MRP lists, and collective displays to sort, filter, and prioritize exception messages for effective materials planning.

But first, we want to make clear the difference between Transaction MD06 and Transaction MD07 (or Transaction MD05 and Transaction MD04).

The Difference between Transaction MD06 and Transaction MD07

The difference between Transaction MD06 and Transaction MD07 is an important one and, if understood and correctly applied, can make a world of a difference in the way you monitor your exceptions. Transaction MD07 is a list of dynamically generated stock/requirements lists as they represent themselves right at the moment you call it up. Transaction MD06 is a collective list of snapshots of what the stock requirements list looked like at the very moment when the MRP run created it. If you enter Transaction MD06 with a date, then you'll only get the items touched by the MRP run on that date. Therefore, Transaction MD06 should be run if you have a daily monitoring process in place. Of course, you should start the process first thing in the morning (otherwise you get outdated MRP lists) so that you only look at those items that were planned since yesterday's planning run—and not the entire portfolio.

Don't forget to enter the Transaction MD06 with today's date (if NETCH MRP runs after midnight). That way, you're presented with a list of items that were planned this morning—and nothing else.

Transaction MD07, on the other hand, is the transaction to use throughout the rest of the day because it's always current and dynamically built every time you look at the situation. There is a REFRESH button in Transaction MD04 (the transaction that pops up when you double-click on an item in the list display of Transaction MD07), and even though you can view exception messages there, it's not the primary transaction to *monitor* exceptions. Also note that in Transaction MD07, you won't receive any messages related to newly created proposals or abnormal ends (usually found in groups 4 and 8). These are only visible in Transaction MD06/Transaction MD05.

Transaction MD06 and Transaction MD07 are both important transactions in their own right. But they do different things, and you'll have to understand their meaning to use them the right way for utmost efficiency in your planning and monitoring process.

Working with Transaction MD07

In Transaction MD07, you get a complete list of all materials assigned to your MRP controller portfolio. That list has, among other information, red, yellow, and green traffic lights. The materials are usually sorted that way: red lights first, then yellow, then green (you can change that sorting sequence) specifying where a material falls in terms of its stock days of supply. Therefore, you can see at a glance where you fell short in delivering and where you carry too much stock. That is very good information for your daily monitoring. You could use Transaction MD07 at any time of the day (remember, it's a dynamically created, current stock requirements situation) and take a quick look at red lights (dangerously low inventory) or do something about your green lights (inventory reduction).

So Transaction MD07 doesn't really represent your exception monitor. Despite the fact that it shows exception messages and you can sort your list by them, it's not a good transaction to monitor exception messages because it lacks focus for effective tending to exception messages. Transaction MD07 with its complete list of all materials assigned to an MRP controller key is an excellent transaction to find outdated elements that are in the way of the MRP run being able to generate meaningful exception messages. To use Transaction MD07 for housecleaning, go into the list, and click on the binoculars icon as shown in Figure 7.15.

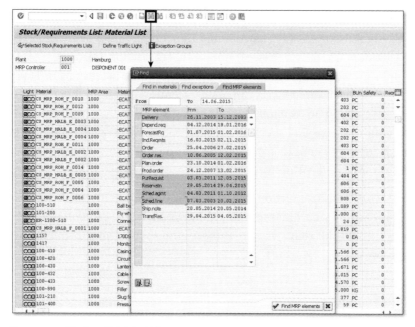

Figure 7.15 Finding Outdated Elements*

Full-Color Figures

Full-color versions of figures marked with an asterisk (*) are available in the supplemental downloads for this book at *www.sap-press.com/3745*. The figures in the e-book are also full-color.

Clicking the binoculars icon brings up a window where you can go to the ELEMENTS tab and fill in a date in the To field. That means you want to select all materials that have elements older than said date. You can even pick the specific elements you want to investigate. As a result, you'll see the screen shown in Figure 7.16.

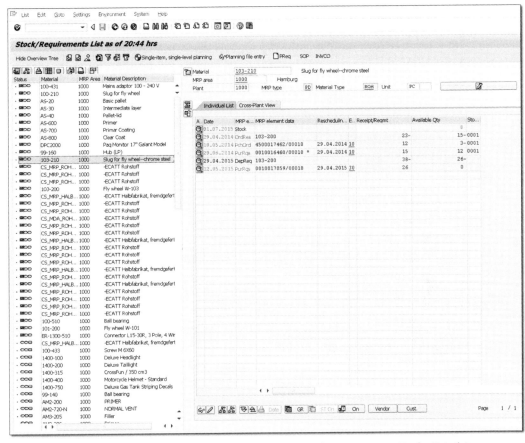

Figure 7.16 List of Materials with Outdated Elements and the Stock Requirements List for Details*

You can see a list of all the materials that have at least one of the outdated elements selected earlier. You can now go through the list and view the details. The outdated elements are now marked in blue within the STOCK/REQUIREMENTS LIST screen.

You can also use Transaction MD07 to see, at a glance, how you're doing with your safety stock planning. If you're working in an MTS environment, you should forecast your product's sales and cover any variability—the difference between forecasted and actual sales, the lack of adherence to planned lead times, and any interruptions—with a safety stock. We highly favor dynamic safety stock over the static safety stock in MRP 2. You can have the dynamic safety stock controlled by way of the coverage profile. That type of safety stock is expressed in days and therefore can be assigned to many products. It's also visible in Transaction

MD07, if you know how to set up and interpret the lights. A range of coverage profile then allows you to set a target safety stock level as well as a maximum stock level. If, for example, you set 5 days as the target and 20 days as the max for a group of products in your warehouse, you're telling the system that there should be enough inventory left over, after you cover your forecast, to get you through 5 days of average sales, if you sell more than what was predicted and forecasted. But the system also cuts the supply (if you have lot sizing EX) so that your inventory never exceeds more than 20 days to be held in stock. If you work with fixed lot sizes or minimum lot sizes, there might be the occasional excess stock (that's when you get an exception 25).

The system is now able to plan for these targets but, as we all know, there is variability, and not everything will turn out to be on par. But you can monitor these levels with Transaction MD07. When calling up your list for the product group for which you've maintained the 5-day target and 20-day max, you can set the traffic lights with a range for the following:

< red >> 5 days >> yellow >> 20 days >> green >

This way, you'll see a display where all the products that have less than 5 days of supply in inventory will be on top of the list with a red light. All the products that have inventory which lasts for at least 5 days and less than 15 days will be in yellow, and all the products with excess stock over 15 days will have a green light at the bottom of the list.

Using Transaction MD06 as Your Exception Monitor

Many people use Transaction MD07, and almost everybody uses Transaction MD04, but not many people use Transaction MD06 or Transaction MD05. You might wonder why you should use Transaction MD06 when the information is already outdated because Transaction MD06/Transaction MD05 is a snapshot in time, that is, a stock/requirements list as it was created at the time of the last planning run. It's called the MRP list because it has the time stamp of the last MRP run. When you use Transaction MD07, you'll get a list with all materials belonging to an MRP controller (or a product group) and their associated, dynamically created stock/requirements lists. This is a good thing if you're cleaning up outdated elements, but not if you want to get in the mode of an exception-minded business and want to tend to those things getting off plan only. Transaction MD06 is the transaction to use for that because you have the ability to limit the list to a certain date (other than in Transaction MD07 where you're asked to provide a FROM and a TO date in the initial screen).

Because the planning run creates the MRP list as the last step of the planning sequence, the MRP list has a time stamp and is, or was, valid only at that specific time and date. By entering yesterday's date, you'll only get MRP lists that were created yesterday. Therefore, you get a list of all materials that were planned yesterday—and no others—which is a great thing because no one wants to work off a list that includes both materials you need to look at and materials you don't. Why look at materials that were not planned and therefore haven't received an MRP-relevant change since the last time you looked at it?

As in Figure 7.17, call up Transaction MD06 first thing in the morning with yesterday's date if the MRP run runs before midnight (and with today's date if MRP runs after midnight).

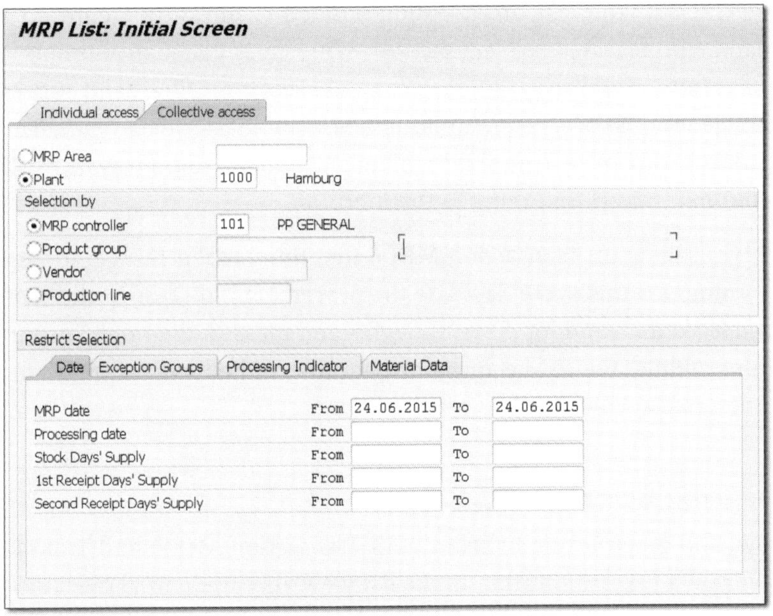

Figure 7.17 Initial Screen of Transaction MD06

The list that will come up is limited to only those materials planned by the MRP date on the date indicated. As shown in Figure 7.18, only nine materials were planned on 24.06.2015. And that is all you need to look at and worry about.

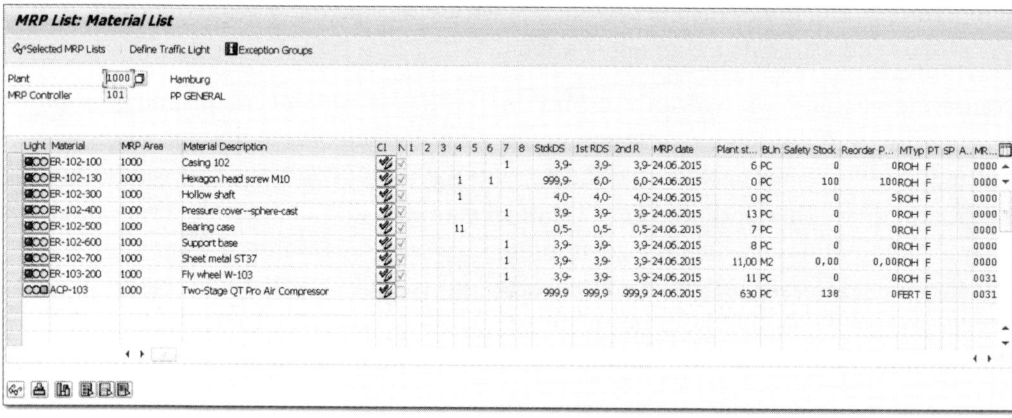

Figure 7.18 MRP Lists Generated on 24.06.2015*

It becomes apparent that if you work the right way with Transaction MD06, you'll move much closer to being an exception-minded business. In Figure 7.18, you can see that the initial screen of Transaction MD06 gives you many options to limit the list of materials you're looking at. You can prioritize, filter, and sort by exception message groups, processing indicator, or even master data fields. This will give you utmost control and the ability to build a preconfigured way of working through your exceptions first thing in the morning.

Get in the habit of calling up Transaction MD06 first thing when you get to your desk in the morning. Do this every day! Use the processing indicator to check off those items you looked at, and jot down thoughts and ideas in the notes section. After you do this awhile, the list becomes manageable and allows for quick and focused exception management.

Setting Up the Traffic Lights

The red, yellow, and green traffic lights in both Transaction MD06 and Transaction MD07 give you a quick indication in the list view about potential overstocking or understocking. A red light will come up if you have a demand in the past that is still unfulfilled. How far in the past this demand element lies is specified by the negative days of supply shown in a column in the list display. A green light, against common belief, doesn't mean everything is in order. It means that there is more stock than we need to fulfill requirements in the future. Green lights, therefore, can alert you of too much inventory held. Yellow lights are assigned to materials where demand and supply is in perfect balance.

SAP allows you to change the traffic light settings to tell the system when you want to be alerted with a red or green light and what range is acceptable to have an item with a balanced demand and supply. The standard setting for the traffic lights looks is shown in Figure 7.19.

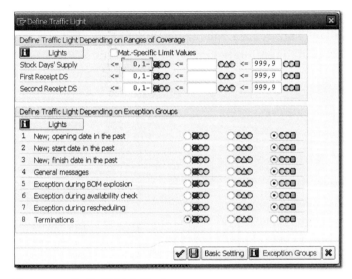

Figure 7.19 Traffic Light Setting*

Now, you can set up these traffic lights as you wish and build a list that works to your advantage and gives you the most information at a glance. For example, a certain client developed their own particularly useful traffic light system particularly useful. In this system, they set up the list so that it's sorted from most urgent materials handling down to long-term opportunities. Therefore, they set the monitor so that materials with stock days of supply below safety levels (and not only after they are overdue) have a red light. Anything that has receipts coming in to cover demand within an acceptable time frame gets a yellow light, and anything that has too many receipts coming too early—and therefore needs to be expedited out—gets a green light.

Even better is that those annoying situations where they have little inventory and no demand anytime in the future (you know, the ones with 999.9 days of supply) get no traffic light at all. So, in essence, they created a fourth light.

Notice in Figure 7.20 how they set the limits so that they sort materials according to their STOCK DAYS' SUPPLY (anything that has fewer than 2 days to cover demand gets a red light). Then every material that gets covered for 11 days of demand—with receipts or actual inventory—gets a yellow light, and everything that's covered up to 19 days is green. All materials that have coverage for more than 19 days, or no demand at all, will not get any light at all. Therefore, the last category isn't really urgent but poses an opportunity for inventory reduction.

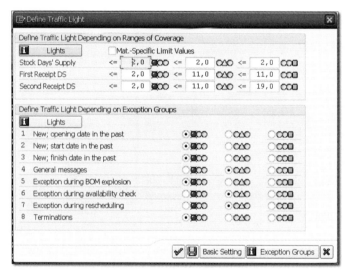

Figure 7.20 Customized Traffic Light Setting*

They also use the traffic lights for exception messages—so that the exception groups they consider more important are sorted above the ones that aren't so urgent combined with the ranges of cover (Figure 7.21).

Even though we prefer to work in the monitors without sorting and without checking off materials from the list, this provides a great solution for when you want to go through the list from top to bottom and check off the materials you consider "done."

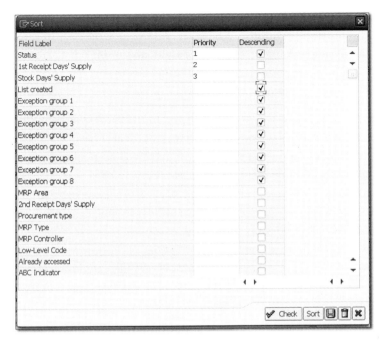

Figure 7.21 Sorting in the Monitor

7.2.4 Putting It All Together

Exception monitoring, the third pillar in our system of effective materials planning with SAP, can be a daunting, if not overwhelming task because of the sheer amount of materials, exceptions, and notifications a planner has to deal with on a daily basis. Often, the overwhelming majority of these messages are meaningless and generated out of erroneous basic data settings, outdated documents, and missing procedural control.

It's therefore essential to streamline and organize the materials planner's workload to deal with exceptional situations after planning is done and the real world sets in. Without a well-thought-out system of intelligent exception monitoring, the materials planner will always struggle to keep on top of the replenishment process, and it's nearly impossible to holistically optimize service and inventory levels.

What does such a system look like? For one, you must provide some time during the busy day to tend to exception monitoring. Monitoring exceptional situations must happen every day. The best time of day to do this is most likely the first 20 to 30 minutes in the morning right at the beginning of your workday. In most organizations, the MRP run is doing its magic overnight, so the MRP lists are still current, and Transaction MD06 provides an excellent means to sort out and build your task list for the day to come.

Then, this system must provide a way to filter, sort, and prioritize the exception messages according to their urgency and importance. Note that if basic data is set up correctly, and the process is executed properly, there are no negligible messages. They all do mean something and have their own right to exist and alert you of an exception—a situation where the actual result strays from what was planned for. Still, there are exceptions that are less urgent and less involved than others, and the materials planner can't possibly look at every message for every material every day. SAP has already done a great job in assigning exception messages to standard groups. All expediting messages, for example, are allocated to group 7. You can easily use these exception groups for your prioritization and work the "late in finishing" messages first, then the "late in staring" messages second, and eventually expedite orders in the afternoon. Of course, you can define your own groups, but the standard provides a brilliant starting point for your sorting, filtering, and prioritization.

There are other tasks that need to be taken care of in the busy day of a tactical materials planner: converting order proposals into fixed receipts, expediting late or early deliveries, and avoiding stock-outs at all cost. But don't forget to leave some time at the end of the day to reduce superfluous inventory. The items with green lights in Transaction MD07 have too much inventory too early, and there are lots of opportunities to reduce your dead stock and overall inventory levels. The latter task mostly falls through the cracks as the planner is busy doing "more important" things such as firefighting. It's an absolute must that you organize your day ahead of time so that you get to perform all necessary tasks of a tactical materials planner and don't get bogged down with fabricated urgencies and seeming disasters.

Now, let's talk about an example of how you could start building such a system of intelligent exception monitoring. Figure 7.22 portrays a possible day in the life of a tactical materials planner. Obviously, this is a suggested approach to exception monitoring and other daily tasks that can be customized to your own needs. A lot more detail can be added to this poster, and we recommend standardizing the procedures in this or a similar way for all planners across the plant or even throughout the company. By no means do we suggest limiting the materials planner's creativity in dealing with exceptional situations, but rather we provide a basic approach for reacting and curing exceptional situations when execution strays from the plan.

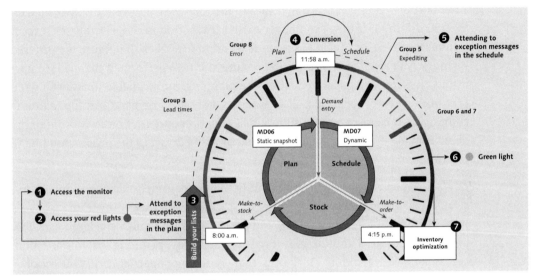

Figure 7.22 A System of Daily Exception Monitoring

In this example, the planner could get started in the morning with Transaction MD06 ❶ and tend to the red lights first ❷. These are materials where we're getting awfully close to running out. Then we'll start prioritizing by exception messages, or better, exception groups ❸. Group 3 contains exceptions dealing with late finishes. As stated previously, these are the most critical exceptions. Group 2 messages are next in line as these are late in starting—a conversion date was missed, or a purchase order was not send out. Then we'll look at all those materials where the planning run abruptly stopped because of some issues with the basic data. Do you have a material in the last run that was marked for deletion? Was there a status that called for different processing?

As the day moves on, our Transaction MD06 display becomes outdated, and it's time to toggle over to Transaction MD07 ❹. After you switch, you'll be faced with a complete list of all the materials for your MRP controller key. Any red lights you see now are either leftovers from yesterday or something happened previously in the morning that caused the red light to come on. Other than that, there should either be yellows or greens. As we mentioned before, the yellow lights are for materials where demand is in perfect balance with supply. However, there might be some materials for which you must turn an order proposal into a fixed receipt (purchase order or production order) today.

After that is all done, expediting comes to the forefront, and vendors are called ❺. We can ask them if they can deliver earlier (exception message 10), later (exception message 15), or cancel the order (exception message 20) because the ordered quantity isn't needed anymore. Expediting is a task performed manually. Expediting messages are generated when the planning run is unable to adjust a fixed receipt or fixed order proposal, so it meets a changed demand. All the planning run can do is notify you of a suboptimal situation and ask you to do something about it manually—picking up the phone or going down to the production line to interfere.

Toward the end of the day, we hopefully find some time to deal with inventory-related exceptions (dipping into safety stock [96] or excess inventory above a maximum range of coverage [25]) and green lights (too much stock too early) ❻. This is something that often gets forgotten, and most planning systems are more concerned with avoiding stock-outs than reducing superfluous inventory on a regular basis. Yes, there is the occasional inventory-reduction program, but only rarely do we see steps and procedures in place to continuously optimize inventory levels ❼ and diligently monitoring upper control limits for inventory holdings.

The day in the life of a tactical materials planner as shown here may or may not work in your organization. It doesn't matter. What matters is that you have some system that your planners can get started with and eventually improve. Without any guidance or understanding of the various elements and piecing it together, the materials planner will develop his own system to get by—with varying degrees of success. Within such an organization that is in survival mode, there is no accountability or standardization. Success is hard to measure because you have nothing to measure against.

To have an effective system, you must ceaselessly avoid red lights, relentlessly reduce exception messages, and continuously scrutinize green lights. After you make it a habit, it will become easy, and you'll open up an enormous amount of free time to tend to analytics and strategies (policies). Besides, being in control and managing variability is much more fun than "transacting" all over the place, not knowing what's causing you trouble and being unable to make a difference.

7.3   Using the SAP Add-On Tool MRP Exception Monitor

The Exception Monitor is an SAP add-on tool and therefore not available in the standard SAP ERP. But it's an SAP transaction that was developed within the SAP namespace, by SAP Consulting in Germany, and it can be used without interfaces or data migration. In fact, it's a collection of standard transactions and reports so that you can manage exceptions in one place. The MRP Exception Monitor is a report with which you can not only view exceptions but also take action, all conveniently available in one place. Its primary purpose is to provide you with an all-encompassing cockpit to attend to the following situations:

- Critical sales orders (not yet confirmed, late)
- Critical production orders (missing parts, backlog)
- Erroneous goods movements
- Critical purchase orders (delayed, excess quantities, current backlog, future backlog, push in, push out)
- Undercoverage or overcoverage
- Missing parts

The MRP Exception Monitor provides an overview of exceptions in operational MRP and displays relevant MRP data. These include general error messages from the stock-/requirements list, for example, based on master data checks (material master, info records, etc.), or due to overcoverage, undercoverage, or delays. Therefore, it provides a very detailed extension to our system of exception monitoring with, primarily but not limited to, Transaction MD06. With the MRP Exception Monitor, you'll get an overview to all the movement data and its current state. Movement data that has critical planning status (such as delayed sales orders or production orders with missing parts) are aggregated and displayed with the possibility to drill down into further detail. MRP controllers therefore have an excellent overview of any errors, warnings, or notifications in their stock, requirements, and supply elements.

The following screenshots show the reporting functionalities in the MRP Exception Monitor, so you can see how this tool may be integrated into your system of intelligent exception monitoring.

First, in the SELECTION SCREEN, you can limit the display of exceptional situations to your specific choice and situation (see Figure 7.23).

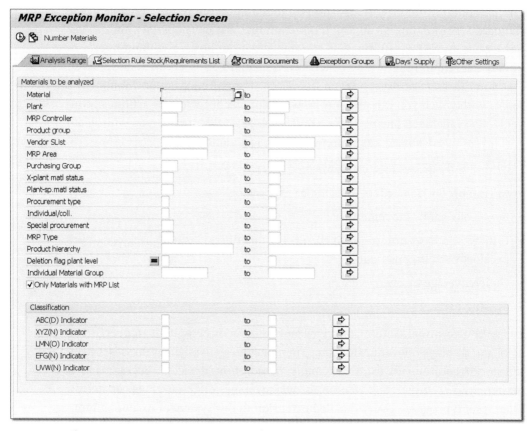

Figure 7.23 MRP Exception Monitor – Selection Analysis Range

Of course, you can limit the range of materials you want to display exceptions for. Figure 7.24 shows the inclusions and exclusions you have at your disposal. Note that you can select by classification and therefore limit the display, for example, to AXE materials only.

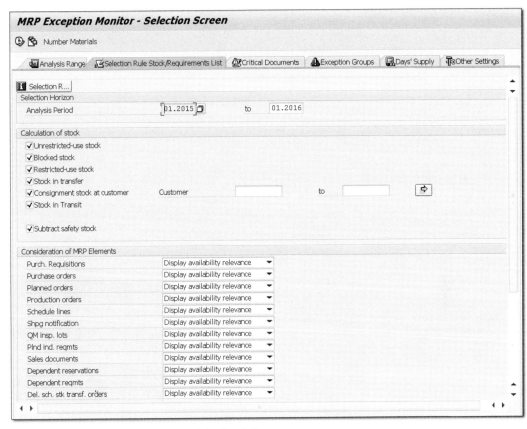

Figure 7.24 MRP Exception Monitor – Selection Rules

Furthermore, you can select by rule as shown in Figure 7.25. Define what types of stock you want to take into focus, and select what MRP elements from the stock/requirements situation you want to consider and how these are to be displayed in the result screen.

A very useful function is the ability to select only those documents you deem critical for the specific situation you want to analyze. This way, you can focus on sales or display supply elements and its exceptions only. The results screen therefore can be customized to the specific role a planner wants to take on. For instance, if you check the DELAYED PURCHASE ORDERS checkbox, then all purchase orders (in the time range you've defined in the selection rule) from a delivery date in the past in Transaction MD04 are analyzed.

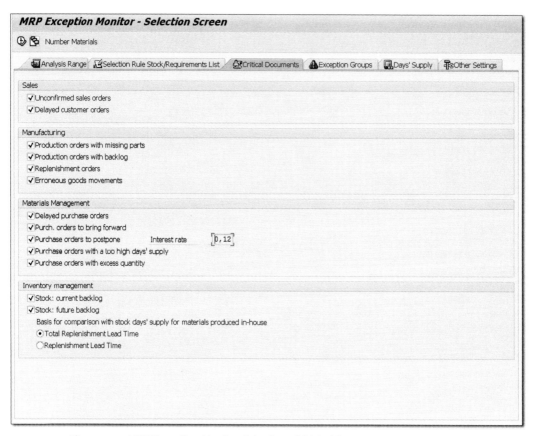

Figure 7.25 MRP Exception Monitor Selection of Critical Documents

As shown in Figure 7.26, you can also select by exception groups. This feature is also available in Transaction MD06 and provides the basis for prioritized exception monitoring. In addition to the Transaction MD06 selection, you might further prioritize your display (the way exceptions are sorted) with the assignments of exceptions to another grouping by DELAYS, OVERCOVERAGE, UNDERCOVERAGE, MASTER DATA, MISSING PARTS, OTHERS, and CHANGED PURCHASE PROPOSALS.

In the DAYS' SUPPLY tab (Figure 7.27), you define the traffic light settings for the material view, determine the intervals for the coverage/replenishment time matrix in the coverage view, and specify the days' supply limits for purchase orders with long days' supply.

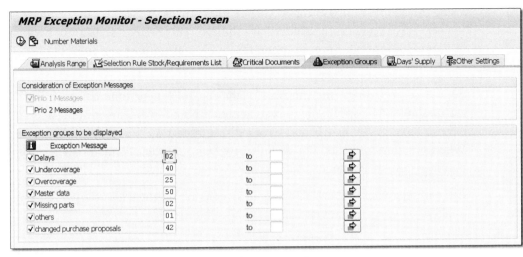

Figure 7.26 MRP Exception Monitor – Selection by Exception Group

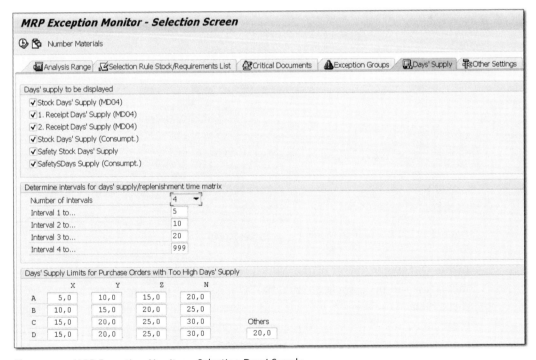

Figure 7.27 MRP Exception Monitor – Selection Days' Supply

Using the color settings of the MATERIAL VIEW, fields of the relevant columns of the MATERIAL VIEW can be colored as required. This increases visibility because in Transaction MD06, not all exception or critical statuses are available for all materials.

Besides color settings, the intervals of the replenishment time/coverage matrix can be shown. The specified intervals apply for both replenishment-time-axis and coverage-axis of the matrix and have a direct impact on the result in the matrix. When defining intervals, the bounds in which the relevant materials are compared are also determined.

After all selections are made, the result screens are displayed, as shown in Figure 7.28.

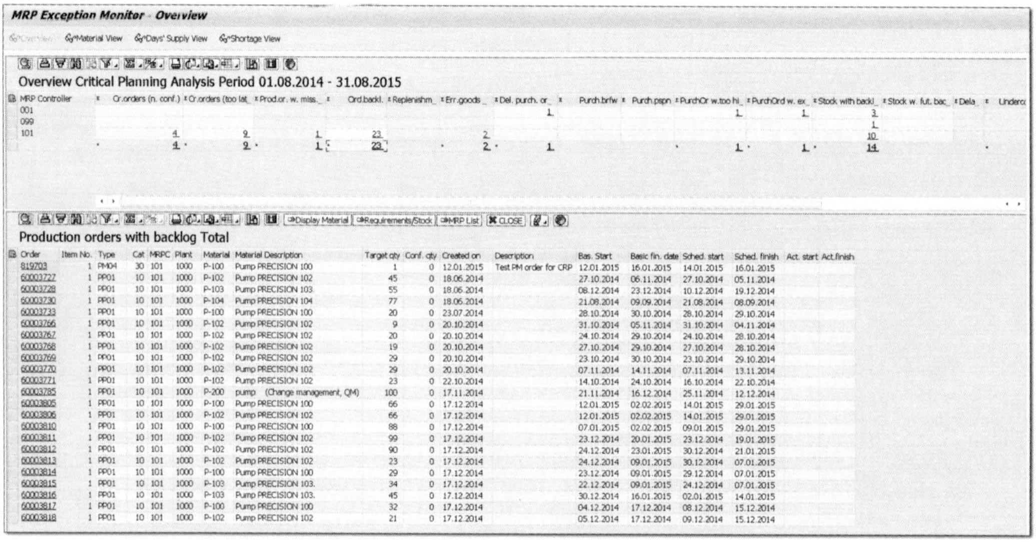

Figure 7.28 MRP Exception Monitor – Overview Screen

In the OVERVIEW screen of the MRP Exception Monitor, you can select specific messages, and the associated materials will come up in a list on the lower part of the screen. For example, we selected 23 messages in the ORDBACKL (order backlogs) column, and the related materials details are listed accordingly.

To navigate to the material view of the MRP Exception Monitor, select an MRP controller number and click MATERIAL VIEW. The Material View (Figure 7.29) allows all the materials of an MRP controller to be displayed with the relevant planning status. In addition to standard information for the material, the relevant MRP exceptions and movement data errors are also listed. Differentiated and configurable coverage and demand information indicates the past and future stock situation.

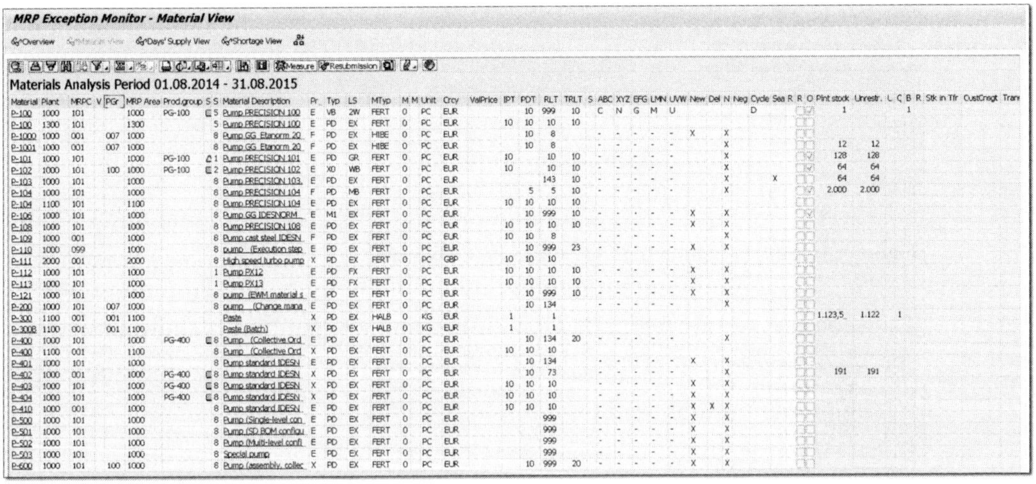

Figure 7.29 MRP Exception Monitor – Material View (Part 1)

In Figure 7.30, you can see more information in the MATERIAL VIEW by scrolling to the right.

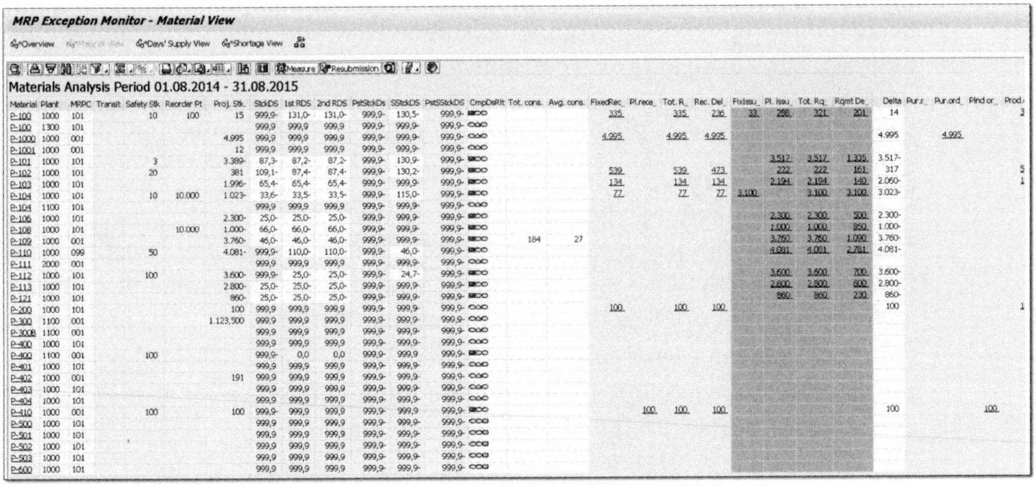

Figure 7.30 MRP Exception Monitor – Material View (Part 2)

Aside from many other views for various analytics, the MRP Exception Monitor also provides an overview to missing parts or shortage situations as depicted in Figure 7.31.

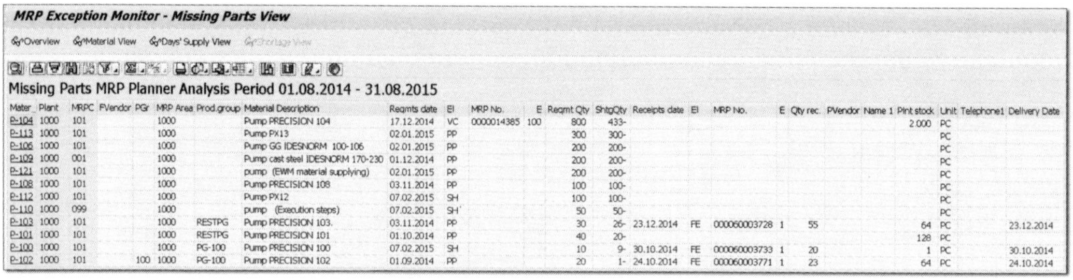

Mater	Plant	MRPC	FVendor	PGr	MRP Area	Prod.group	Material Description	Reqmts date	El	MRP No.	E	Reqmt Qty	ShtgQty	Receipts date	El	MRP No.	E	Qty rec.	PVendor	Name 1	Plnt stock	Unit	Telephone1	Delivery Date
P-104	1000	101			1000		Pump PRECISION 104	17.12.2014	VC	0000014385	100	800	433-								2.000	PC		
P-113	1000	101			1000		Pump PX13	02.01.2015	PP			300	300-									PC		
P-106	1000	101			1000		Pump GG IDESNORM 100-106	02.01.2015	PP			200	200-									PC		
P-109	1000	001			1000		Pump cast steel IDESNORM 170-230	01.12.2014	PP			200	200-									PC		
P-121	1000	101			1000		pump (EWM material supplying)	02.01.2015	PP			200	200-									PC		
P-108	1000	101			1000		Pump PRECISION 108	03.11.2014	PP			100	100-									PC		
P-112	1000	101			1000		Pump PX12	07.02.2015	SH			100	100-									PC		
P-110	1000	099			1000		pump (Execution steps)	07.02.2015	SH			50	50-									PC		
P-103	1000	101			1000	RESTPG	Pump PRECISION 103.	03.11.2014	PP			30	26-	23.12.2014	FE	000060003728	1	55			64	PC		23.12.2014
P-101	1000	101			1000	RESTPG	Pump PRECISION 101	01.10.2014	PP			40	20-								128	PC		
P-100	1000	101			1000	PG-100	Pump PRECISION 100	07.02.2015	SH			10	9-	30.10.2014	FE	000060003733	1	20			1	PC		30.10.2014
P-102	1000	101		100	1000	PG-100	Pump PRECISION 102	01.09.2014	PP			20	1-	24.10.2014	FE	000060003771	1	23			64	PC		24.10.2014

Figure 7.31 MRP Exception Monitor – Missing Parts View

The shortage, or missing parts view, lists materials that have a shortfall within a specified time period. To get to this view, select an MRP controller, and click SHORTAGE VIEW.

Detail views can also be displayed for all materials and movement data, which list the elements of the aggregated views. There are also further options for navigating to the standard transactions, Transaction MD04 and the like, of the respective data objects.

The MRP Exception Monitor represents an excellent extension and addition to round out your system of intelligent exception monitoring. With the MRP Exception Monitor, the materials planner is empowered to manage exceptional situations and close the gap between planned and actual results.

7.4 Summary

Exception monitoring represents the third pillar in our system of effective materials planning. As you set effective policy, your exceptions become more meaningful and significant. Now it's up to the planner to deal with these exceptional situations. We can't ignore any of the exceptions anymore. They all need to be analyzed and cured, and it becomes more important than ever that we wisely sort, filter, and prioritize the way we look at them.

You can build your own system of regular exception monitoring. There is an abundance of tools, features, and riggings that can be used in standard SAP to round out an organism of, not only monitoring, but also curing exception messages. Managing and dealing with exceptions is important, especially if you want to move your organization to a more exception-minded business. In an exception-minded business, the rule and principles stay (the strategy is adhered to and survives) while the exceptions breaking the rules are analyzed and cured to improve the rule or strategy. That is a very important aspect of an effective system of materials planning.

If you find that there isn't enough automatism in the SAP ERP approach to exception monitoring, take a more thorough look into what the MRP Exception Monitor provides.

Inventory optimization isn't a project—it's an ongoing effort.

8   Sustainable Inventory Optimization

Inventories have been the subject of discussions around operational excellence for quite some time now. Unfortunately, the initiatives aren't always aligned and integrated with an overall optimization effort. All too often, inventory changes are perceived as quick fixes, and if a balance sheet or profit and loss (P&L) statement needs improvement, managers quickly opt for inventory reduction as a solution. This is a dangerous thing to do because companies very often spiral into a death trap framed by excess inventory and frequent stock-outs.

Situations change, and any change might have an impact on the inventory. If the change isn't considered right away, it might cost you a lot of money in the form of stock-outs, lost sales, or excess inventory and cash being tied up and not available for other investments. The old adage of chasing the forecast is a specifically costly one. If you keep adjusting and modifying the forecast and everything that follows through the bill of materials (BOM), you're scheduling in, then scheduling out, and scheduling in again, and so on. At some point, you'll have to fix your orders and your outside vendors, and inside production managers will run back and forth with you for only so long before they will or will not deliver the goods to your inventory. All of that chasing the forecast actually doesn't represent any kind of planning but rather introduces unnecessary, unmanageable, and costly noise into the system of replenishment and inventory holdings.

The solution to the problem of forecast hunting is buffering. Materials planners have three buffers available:

▶ **Inventory**
A safety stock, or additional quantities of a material to buffer unforseen requirements.

▶ **Capacity**
Additional shifts (e.g., on Saturday morning), or increased supplier performance.

▶ **Time**

Waiting for the next receipt to cover additional demand.

Buffering in these three areas is what intuition will call for to counter the unknown for us in materials planning. The idea is to build a system of repeatable tasks so that we're using the three buffers of time, capacity, and inventory in the most effective way for any given situation at any given time.

Inventory Optimization Isn't a Project

Projects have a beginning and an end; inventory optimization doesn't. As pointed out previously in this book, a system of effective materials planning has four parts:

▶ Portfolio management and housecleaning of basic data and supply elements

▶ Policy setting after segmentation and classification of your materials portfolio

▶ Exception monitoring in the exception-minded business to avoid having to look at every part every day

▶ Inventory optimization to continuously and sustainably provide excellent service levels with minimum inventory investment

The last part, inventory optimization, is the ongoing effort to provide maximum availability with minimum stock holdings for any given demand situation. And because the demand situation changes all the time, the policies that were driving that balance when you went live with the SAP system may not hold water anymore. What's keeping your inventories optimized is the correct maintenance of basic data—replenishment type, lot-size procedures, safety stock settings, forecast parameters, lead times, and more—to the situation the individual item is under. Do we have consistent consumption, and are we able to forecast the demand? Does the item contribute a lot of value to our business or not? Does it have a short lead time? These and other questions will have to be answered before you can set the optimal parameters that drive automation and inventory optimization.

But if you answer the questions only once and don't adjust the parameters as the answers to these questions change over time, your parameters won't support automation or optimized inventory levels any more. The MRP run will generate supply proposals that don't conform to the paradigm of good service with minimum stock.

What usually happens during an SAP implementation is that due to the limitations in budget and time to go-live, only the most basic parameters are set up so the SAP system can be activated. Typically, the basic parameters are MRP type PD (maybe the occasional manual reorder level type, VB), lot-size procedure EX, and a static safety stock that's guesswork. The planned delivery time is a big unknown and will be set generously so that you'll usually receive the item way ahead of its requirement date. Then, after you've been using SAP for a while, the "inventory optimizers" come in and sell you a six-month project to get your basic data straight. This is a noble effort and yes, your planners need to understand all the parameters and how to set policy. But if you go through the tedious task to analyze and set up each individual part, your MRP controllers will learn a great deal about all the fields in the material master record, but they will also have to leave their families to move into the office.

And after all the materials are finally set up with the right policy, the situation changes. What was consistent consumption is no more; the material is procured from a different supplier, and therefore a different replenishment lead time takes effect; and the item becomes a slow mover and is replaced by another part. In the end, you'll have to start from the beginning. By that time, the inventory optimizers are long gone. As shown in Figure 8.1, these inventory optimization projects are very costly, both in inventory holdings as well as consulting, and they deliver only temporary improvement.

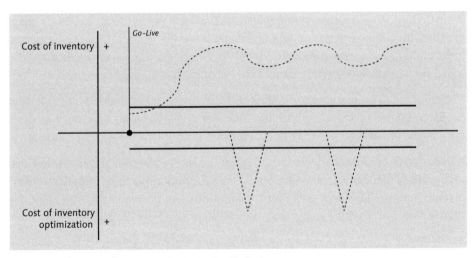

Figure 8.1 The Cost of Inventory Optimization Projects

So what should you do? Implement effective materials planning with portfolio management, automated policy setting on a periodic basis, continuous exception monitoring within the framework of the exception-minded business, and inventory optimization via an automated process that will become second nature to your MRP controller. Automation is key here, and so is managing by exception. If you have to look at each item every day and set up each item manually, you won't be able to keep control over your inventory and service levels.

The first one of a number of tasks we want to discuss is to analyze the historical behavior of our inventory.

8.1   Performing Inventory Analysis

Inventories can be analyzed in groups of materials or by individually material. The ultimate goal of inventory analysis is to derive a future strategy from inventory activity and behavior in the past. We want to look at whether we can detect consistency, a seasonal pattern, irregular replenishment, or spikes and long periods of no consumption. Depending on what is found, we can construct a fitting strategy or policy for replenishment in the future and make it as automated as possible. Inventory analysis may be performed in a number of ways and typically every planner has to build his own system to do it. It isn't really common that a company delivers a comprehensive, clearly defined, and useful key performance indicator (KPI) framework to their planners within which inventories may be evaluated. More often than not, vague directions are thrown out, and every planner does inventory evaluation and optimization to the best of his knowledge and independent from each other. The result is a hodgepodge of different activities based on various interpretations and inconsistent strategies.

The topic of KPIs and measurements will be discussed elaborately in the next chapters, but let's focus on where the information for a sound inventory analysis can come from and how it may be interpreted to fit into a measuring framework.

A very useful graphic that you should make extensive use of is the inventory history graphic that can be called up out of many transactions in the Logistics Information System (LIS) and document evaluations. As an example, you may use Transaction MC.9 with a data range of your liking and proceed as follows.

In the result screen, you follow the menu path EXTRAS • DETAILED INFO • STOCK LEVEL, and then choose either STOCK QUANTITY or STOCK VALUE to see the historic inventory levels in a graphic (see Figure 8.2).

Figure 8.3 shows an example of the inventory history graphic, from which you can derive a number of interpretations and receive a lot of valuable information.

The main line depicts the historical course of the inventory over time. As you can see, there is a timeline (x-axis) and a quantity scale (y-axis). Hence, it's possible to plot the inventory levels of a specific material (or a group of materials as a total) over the calendar. When the line goes up, it shows an increase of inventory on that day caused by the posting of a goods receipt or a return. On the other hand, when the line goes down, it shows a reduction of the inventory usually due to consumption (maybe to a production order or, in the case of a finished product, to a sales order).

Figure 8.2 Navigation to the Inventory History Graphic

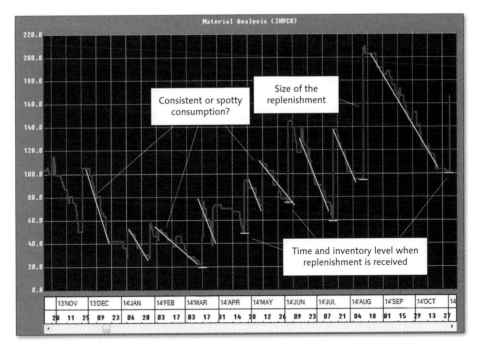

Figure 8.3 Inventory Graphic with Markings*

In this graph, we're looking at a purchased part, and therefore the increase of inventory came from a goods receipt from purchase orders, whereas the reduction of inventory (line going down) came from production orders that consumed the purchased part. As you can see, the consumption happens in smaller quantities over a longer period of time, while the receipts are coming in lot sizes to make the inventory jump up in one day. This is consistent with the behavior of a company that buys parts from vendors in lots to fill up inventory (and hold a safety stock) so that their production lines may consume the parts gradually over time before the next receipt comes in.

Let's see what we can learn from such a graphic. For better viewing, we've added some markings and lines (these don't show in the SAP graphic). As for the interpretation of the graphic, we can then derive some clues. First, if we look at consumption depicted by the main line moving downward, these might go down at the same angle from period to period, or they might not. In the latter case, the consumption in the past was very inconsistent and unpredictable, and it included spikes and relatively long periods of low or no usage. If, however, the lines between the receipts come down in always the same patterns or angles—as can be seen in our screenshot—then we know that the part underlies a consistent consumption pattern that most likely repeats itself into the future. Most people would classify such a behavior as a part that is "X" according to an XYZ analysis.

The other clue we're getting from the graphic lies in the replenishment pattern. It answers the questions, "How often did we receive the part?" "How much did we receive from the various purchase orders?" and "At what level of inventory did we receive a certain quantity of the part?" In Figure 8.3, the points where the replenishment was received is marked with a short, horizontal line. And we can see that sometimes a quantity of the materials was received when there was still plenty of inventory. It also seems as though the timing of the receipts is irregular too. Sometimes there is a short cycle, and sometimes there is a very long one.

There are many more clues you can take from such a graphic and because no KPI is available in the LIS to give you a dead stock value (there is, however, dead stock calculation in the document evaluations), you can analyze it in the inventory graph. Dead stock is an indication of how much inventory doesn't turn. Dead stock is measured over time, so you'll have to identify the period for which the dead stock value is relevant. In Figure 8.4, for example, the dead stock value for the fiscal year 2009 was at about 2500, whereas the dead stock during 2008 was much higher at 6000.

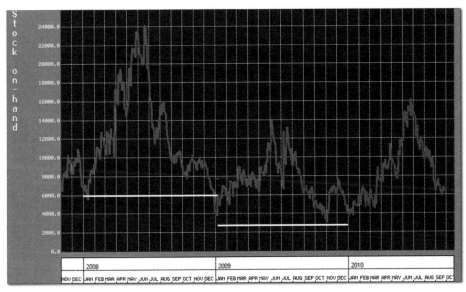

Figure 8.4 Depicting Dead Stock Value for Different Periods*

You can get much more from this graphic, and it's certainly worthwhile to use it for your inventory analysis of individual parts or products.

8.1.1 SAP ERP's Logistics Information System

If you seek help in the area of inventory analysis and, for whatever coincidence, come across SAP ERP's Logistics Information System (LIS), chances are that someone will tell you that SAP has stopped supporting the LIS. For most consultants and users, the LIS is outdated, unappealing, and faulty. Although the LIS is old and unappealing, which have nothing to do with its effectiveness, the LIS isn't faulty! It might have been misinterpreted for a long time, but it certainly delivers correct results. That is why SAP doesn't have to support it anymore. Upgrades aren't necessary and bug fixes aren't required because it's not broken. The LIS has been there for analysts to use for many years, and to this date—and probably many more years to come—it provides you with many valuable insights, great decision-making support, and lots of inventory KPIs.

You own it, and it works. Why not use it? You just have to know a few important things to make it run to your advantage. First, LIS is made up of the following subcomponents that provide insight according to the areas of functionality:

- Sales Information System (SIS)
- Purchasing Information System (PIS)
- Inventory Controlling (LIS)
- Shop Floor Information System (SFIS)
- Plant Maintenance Information System (PMIS)
- Quality Management Information System (QMIS)
- Retail Information System (RIS)
- Transport Information System (TIS) [Ext.]

The information systems that belong to the LIS have a modular structure, and a variety of techniques (sorting, filtering, grouping, aggregation, and disaggregation) allow you to evaluate data.

The LIS permits you not only to evaluate actual data but also to create planning data. These systems provide an easy-to-use planning function that is also supported by a forecasting function. In earlier SAP versions (from release 3.0 on), the planning functionality of the information systems and the component Sales & Operations Planning (SOP) were combined and enhanced to make one central planning and forecasting tool. You can use the Logistics Data Warehouse in Customizing to design the LIS to meet your own requirements. This tool provides functions to customize the setup of the data basis for your information system to define the rules for updating the data and to generate the standard analyses for evaluating the data.

The LIS also includes an Early Warning System that is integrated into all of the information systems and is based on their key figures. The Early Warning System supports the decision-making process by allowing you to target and monitor weak areas in logistics. It searches for exceptional situations and helps in the early detection and correction of undesirable situations. The Logistics Information Library is a further component of the LIS. The Logistics Information Library makes it possible to access key figures in LIS by using simple search strategies. In addition, it allows you to catalog the key figures.

As illustrated in Figure 8.5, the LIS represents a framework of reference and the complete data basis for inventory analysis. The Logistics Information Warehouse provides all data needed for the calculation of valuable KPIs and for building reports and data extracts you may slice and dice to your liking and save as variants to call up whenever you need them.

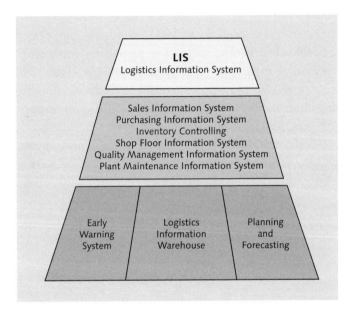

Figure 8.5 The LIS and Its Subcomponents

The Early Warning System and Planning and Forecasting parts are very useful by-products of the LIS. The main feature of the LIS, however, is that all the information systems provide you with all the information you may ever need.

Infostructures and Characteristic Values

LIS is built on infostructures with characteristics and characteristic values. Info-structures are files of special statistics data that constitute an important element of the information systems. They form the data basis for the standard analyses. The various information systems collect specific—according to their functional area—transactional data over time as they are posted into the infostructure. For example, the Shop Floor Information System collects confirmations to production orders, the Purchasing Information System collects goods receipts to purchase orders, and Inventory Controlling collects goods movements of all types.

An infostructure defines a group containing information that is used for the aggregation and subsequent evaluation of data from the operative application. The standard system provides infostructures for every information system, which includes valid key figures for all of the analyses in the application area. Customizing allows you to create your own infostructures so you can add your own enhancements to the information systems.

As illustrated in Figure 8.6, date is displayed across time periods and aggregated into relevant key figures. Every infostructure has its own periodicity and a set of key figures that can be analyzed on various levels of aggregation. Therefore, infostructures provide an excellent platform for the structuring and sorting of useful data. Inventory Controlling abounds with KPIs that you can use for your reports and analytics. For example, you may aggregate and view valuated stock receipts, average consumption, total consumption value, number of material movements, and much more. We'll get into some of the preconfigured and provided KPIs in more detail in Section 8.2.

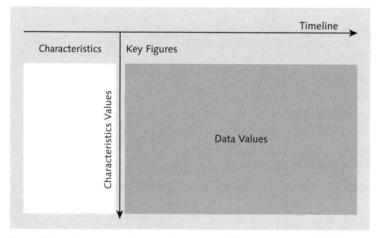

Figure 8.6 Infostructure Displayed in the LIS Table

Calculating Key Figures in the LIS

The "old" LIS can collect data concurrently as it's updated through the operational transactions that are executed on a daily basis. For the collection of information, the following infostructures are available in Inventory Controlling:

▶ **S031 Movements**

All key figures relating to material movements involving current valuated stock and vendor consignment stock are updated to this infostructure. The period unit in this infostructure is "month."

▶ **S032 Stocks**

The current valuated and vendor consignment stocks are updated to this infostructure when a goods movement takes place. Stock values are also updated to this infostructure when a goods movement and invoice verification/revaluation take place. This infostructure doesn't contain a period unit.

▶ **S033 Movements (individual records)**

To gain specific results from an analysis, such as determining the date of last consumption, displaying informative receipts/issues diagrams, or obtaining reliable mean stock values, updating of the statistical data must take place on a daily basis. Infostructure S033 satisfies this requirement because it's supplied with data every day. Structurally, Infostructure S033 is identical to Infostructure S031, yet also includes the characteristic "document number." Updating is carried out on a daily basis at the document level.

▶ **S034 Movements (Batches)**

The key figures relating to material movements at plant, storage location, material, and batch levels are updated to this infostructure.

▶ **S035 Stocks (Batches)**

The current valuated and vendor consignment stocks are updated to this infostructure when a goods movement takes place. This infostructure doesn't refer to any period and is set up in the same way as Infostructure S032, yet also contains the additional characteristic "batch."

▶ **S039 Planning**

This infostructure includes all of the key figures that are available in Inventory Controlling, including all of the extra key figures (range of coverage, inventory turnovers, key figures that are calculated using the mean value). No actual data is written to this infostructure. This infostructure provides the basis for flexible planning.

Data is written to the standard Infostructures S031, S032, and S033 when goods movements and invoice verification/revaluation take place. The data flows from the document structure to the infostructures. Goods movements are divided into the following types: goods receipt, goods issue, stock transfer, transfer posting, and inventory differences.

The updating process for specific, individual movement types can be switched off in Inventory Management or in one of the subsequent applications in the logistics chain. Amounts are always updated in the local currency, which is assigned to the company code in Customizing. Quantities are updated in the base unit of measure. The base unit of measure is the unit of measure in which the system manages the material stocks, and it's determined in the material master.

So every goods movement is updated into the infostructure with its according time stamp, and the LIS can then make available or calculate KPIs within the various components, such as the Purchasing Information System, Shop Floor Information System, or Inventory Information System. Next, let's discuss how some of the KPIs are figured.

To evaluate stocks in the LIS, you can evaluate key figures for the stock types, valuated stock, and consignment stock (vendor consignment goods). The entire valuated stock of a material is a result of the sum of stocks that can be used in any way, stock in quality inspection, stock in transfer on the storage location and plant level, blocked stocks, customer consignment stocks, customer returnable packaging, and subcontracting.

From this you can get the following key figures:

▸ Total Stock, which is the sum of valuated and consignment stock
▸ Quantity of Valuated Stock
▸ Quantity of the Consignment Stock
▸ Safety Stock
▸ Stock at Receipt
▸ Value of Valuated Stock
▸ Value of Stock at Receipt

There are also zero stock figures that show how often the stock quantity reaches zero. With regard to zero stock, the following key figures can be evaluated:

▸ Number of Valuated Stocks at Zero
▸ Number of Total Stocks at Zero
▸ Number of Consignment Stocks at Zero

Then, there are the average values calculated when the standard analysis for the designated time period is carried out. With regard to the quantities, the following average key figures can be evaluated:

- Average Valuated Stock
- Average Total Stock
- Average Consignment Stock

Average stock is calculated from the sum of beginning stock and ending stock within the time frame of the analysis and then divided by two. With respect to values, the key figure Average Stock Value of Valuated Stock can be evaluated. The average stock value of the valuated stock is the sum of beginning stock and ending stock within the time frame of the analysis divided by two.

There are key figures for usage as well, which are categorized as planned and unplanned usage. (Planned usage is updated when material is taken from the warehouse as a result of a reservation. Unplanned usage is updated when material is taken without a reservation.) These key figures include the following:

- Total Number of Times Used
- Number of Times for Unplanned Usage
- Total Usage Quantity
- Unplanned Usage Quantity
- Unplanned Usage Value
- Total Usage Value

Of course, you'll also find a number of key figures for goods receipt and goods issue postings:

- **Number of Receipts of Valuated Stock**
  The system cumulates the number of occurances of a receipt, when valuated stock is received.
- **Quantity of Goods Received of Valuated Stock**
  The quantity of all receipts during a given period, when valuated stock was received.
- **Receipts Value of Valuated Stock**
  The receipts value of valuated stock is calculated from the delivery quantity of valuated stock, valuated with the standard price or the average moving price. When a goods receipt for a purchase order is made, it results in the receipt

value, which is derived from the quantity of valuated stock that was valuated with the net order price. If an invoice was posted for a purchase order before the goods receipt, then the invoice price is taken into account for valuation.

▸ **Average Receipts of Valuated Stock**
The average receipts of the valuated stock is derived by dividing the quantity of goods received by the number of receipts of valuated stock.

▸ **Value of Average Receipts of Valuated Stock**
The value of the average receipts of valuated stock is calculated by dividing the receipts value by the number of receipts.

▸ **Number of Issues of Valuated Stock**
The system cumulates the number of occurences of an issue, when valuated stock is received.

▸ **Issue Quantity of Valuated Stock**
The quantity of all the issues during a given period, when valuated stock was received.

▸ **Issue Value of Valuated Stock**
The issue value of valuated stock is derived from the current price (purchase order price, invoice price, or the price from the material master) of the valuated issues quantity of valuated stock. This also applies to materials with a standard price as for materials with a moving average price. This key figure is updated on the posting date.

▸ **Average Issues of Valuated Stock**
The key figure is calculated by dividing the issues values of valuated stock by the number of issues of valuated stock.

▸ **Value of Average Issues of Valuated Stock**
The key figure is calculated by dividing the issues values of valuated stock by the number of issues of valuated stock.

Of particular value are the key figures for range of coverage because you can get valuable insight into your stock holdings. A simple stock value doesn't provide as much awareness as the knowledge about how long a particular stock will last does. If you're comparing current stock holdings with future requirements or past consumption, you can derive valuable information on whether you're holding too much or too little in stock to get by efficiently. Range of coverage for a particular stock is calculated by dividing the average total usage per day by the stock holding. From this, two range of coverage key figures can be evaluated:

- ▸ Range of Coverage of Valuated Stock
- ▸ Range of Coverage of Total Stock

And the average range of coverage is calculated by dividing the average total usage per day by the average stock holding. Therefore, you'll get two more key figures:

- ▸ Average Range of Coverage of Valuated Stock
- ▸ Average Range of Coverage of Total Stock

Another important inventory KPI is inventory turnovers. The formula for inventory turnover is represented by dividing average stock by total usage (usually over a year). Average stock is calculated by adding the beginning stock and the ending stock in the period to analyze and dividing it by two. Consequently you have at your disposal the following key figures:

- ▸ Inventory Turnover of Valuated Stock
- ▸ Inventory Turnover of Total Stock
- ▸ Average Inventory Turnover of Valuated Stock
- ▸ Average Inventory Turnover of Total Stock
- ▸ Inventory Turnover of Valuated Stock per Year
- ▸ Inventory Turnover of Total Stock per Year

Lastly, you can also get some key figures telling you about materials movements:

- ▸ Inventory Turnover of Valuated Stock per Year
- ▸ Inventory Turnover of Consignment Stock per Year
- ▸ Inventory Turnover of Total Stock per Year

All these KPIs are available for your analysis in the LIS transactions (e.g., in Transaction MC.9), and you can now start building your lists with sorting, filtering, and even a graphical display of the data as we'll describe in the next section.

Inventory Graphics in the LIS

LIS also has many useful graphics that you might want to explore if you're the more visual type of analyst. Of course, you can view the graphics directly from an LIS transaction, but when analyzing individual materials, we like to use navigation profiles and work from within Transaction MD04 (Stock/Requirements List).

Depending on which navigation profile you're using, you can access LIS transactions and the graphics we're about to discuss from within the STOCK/REQUIREMENTS LIST. Click the INVCO button shown to the right of Figure 8.7 to access an LIS transaction.

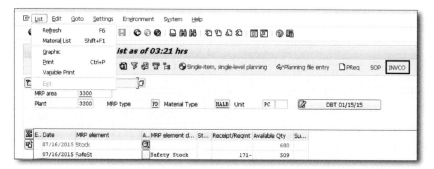

Figure 8.7 Accessing LIS Graphics by Using a Navigation Profile from within Transaction MD04

Inventory History Graphic

You can call up an inventory history graphic from an LIS transaction by following the menu path shown in Figure 8.8 to plot stock quantities or stock values over the time horizon you've selected in the initial screen of the transaction.

Figure 8.8 Calling Up the Inventory Graphic from an LIS Transaction

Figure 8.9 provides an example of the development of stock quantities over the periods selected in the initial screen. It shows receipts, consumption, and the resulting stock levels on every day from May 2013 through July of 2015. The graphic relates to a single material and plots the daily net of receipts and issues.

Figure 8.10 plots the inventory development for multiple materials—maybe for all stock levels of all materials accumulated for an entire plant code.

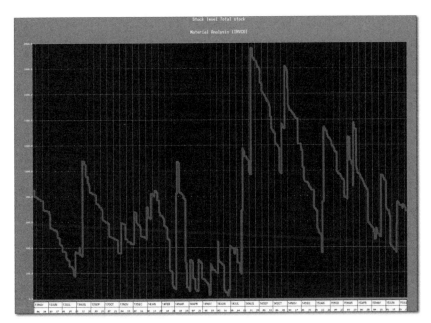

Figure 8.9 Inventory History for a Single Material*

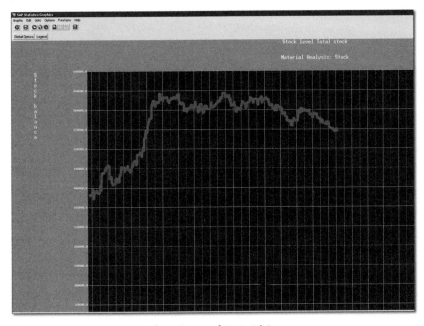

Figure 8.10 Inventory History for a Group of Materials*

We can take a number of insights from these inventory history plots. As shown in Figure 8.11, when the line moves down, it indicates the net consumption of a given day. Analyzed over a longer period, its slant provides clues on whether consumption is fairly consistent or not over time. When the line moves up, however, it represents a goods receipt from, maybe, a purchase order on that day. Receipts usually don't occur every day, so when the downward trend is interrupted by a receipt, you know on what day that receipt occurred. From this, you can take valuable information about the timing of your replenishment.

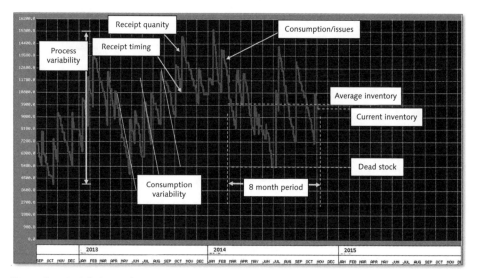

Figure 8.11 Insights into the Inventory History*

The LIS doesn't provide a KPI for dead stock, but from the graph, you can take the value over a specific period of time. In the example, we've chosen a period of roughly eight months, and the lowest point during that period represents the dead stock value over that period.

You can also see the current inventory value and estimate the average inventory held over a certain period of time. Looking at the angle produced by daily issues, you can take very valuable insight into the consistency of consumption.

Finally, it's recommended to evaluate the process stability or lack thereof. A well-defined and correctly setup replenishment process is automated and produces regular receipt patterns. Receipts occur in regular time intervals with the same or similar receipted quantities. If the receipts occur at different time intervals with different quantities and at different stock levels, you should think about fine-tuning the policy by using some of the techniques described in this book to optimize the balancing of supply and demand.

After you fine-tune the policy for an improvement on the process stability, you can simulate the changes in a graphic within Transaction MD04 (Stock/Requirements List). Policy is adjusted mainly in the four MRP views of the material master record, which may also be accessed directly out of Transaction MD04. After the master data like lot size procedure, safety stock settings or MRP type have been optimized, you run MRP on the item to adjust the future replenishment process. The new stock/requirements situation in Transaction MD04 can now be plotted into the future by calling up the respective graphic.

Choosing LIST • GRAPHIC, as shown in Figure 8.12, will access a graphic showing the result of the MRP run after netting demand with supply. This is a great way of simulating policy in Transaction MD04.

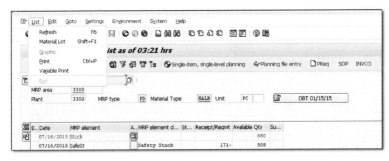

Figure 8.12 Menu Path for a Graphic Depicting Future Inventory Development

As shown in Figure 8.13, inventory levels will settle into a range driven by policy after the fixed receipts are replaced and adjusted by order proposals in line with integrated net requirements planning.

Actual and planned or forecasted demand is covered by receipt proposals generated by the MRP run. The quantity and time of these receipt proposals are influenced by safety stock settings, lot-size procedure, and MRP type maintained in the material master record (the policy). Therefore, this graphic is an excellent representation of the expected outcome of a policy adjustment and serves as a brilliant simulation tool.

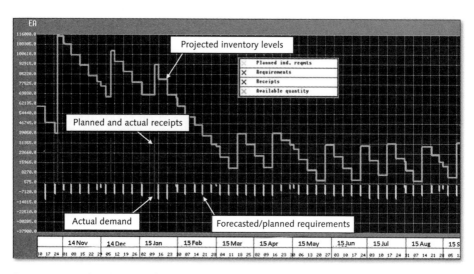

Figure 8.13 Simulated Result of the Policy in Transaction MD04 Graphic (Not an LIS Graphic)*

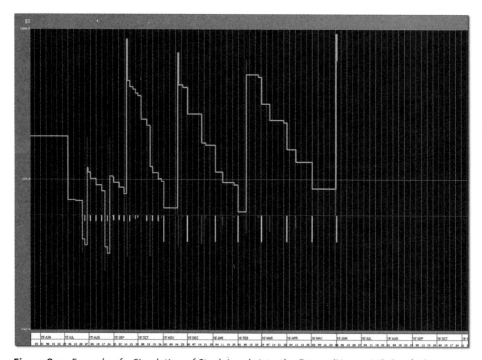

Figure 8.14 Example of a Simulation of Stock Levels into the Future (Not an LIS Graphic)*

Figure 8.14 is another example of a graphic showing future inventory levels. As we know by now, the green line (please refer to the full-color version of this figure from the book's supplemental downloads at *www.sap-press.com/3745*) represents future inventory levels, whereas blue lines (going up) show the receipts, and yellow lines (going down) show planned or forecasted demand. Note that the red lines (going down) are also demand. However, these are actual demand such as an order reservation (from production or sales orders), and these might consume the yellow lines (the forecast).

Graphics, as you can see, are available in different areas of SAP ERP. These examples showed simulation graphics from Transaction MD04. Let's return to the LIS to view some more.

Receipts/Issues Diagram

The historic inventory graphic we discussed earlier can also be displayed together with cumulative receipts and cumulative issues all in one graph. This increases your inventory when you don't have the corresponding consumption.

Picture the following situation: Your planning department has forecasted a higher than usual consumption of raw materials because an increase in finished product sales was anticipated. The materials controller therefore planned for higher supply, and purchasing increased its order quantities. However, the increased sales didn't materialize, and the warehouse got stuck with too much inventory.

This type of situation happens very often if planning is deterministic—meaning that people react to forecast changes all the time and don't use buffering strategies. When we see problems like this, we pull out the issues/receipts diagram and show that consumption kept on going up at the same degree (consistent) while receipts increased dramatically all of a sudden. If you can see this type of thing happening often over the period of evaluation, you might come to the conclusion that it's better to ignore the frequent changes in finished goods forecast and stick with your consumption-based replenishment policy. To view the receipts/issues diagram, follow the menu path shown in Figure 8.15 in any of the respective LIS transactions, such as Transaction MC.9.

Figure 8.16 provides an example of the receipts/issues graphic. As you can see, the inventory history graphic is plotted as well at the bottom of the graph. It's a bit cramped because of the scale of the cumulating of issues and receipts, but you get a good idea of when stock goes up and when stock goes down.

Figure 8.15 Navigating to the Receipts/Issues Diagram

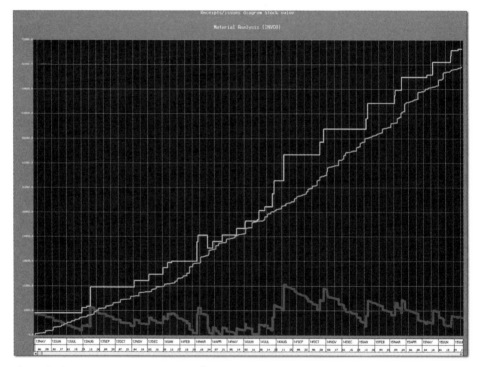

Figure 8.16 Receipts/Issues Diagram in the LIS*

The green line then shows the cumulated issues (or consumption) over time from the past. In this example, the curve rises pretty consistently, which means that consumption doesn't change much in value from week to week. The blue line then shows how this material was receipted. Every time a goods receipt (maybe from a purchase order) is posted, a straight line the size of the receipted quantity goes up. If you take a closer look, you can see that from April through July of

2014, there were regular receipts of about the same small quantity. Because consumption was consistent too, the inventory moved up and down around a small, average value (as can be seen with the red line). However, toward the end of July and throughout August, inventory started climbing up to very high levels, and receipts were posted at times when there was plenty of stock available.

When we analyze this kind of thing, planners usually wonder how they could have ordered so much when they were holding so much already. The problem is that there is a lead time between the time you order and the time you receive the order. If there is an anticipated, unusually high demand in the future, and the materials planner reacts to it, he has to order the additional quantity much earlier than when it needs to be received. And at the time the supplier delivers the goods, the unusual demand has disappeared, and no one knows why so much was ordered.

This is why sometimes we're much better off using buffers (safety stock or time) to counter variability instead of trying to catch the ever-changing forecast.

In any case, the receipts/issues graph provides lots of insight and serves as an excellent analysis tool because it shows receipts, consumption, and resulting inventory levels all in one screen. Watch for widening gaps between the issues and receipts lines. These usually indicate that we're buying too much too early and receiving more than we need (of course, if the cumulated issues curve exceeds the cumulated receipts curve, then we're buying less than what we need).

Key Figures

Using the menu path shown in Figure 8.17, you can display important key figures from the LIS transaction.

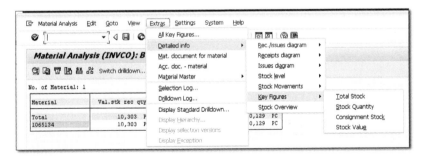

Figure 8.17 Navigating to Important Key Figures

Using this function, an overview to important key figures is given, and you can analyze specific dates and values as shown in Figure 8.18.

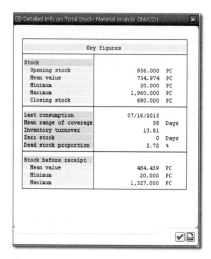

Figure 8.18 Important Key Figures in the Logistics Information System

Of particular interest in your analysis may be the date of the LAST CONSUMPTION or the number of days with ZERO STOCK when you look for slow-moving parts. In combination with MEAN RANGE OF COVERAGE and the DEAD STOCK PROPORTION, you get a true picture of a part's position in your portfolio.

Portfolio Graphic

You can use the portfolio graphics to gain a quick overview of the interrelationships and interactions between two key figures for particular characteristic values. The portfolio graphic provides an overview of the concentration of the characteristic values with regard to these two key figures. The characteristic values are displayed on the x-/y-axis, and in the example in Figure 8.19, the number of average stock issues is displayed over the average, valuated stock holding.

Consequently, you can see that there is a high concentration of parts with a low number of issues and low average stock holdings in this example. There's nothing wrong with that, but you might want to analyze the parts further to the right and lower on the y-axis. These parts don't get used much, but they exhibit high average stock holdings over time.

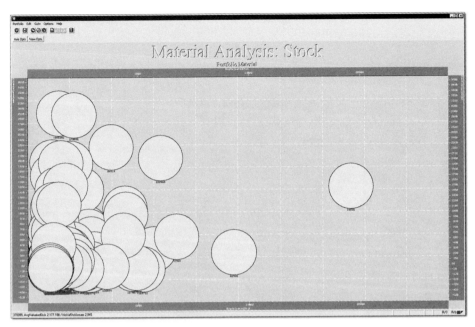

Figure 8.19 Portfolio Graphic in the LIS

To call up the portfolio graphic, follow these steps:

1. From the standard analysis, select GOTO • PORTFOLIO GRAPHIC. A dialog box appears containing the key figures in the list.

2. Select the two key figures that you want to display in your portfolio graphic, and press [Enter]. The portfolio graphic appears.

Cumulative Frequency Curve

At every list level, key figure data can be represented in the form of a cumulative frequency curve. The cumulative frequency curve provides information about the concentration of characteristic values. Individual key figure values are expressed as totals in descending order. The number of characteristic values is plotted on the x-axis, and the cumulative values of the specified key figure on the y-axis.

The cumulative frequency curve is displayed in either absolute or percent values depending on the selection you've made. The characteristic values on X combine the cumulative key figure values Y. Thus, the graph offers an overview of the extent to which a large proportion of a key figure's total value is concentrated on a few characteristic values. In Figure 8.20, you can see an example of a cumulative curve for stock values.

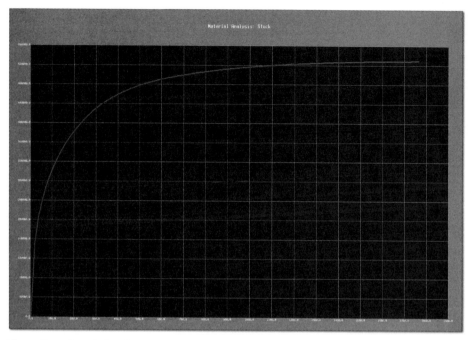

Figure 8.20 Cumulative Curve*

For example, you might want to check the distribution of orders for particular materials. In the table in Transaction MC.9, you can select the key figure ORDER QUANTITY. The list then shows selected materials and key figure ORDER QUANTITY. After you generate a cumulative frequency curve for this list, the graphic could, as an example, provide the following information: 10% of all materials make up 65% of the cumulated order quantity. In other words, relatively few materials make up a large portion of the order quantity.

In another example, you might want to check how the value of the valuated stock is distributed over your materials. Perform a material analysis, and select the key figure VALUATED STOCK. The resulting list shows the particular materials and the key figure VALUE OF VALUATED STOCK. You then create a cumulative frequency curve for this list, and the graphic provides you with the following insight: 15% of all materials make up 50% of the stock value; that is, in this case, relatively few materials make up 50% of the total stock value.

Correlation Curve

A correlation curve is used to identify the interrelationships between two, three, or more key figures. The number of characteristic values in the list is plotted on the x-axis, and the key figure values are scaled to a range of 0 to 1 on the y-axis. The value 0 is assigned to the smallest key figure value, and the value 1 is assigned to the largest key figure value.

As an example from the Purchasing Information System, you may want to check how the development of the key figures Order Value and Invoiced Amount is distributed over specific periods for a specific vendor. You generate a drilldown list according to periods during the vendor analysis and use the correlation curve to view the interrelationship between the key figures Order Value and Invoiced Amount for the designated periods.

Or you might want to check the development of the receipts quantity and the issue quantity of the valuated stock and how they are distributed over select periods for a particular material. Here you can use the correlation curve to view the interrelationship between the key figures Receipts Quantity and the Issue Quantity of the Valuated Stock for the designated periods. Figure 8.21 shows an example of a correlation curve using three key figures.

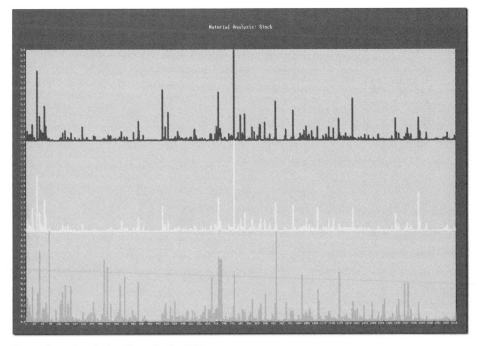

Figure 8.21 Correlation Curve in the LIS*

ABC Analysis with the Logistics Information System

SAP ERP provides functionality to perform an ABC analysis within the LIS and its data stored in infostructures. The ABC analysis can be used to classify characteristic values in order of importance for particular key figures. An ABC analysis can divide items into three categories:

▶ A: Important

▶ B: Less important

▶ C: Relatively unimportant

Figure 8.22 provides an example for an ABC analysis in inventory controlling. The strategy that was applied relates average valuated stock values and categorizes materials into three groups. In this example, 181 materials make up 70% of the total average valuated stock value. These materials were therefore classified as A items. The next 20% were classified as B items, and the remaining 1,276 materials were classified as C items.

Segments	Material		AvgValuatedStck in segment	
A segment	181	10.25 %	370,772.699	70.07 %
B segment	308	17.45 %	105,471.709	19.93 %
C segment	1,276	72.29 %	52,868.648	9.99 %
Total	1765	100.00 %	529,113.056	100.00 %

Figure 8.22 ABC Analysis for Average Valuated Stock Value

We can also see the totals for the materials in scope of the exercise. Note that about 10% of the materials make up over 70% of the total average stock value, whereas 72% of the materials in scope make up only about 10% of the total value.

You can double-click on any one of the segments to call up a list of materials belonging to that class. The result is shown in Figure 8.23.

The ABC analysis is an important part of segmentation for policy setting. However, it isn't the only one. Only when using additional classification according to usage value, price, lead time, and possibly lifecycle will you get a full picture of a material's story.

List A segment		
ABC ind.	Material	AvgValuatedStck
A	24555	27,140.125
A	02938	16,627.000
A	72968	11,460.375
A	222460	10,027.000
A	08085	9,405.375
A	369792	8,405.250
A	379720	7,820.938
A	1074075	7,473.188
A	397780	6,852.313
A	01516	6,787.188
A	54333	6,615.438
A	04414	5,545.813
A	30406	5,326.438
A	630094	5,140.188
A	86866	4,991.188
A	09005	4,843.250
A	386987	3,961.313
A	1066063	3,886.750
A	360801	3,698.313
A	46800	3,680.563

Figure 8.23 A Segment of the ABC Analysis

Dual Classification with the Logistics Information System

Dual classification allows for classification using two key figures at the same time. It divides characteristic values into classes with reference to specific key figures (two of them). Materials are then assigned to classes, which are quantified using class limits. This way, you may, as an example, specify that all materials with less than $200 of average stock value and more than 620 goods issue postings are categorized into a particular dual class.

In dual classification, any two key figures available in the infostructure can be used, and you can customize how many class limits you want to use and specify what the class limits will be.

The example in Figure 8.24 shows a dual classification for the key figures AVGVALUATEDSTCK (Average Valuated Stock Value) and NOVALSTCKISSUES (No Valuated Stock Issues) using six class limits for each.

Double-clicking on any one of the classes opens up a window with a list of the materials belonging to that dual class.

```
                    Overview of segments - Material


                           ┌──────────────────────────────────────┐
                           │          NoValStckIssues              │
         AvgValuatedStck     100     230     360     490     620     >      Total

                200        1,188      99      21      11       3       6     1,328
                800          193      46      18      10       7      15       289
              1,400           37      21       8       2       1       9        78
              2,000           11       1       4       8       1       4        29
              2,600            2       3       1       0       1       1         8
                  >           11       4       4       1       1      12        33

         Total             1,442     174      56      32      14      47     1,765
```

Figure 8.24 Dual Classification Using the Two Key Figures

As an example from purchasing, you can divide materials into classes for the key figures Number of Order Items and Order Value. This then illustrates relationships between these key figures and helps you detect possible problem areas, such as materials with a relatively low order value and a high number of order items. Materials that lie in the upper classes with regard to both key figure values aren't critical.

You can also classify customers for the key figures Number of Orders and Invoiced Sales. This helps to detect relationships and possible problem areas, such as customers with relatively low invoiced sales but a high number of orders. In inventory controlling, materials can be classified with regard to the key figures Value of the Average Stock at Receipt and Range of Coverage of the Average Stock at Receipt. Those materials that lie in the upper classes with regard to both key figure values might represent opportunities for inventory reduction through reduced order lot sizes.

To view the materials belonging to a particular segment, position the cursor on the intersection in the matrix for the combination of classes you require, and double-click on the number. A segment list containing detailed information on the selected combination of classes appears as shown in Figure 8.25. The segment list shows all the characteristic values for the chosen combination and the value of the two key figures.

```
                         List Segment 1/5


 Segment   Material     AvgValuatedStck          NoValStckIssues

   1/5     201013          198.750                   507
   1/5     575603          147.813                   507
   1/5     603538           55.500                   538
```

Figure 8.25 Listing of a Segment in Dual Classification

The graphics function then displays the data in the list graphically.

Comparing Results

In the LIS, you can also compare results. Planned and actual figures can be compared or a previous year equated to the current year. Planned/actual comparison can aid the decision-making process by comparing the list displayed on-screen with planned and actual data for all characteristic values with reference to one key figure. This is only possible if you've saved planning data as a planning version for the characteristic and key figure in question. The planned data is then compared with the actual data for the same selection period.

For example, you could have created a list that displays vendors and the key figure Order Value and Invoiced Amount. In the planned/actual comparison, the actual data and the planned data (in a planning version) of all the vendors shown in the list are compared with reference to a specific key figure. Or you generate a list with material groups and the key figure Total Usage. In the planned/actual comparison, the actual data and the planned data (in a planning version) of all material groups listed are compared with reference to the key figure Total Usage.

Previous year comparisons may also be performed. If you do this with regard to a key figure that is displayed in the list, this function allows you to compare (for one key figure) the data that is currently displayed on the screen with the respective data in the same selected time period of the previous year.

In the example shown in Figure 8.26, the average valuated stock quantity is used as a key figure.

335

Comparison with previous year

Key figure AvgValuatedStck

Material	Previous year		Current		Difference		%
Total	421,132.869	***	529,112.620	***	107,979.751	***	
00500-1	198.750	PC	123.375	PC	75.375-	PC	37.92-
00500-10	652.438	PC	590.813	PC	61.625-	PC	9.45-
00500-15	256.563	PC	418.375	PC	161.812	PC	63.07
00500-4	487.563	PC	398.938	PC	88.625-	PC	18.18-
00910	165.750	PC	202.313	PC	36.563	PC	22.06
00911	1,363.188	PC	3,250.375	PC	1,887.187	PC	138.44
00912	809.563	PC	688.063	PC	121.500-	PC	15.01-
00915	99.125	PC	138.500	PC	39.375	PC	39.72
00916	197.625	PC	212.688	PC	15.063	PC	7.62
00918	325	PC	286.625	PC	38.375-	PC	11.81-
00919	42.313	PC	28.375	PC	13.938-	PC	32.94-
00926	666.125	PC	707.938	PC	41.813	PC	6.28
00927	841.750	PC	1,705.188	PC	863.438	PC	102.58
00928	1,808.813	PC	2,003.500	PC	194.687	PC	10.76
00930	161.938	PC	124.250	PC	37.688-	PC	23.27-
00954	354.250	PC	289	PC	65.250-	PC	18.42-
00960	800.563	PC	270.563	PC	530-	PC	66.20-
00966	81.500	PC	149.688	PC	68.188	PC	83.67
01139	259	PC	179.938	PC	79.062-	PC	30.53-
01314	6,343.250	PC	1,454.375	PC	4,888.875-	PC	77.07-
01409-1	7.313	PC	36.813	PC	29.500	PC	403.39
01429	24.250	PC	27.188	PC	2.938	PC	12.12
01433-1	64.688	PC	66.688	PC	2	PC	3.09
01513	968.688	PC	478.063	PC	490.625-	PC	50.65-
01516	5,800.500	PC	6,787.188	PC	986.688	PC	17.01
01543	3,099.375	PC	2,893.063	PC	206.312-	PC	6.66-
01697	215.063	PC	594.813	PC	379.750	PC	176.58
01998	9.625	PC	19.125	PC	9.500	PC	98.70
02129	98.625	PC	80.438	PC	18.187-	PC	18.44-
02141	85.750	PC	59.625	PC	26.125-	PC	30.47-
02247	5.500	PC	9.688	PC	4.188	PC	76.15
02363	58.063	PC	23.375	PC	34.688-	PC	59.74-
02384	596.750	PC	660.500	PC	63.750	PC	10.68
02431	56.250	PC	190.563	PC	134.313	PC	238.78
02464	49.438	PC	72.375	PC	22.937	PC	46.40
02469	38.438	PC	32.563	PC	5.875-	PC	15.28-
02485	197.750	PC	114.438	PC	83.312-	PC	42.13-
02549	4.750	PC	20.563	PC	15.813	PC	332.91
02643	19.750	PC	16.438	PC	3.312-	PC	16.77-
02644	5	PC	3.375	PC	1.625-	PC	32.50-
02711	6.250	PC	5.938	PC	0.312-	PC	4.99-
02912	42.438	PC	34.625	PC	7.813-	PC	18.41-
02938	17,457.813	PC	16,627	PC	830.813-	PC	4.76-
02940	57.688	PC	116.938	PC	59.250	PC	102.71

Close

Figure 8.26 Comparing Results in the LIS

You can use the graphics function to view a graph of all the key figure values that are shown in the list.

8.1.2 Analyzing and Monitoring Stocks with Document Evaluations

Document evaluations enable you to monitor stocks without updating statistical data into infostructures in the LIS. The data is read directly from the documents, and all the KPIs are calculated using specific routines. This way, KPIs such as dead stock, average inventory values, or inventory turnover are determined and listed according to the selection criteria you define in the initial screens of the document evaluation transactions. This, in some cases, takes much longer to calculate than the LIS routines that access data directly from the infostructure.

Figure 8.27 shows the menu path to access document evaluations and its transactions.

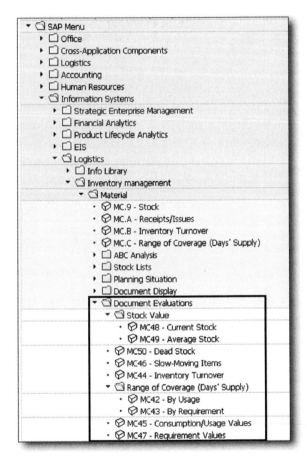

Figure 8.27 Accessing the Document Evaluations from the SAP Menu

The following document evaluations can be carried out:

- STOCK VALUE (current stock value, average stock value)
- RANGE OF COVERAGE (according to usage, according to requirement)
- INVENTORY TURNOVER
- SLOW-MOVING ITEMS
- DEAD STOCK
- USAGE VALUES
- REQUIREMENT VALUES

When using the analyses that are usage-based (analyses for RANGE OF COVERAGE, INVENTORY TURNOVER, SLOW-MOVING ITEMS, USAGE VALUE), you can also precisely analyze the usage or consumption.

Stock Value

This analysis is based on the stock value of a material and allows for the selection of materials with high inventory holdings. The analysis is based either on current stock value or average stock value (see Figure 8.28). Naturally, current stock value is calculated by multiplying the stock level with the current price, and average stock value is calculated by multiplying the average stock level with the current price.

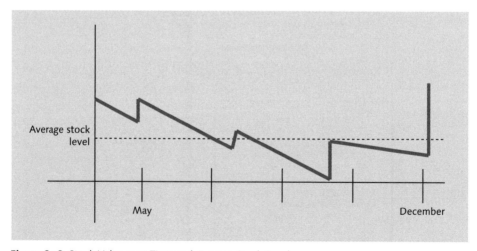

Figure 8.28 Stock Value over Time and Average Stock Level

When interested in current stock levels, call Transaction MC48 from the document evaluations. The result—shown in Figure 8.29—lists materials with stock values as of the date of the analysis and cumulates the percentage proportion of the total stock value of the analysis date. Current stock value doesn't provide any insight to the history of a materials inventory development and simply tells the inventory level as of today.

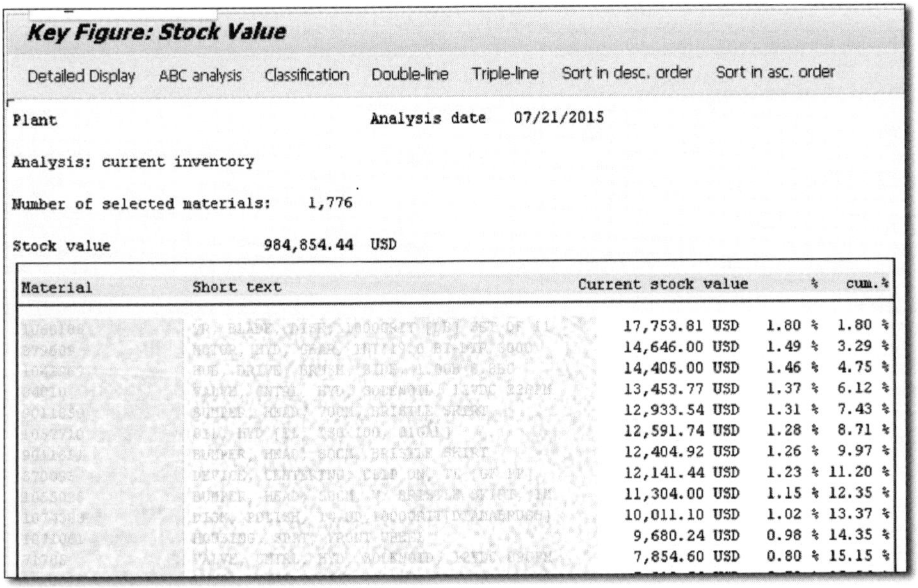

Figure 8.29 Transaction MC48 Current Stock Value

Besides listing current stock values for individual materials, Transaction MC48 also shows the total, current stock value of all materials in the list and indicates the proportion of an individual materials' value in relation to the total stock value. Furthermore, it cumulates this proportion so that you can, as in this example, see the top seven materials that make up 10% of the total stock value. This provides a good opportunity to find "low hanging fruit" for inventory reduction. However, beware that the current stock value doesn't provide the complete picture of a material's inventory performance. A more telling analysis is given by the document evaluation Average Stock Value, which we'll discuss next.

Transaction MC49 delivers the key figure Average Stock Value for individual materials and as a total of the list. As shown in Figure 8.30, proportions are calculated and displayed also.

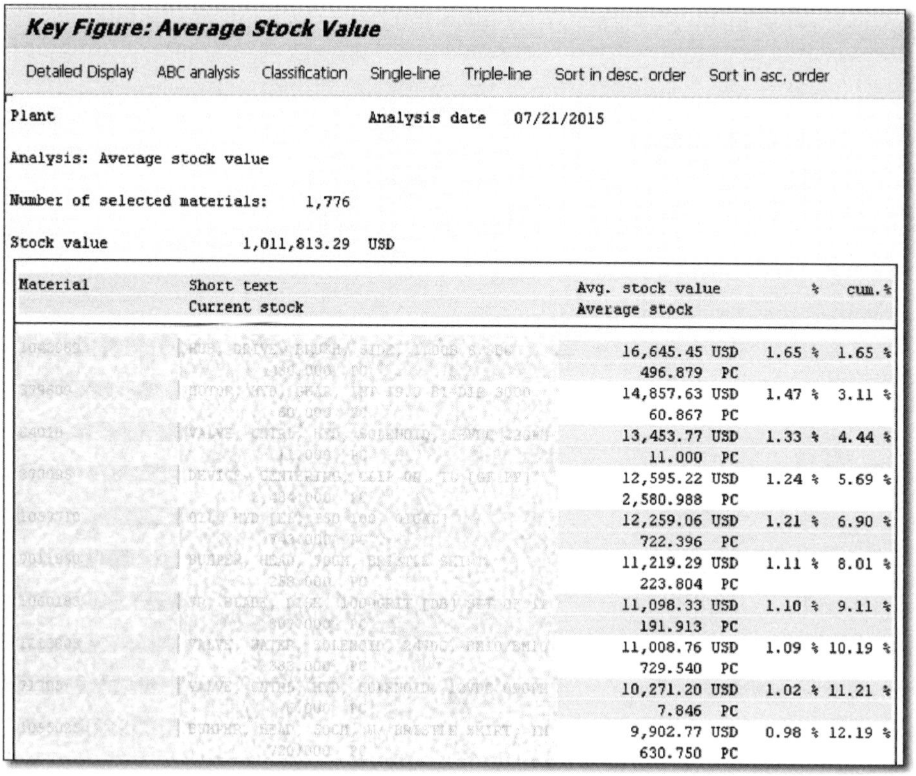

Figure 8.30 Transaction MC49 Average Stock

The double-line view of the evaluation is shown here. By choosing EDIT and then SINGLE LINE, DOUBLE LINE, or TRIPLE LINE, you can select either a single, double, or triple line display for the list you want. The single-line display of the material list shows the materials and the inventory turnover in days. The double-line display shows the material list for each material in addition to the following values:

▸ Current/average stock value

▸ Percentage of total stock value

▸ Cumulated percentage of total stock value

The triple-line display shows the following values for each material:

▸ MRP

▸ MRP type

▸ ABC indicator (only for the analysis object plant)

▸ Material group

▸ Material type

▸ Purchasing group

Dead Stock

Dead stock is that part of the inventory that hasn't been used for a certain period of time. Dead stock is always selected for a very specific time period and represents the lowest point of inventory during that time as illustrated in Figure 8.31.

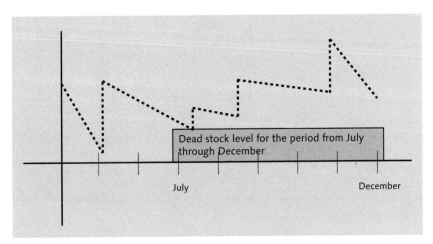

Figure 8.31 Dead Stock for the Period from July through December

The dead stock value is calculated by multiplying the dead stock with the current price. A dead stock analysis allows for the identification of materials with inefficient and superfluous amounts of stock. Surplus stocks of the material can be viewed, and important control parameters such as safety stock can be further evaluated. Figure 8.32 displays the dead stock evaluation in triple line view:

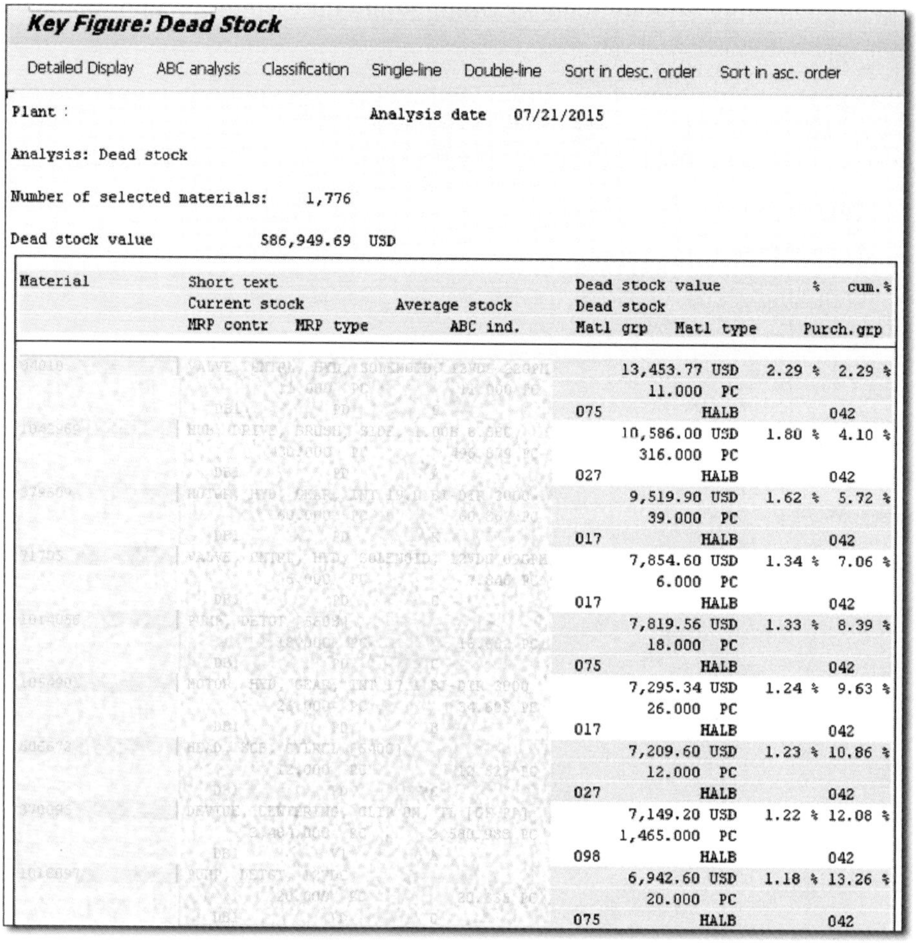

Figure 8.32 Transaction MC50 Dead Stock

The dead stock value by itself provides only basic information about a material's inventory "wellness." Once cross-referenced with average inventory levels and calculated as a proportion of the same, it becomes more meaningful. For example, in certain industries, a dead stock proportion of over 25% of average inventory value over the same period of time is perceived as too high and inefficient.

The Dead Stock document evaluation provides an excellent opportunity to build a hit list with the worst performers and concentrate your optimization efforts on that hit list to pick up on the low hanging fruit. As shown in Figure 8.32, you may work on the first seven materials that make up almost 11% of the total dead stock value of all the materials in the list.

Slow Movers

Materials that have been consumed little or not at all over a long period of time are referred to as slow-moving items. Every organization has inventory for slow-moving items that develops over time from safety stocks, a bad forecast, or some unforeseen events in the way these items are used in production. Slow-moving items' inventory levels are hard to reduce just because these items are moving slowly and have low consumption. It's therefore an important part of any inventory analysis to identify the slow movers so that appropriate action can be taken.

The main criterion for this analysis is the date of the last usage. This analysis enables you to identify materials that aren't currently in use (see Figure 8.33). You can, therefore, determine which stocks aren't required and, if necessary, remove them.

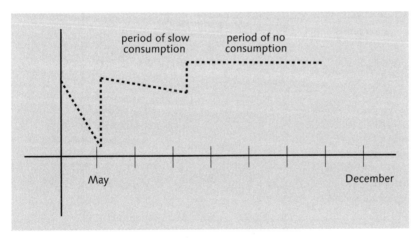

Figure 8.33 Inventory Development for a Slow-Moving Item

In the initial screen for the slow-moving items evaluation (Figure 8.34), select plant codes and MRP CONTROLLER keys and the number of days you want to go back for the last inventory movement (NO. OF DAYS UP TO LAST CONSUMPTION). The resulting list will allow you to select you slowest movers and take appropriate action.

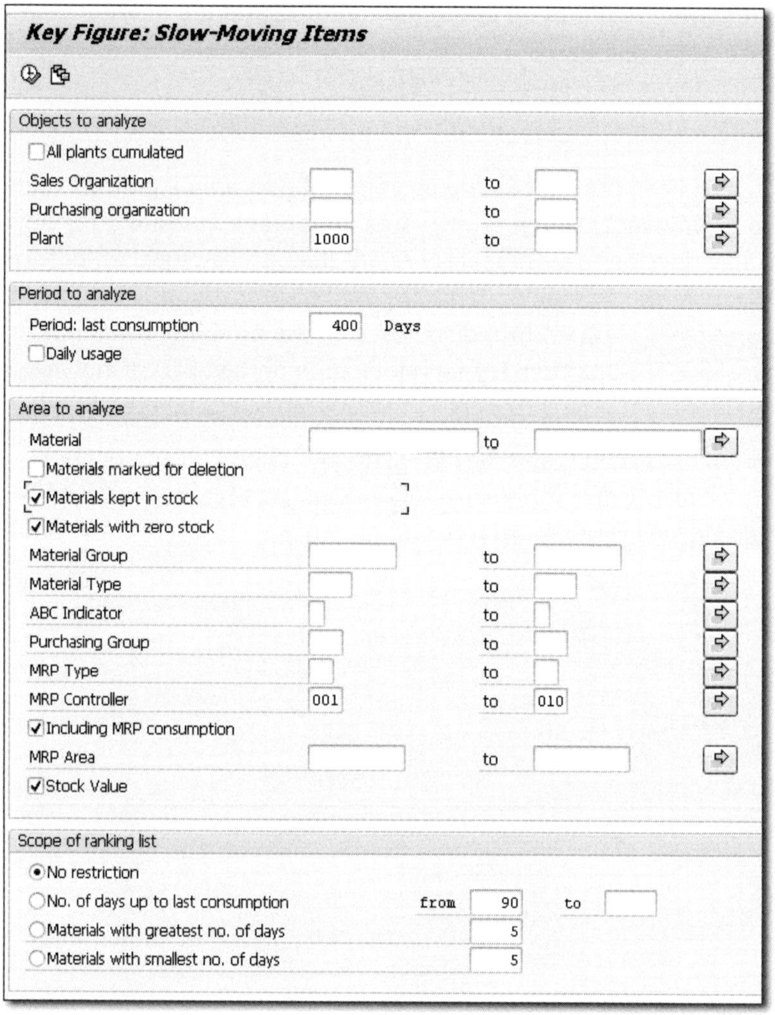

Figure 8.34 Initial Screen of the Transaction MC46 Slow Mover Report

Inventory Turnover

The key figure Inventory Turnover specifies how often average stock has been consumed. Inventory turnover is calculated as the ratio of cumulative usage to average stock level. An inventory turnover analysis allows for the identification of slow-moving items to see how effectively fixed capital has been used.

A low turnover rate may point to overstocking, obsolescence, or deficiencies. However, in some instances, a low rate may be appropriate, such as where higher inventory levels occur in anticipation of higher consumption. Conversely, a high turnover rate may indicate inadequate inventory levels, which may lead to a loss in business as the inventory is too low. This often can result in stock shortages. Generally speaking, you may want to reach at least an inventory turnover rate of 6 to 8, which means you're turning that material's inventory 6 to 8 times a year. Anything less is considered ineffective.

Naturally, an item whose inventory is consumed (turns over) only once a year has higher holding cost than one that turns over twice, or three times, or more in that time. Stock turnover also indicates the briskness of the business. The purpose of increasing inventory turns is to reduce inventory for the following three reasons:

▶ Increasing inventory turns reduces holding cost. The organization spends less money on rent, utilities, insurance, theft avoidance, and other costs of maintaining a stock of goods to be sold.

▶ Reducing holding cost increases net income and profitability as long as the revenue from selling the item remains constant.

▶ Items that turn over more quickly increase responsiveness to changes in customer requirements while allowing the replacement of obsolete items.

When comparing organizations, it's important to take note of the industry, or the comparison will be distorted. Comparing a supermarket and a car dealer isn't appropriate because supermarkets sell fast-moving goods such as candy, snacks, and soft drinks, so the stock turnover will be higher. However, a car dealer will have a low turnover due to vehicles being slow-moving items. As such, only intra-industry comparisons are appropriate.

Inventory turnover represents one of the most important KPIs for the evaluation of your inventory effectiveness and is therefore crucial in your analysis and opportunity identification. Figure 8.35 shows an example of a list of materials with respective turnover figures, sorted in descending order and as a single line display.

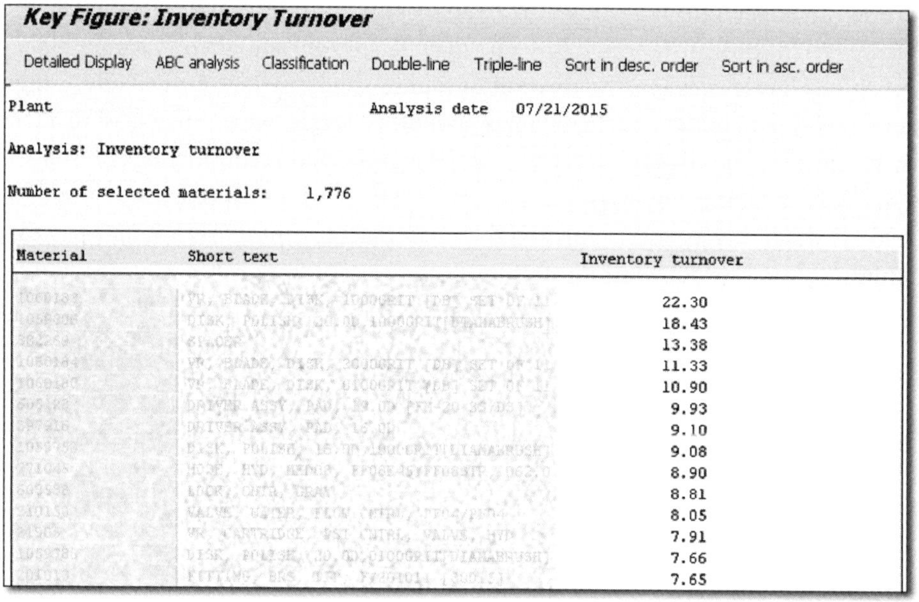

Figure 8.35 Transaction MC44 Turnover

Range of Coverage

The key figure Range of Coverage provides information on stock levels in relation to demand. It informs about how long a stock amount will last, given a specific average daily requirement.

Figure 8.36 illustrates range of coverage. In this example we have a coverage of more than three months. Lead time is an important cross reference for the assessment of the range of coverage. If the range of coverage is less than the replenishment lead time, stock-outs are imminent. Conversely, if the lead time to replenish is much shorter than the range of coverage, you're most likely holding too much inventory.

The analysis according to range of coverage can be executed for usage and requirements. The range of coverage for usage is calculated by dividing the current stock by the average usage per day. The range of coverage for requirements value is calculated by dividing current stock by the average requirement per day. Figure 8.37 and Figure 8.38 show an example for the range of coverage reports (based on usage or requirements).

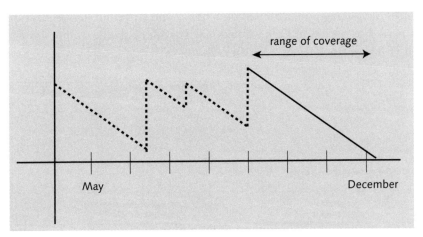

Figure 8.36 Range of Coverage

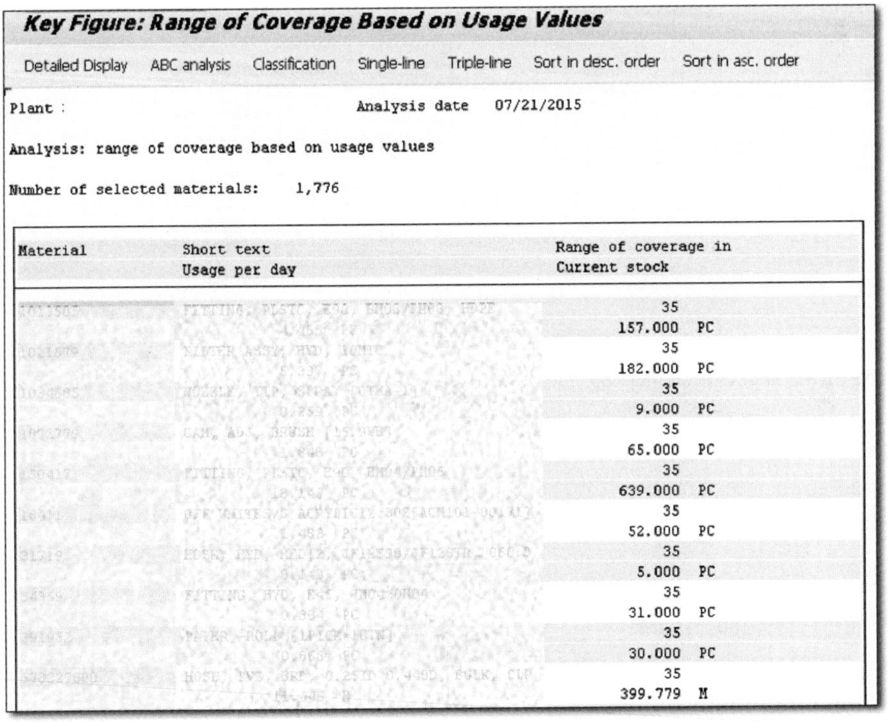

Key Figure: Range of Coverage Based on Usage Values

Detailed Display   ABC analysis   Classification   Single-line   Triple-line   Sort in desc. order   Sort in asc. order

Plant :   Analysis date   07/21/2015

Analysis: range of coverage based on usage values

Number of selected materials: 1,776

Material	Short text Usage per day	Range of coverage in Current stock
		35 157.000 PC
		35 182.000 PC
		35 9.000 PC
		35 65.000 PC
		35 639.000 PC
		35 52.000 PC
		35 5.000 PC
		35 31.000 PC
		35 30.000 PC
		35 399.779 M

Figure 8.37 Transaction MC42 Range of Coverage Based on Usage/Consumption

Use the range of coverage report based on usage if you had consistent consumption from period to period in the past because it produces better results for the calculation of future stock levels (see Figure 8.38).

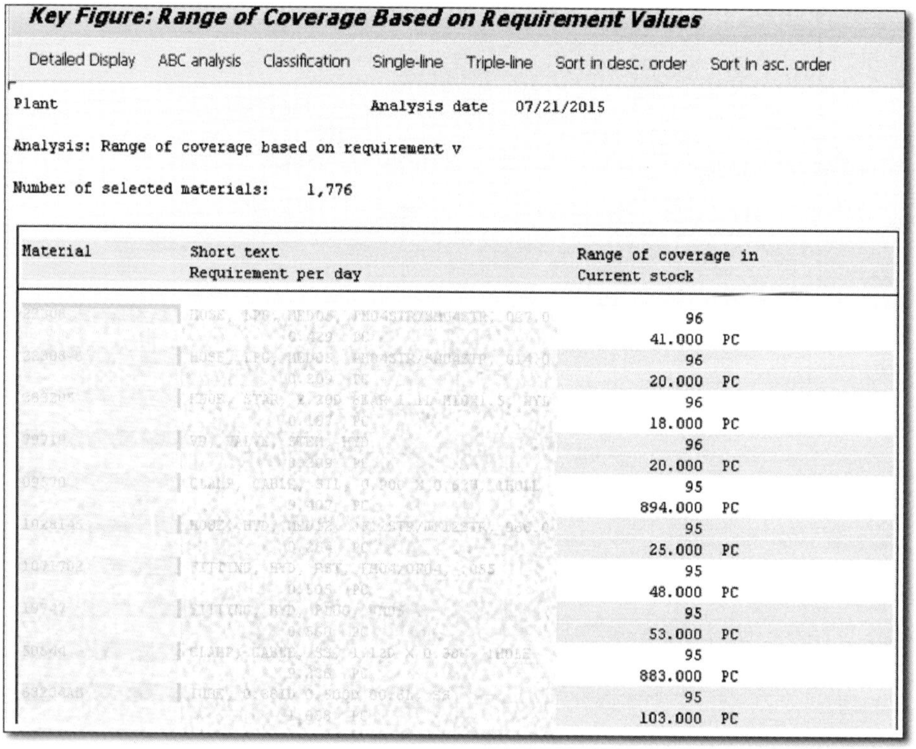

Figure 8.38 Range of Coverage Based on Requirements

Use the range of coverage report based on requirements if you're more concerned about meeting the forecast.

Usage Value

By using the analysis on usage value, you can select materials that have a high level of usage value and a high capital lockup. The usage value is derived from the average usage of a material within a period of time in the past. Figure 8.39 provides an example.

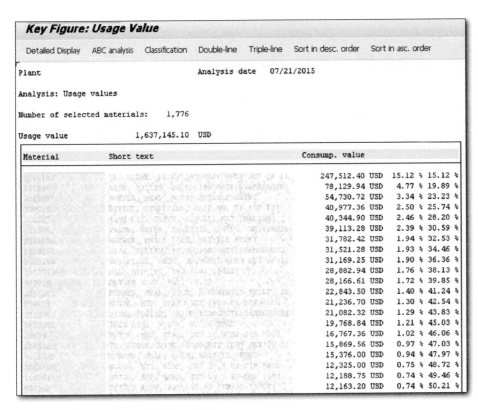

Figure 8.39 Transaction MC45 Usage Value

Requirements Value

By using the analysis on requirements value, you can select materials that have a high level of requirements value and a high capital lockup in the future. The requirements value of a material is derived from the current price of valuated requirements within a period of time in the future. Figure 8.40 provides an example of requirements values in a double-line display.

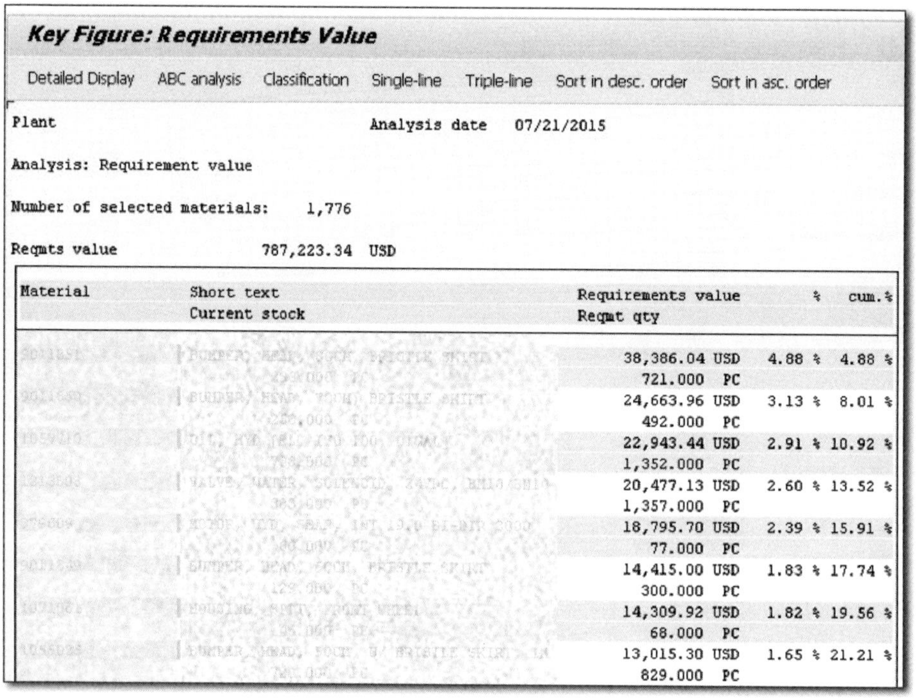

Key Figure: Requirements Value

Detailed Display   ABC analysis   Classification   Single-line   Triple-line   Sort in desc. order   Sort in asc. order

```
Plant                              Analysis date    07/21/2015

Analysis: Requirement value

Number of selected materials:    1,776

Reqmts value              787,223.34  USD
```

Material	Short text Current stock	Requirements value Reqmt qty	%	cum.%
		38,386.04 USD 721.000 PC	4.88 %	4.88 %
		24,663.96 USD 492.000 PC	3.13 %	8.01 %
		22,943.44 USD 1,352.000 PC	2.91 %	10.92 %
		20,477.13 USD 1,357.000 PC	2.60 %	13.52 %
		18,795.70 USD 77.000 PC	2.39 %	15.91 %
		14,415.00 USD 300.000 PC	1.83 %	17.74 %
		14,309.92 USD 68.000 PC	1.82 %	19.56 %
		13,015.30 USD 829.000 PC	1.65 %	21.21 %

Figure 8.40 Transaction MC47 Requirements Value

Graphical Display in Document Evaluations

As with the LIS, you can analyze key figures in the document evaluations as well. To get the graphic, first click on the item ❶ for which you want to display the graph (see Figure 8.41) . Then click the DETAILED DISPLAY button ❷. Choose the STOCK LEVEL radio button ❸, and a new window with the past inventory graphic appears.

Note that the period of evaluation isn't limited by the date range that was selected in the initial screen of the transaction; rather, it shows the entire history of the material in question.

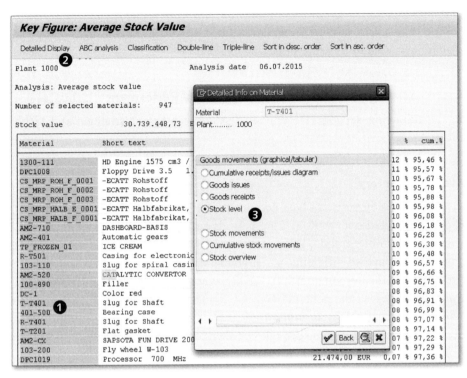

Figure 8.41 Calling Up the Inventory History Graphic from a Document Evaluations Transaction

8.2 Employing Inventory Strategies with Meaningful Key Performance Indicators

As we discussed earlier, a well-defined inventory optimization strategy must include periodic evaluations of the organization's supply chain so that inefficiencies can be addressed. After the analysis functions are defined, you should then map out the process to determine areas for improvement and establish standardized operating procedures to improve on the current situation.

Technology can be helpful in enabling inventory optimization programs. However, organizations must see technology as a supplement to stable inventory planning processes so that the processes, not the technology, are the drivers of performance. What technology provides primarily is the calculation of useful KPIs. Picking the right KPIs and putting together a benchmarking process for continuous and sustainable inventory optimization has been a major challenge. The following is meant to provide explanation for some of the KPIs, gauges, and levers that are available to measure performance.

8.2.1 Strategic and Tactical Inventory Key Performance Indicators

In the following sections we will discuss some relevant strategic and tactical inventory KPIs:

Average Inventory

Trends and predictions are best done using the key figure Average Inventory. It can be calculated over various time periods and depicted in a graphic so that it shows and exhibits trends. What you gain by looking at averages as opposed to specific levels at a specific time is that you're smoothing outliers and normalizing the history of the item in question. We use average inventory to get an idea about the effectiveness of the policies being set. If an item was identified as holding too much inventory, it may be optimized using a different policy. Monitoring the average inventory over time provides you with a very effective tool to spot reductions if the policy works or to increase values if it doesn't.

Dead Stock as a Percentage of Average Inventory

Average inventory may also be used to make the dead stock value meaningful. A dead stock value of $20,000 by itself means nothing. But if an item with an average inventory holding of $100,000 has $20,000 lying around in unused stock, we can say that for that item we're holding 20% of dead stock. This simply means that over the defined period, the stock holdings included $20,000 that we've never even touched in that period. In other words, 20% of our inventory remains unturned.

Generally speaking, we can say that about 20% to 25% of dead stock average inventory remains within an acceptable range. However, this varies with your industry as well as the classification of the specific item.

Inventory Turns

Monitoring how often the inventory turns represents a very effective means to make good decisions in policy setting. The basic definition of inventory turns is defined with the formula shown in Figure 8.42.

$$\text{Inventory Turns} = \frac{\text{Cost of Goods Sold}}{\text{Average Inventory}}$$

Figure 8.42 Formula for Inventory Turns

In materials planning, however, we deal with consumption of raw materials and purchased parts; therefore, the equation may be formulated as shown in Figure 8.43.

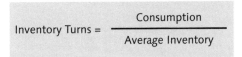

$$\text{Inventory Turns} = \frac{\text{Consumption}}{\text{Average Inventory}}$$

Figure 8.43 Inventory Turns Calculated for Purchased Parts or Raw Materials

Out of this, we can conclude that the only two ways of improving (increasing) turns is by either increasing consumption or reducing average inventory. A materials planner can't easily increase consumption, so the materials planner's tactics to increase turns lies in a reduction of average inventory.

Too often, averages are reduced without proper strategies (or policies), and more often than not, these reductions result in stock-out because it's not really clear where exactly the surplus resides. Fixing this problem with the KPI Inventory Turns provides a far more controlled, smart, and efficient way to relate consumption with average inventory holdings and therefore the ability to better control the outcome of an inventory optimization.

Inventory Quality Ratio

The Inventory Quality Ratio (IQR) is a simple and straightforward way of measuring inventory performance, managing inventory dollars, and identifying inventory reduction opportunities. The IQR logic was developed collectively by a group of materials planners from various companies who had huge successes in reducing inventories and improving on-time delivery using IQR.

Using the data from SAP ERP, the IQR logic first divides inventory into three groups: items with future requirements, items with no future requirements but with recent past usage, and items with neither. The items in these groups are then stratified into typical ABC-type classifications based on their future dollar requirements, their past dollar usage, or their current dollar balances, respectively. A target inventory level expressed in days' supply is set for each item based on its classification. The balance on hand of each item is compared to the target, and the dollars of each item are categorized as either active, excess, slow moving, or obsolete. These are called the inventory quality categories. Figure 8.44 represents such a system.

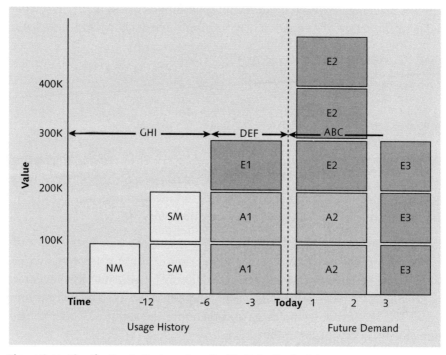

Figure 8.44 Classification in the Inventory Quality Ratio Methodology

As shown in Figure 8.45, the IQR is the ratio of the active inventory dollars (the materials you need now) to total inventory dollars (the active inventory plus all the other stuff you hold on hand). In a theoretically perfect situation (i.e., with no excess, slow-moving, or obsolete inventories), the IQR would be 100%.

$$IQR = \frac{\text{Active Inventory Dollars}}{\text{Total Inventory Dollars}}$$

Figure 8.45 Inventory Quality Ratio Formula

IQR incorporates the best practices of periodic reviews and ABC analysis with forward-looking days' supply and user-defined parameters. It provides inventory managers with a dynamic methodology to review and reassess lead times, safety stocks, order quantities, and replenishment cycles on a weekly or monthly basis. IQR also enhances existing MRP systems by adding a dollar focus to prioritize current reduction opportunities.

IQR, like many new methodologies, isn't part of the standard delivery of SAP ERP. However, if you're part of the continuous enhancement program by SAP Consulting and own the SAP add-on tool Inventory Cockpit, you can use the method, formulas, and functionality that comes with it to calculate your own IQR.

Range of Coverage Over Replenishment Lead Time

Categorizing materials' inventory levels by looking at range of coverage and the materials' total replenishment lead time is a very effective way to quickly see if you're holding excess stock. Obviously, if a material has a short lead time, you don't need as much coverage into the future as when the material has a long lead time to replenish. Figure 8.46 shows a graphic that performs such a categorization using the Inventory Cockpit.

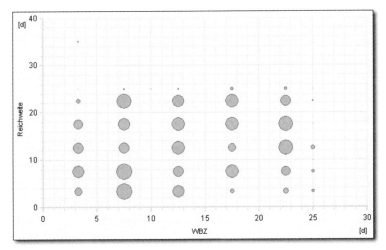

Figure 8.46 Range of Coverage Over Replenishment Lead Time in the Inventory Cockpit

The chart shows the distribution of materials in a replenishment lead time/range of coverage graph. The bigger the sphere, the more materials belong to the respective group. By clicking a sphere on the graph, you can display the corresponding materials as shown in Figure 8.47.

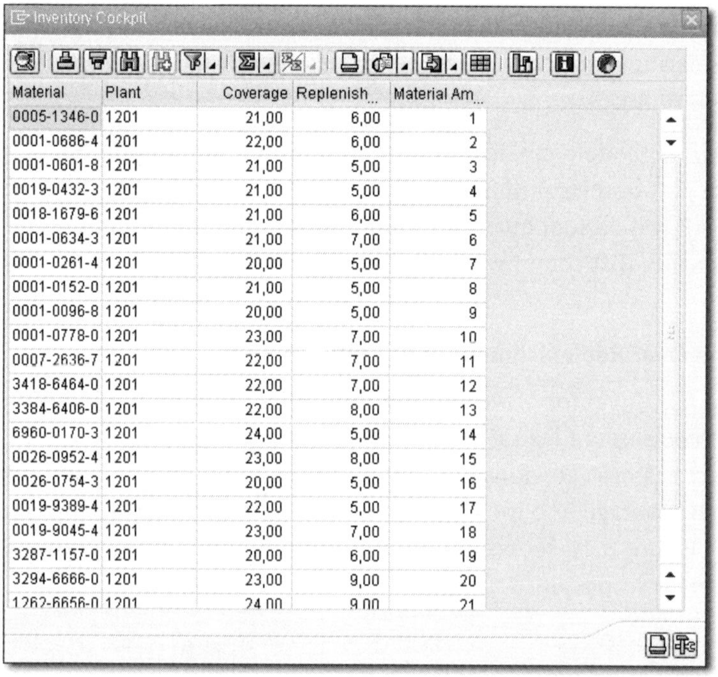

Material	Plant	Coverage	Replenish...	Material Am...
0005-1346-0	1201	21,00	6,00	1
0001-0686-4	1201	22,00	6,00	2
0001-0601-8	1201	21,00	5,00	3
0019-0432-3	1201	21,00	5,00	4
0018-1679-6	1201	21,00	6,00	5
0001-0634-3	1201	21,00	7,00	6
0001-0261-4	1201	20,00	5,00	7
0001-0152-0	1201	21,00	5,00	8
0001-0096-8	1201	20,00	5,00	9
0001-0778-0	1201	23,00	7,00	10
0007-2636-7	1201	22,00	7,00	11
3418-6464-0	1201	22,00	7,00	12
3384-6406-0	1201	22,00	8,00	13
6960-0170-3	1201	24,00	5,00	14
0026-0952-4	1201	23,00	8,00	15
0026-0754-3	1201	20,00	5,00	16
0019-9389-4	1201	22,00	5,00	17
0019-9045-4	1201	23,00	7,00	18
3287-1157-0	1201	20,00	6,00	19
3294-6666-0	1201	23,00	9,00	20
1262-6656-0	1201	24,00	9,00	21

Figure 8.47 List of Materials from a Range of Coverage/Replenishment Lead Time Analysis

Looking at inventory in this way provides a far more telling story about a material's low or high stock holdings than simple current or average figures.

8.2.2 Parameter Controlling with Dual Classification

Parameter controlling provides the opportunity to optimize material parameters on the basis of statistical data in Inventory Controlling and the LIS. It has the potential for optimization with regard to individual material parameters such as lot size and safety stock. Parameters controlling includes a deviation analysis with which a modification of the parameters can be carried out, and it uses a cause-oriented approach to reach the goal of inventory optimization and reduction of capital lockup.

Parameters controlling is implemented in the form of five predefined dual classifications. In these dual classifications, the characteristic values (materials) are always classified with regard to two key figures. The segments that are generated in this way can then be evaluated more precisely with regard to the characteristic values they contain. This makes interrelationships between key figures more meaningful and allows for the quick detection of possible problem areas. The five predefined dual classifications in parameters controlling are described in the following subsections. You can find the dual classifications in any initial or drilldown list in the LIS under the EDIT menu option.

Lot Size

The key figure Range of Coverage of the Average Receipt and the key figure Value of the Average Receipt are compared in this report. Naturally, if a material is ordered or produced in lot sizes that are too large, it may lead to excessive average stock levels. The lot size must, however, be seen in relation to the consumption. A high level of consumption justifies a large lot size. For this reason, a key figure that takes both the lot size and consumption into account would prove to be very telling. This KPI is the range of coverage of the average receipt in days. If the range of coverage of the average receipt is large, then the lot size, and thus the average stock, can be reduced. To perform this dual classification, start from an initial or drilldown list, and select EDIT • CHECK PARAMETERS • LOT SIZE.

Materials that are assigned to the upper class limits with regard to both key figures will be easily visible. These materials have a high range of coverage of the average receipt and display a high value of the average receipt. This means that a reduction of the lot size is recommended because the current lot size has a high value at receipt, thus causing a high stock value and a high capital lockup.

Stock at Receipt

In this dual classification, the key figure Range of Coverage of the Average Stock at Receipt and the key figure Value of the Average Stock at Receipt are compared. If the goods receipt posting of a material takes place when a large quantity of the material is still available in the warehouse, it leads to a disproportionately high average stock value. As the amount of stock at receipt should be evaluated in relation to the items' consumption, we should judge the stock level by the amount of time it can last. The decisive key figure here is therefore Range of Coverage of the Average Stock at Receipt.

A high stock level is often the result of premature procurement. You should check for the following to find the cause for excessively high stock at receipt:

▶ Does the lead time in the material master correspond to the actual lead time?

▶ If safety sock has been entered manually, can the safety stock be reduced?

▶ If safety stock has been calculated automatically, is the preset service level justified?

▶ Do forecasting and planning provide realistic requirements?

To perform this dual classification, select EDIT • CHECK PARAMETERS • STOCK AT RECEIPT from an initial or drilldown list.

Materials that show both a large range of coverage of average stock at receipt and a high value of the average receipt have high inventory value at the time of the receipt in relation to its consumption and should therefore be examined more closely.

Safety Stock

Key figures Value of the Average Stock at Receipt and Stock Factor' are compared in this dual classification. The key figure Stock Factor is calculated by dividing the average stock at receipt by safety stock and should ideally be 1. To optimize stock levels, and at the same time observe the safety factor, it's advisable to reduce the average stock at receipt to correspond with the safety stock. The optimum level is reached when the average stock at receipt and the safety stock are equal. If the average stock at receipt is larger than the safety stock, it leads to an unnecessarily high stock level; if it's smaller, then there is the danger of a shortage. If you want to optimize the average stock at receipt, you should ask the following questions:

▶ Does the lead time in the material master correspond to the actual lead time?

▶ Do forecasting and planning provide realistic requirements?

In reorder point planning, a purchase order is always triggered when the reorder point is broken. The reorder point consists of the safety stock and predicted consumption during replenishment lead time. If the average stock at receipt is always higher than the safety stock, it might indicate that the replenishment lead time (PLANNED DELIVERY TIME in the MRP 2 screen of the material master record) had been set incorrectly, that orders were been placed too early, or that the safety stock level is too high.

To perform this dual classification, start from an initial or drilldown list, and select EDIT • CHECK PARAMETERS • SAFETY STOCK .

Parameter controlling of this type is most effective when you look out for materials that deviate greatly with regard to both key figures and that show a stock factor higher than 1. The potential lies in improving the consumption forecast or fixing the lead time set in the material master.

Safety Stock Buffer

The key figure Range of Coverage of the Average Receipt and the key figure Range of Coverage of the Average Stock at Receipt are compared. Both of these key figures represent the safety stock buffer, which is one of the most important parts in a system of effective inventory optimization or materials planning.

Avoiding stock-outs is one of the key objectives of Inventory Management. You can make use of two strategies to achieve this goal:

▶ High safety stocks and therefore high average stock at the time of the receipt

▶ Large lot size and therefore high range of coverage at the time of the receipt

If the decision is made in favor of high safety stocks, you should check whether the lot size and the average stock at receipt can be reduced. On the other hand, if you choose larger lot sizes for reasons of cost, then you should consider reducing safety stocks and the average stock.

To execute this dual classification, start from an initial or drilldown list, and select EDIT • CHECK PARAMETERS • SAFETY STOCK BUFFER.

You should pay particular attention to characteristic values that are in the upper class limits for both key figures. The combination of a high lot size (represented by the key figure Range of Coverage of the Average Receipt) and high safety stocks (represented by the key figure Range of Coverage of the Average Stock at Receipt) indicates problems in planning and parameter setting.

As a general rule, you might say that if you're aiming for high lot sizes, then a small safety stock is sufficient. But if your strategy calls for high safety stocks, smaller lot sizes are sufficient.

Slow-Moving Items

For this dual classification, we're using the key figure Value of the Last Consumption and the key figure Days without Consumption. The key figure Days without Consumption is derived from the time difference between the date of the last consumption and the current date.

Slow-moving items are those materials for which the last consumption posting is far in the past. Slow-moving items incur unnecessarily high cost, and if you can pinpoint and separate these, there is ample opportunity for improvement.

To perform this dual classification, select EDIT • CHECK PARAMETERS • SLOW-MOVING ITEM from an initial or drilldown list.

Materials showing high values for both key figures are good candidates for parameter optimization.

8.3   Making Inventory Optimization Sustainable

As we all know, inventory optimization programs abound, but rarely do inventories that have been optimized remain that way. Much too often, the initiative is abandoned, left without results, or, in the worst cases, considered a success when in actuality the perceived inventory reduction will lead to stock-outs, lost revenue, and starving production lines.

In the following subsections, we'll discuss a number of situations where a change in thinking and behavior may make all the difference and falling back to old habits can be avoided. There are certainly ways to make inventory optimization sustainable and lasting.

8.3.1   Fine-Tuning the Policy

The second pillar of our system of effective materials planning is automated and periodic policy setting. In fact, policy lies at the heart of a materials planning system. A policy, among many other functions, drives inventory levels dynamically. Many parts of a policy such as lot-size procedure, safety stock settings (static and dynamic), MRP type, and strategy groups have a major impact on the way inventory rises or falls. Therefore, it's a good idea to check on the policy when you find an item that has suboptimal stock levels.

When building a hit list of items for a targeted inventory optimization, you should look at the individual settings in the policy first and at the holistic outcome of the policy second. There are tools to simulate a policy (see the description of the SAP add-on tool MRP Parameter Simulation in Section 8.4.3) so that you can anticipate and compare different outcomes for specific inventory KPIs through various policies. As you run that simulation, you might want to switch an MRP type, reduce the safety stock, or use an optimizing lot-size procedure. And whatever works for you will be saved as a revised or possibly a new policy in your collection. This way, you're building a library of tested and proven policies so that you soon will have an answer to any problematic situation.

However, at the same time, you should be cautious. Don't fiddle too much with the policy. If you end up changing the reorder point three times a day, you'll never know what works and what doesn't.

8.3.2 Performing Daily Exception Monitoring for Continuous Attainment of Good Results

Get into the routine to check your exceptions daily and work through all of them in a prioritized way. It's best if you start first thing in the morning. In Chapter 7, in which we discuss intelligent exception monitoring—the third pillar—we provide one way of managing exceptions, but there are many more. It's strongly recommended that you build your own prioritized way of looking and dealing with exception messages. Standardize your remedies and see that you get through the list completely every day. You'll be rewarded with many fewer exceptions; however, just laboring through them day by day would be a waste of time if there are too many faults in the processes causing the exceptions.

Both exception handling as well as process design must be considered, but without effective and routine exception monitoring, your inventories soon start getting out of bounds again.

8.3.3 Keeping the Basic Data and Supply and Demand Elements Clean

Outdated elements falsify the stock/requirements situation and trick the MRP run into generating wasteful order proposals. Only when you post goods movements as close as possible to when they occur will you provide a good basis for inventory management. If you don't and also don't adjust the delivery date of a late purchase order, you're taking away the system's ability to provide you with good information.

8.3.4 Getting Management to Sign Off on Meaningful Supply Chain Strategies

Without consensus and direction, it's very difficult to maintain integrity with management and deliver what they expect. If the only mandate a planner receives is an occasional reduction of inventory by 20%, there might be too much of the wrong materials and not enough of the right materials in the warehouse at any given day.

The planner should define performance boundaries (what service level do we desire for AX parts, what coverage do we need for short lead time items, etc.) and submit the document to management so they can sign off on it or revise it. Chances are that when you ask management to build the strategy themselves, you might need to wait awhile. But if you proactively force the issue, chances are much better for you to work with clarity and without the need for countless discussions about service level and safety stock settings.

8.3.5 Performing Capacity Sequencing, Leveling, and Scheduling

Did you know that the MRP run doesn't care at all if the order proposals fit into the available capacity profile? When MRP generates order proposals for production, the end dates of the orders covering a demand are all set up with the same delivery date; just before the demand needs the supply. From there, backwards scheduling takes place, and you'll end up with a bunch of planned orders all with the same end dates.

Capacity scheduling is now needed, and after it's done, most of the planned orders will be rescheduled to a different point in time. Because every order needs raw materials to be available to get started, material requirements dates will be different before capacity scheduling than they are after capacity scheduling.

Make sure capacity planning is done—and at the right time—otherwise, you'll procure purchased parts to the wrong requirements dates and end up with stockouts in some cases and surplus inventory in others.

8.3.6 Respecting the Planning Horizons

SAP software provides excellent planning functions and capabilities. But before you can effectively use them, you must define the planning horizons. Some people don't necessarily mind if they're in the long-, mid-, or short term for what transactions and tasks they perform.

For example, a scheduler might turn a planned order into a production order several weeks or even months before production of that order starts, or the forecast is worked by the MRP run (and subsequently planned orders are generated) way beyond the short term or even midterm. These and other misconducts cause problems for your inventory planning. Figure 8.48 summarizes how a planner can move his activities through the planning horizons to ensure good results in the end for inventory holdings.

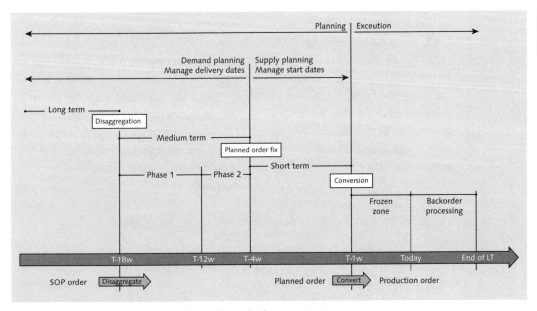

Figure 8.48 *Moving Activities and Objects Through Planning Horizons*

There are two major rules that are valid in such a planning system:

▶ **Rule of Planning #1: There is a point in time after which planning activities end.** This point in time isn't today! It comes before today, exactly at the point where the frozen zone begins. In the frozen zone, you're working with production orders. And production orders are supply elements that we aren't planning with anymore. We're expediting on them and rescheduling them, rerouting operations to different workstations, and reacting to exception messages they received from the MRP run when actual results differ from the plan. If you find yourself looking for a tool to automatically reassign and reschedule within the frozen zone, you either don't have a frozen zone, or you're under the wrong assumption that the planning system should not only plan but also fix deviations from the plan. These deviations are due to variability, which can only be buffered—not planned— especially *after* it occurs.

▶ **Rule of Planning #2: To plan your resources in the mid- and longterm, level and manage demand; to plan your resources and sequence in the short term, level, schedule, and manage supply.**
It doesn't make sense to reshuffle planned orders in the long term. You shouldn't have any in the first place. In the long term, you're working in SOP and therefore with a planning hierarchy, monthly demand figures, and SOP orders that cause rough capacity requirements (and not detailed capacity requirements). In SOP, you move the demand so that capacity violations are resolved. In the midterm, you should work with long-term planning (LTP) and its planning scenarios. A planning scenario contains a demand program that you can simulate (with simulated planned orders) for midterm capacity planning. Here you should also work with the demand program until you find one that generates simulated planned orders that fit into your available capacity program. That is the demand program (planning scenario) that you activate into the short term. Now you can run MRP on those planned independent requirements, and the resulting planned orders can be sequenced, leveled, and scheduled in capacity planning. The latter activity was managing and scheduling supply, whereas the previous activities were concerned with leveling demand.

Those two rules we've persistently respected and followed in our efforts to build a standardized and integrated planning system everyone in the organization is using and looking at for continuous improvements. The sales planners enter their forecast into product groups within a planning hierarchy. SOP orders, statistical work centers, and rough-cut planning profiles are used to analyze the capacity situation for a horizon of 18 months out up to 5 years. If we encounter a problem, we move the entire product group demand into a previous, less capacity constrained period or fill out a request for more capital expenditure to increase capacity and meet increasing customer demand.

When the leveled demand is disaggregated from the product group level to the actual product, we then transfer the demand profile into LTP where we simulate various demand programs and generate simulative supply. Requirements are determined for long lead time items, and the procurement process is started if necessary. During Phase 1 of the midterm—12 months to 18 months out in this example—we let demand changes from the SOP flow in and integrate these into the demand programs. In Phase 2 of the midterm, we perform detailed capacity planning with simulative planned orders and find the best demand program that fits into our available capacity.

The activation of the demand program (transfer of planned independent requirements into MRP) indicates the move from the midterm to the short-term planning horizon. After MRP is run, planned orders are generated that we can sequence, level, and schedule within available capacity on the bottleneck work center.

The last planning activity then is to take all leveled and sequenced planned orders of, say, one week and perform a collective material availability check. Now you've ensured that all materials and the capacity are available for all the orders to be executed, and you're ready to move these orders into the frozen zone by collectively converting the planned orders into production orders for the next week. From then on—within the frozen zone and into backorder scheduling—all planning has stopped. Anything that happens against the plan needs to be adjusted manually. If a work center is down, an alternative work center will have to be found, and the sequence in the work order must be changed manually.

This last point is especially important because people often ask if they can automate this function. This is an impossible proposition because you would have to build all possible cures to an exception into the basic data (production versions, alternative BOMs or routings, etc.), and you can't possible do that. It's much better to have someone who is close to the exceptional situation pick an alternative and just change it into the order. After all, that is the whole reason why we're comparing actuals to the schedule and the plan.

8.4   SAP Add-On Tools for Inventory Optimization

As we mentioned previously in this book, SAP Consulting has been enhancing standard SAP ERP software functionality with a series of add-on tools. These cockpits, monitors, and simulators came out of customers' requirements to facilitate (combine transactions into one central monitor for faster access of information), improve (keep adding functionality to the existing SAP ERP 6.0), and generally make the overall SAP experience more effective, more convenient, and more exciting.

In the following subsections, we'll introduce three SAP add-on tools that provide excellent functionality for inventory analysis and optimization.

8.4.1 Analyzing Stocks with the Inventory Cockpit

The Inventory Cockpit makes it easy to analyze and display key figures on various aggregation levels. You can run a multitude of comparisons and display the result in tables and graphics. Instead of having to gather information from countless individual transactions in the LIS or the document evaluations, you have all the data readily available in one place. Sorting, filtering, and listing are a breeze, and data may be exported into Excel spreadsheets for further slicing and dicing.

Its most taunting function lies in the ability to set a target inventory level with which you can set a benchmark for periodical comparison to your actual levels. With the Inventory Cockpit the user gains control over inventory performance and, through better transparency, can find critical items and build hit lists for improvement activities.

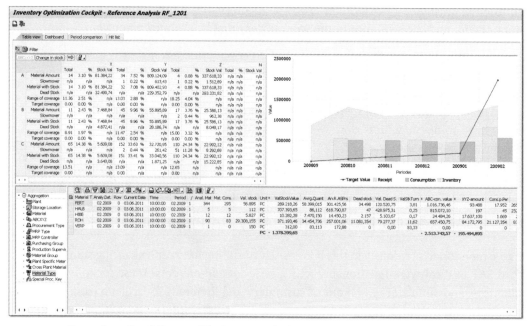

Figure 8.49 Result Screen of the Inventory Cockpit

The Inventory Cockpit can be run month by month. The results screen is shown in Figure 8.49.

As you can in this figure, the results screen provides a classification grid where specific inventory KPIs are displayed according to an ABC/XYZ classification. Downloadable graphics show inventory developments of the past, a target inventory line, and bar charts for receipts and issues in the select periods. You can aggregate to the MRP CONTROLLER KEY, PLANT, MATERIAL, MRP TYPE, and many more. Filtering is possible so that, for example, dead stock, average values, and current values can be aggregated to materials set to a reorder point procedure and then filtered for a specific materials planner so that you can monitor the effectiveness of a specific policy.

Figure 8.50 shows some examples of the graphics you may employ using the monitor.

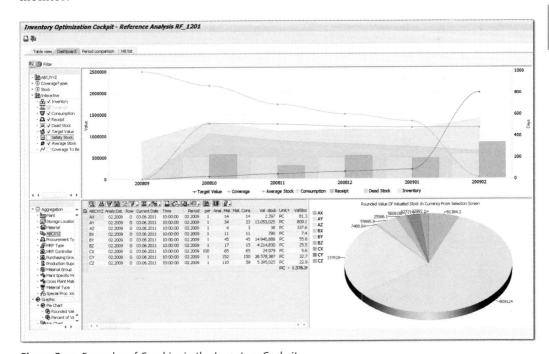

Figure 8.50 Examples of Graphics in the Inventory Cockpit

The PERIOD COMPARISON tab in the add-on tool is dedicated to performing comparisons. As shown in Figure 8.51, you can compare various aggregation levels such as MATERIAL TYPE or MATERIAL GROUP over the period of evaluation.

You can show totals, and the fields to be displayed are freely configurable so that you can save your own, user-defined layouts.

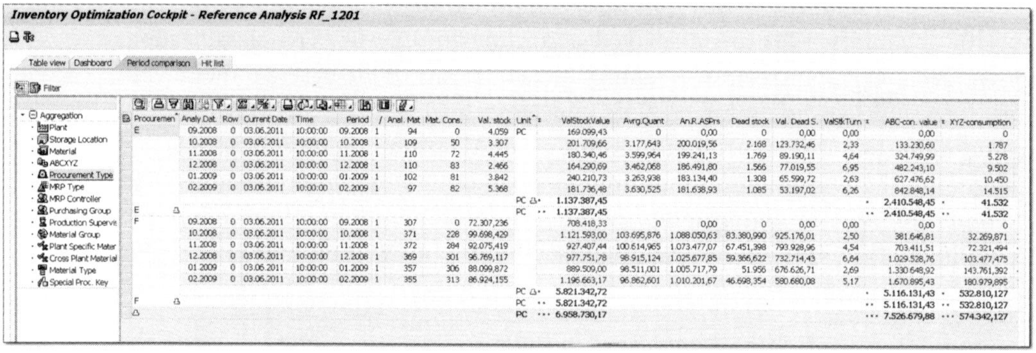

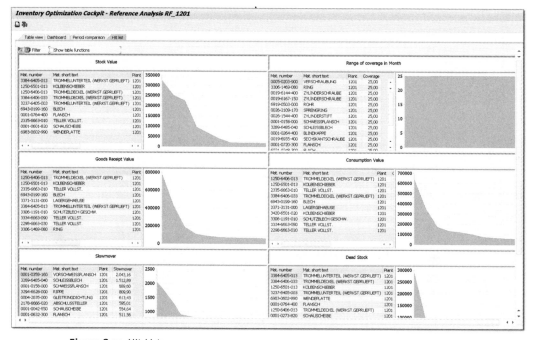

Figure 8.51 Period Comparisons on Different Aggregation Levels

Finally, the Inventory Cockpit generates hit lists for you to put together targeted and focused improvement programs (see Figure 8.52).

Figure 8.52 Hit Lists

These hit lists can be built for the 10 materials with the highest dead stock value or the worst 20 performers in terms of range of coverage. Measures and resubmissions can then be maintained for these materials, and a future target can be put up to be met.

8.4.2 Simulating Lot-Size Procedures, Safety Stock Levels, and Reorder Points

Within the suite of available SAP add-on tools, there are two simulators: the Lot Size Simulation tool comes up with the optimum lot-size procedure for a specific demand situation, and the Safety Stock and Reorder Point Simulator calculates safety stocks and reorder points for a series of service levels.

Both tools can mass update the optimum results into the material master records, and either one can be called up separately or directly out of the MRP Monitor.

With the Lot Size Simulation Tool, it's possible to calculate the cost effects of various lot-size procedures. The tool uses the existing demand situation of the materials in scope and performs a simulative MRP run for all the lot sizes to be tested to calculate the resulting ordering cost and compare it to the necessary stock holding cost.

Figure 8.53 displays the result screen of the simulation. In the PARAMETERS FOR ALL MATERIALS area ❶, parameters are set for the simulation; the list on the upper-right side of the screen ❷ allows for the selection of different lot-size procedures; and the bottom area of the screen ❸ shows the result of the simulation. The Lot Size Simulation Tool sorts the results in a way that the lowest cost procedures are displayed in a column that can be selected and used to update the material master record. Therefore, the Lot Size Simulation Tool serves as a great opportunity to keep your lot size most cost effective at any time under changing requirements.

The Safety Stock and Reorder Point Simulator allows you to determine safety stock levels and safety stock values for alternative service levels. You can then compare the result with the current material master setting. After the data has been compared, the best option can be saved in the material master.

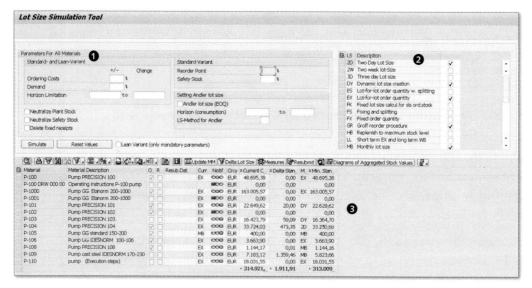

Figure 8.53 Results Screen of the Lot Size Simulation Tool

There are three calculation methods possible for the determination of safety stocks and reorder points:

▶ The ERP method in calendar days, which uses standard SAP functionality as in the forecast screen of the material master record

▶ The ERP method in working days, which uses the same formulas and functions as the previous list item but calculates the lead time in working days

▶ The Advanced Method, which allows for two additional parameters to be used in the calculation: variation in demand and variation in lead time

Figure 8.54 shows the results of a safety stock and reorder point simulation. The lower window contains all simulated results for all the service levels selected. KPIs such as the value of the safety stock for a material can be totaled so that, for example, you may want to display the cost effect of a service level of 97% and compare it to the effect of a service level of 99%. This function has great merit for our system of effective materials planning because an organization can agree on a service level strategy for, let's say, CX items and then make the decision part of the standard policy so that you achieve commonality and standardization across the board.

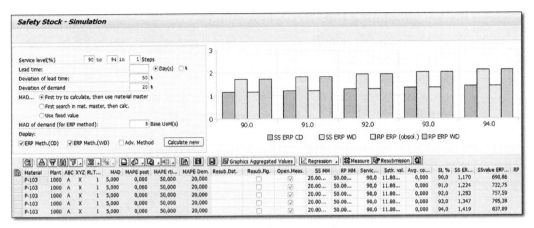

Figure 8.54 Results Screen of a Safety Stock and Reorder Point Simulation

Another function of the safety stock simulator is displayed in Figure 8.55. Safety stocks are plotted over service levels, and you can clearly see the exponential growths of a safety stock requirement as the service level approaches 100%. If you plot a regression line as shown in Figure 8.55, it's recommended to consider a service level where the safety stock starts breaking above the regression line. In our example this service level is in the neighborhood of 93 to 94%.

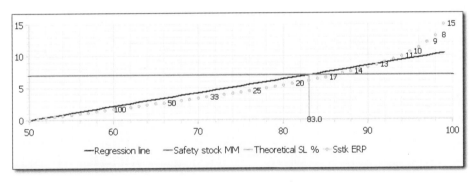

Figure 8.55 Regression Analysis Using Various Service Levels

After the optimum service level for the best safety stock has been determined, the respective material master records can all be updated collectively, by clicking MATERIAL UPDATE. Here, service levels, safety stock settings, and reorder points can also be set in the materials.

8.4.3 Simulating the Effects of a Policy

The MRP Parameter Simulation is an SAP add-on tool containing functionalities to predict the future outcome of a policy. The MRP Parameter Simulation is based on simulative data to support your strategic decision making. It enables you to perform planning runs on different planning and demand scenarios form LTP and calculates specific inventory KPIs for a future date. The results are presented shown in Figure 8.56.

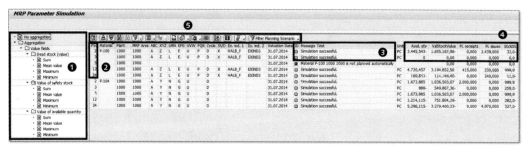

Figure 8.56 MRP Parameter Simulation Results

On the left side of the results screen, you can find a tree structure so that you can perform aggregations ❶. Here, simulations can be conducted for various materials, for all LTP Planning Versions ❷. Messages about successful simulations are also located on this screen ❸, and the resulting KPIs are displayed with their respective values ❹. At the top of the screen buttons can be found to filter, search, and sort the list ❺. Aggregation is possible for various KPIs. Apart from total and mean value, the maximum and minimum of every KPI for each material can be shown for the simulated scenarios.

As the MRP Monitor add-on tool comes with a policy table, you can simulate the demand program from LTP with various policies. Therefore, the MRP Parameter Simulation tool serves as a superior tool for long-term and midterm materials planning.

8.5 Summary

Sustainable inventory optimization, the fourth pillar in our system of effective material planning, is only possible if it isn't viewed as a one-time affair or project but as a continuous set of activities to analyze, monitor, and optimize the replenishment policy of a purchased part. Effective tools, transactions, and reports are essential to manage the inventories of thousands of parts, and SAP provides a wealth of information through its LIS.

The LIS, with its infostructures, has all the data required to perform inventory analysis. However, the data needs to be evaluated in a meaningful way, and with the various graphics, tables, and classifications it provides, an informed user gets all the information necessary to make good decisions.

Graphical analysis, dual classification, parameter controlling, and document evaluations are, no matter how long ago they were developed, essential tools in the box of a conscientious material planner and analyst. Additionally, KPIs such as inventory turns, range of coverage, dead stock value, and averages help to round out the meaningful big picture the analyst gets when he connects the dots and figures out dependencies and correlations.

Lastly, SAP add-on tools represent one of the last efforts to enhance and further develop SAP ERP functionality. Using these capabilities for mass updates, simulations, and spot analysis makes the life of a materials planner a better one.

PART III

Evaluating, Measuring, and Improving Materials Planning

Darkness can't drive out darkness; only Light can do that.
—Dr. Martin Luther King

9   Key Performance and Supply Chain Indicators

Since the dawn of enterprise resource planning (ERP) systems, companies have tried to evaluate whether they are on the right track implementing and using the software that runs their operations. Measuring progress in the implementation and use of the software is a challenge. It's hard to know if you're improving, and it's tricky to compare one state of efficiency with another. One of the greatest challenges is picking the right indicators and measures. There are probably more key performance indicators (KPIs) than you could wish for, and picking the ones that provide useful results is difficult to say the least. Some KPIs are measurable in numbers, whereas others need interpretation and a lot of experience to determine the rating.

Materials planning, like any other discipline in supply chain and operations management using SAP ERP, needs to be evaluated, constantly analyzed, and measured. Organizations of all sizes in all industries spend enormous efforts on putting together their own systems (with more or less success) to do the following:

▶ Measure progress.

▶ Identify improvement opportunities.

▶ Monitor the implementation and effectiveness of strategies and policies.

▶ Allow for measurement of accomplishments (not just the work that has been done).

▶ Provide a common language for everyone to understand.

▶ Identify the gap between a target and the actual result of actions performed.

Whether these actions, improvement activities, and initiatives are organized in an effective manner, pursue valuable results, and work commonly toward the overall goals of the company is a very different question. This chapter strives to provide a common understanding about what a framework of measurement could look like for an organization that runs its operations and materials planning with SAP software.

Supply chain KPIs evaluate the success and progress of a particular activity we define in an improvement or for a daily process. Often, success is simply the repeated periodic achievement of some levels of operational goal, and sometimes success is defined in terms of making progress toward strategic goals. Accordingly, choosing the right KPIs relies on a good understanding of what is important and what is valuable to the process and the entire organization. What is important often depends on the department measuring the performance—for example, the KPIs useful to finance will be much different from the KPIs assigned to inventory planning. Because there is a need to understand what is important, various techniques to assess the present state of the business, and its key activities, are associated with the selection of valid, valuable, and meaningful KPIs. These assessments should lead to the identification of potential improvements, so KPIs are routinely associated with performance improvement initiatives. A very common way to choose KPIs is to apply a management framework such as the Balanced Scorecard (BSC) or the Supply Chain Planning Index framework we'll discuss later in this chapter.

9.1   The Balanced Scorecard

The Balanced Scorecard (BSC) is a measuring system that was used by organizations for quite some time and still is one of the preferred methods to evaluate a company's performance. In its essence, it combines financial and nonfinancial metrics to track progress.

The BSC is a strategy performance management tool—that is, a strategic planning and management system—used extensively in business and industry, government, and nonprofit organizations worldwide to align business activities to the vision and strategy of the organization. Companies strive to improve internal and external communications and to monitor their processes using the BSC.

The BSC went through three generations of development. The first generation used a four-perspective approach. These perspectives evaluated information from the view of finance, the customer, internal business processes, and learning and growth. The idea was that managers would pick more detailed KPIs to aggregate a measurement to each of these four perspectives. The designers of this first generation of the BSC, Kaplan and Norton, however, were primarily thinking of non-divisional, commercial organizations in their first design. For multidivisional or multinational organizations, the first-generation approach proved to be a problem because the managers of large organizations did not always pick the right measures under the respective heading of the four perspectives. This resulted in many users abandoning the method. They weren't confident that the measures were well chosen, and consequently confidence in the information it provided diminished. This means that first-generation BSCs aren't easy to design or accepted.

In the mid-1990s, a new method was designed using strategy maps. Strategy maps are used to tell a story. They communicate how value may be created for the organization and show logical connections between strategic objectives. As in systems thinking, these connections are made visible by causal chains. Simply speaking, when performance is improved in the objectives for learning and growth, the internal process improves with it. Likewise, you'll experience automatic advances in the customer and financials perspectives.

Select measures are plotted and linked on these maps to form a visual representation of strategic direction based on objectives and measures. However, the flaw in the second-generation design was that it didn't really depict causality as a system thinker would expect from a complete and useful measuring framework. Missing causal loops and feedbacks disallowed the complete understanding of what caused the problem and therefore restricted the user in the development of a sound future plan.

Therefore, the third generation (see Figure 9.1) of the BSC included a vision or destination statement that was based on causalities visualized by system thinking (we discuss system thinking further in Chapter 12, Section 12.2). These statements describe what strategic success looks like and can guide the entire organization on working toward the same goals using the same measures with a structured set of activities. Interestingly enough, a strategy map can be viewed from either top down or bottom up. If you look from the top, you would ask "how" questions regarding the way to achieve the specific financial and customer perspectives targets. On the other hand, looking up from the bottom, you would ask, "if/then" questions to make decisions regarding learning and on your internal processes so that the desired goals are reached.

As depicted in Figure 9.1, the third-generation BSC answers two major questions. The first asks the following: *If* an objective changes from the bottom upwards, *then* will the causal connection improve? The second question asks the following: *How* does the causal structure logically connect from top down.

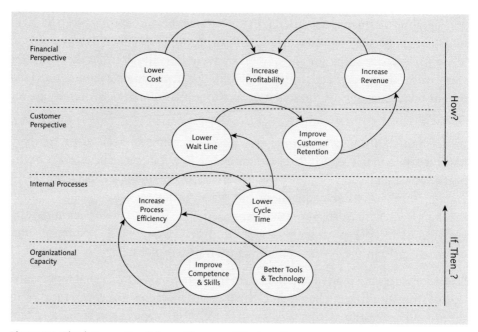

Figure 9.1 Third-Generation Balanced Scorecard Strategy Map

Because the focus of this book is materials planning, for purposes of the BSC, we'll focus on the internal process improvements perspective and the associated quest for more efficiency, which can be formulated as the following:

Efficiency = Performance ÷ Cost

From this equation, we can conclude that higher efficiency is directly related to better performance with lower cost in the process. This really doesn't come as a surprise, but, nevertheless, it's disturbing how little this formula is applied in projects that are in existence primarily because they're supposed to raise said efficiency. The former statement sounds very trivial, so initiatives often are set up to increase performance without regard to the increasing cost in the processes supporting the performance improvements. Or, even worse, cost reductions in the process bring about direct performance reductions. For example, when a production manager decides to increase production lot sizes to save on setup cost, agility in the supply chain will go down proportionally.

There are many more examples in industry which prove that a more holistic and analytical view of the effects of various activities is leading toward the desired results.

Another focus point should be the increase of competence and the proper use of tools and technologies, which will help increase efficiency and in turn reduce the cycle times, optimize inventory and service levels, and drive the targets for the customer perspective and the financial perspective.

Because we'll apply some customization to the fourth-generation BSC so that it better fits with our efforts to monitor a system of effective materials planning with SAP, we'll now refer to it as the Supply Chain Performance Index. The Supply Chain Performance Index is made up of a comprehensive framework of critical KPIs as we'll explain in further detail in the following section.

9.2   The Supply Chain Performance Index Framework

After SAP ERP software functions are implemented and running, it's time to start measuring progress and success. If there is no clearly defined basis upon which measurement can take place, then the first step we need to take is to define a benchmark.

The Supply Chain Performance Index provides such a benchmark. It looks at 10 major measurements to benchmark how well your SAP investment drives your supply chain. Each measurement is supported by various KPIs, and the final result—the index—visualizes the benchmark (Figure 9.2).

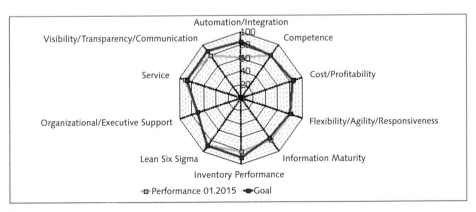

Figure 9.2 Benchmarking Visualized

The following 10 areas are of interest in the Supply Chain Performance Index:

- Automation/Integration
- Competence
- Cost/Profitability
- Flexibility/Agility/Communication
- Information Maturity
- Inventory Performance
- Lean Six Sigma
- Organizational/Executive Support
- Service
- Visibility/Transparency/Communication

Without such a framework (it doesn't have to look exactly like the one described here), reliable, accurate, and useful measuring often fails because the appropriate indicators aren't thought through very well or they don't allow for accretion to the bigger picture. Measuring systems work well when the indicators can be aggregated from lower, more detailed levels to a summarized point of view and, vice versa, disaggregated from higher, summarized levels.

The accrued data can be further evaluated by drilling down to the source of the result. However, a simple, linear structure doesn't, in most cases, deliver the desired results. Mixing tangible measurements such as cycle times and inventory levels with intangibles such as competence and transparency further complicate the task at hand. Considering all the difficulties, we've developed a measuring framework that allows for the following:

- Aggregation and disaggregation up and down a customizable, nonlinear hierarchy
- Comparisons between manufacturing plants and distribution centers within an organization
- Comparisons to other business units within the organization
- Comparisons to industry standards and other organizations
- Goal setting and actual/plan comparison
- Definition of opportunities and the associated actions and tasks

Central to our Supply Chain Performance Index framework is the idea of improving efficiency. Efficiency, as stated earlier can be defined as the following:

Efficiency = Performance ÷ Cost

As performance isn't to be confused with outcome, we can say that efficiency (more closely related to outcome) is determined by how well we make use of someone's performance. In other words, just looking at someone's great performance doesn't conclude that the work done is also efficient. Efficiency is sometimes defined as "accomplishment of or ability to accomplish a job with a minimum expenditure of time and effort." Productivity, however, is simply defined as the ratio of outputs over inputs and therefore doesn't include the intangible elements of the equation that performance will provide. We conclude that for the purpose of materials planning, we want to measure and strive for more efficient internal processes as defined by the performance of our resources (man and tools) and the cost (energy) we put into the process.

From this, we can also define the previously mentioned efficiency formula as the following:

Efficiency = degree of automation, transparency, integration, flexibility, and responsiveness ÷ the amount of competence, quality of data, and capital tied up in inventory

This just confirms that for the purposes of materials planning, the measure of efficiency will pose the central objective and starting point. The Supply Chain Performance Index therefore is a measure of overall efficiency. We'll go into the details about what makes up the index next.

9.2.1 The Supply Chain Performance Index Spider Graph

To visualize efficiency measurements with Supply Chain Performance Index and provide an overall idea of the performance of a supply chain, the results are depicted as a spider graph (see Figure 9.3). Ten major categories or success factors break down into individual KPIs. Through a carefully designed weighting system, the individual ratings aggregate to the category evaluation, which provide the overall Supply Chain Performance Index. Once aggregated, the Supply Chain Performance Index can be evaluated on every level and compared to previous states or to another entity. The Supply Chain Performance Index provides an excellent basis to uncover weakness and suboptimal states in your SAP ERP supply chain. It also supports the definition of activities and projects to optimize the use and efficiency of your planning configuration, measuring the progress to achieve previously defined goals and targets.

The Supply Chain Performance Index can be measured for an individual plant or warehouse, and you can also apply it to your entire organization. Of course, it's possible to compare various entities inside your organization and compare your organization to the industry standard.

In the Supply Chain Performance Index spider graph, an aggregated view is presented of performance to compare current performance with desired performance. The red line depicts the current performance, while the green line provides a target or goal that should be achieved when using various optimization efforts.

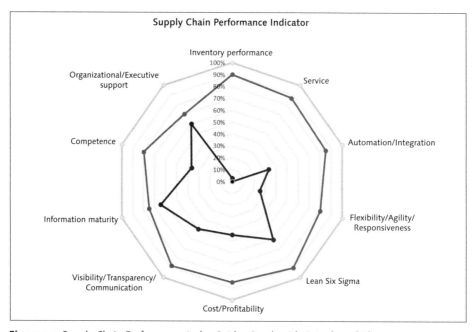

Figure 9.3 Supply Chain Performance Index Spider Graph with Actuals and Plan

The Supply Chain Performance Index spider graph is built based on the 10 success factors we listed earlier. Each one of the success factors is built based on its own more detailed measurements, KPIs, and a weighting factor. This way, the Inventory Performance success factor is weighted more heavily by the number of inventory turns achieved in the past 12 months and less with the measure of dead stock over that period. Those two KPIs might be interrelated, but it's crucial that we're not simply aggregating important and not so important measures together.

As mentioned before, a supply chain measuring system isn't linear and shouldn't be oversimplified.

As shown in Figure 9.4, the Supply Chain Performance Index allows for the measurement of current performance as well as the setting of goals for each success factor. Goals may be set on any level of the hierarchy, and performance should be measured in regular intervals and saved for comparisons over time.

	SCPI Score	
	current	goal
1. Inventory performance	35%	90%
2. Service	70%	85%
3. Automation/Integration	25%	85%
4. Flexibility/Agility/Responsiveness	25%	85%
5. Cost/Profitability	70%	85%
6. Visibility/Transparency/Communication	35%	90%
7. Information maturity	50%	90%
8. Competence	50%	90%
9. Organizational/Executive Support	60%	80%

Figure 9.4 Supply Chain Performance Index Score with Planned and Actual Ratings*

The individual measurements can be retrieved from the SAP ERP Logistics Information System (LIS), from the SAP Business Warehouse (SAP BW), or via the SAP add-on tools MRP Monitor and Inventory Cockpit. After all measurements are in, we can give an overall rating for each of the 10 major KPIs and plot a spider graph as shown earlier in Figure 9.3. Some of the optimization efforts that may drive your SAP supply chain toward your perceived targets include the following:

▸ Managing inventories using policies and exception monitoring

▸ Optimizing availability checks and transfer of demand

▸ Improving forecast accuracy

▸ Defining and using buffering strategies to counter variability

▸ Automating replenishment and procurement

▸ Using better production/capacity scheduling methods

▸ Introducing a system for materials planning, portfolio management, exception monitoring, and policy setting

▸ Maintaining a usable KPI framework and reporting tools

► Performing optimized Sales & Operations Planning (SOP) and forecasting/ rough resource checks

► Using more integrated, standard SAP functionality for delivery and distribution

The ratings might not perfectly represent the actual situation—it's an approximation—but it's still so much better than moving in the dark and trying to find that magic handrail to guide you in the right direction. Application of improvement activities based on a well-designed measurement system can raise your benchmark significantly. Let's dive into more detail on the 10 success factors.

9.2.2 Inventory Performance

Inventory is the lifeblood of any supply chain. Very often inventory is simply viewed as a liability with efforts to reduce it for increased financial performance. Some lean practitioners strive to achieve zero inventory but as the Factory Physics theory and many other rightfully preach, without inventory, there will be no throughput. Inventories need to be optimized, not simply reduced. The delicate balance between availability (service) and inventory is dynamic, and therefore the way you evaluate whether you have too much or too little of the right item in the right place at the right time is of utmost importance. Measuring inventory is tricky and requires careful designing of its individual KPIs.

For example, dead stock is a very good measure of how well your inventory performs. But by itself, the measure is worthless. For example, a $30,000 dead stock value doesn't tell you much, but if you relate it to your average inventory holding and consumption, you'll get some answers. As soon as dead stock represents more than 25% of your average inventory holding, you have room for improvement. Individual KPIs define improvement and optimization activities. The preceding situation, as an example, calls for better safety stock planning on X items (materials with consistent and predictable consumption). Overall, we can derive that the inventory is too high for what is actually required. There aren't many stock-outs, the availability check finds stock regularly, and the safety stock values are high. An inventory reduction effort is in order as long as the high availability and low stock-out rating is kept. This can be achieved with better replenishment policies and the introduction of an exception monitoring method.

Additionally, the Supply Chain Performance Index measures turns, safety stock values, days of supply, and stock-outs, and relates the result with a weighting system to derive a meaningful inventory performance measure. Some examples shown in Figure 9.5.

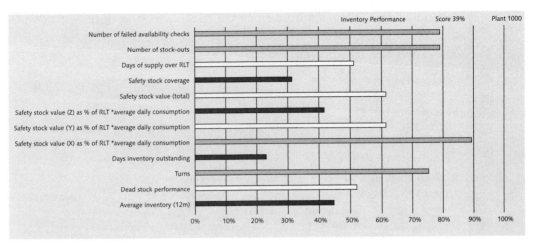

Figure 9.5 Inventory KPIs in the Supply Chain Performance Index

Many of the KPIs come from the standard SAP LIS, but some others, such as safety stock value, inventory developments, and different coverages, come from the Inventory Cockpit. This SAP add-on tool, combined with the Safety Stock and Reorder Point Simulator, Lot Size Simulation Tool, and the MRP Monitor, define sustainable and continuous optimization efforts.

Inventory performance for finished goods in the warehouse is measured separately from raw materials and work in process (WIP). Evaluating each category individually allows targeted measures and activities to be defined and executed. Eventually, the various KPIs are aggregated with a weighting system to derive the overall rating for your company's inventory performance (see Figure 9.6).

1 INVENTORY PERFORMANCE

KPI	result		rating	weight	total
purchased parts in Mount Pleasant (2150)				0.3	◑43%
average inventory (12m)	400	from MRP Monitor	55%	0.1	6%
dead stock	50	from MRP Monitor	65%	0	0%
dead stock % of average	13%		65%	0.2	13%
turns		Measures how many times a company's inventory has been sold (turned over) during a period of time." It equals "the cost of goods sold, divided by the average inventory level of inventory on hand.	54%	0.2	11%
safety stock value (X)		from MRP Monitor	100%	0	0%
safety stock value (X) as % of RLT*average daily consumption		from MRP Monitor	100%	0.1	10%
safety stock value (Y)		from MRP Monitor	74%	0	0%
safety stock value (Y) as % of RLT*average daily consumption		from MRP Monitor	76%	0.05	4%

Figure 9.6 Weighting System to Aggregate to Inventory Performance Success Factor

Each individual KPI is rated from either the result in SAP or, in case of a nondescript KPI, from a guesstimate provided by people. The latter, of course, requires some experience and good judgement.

Some Helpful Inventory KPIs

▶ **Inventory Turns**
This KPI is a measure of the number of times inventory is sold or used in a time period such as a year. The equation for inventory turnover equals the cost of goods sold divided by the average inventory.

▶ **Dead Stock as a Percentage of Average Inventory**
This KPI makes the dead stock measure meaningful. Dead stock is always measured over a specific time period and is that portion of the inventory that is never used during that period. Dead stock isn't to be confused with safety stock, as a safety stock has a positive connotation with its buffering features, and dead stock doesn't.

▶ **Replenishment Lead Time over Range of Coverage**
This KPI relates the lengths of time inventory will last to the time it takes to replenish a void. You should never carry much more inventory than you can fill up quickly.

9.2.3 Service

Service measures how well customers receive product to their requested delivery date and how well promises are kept. But it can also measure the service level from production to the warehouse (how well the planning strategies work), from the raw materials warehouse to the shop floor (how well purchasing performs in supplying production with good availability and low stock holdings), and the service from suppliers (how well suppliers perform to orders from your purchasing department).

The Supply Chain Performance Index can aggregate these service measures to a chart as shown in Figure 9.7 but, of course, allows for drilldown to evaluate the details behind each service category.

All too often, organizations only focus on the customer delivery service and neglect service performance to the production lines. However, that specific service is a very important one because on top of inefficient scheduling methods, the customer service badly degrades when the production lines are starving due to insufficient raw material availability. Bad service levels in that area have a negative impact on many other success factors such as flexibility, agility, and finished goods inventory performance (more finished goods safety stock is needed to buffer inefficient supply).

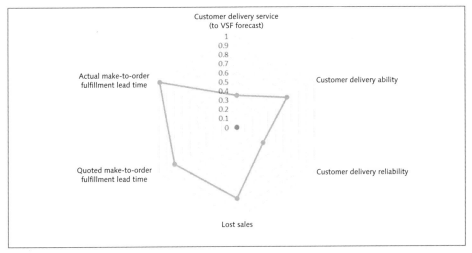

Figure 9.7 Graphical Representation of Various Service Levels

For each of the service ratings in the Supply Chain Performance Index, there are three specific KPIs:

▶ **Delivery Service**
Gauges how well you deliver in full and on time.

▶ **Delivery Ability**
Measures to what degree you can confirm to the customer's requested delivery date.

▶ **Delivery Reliability**
Determines to what degree you keep the confirmed date and quantity.

If, for example, a sales order is delivered three days after the customer's requested delivery date, the Delivery Service KPI degrades. However, it could have been possible that at the time the order was received, the sales representation was able, during the availability check, to confirm the order to the requested delivery date. In that case, the same order would receive a 100% rating for the Delivery Reliability KPI. Consequently, the third KPI, Delivery Reliability, would degrade because the confirmed date wasn't kept.

The Supply Chain Performance Index works with add-on tools native to SAP (we describe these in detail at the end of each chapter), displaying detailed results generated by the individual ratings of the KPIs, and determining your service rating (see Figure 9.8).

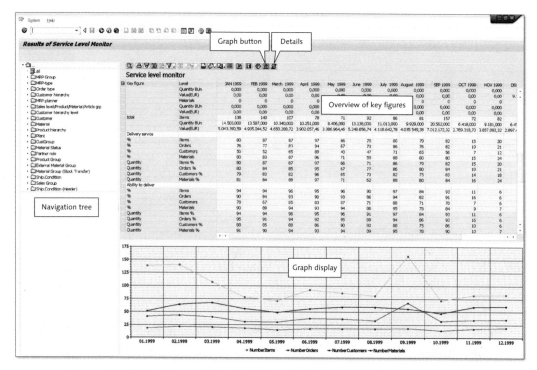

Figure 9.8 SAP Service Level Monitor Add-On Tool

Each entity (plant or distribution center) can be evaluated separately, and an overall score is determined based on a weighting system and aggregation of the individual KPIs and entities. Again, you may want to design improvement activities and optimize configuration settings based on the details of the ratings.

9.2.4 Automation/Integration

The level of automation—using SAP transactions and functions—poses many improvement opportunities. Using a higher degree of automation moves you more toward higher efficiency because automation relieves cost (energy and workload) in the efficiency equation of *Performance ÷ Cost*.

For example, planned orders can automatically convert into a production program, packaging materials can be automatically procured, policy-setting methods may be applied regularly, and the resulting exception messages can be monitored in a well-configured system of prioritized management by exception. Many firms don't use these helpful standard transactions (such as auto PO, collective conversions of planned orders, and collective availability checks) available in the SAP functionality. Automation can be increased easily by implementing some of the standard functions available in SOP, MRP, production scheduling, and procurement of your current SAP system. Even though automation and integration are to some degree subjective measures, they can certainly be measured and provide valuable information in our quest for efficiency.

Figure 9.9 graphically depicts some examples for the automation and integration success factors with traffic light colors to provide an overview of what areas need improvement.

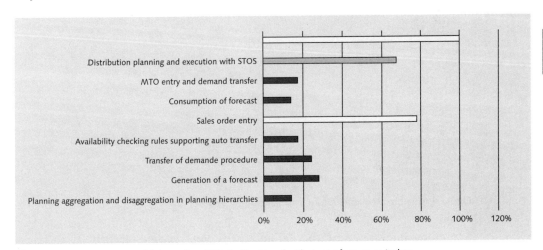

Figure 9.9 Automation and Integration KPIs in the Supply Chain Performance Index

If the interface between sales and distribution and production planning is executed manually, it's not driven by automation and therefore loses the benefits of integration. Integration provides the ability to define activities that implement appropriate planning strategies, effective availability checking rules, and an optimized and correctly configured transfer of demand. People can't make those volumes of sophisticated calculations, but your SAP system can—accurately and quickly.

Automation and integration are defining measures for the areas of MRP, PP, sequencing and scheduling, and procurement. Seamless integration of these functions is essential to any functioning supply chain. Figure 9.10 visualizes how forecasting drives MRP, which needs capacity planning to drive a production schedule so that purchasing receives correct requirements dates. Without such integrated information flow, the material flow will fail, and inventories will pile up as buffers or fail to drive performance.

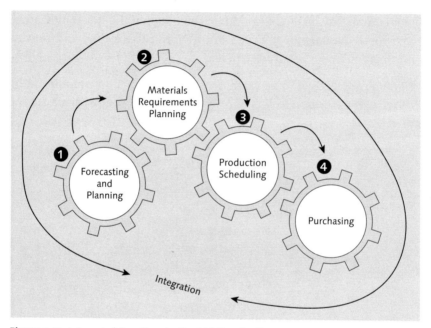

Figure 9.10 Integrated Functions in the SAP Supply Chain

Therefore, integration can be defined as by your system's capability to create information flow and material flow. To that extent, you can measure integration well and also derive from it the degree of automation that it generates or is generated by.

A Useful KPI for Automation and Integration

The Average Time Spent to Convert a Purchase Order KPI provides evidence on your degree of automation in the purchasing department. Make sure you're clearly identifying the interface between the tasks of materials planning and purchasing as there is often confusion about the responsibilities associated with replenishment (When? How much? From whom?).

9.2.5 Flexibility/Agility/Responsiveness

An agile supply chain is defined by its ability to react quickly to a changing environment. Fluctuating customer demand, irregular lead times, and short product lifecycles require flexibility to keep the service levels high. To increase flexibility, various activities such as implementing the SAP Variant Configurator (VC) can widen the product spectrum to the customer.

The degree of flexibility becomes apparent when looking at the way the planning (information) and material flow is designed. Such flexibility can be achieved with the introduction of decoupling or an inventory/order interface, and the resulting buffering of inventory before the final assembly or packaging lines. The strategic placement of the inventory/order interface with a resulting finish-to-order (FTO) policy has a positive effect on your rating, as does using the correct scheduling option and an optimized mix of the inventory, time, and capacity buffers.

4 FLEXIBILITY / AGILITY / RESPONSIVENESS				
KPI	result	rating	weight	total
Responsiveness		0.5		☐ 35%
forecast accuracy	taken from Lean Six Sigma	70%	0.2	14%
responsiveness to change in strategic direction / change of policy	there is really not a process in place where an executive direction would result in the adoption and setup of the appropriate policy. Any reaction would be implemented manually with a high probability of error	15%	0.1	2%
are the correct scheduling options used	there is not much flexibility in the production program. Often the lines are scheduled with a planned utilization of 100% or more and leave no room for a rush order or change in production	32%	0.2	6%
use of buffers capacity / time / inventory	currently the only buffer that is being used is inventory. The time buffer is eliminated by the sales availability check, which promises always after the replenishment lead time. There is also no process in place to effectively increase capacity in order to buffer variability in demand.	33%	0.2	7%
is there WIP control in a pull system	no	22%	0.05	1%
inventory / order point strategically optimized	order based thinking is prevelent. This results in a lot of noise in the production program... especially in upstream operations. If chsanges in finished goods demand are propagated through the entire BoM structure, it is impossible to smooth and level out the supply program	21%	0.2	4%
effectiveness of availability checking procedure and transfer of demand from STO	the better the demand transfer conveys the requirements, the more responsive the supply chain can act. Here the demand transfer does not convey any information about the actual reuired delivery date	25%	0.05	1%
			1	
Agility		0.5		☐ 15%
variety in SKU portfolio	a lack of configuration functionality in the Sales Order makes it hard to give the customer more choices.	60%	0.2	12%
MTS versus MTO split	today there is no clear differentiation between MTS and MTO	33%	0.1	3%

Figure 9.11 Some Examples of Flexibility and Responsiveness Key Performance Indicators with Weighting and Ratings

Using SOP functionality with flexible planning of product hierarchies and performing rough resource checks, the resulting forecast figures can be placed on an inventory point upstream from the final assembly or packaging lines. This enables the downstream lines to be scheduled with a demand-driven pull system,

393

and the resulting agility will increase service levels and drastically reduce safety stock or days of cover requirements.

The more often used method of placing an unchecked forecast on the finishing lines and the subsequent conveyance of every finished product forecast to the bulk level leaves very little room for responsiveness to quickly changing demand. Very low flexibility to counteract forecast errors is compensated for by changing the forecast of the near future. This poses a number of issues to the production scheduler, and the additional problem of ever-changing, "un-fixed" stock transport requisitions from the warehouse makes it almost impossible to put together an agile production program.

Categorizing the product portfolio to set an MTS versus an MTO strategy is as important as the integration between the sales and production scheduling departments, which is driven by an optimized availability checking rule and the resulting transfer of demand.

9.2.6 Lean Six Sigma

A lean supply chain is defined by its low degree of producing or causing waste. For example, the waste of overproducing finished goods to the warehouse can be induced by a high forecast error or a faulty transfer of demand.

Additionally, ineffective planning procedures may lead to ineffective supply programs that produce lots of waste. Another form of waste lies in long cycle times. If, for example, production orders are released to the shop floor without performing all necessary steps—such as an availability check for components, capacity leveling, and proper sequencing of jobs—the orders remain on the line unprocessed, block valuable machine time, and reserve raw or packaging material that other orders could use.

Six Sigma mostly measures defects and strives to introduce processes that will reduce the number of defects to avoid waste and achieve a lean supply chain with a high sigma—or low number of defects for high quality in process and product.

A lot more effort is required to truly measure lean Six Sigma, but a lot of waste and defects are caused by a lack of fitting scheduling methods combined with high forecast errors and a complete lack of buffering strategies to counter variability. Also, in the process industry, ineffectively transferring and placing demand coupled with not providing a good process to reintroduce by-product into the process builds up inventory that expires unused.

The use of an incorrect production type, as can often be seen if a process manufacturer works with production orders, routings, and BOMs, results in the inability to calculate precise yield factors. Additionally, incorrect plans and false requirements for ingredients are a further hindrance of productivity.

9.2.7 Cost/Profitability

Profitability is the ability of an organization to make a profit. Profit is what's left of the revenue after you subtract cost. And a profitable supply chain delivers high value with low cost. How to measure the components of this equation is a subject far exceeding the scope of this book. As we intend to motivate you to build your own system of performance measurement and monitoring with the Supply Chain Performance Index, we want to leave this section open for your own definitions, structures, and KPIs.

Increasing Profitability Requires Dealing with Conflicting Goals

Have you ever wondered why your "continuous improvement" program feels like you're moving in circles? This might be because you have to deal with conflicting goals in the quest for increased profitability. On one hand, costs need to be reduced, and on the other hand, you need to increase income, revenue, or sales.

To reduce cost, companies usually strive to reduce working capital (WIP, stocks, resources), save on the cost of procurement or production, and optimize their planning processes so that they can execute more efficiently. To get the expected result, you require low inventories in raw, semi-finished, and finished goods; high utilization of resources; and less variability in demand and supply.

The other side of the coin is the desired increase in sales, which can be achieved by quickly responding to customers' wishes, delivering on time, producing high-quality products with less waste, and offering a wide variety of options and customized features in the finished product. Logically, this requires ample supply of all variants of the finished good and ample capacity on the production lines so rush orders can be attended to quickly. The result is a lot of variability.

The key to dealing with these conflicting goals is to find the perfect balance between cost reduction and revenue increase. Practical science such as the Factory Physics theory we've mentioned several times provides a great framework to find that balance. In Factory Physics, tools such as the flow optimizer or efficiency curve in conjunction with the application of Little's Law, the VUT equation (which relates the three buffers of inventory, capacity, and time), and the determination of the variability in lead time demand help a great deal to optimize capacity, WIP, inventory, and cash flow, as well as determine the policies that support the strategy your company pursues.

It's those policies that we can use in the SAP supply chain. Although it's beyond the scope of this book to describe the details of how to use Factory Physics to derive sensible policies that support strategy, it's certainly worthwhile to look further into it, especially when you're looking for what to do to get better results!

9.2.8   Visibility/Transparency/Communication

The way the system creates visibility up and down the supply chain is of major importance. Material planners need to be able to "see" when plans and actuals are about to differ (see Figure 9.12).

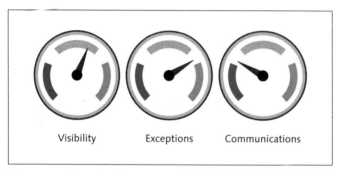

Figure 9.12 Measuring Transparency and Visibility

They need transparency in the replenishment cycle and need to have an idea about when demand falls off the planning chart (see Figure 9.13). A production scheduler should be aware of delays in suppliers' deliveries or changes in demand of an important customer. Sales representatives must be updated on finished goods inventory levels and progress on production lines.

To determine the degree of the exception-minded business, we look at the procedures and tools available to the materials planners in managing exceptional and unforeseen situations such as a delivery delay, unusual demand, changes in lead and cycle times, and dangerously low or excessive inventory levels. We measure the ability of the planner to handle the (possibly overwhelming) number of exceptions occurring every day. High ratings are given for the effectiveness of a process put in place to enable the planner to manage and handle exceptions every day. Figure 9.14 provides an example of a system of effective exception monitoring.

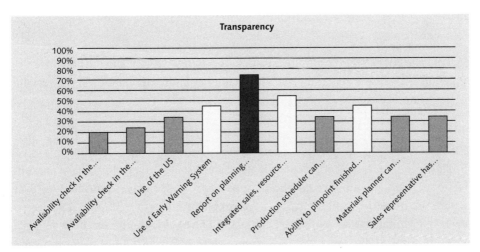

Figure 9.13 Some Examples of Visibility and Transparency Key Performance Indicators in the Supply Chain Performance Index

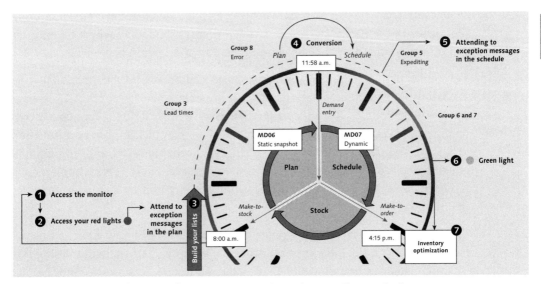

Figure 9.14 A System of Prioritized Exception Monitoring to Improve Communications

Communication is crucial for a well running supply chain. This indicator evaluates how information flows from one department to the other and whether regular meetings or activities are scheduled, so that exceptions, additional demands, or delays can be addressed across the entire supply chain and not just in the specific department.

If it turn out that the communication rating is low, regular meetings might be scheduled to align a demand plan with a supply plan under conditions of variability and uncertainty.

9.2.9 Information Maturity

SAP's basic data setup represents the most important driver of accuracy and efficiency for replenishment and planning policies. It also drives automation. Basic data is expressed in policies that drive replenishment in economic lot sizes to achieve optimal service and inventory levels. Here we can measure how well policies are defined and used by the planner.

SAP's basic data includes material master data, routings, work centers, resources, production versions, and BOMs. It needs to be evaluated on a regular basis, and changes must be coordinated between the affected departments. The sum of all settings in SAP's master (or basic) data represents a policy by which inventories and orders are filled, service levels are met, and automation happens.

Very important decisions in regards to basic structures and data maps must be made during the implementation. The best possible type or grouping isn't always used, and sometimes it's difficult to change what was designed and configured before. Additionally, one size doesn't fit all! For example, if discrete production orders are set up for process manufacturing, it's probably better to go through the effort to replace discrete routings with the more accurately representing recipe, rather than moving on without the possibility of any improvements or increases in efficiency.

The information maturity category provides evidence about how well the existing basic structures reflect the physical process or supply chain activities. Using this indicator, you can pinpoint inefficient data and define activities to improve the accuracy and effectiveness of the data structures.

9.2.10 Competence

Competence is hard to evaluate but essential for a well-running materials planning system. Without user competence, any tool, well-defined process, or standard operating procedure is useless and unnecessary. When competence is measured, you need to ask the following questions:

- How much training was provided for the user?
- What was the level of detail and quality of the training?
- Is the system perceived to drive value?
- What is the level of user acceptance?

You should use questionnaires and tests for material planners, forecast planners, production schedulers, sales representatives, and buyers. Based on these results, you can pinpoint the areas where users would benefit from additional coaching, training, and workshops. A detailed educational program can then be defined based on the findings of the evaluation.

9.2.11 Organizational Support

Much attention should be paid to determine the level of organizational support that is given to the SAP user. It's of great importance that executives in the company, the people who made the decision to buy and use SAP software, are in full support of making the best use of the investment. Therefore, executives should be involved to a fairly detailed degree and help support any improvement, sustainability, and optimization projects around a better use of SAP software to drive supply chain excellence.

9.3   Putting It All Together

When you embark on an optimization and evaluation of your supply chain, value stream mapping and building a reference model are very helpful. An SAP value stream map allows you to document the current state of your supply chain. As with any value stream mapping initiative, you can also define a future, more optimized state on the map, which will serve as a guideline for any activities and projects seeking improvements and progress in the efficiency of the supply chain dynamics.

In the material flow of the value stream map, inventory points are represented by material master records. Various KPIs, such as Average Inventory Value, Dead Stock Value, Ranges of Coverage, and Service Level can be captured right here.

The settings of the materials master's four MRP screens can be documented right underneath the inventory point (Figure 9.15, beneath the inventory triangle). This allows policies to be identified that drive automation, optimized inventory levels, and high service ratings. Processing steps and assembly or fabrication operations are also part of the value stream, and the corresponding settings in the SAP work center or resource are captured in the map. Also, routings are identified that represent orders of different types. This way, a distinction can be made to identify where discrete, process, or repetitive manufacturing are best suited to reflect and manage the material flow in the configured and customized SAP software.

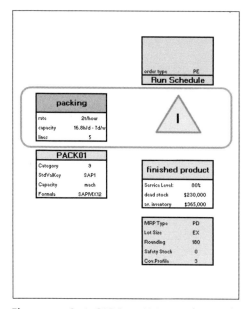

Figure 9.15 Basic SAP Data Maintained in a Value Stream Map*

The information flow is also drawn up in the SAP value stream map. You can define functional areas such as SOP, MRP, scheduling, and purchasing with transaction codes (see Figure 9.16).

As you evaluate the map and its information and material flows, you can now make design decisions for better flow, more automation, increased transparency, and superior inventory performance. In the following example shown in Figure 9.17, inventory between the processes "sieving" and "mixing" was eliminated and a pull system was introduced from the packaging line.

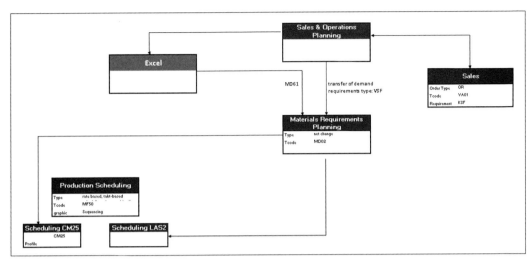

Figure 9.16 Depicting the Information Flow on the Value Stream Map*

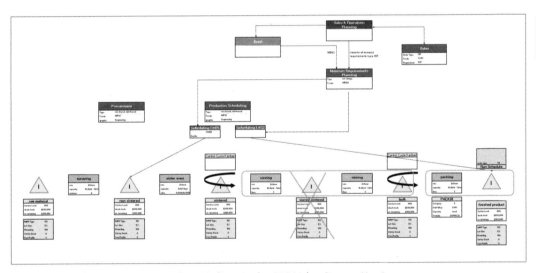

Figure 9.17 Making Decisions Based on Findings in the SAP Value Stream Map*

Various modeling options may now be designed and configured into your SAP system. From there, you can start measuring, identifying, and evaluating the performance of the SAP supply chain and then define the activities necessary to optimize the SAP supply chain and its performance.

The Supply Chain Performance Index allows you to perform an honest and realistic assessment of your SAP supply chain. Even though there are subjective measure involved, with experience and knowledge about what's possible with SAP functionality, a true evaluation is absolutely given. In the end, it's all about finding those weak areas where an improvement effort gives you very large benefits if the activities are well thought through and executed by people who understand the functionality and the process.

The Supply Chain Performance Index is all about getting those benefits and moving toward a high performance SAP supply chain that is sustainable and effective.

9.4   SAP Add-On Tools for Performance Measurement

SAP Consulting also provides some add-on tools to measure a company's performance in the supply chain. These tools are part of the enhancements the division has developed with customers over the years. Seamless integration is provided because the add-on tools are wholly developed in the SAP namespace. The two monitors described next combine and display KPIs, which are hard to get in SAP ERP or SAP APO.

9.4.1   Service Level Monitor

The Service Level Monitor add-on tool allows you to monitor deliveries of sales orders and of internal stock transfers. Confirmations and deliveries for the selected sales order items and stock transfer order items are determined, and the underlying program calculates which quantities were confirmed and delivered on which dates.

The following quantities and dates are included in the results list for each order:

- Requested quantity of the customer
- Requested delivery date
- All confirmations
- All deliveries
- Quantity confirmed on the requested date
- Overall confirmed quantity

▶ Quantity delivered on the requested date

▶ Quantity delivered on the confirmation date

▶ Overall delivered quantity

▶ Requested delivery time (difference between receipt of purchase order and requested delivery date)

▶ Actual delivery time (difference between receipt of purchase order and actual delivery date)

The Service Level Monitor provides three KPIs (listed earlier in this chapter) that are relevant to service levels:

▶ **Delivery Service**
   This KPI answers the following questions:

   ▶ Was the requested quantity delivered in full on the requested delivery date?

   ▶ What proportion of the requested quantity is delivered on the requested delivery date?

▶ **Delivery Ability**
   This KPI answers the following questions:

   ▶ Was the requested quantity confirmed in full on the requested delivery date?

   ▶ What proportion of the requested quantity is confirmed on the requested delivery date?

▶ **Delivery Reliability**
   This KPI answers the following questions:

   ▶ Was the confirmed quantity delivered in full on the confirmed date?

   ▶ What proportion of the confirmed quantity is delivered on the confirmed date?

Each key figure has a "yes/no" and a percentage value for the individual order item. The figures are summarized for each order, customer, and material. Additionally, the monitor counts which proportion of the order items/orders/materials/customers were evaluated with "yes" or "no" for each period, and then calculates the average of the percentage quantities.

Figure 9.18 provides an example of the result screen of the Service Level Monitor. The window on the left allows for various aggregations, and a graphical representation of KPIs is possible too. In our example, the three key figures Delivery Service, Delivery Ability, and Delivery Reliability are displayed along with the number of items and the number of completely delivered items.

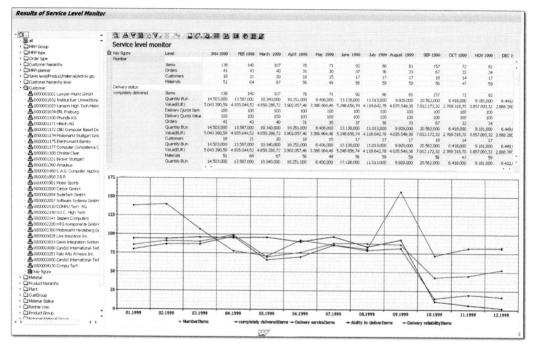

Figure 9.18 Service Level Monitor Add-On Tool

The Service Level Monitor serves as an excellent KPI reporter in the area of service evaluation. It's indispensable for any effective system of materials planning. After the Service to Production Lines KPI (which is in development and available in a near future release) is added to the already comprehensive list of performance measures, the Service Level Monitor should be part of every planner's toolbox.

9.4.2 Supply Chain Performance Cockpit

The Supply Chain Performance Cockpit is a brand new addition to the suite of add-on tools by SAP Consulting. It came out of the necessity to integrate KPIs from different perspectives into one representation of a company's supply chain performance. The Supply Chain Performance Cockpit provides an aggregated view of supply chain health and, at the same time, allows for a drilldown into the details of performance inhibitors and possible inefficiencies. The idea behind the Supply Chain Performance Index is to find improvement opportunities and take action to raise performance while monitoring progress.

Figure 9.19 shows an example of the top-level result screen in the Supply Chain Performance Cockpit. From here, you can drill down into further details.

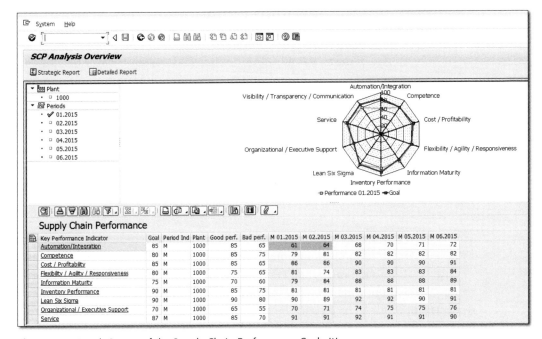

Figure 9.19 Result Screen of the Supply Chain Performance Cockpit'

The Supply Chain Performance Cockpit allows for the customization of your own KPI framework. It comes with a preconfigured set of KPIs, and, of course, you may define your own. Supply Chain Performance Index integrates with standard functions in SAP ERP as well as the other SAP add-on tools such as the Service Level Monitor, Replenishment Lead Time Monitor, and the Inventory Cockpit.

In Figure 9.20, you can see the details to the main category INVENTORY PERFOR-MANCE.

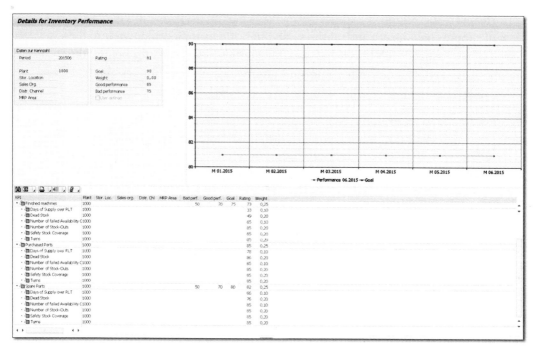

Figure 9.20 Details for Inventory Performance in the Supply Chain Performance Cockpit

The Supply Chain Performance Cockpit allows for the monitoring of tangible KPIs, and you can also include some intangible KPIs such as Planner Competence or Degree of Automation. When taking time and effort to design a well-thought-through KPI framework in your organization, the Supply Chain Performance Cockpit will prove to be an extremely valuable tool.

9.5   Summary

It's an absolute must for any successful organization to monitor and measure the performance of the supply chain. But it has been very difficult to make sense out of the endless number of KPIs found in literature or online. As the BSC has been evolving into a standard approach for performance measurement, it provides an option based on which a KPI framework can be developed.

Another alternative is provided by the Supply Chain Performance Index, which aggregates KPIs into 10 major supply chain indicators.

In the end, you must develop your own framework customized to your company's specific requirements and needs. The benchmark frameworks such as the BSC and the Supply Chain Performance Index only provide a structure and some ideas. The performance measurement system will need to be developed individually, and SAP add-on tools such as the Supply Chain Performance Cockpit provide wonderful functionality to set up such a system.

The first rule of any technology used in a business is that automation applied to an efficient operation will magnify the efficiency. The second is that automation applied to an inefficient operation will magnify the inefficiency.
—*Bill Gates*

10   Traditional Inefficiencies

As we discussed in the previous chapter, our main variable in improving the process of materials planning is efficiency. If you increase efficiency, you're positively enhancing a number of business processes. Your output rates go up, service gets better, cost goes down because fewer resources are required to produce the same yield, and your inventory turns faster because replenishment is done more frequently but not too frequently—in other words, it's done more efficiently.

For the purposes of materials planning, the general definition of efficiency is formulated as the following

Efficiency = Productivity ÷ Cost

This principle can be adjusted to the following various metrics, which we'll explore further:

▸ **Material efficiency**
This is the degree of efficiency to which consumption of raw materials is carried out. What is measured is the manner in which the raw material is transformed into value for the company (e.g., the transformation into a finished good). Often, that process produces more waste than desired and isn't perfect in terms of the point in time consumption happens. Less inventory to produce more product is obviously more efficient, and consuming the material closer to when it was received provides more "bang for the buck." Material efficiency also includes the measuring of how efficient the replenishment process is performed and how effective a certain level of safety stock supports buffering strategies.

Material Efficiency = Service Level ÷ Inventory Cost

With better service levels and availability to the production lines and the right inventory at the right time and right place, materials efficiency will improve drastically.

▶ **Process efficiency**

This is often directly connected to lean efforts because many people consider lean as the ultimate way to raise productivity and efficiency. Be cautious about being hyped up too much with buzzwords because zero inventories, pure pull, and orderless systems don't always deliver the expected results and often end up causing confusion and back peddling. As shown in its formula, process efficiency can be raised by increased automation and a reduction of the transactional or manual workload for planners and schedulers.

Process Efficiency = Automation ÷ Transaction Load

▶ **Ability efficiency**

With this metric, we're concerned with our people's ability to use the tools (SAP software and functionality) and their understanding of general management theories. Often mental models (i.e., perception versus reality) need to be broken down, and new functions and features (often hidden and ready to use in standard SAP) must be introduced. Raising planners', buyers', and schedulers' competence through coaching, education, and training will greatly improve productivity, standardization, and the ability to grow the organization.

Ability Efficiency = Competence ÷ Cost of Managing Change

▶ **Market efficiency**

This may be described as your ability to react purposefully and within an appropriate time frame to customer demand or changes in the marketplace to bring about or maintain competitive advantage. To determine how you can most efficiently operate to fulfill changing market demands, you must work with policies that use an effective combination of the time, inventory, and capacity buffers.

Market Efficiency = Flexibility & Responsiveness ÷ Time × Inventory × Capacity

▶ **Efficiency in decision making**

Is your organization making good decisions? If not, the culprit most likely lies in the fact that your decision makers don't have good information at their fingertips. If you can't "see," you can't make good decisions. Maybe the most important and biggest contributor to a system with high visibility and transparency is the quality of your data. In SAP ERP, we're working with basic data (the material master record, routings, recipes, bills of material [BOMs], work centers, etc.) and transactional data (orders, documents and requirement records), and if either one is out of date or otherwise false, the quality of information, along with transparency, degrades drastically.

Efficiency in Decision Making = Visibility & Transparency ÷ (1/Information Maturity)

In all equations and efficiency measures, variability plays a dominant role. Most improvement initiatives should look to achieve a reduction in variability. We'll explore variability and its ramifications in the next chapter; for now, simply assume that variability is an ever-present fact of life.

Next, we'll explore some of these efficiencies and discuss how they become inefficiencies due to a lack of focus on the business process during the implementation of SAP software.

10.1 Dealing with an Unmanageable Amount of Exception Messages

Firefighting should be done by emergency response units—not by MRP controllers or materials planners who are running an exception-minded business. We do, however, use the term for exceptional situations when a plan failed to materialize because variability got the best of us. An exceptional situation, as the name implies, shouldn't be the norm, but if you have a bad plan, you don't need variability to cause all these exceptions; they will come automatically in great numbers, all the time. And if that happens, your efficiency in decision making degrades (lack of data maturity and with it transparency), process efficiency doesn't exist (because an overwhelming amount of exception messages makes it impossible to automate a process), and ability efficiency goes out the door when frustration takes over and planners give up in the face of an insurmountable task at hand.

10.1.1 Using Exception Messages

In Figure 10.1, you can see exception messages at a glance. Note that there is a reference to the exception group, and the number of exceptions is displayed for each exception message in the column on the right side. If, however, the number of exceptions exceeds 99, the system will give up on you. There is no sense in showing there are exceptions of a certain kind in excess of a hundred or even a thousand. This is just not how this system of managing by exception works.

E	E	Exception Message	Num
1	⊕	Opening date in the past	48
2	06	Start date in the past	17
3	07	Finish date in the past	53
5	52	No BOM selected	2
6	26	Shortage in individual segment	1
6	96	Stock fallen below safety stock level	7
7	10	Reschedule in	15
7	15	Reschedule out	38
7	30	Plan process according to schedule	1
7	63	Production start before order start	99

Figure 10.1 Excessive Number of Exception Messages

10.1.2 Using the Right Transaction Codes

Another issue is how the planner uses the tool to get an overview of what the material situation is like. Just a few of the questions the materials planner should answer every day—preferably first thing in the morning—include the following:

▸ Are we on plan?

▸ Will we, or are we already consuming safety stock?

▸ Will we end up with superfluous inventory?

▸ Is there a new demand sneaking in within the lead time?

▸ Do we have issues with our basic data setup?

To gain an overview of the situation and subsequently work with and remedy the exceptions, planners are taught to use SAP's exception monitor. In SAP ERP, this is perceived to be the collective list of stock/requirements situations, and most instructors or advisors identify Transaction MD07 as the monitor of choice.

Because many people use Transaction MD07 to find the answers to these questions, they often forget what Transaction MD06 can do for them. Both transactions have, of course, their right to exist and fulfill their purpose, but the key to success—and improvement on process efficiency—lies in the correct use of the transactions and knowing in what situation and what time of the day to call upon them.

As mentioned in Chapter 7, you may inquire as to the reason behind using Transaction MD06 when the information is already outdated. Because Transaction MD06/Transaction MD05 provide a snapshot in time of a stock/requirements list as it was created at the time of the last planning run, planners shy away from looking at it. But what isn't always known is that Transaction MD06 provides you with the ability to limit the amount of materials shown in the list. Transaction MD07 lists all materials to a given MRP controller key. Transaction MD06 lists only those materials that were planned yesterday, if you use the transaction correctly. Because this is outdated information, you call up the exception monitor first thing in the morning and mark the items you've worked with. Don't forget to maintain today's date in the initial screen of Transaction MD06; if you don't, you'll get a list of all the materials with the snapshot from when they were planned last—and that could have been weeks or even months ago. Once done right, the list and its exceptions are much easier to manage. What you see then in Transaction MD05 (or with double-click on the material in Transaction MD06) is the MRP list because it has the time stamp of the last MRP run.

Most planners, however, use Transaction MD07/Transaction MD04 all the time. They basically look at every material in their portfolio every day. This is a good thing if you want to clean up your outdated elements or basic data but not if you run an exception-minded business.

10.1.3 Lack of Good Policy

Another reason for an unmanageable list of too many exceptions is the lack of good policy. An inefficient lot-size procedure, MRP type, or false lead times cause exception messages to be generated over and over every day. Instead of tending to the problem at its root, many times planners get into expediting or firefighting mode. For example, we've seen a planner call the supplier every time when the delivery of goods came in too late for the production lines. And the delivery was late *every time*! The item in question was set on a reorder point procedure, and even though purchase orders were sent out every time the system called for it, the item had a very bad record of availability. As it turned out, the problem was too low of a reorder point, so despite the supplier delivering on time, the planner was running out because the inventory at ordering wasn't enough to get them through the replenishment lead time. This represents a typical case where a one-time adjustment in policy cures the problem and alleviates the planner's expediting and firefighting workload.

After you implement a system of effective materials planning and you're performing periodic and automated policy setting based on segmentation and classification, your exception messages, and with it your firefighting, will be drastically reduced. Call Transaction MD06 first thing in the morning with yesterday's date if MRP runs before midnight (and with today's date if MRP runs after midnight). Do this every day, and manage the exceptions and check off the record as being managed. After this is done for a while, the list becomes manageable and allows for quick and focused daily exception management. Then you can expect large improvements in process and material efficiency.

10.2   An Isolated Sales Department

Happy customers are the most important metric for the sales department, and so it should be for the rest of the organization—but not at any price. There is a trade-off, for example, between the amounts of sellable inventory of finished product we can hold and the availability we want to provide to our customers. There is also a trade-off between the lead time we promise to customers and our flexibility to work with quick response times. Both these trade-offs (and much more) are founded in the capabilities of procurement and production. Therefore, there must be communication between the departments of sales, production, and procurement before sales can live up to their promises. Communication must happen on various levels. Meetings need to be held to set performance boundaries, and management needs to provide direction for service-level targets and delivery capabilities. The systematic communication, however, needs to be configured into the system and then taught to the user community before it can work and do its job automatically. That is where the process often fails.

What would you say should happen if a sales representative performs an availability check for a make-to-order (MTO) product and doesn't find anything in inventory? Should additional demand be placed on the production line? Are the planning people to be held responsible? Should we tell the customer that we'll do anything we can to get the ordered product to him immediately? No, no, and no! An item identified as to MTO has no reason to be in stock, readily available to be shipped. It will be made to that order, and therefore the availability check has to tell the customer that he will get it *after* the replenishment lead time has passed. Holding to that lead time is the service we'll measure against.

The example described here presents a mental model (once again, perception versus reality) that needs to be broken down and a working process reinstated. You'll find more on some of these mental models emerging on the interface between demand and supply in the following sections.

10.2.1 Possible Sales Interface Mental Model 1: Not Fixing the Date in the Delivery Proposal of the Sales Availability Check

Every time a sales order is entered by a sales representative, an availability check should be carried out. The availability check tells the sales representative if and when which total or partial quantity of the product can be committed to the customer. The availability check looks for inventory if the item is made-to-stock (MTS). If it doesn't find inventory, the availability check goes out and looks for the next receipt and confirms according to that date—and doesn't put additional demand onto the production line. It therefore avoids the generation of unnecessary noise. That is how the MTS check typically works. If an item is MTO, the availability check should always confirm the item after the replenishment lead time. Because we're making this product *after* the order is received, it will take time to make it, that is, the time to replenish the product to the order.

When you have a committed date for either order, but the sales representative doesn't fix the date (as is shown with an unchecked FIX QTY/DATE indicator in Figure 10.2), then the current date shows up as the material availability date in Transaction MD04, and all hell breaks loose in the exception monitor (of course only if people aren't desensitized by the amount of red lights and exception messages they receive on a daily basis in the materials planning department). One of the main reasons that the date doesn't get fixed is the hope of the sales department that they can deliver before the newly confirmed delivery date. They hope that the production department produces a miracle so they can still deliver to the customer on time. On the other hand, if the date gets fixed with the new delivery proposal, then everything, including the delivery due list, works toward that new fixed date. There certainly may be a situation when the date shouldn't be fixed, but it isn't the rule and should only be done when it constitutes a process necessity—not just because someone wants to keep their options open.

Figure 10.2 Fixing Indicator in the Delivery Proposal of the Sales Availability Check

10.2.2 Possible Sales Interface Mental Model 2: Forecast Reduction

When planning an MTS product, you should put out a forecast against which the production scheduler can plan producing inventory. Usually this is a forecast of the type VSF coming from strategy 40. Standard strategy group 40 in the MRP 3 screen contains strategy 40, which is configured to trigger the consumption of forecast with incoming sales orders. When entering strategy 40 in MRP 3, you can also maintain consumption parameters as shown in Figure 10.3.

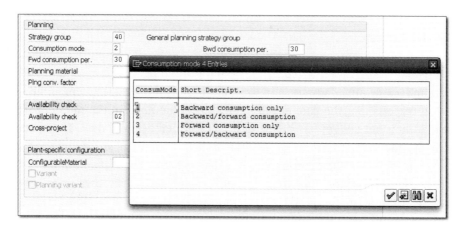

Figure 10.3 Strategy Group and Consumption Parameters in the MRP 3 Screen of the Material Master

The following options are available to consume a forecast (through incoming actual sales orders):

▸ Going forward in time a certain number of working days

▸ Going backward in time for a number of working days

▸ Going backwards first and then looking forward

Now let's think about this situation: Assume there is a monthly forecast, which means there is a VSF forecast with a negative quantity (a demand element) standing at the first working day of every month. The planning run will cover that demand by creating a supply element (usually a planned order) to bring in the quantity just before the first working day of the month. This will ensure that enough inventory is available at the first working day of the month, so that you can sell (with actual sales orders) that forecasted and produced to inventory throughout the month (plus a safety stock).

Naturally, every sales order coming in during the month is reducing the inventory and should reduce the forecast—but only the forecast that was created for it, right? You achieve that by maintaining a consumption strategy that consumes in a backward direction of no more than 22 working days. If your consumption strategy consumes backward and then forward, after you sell more than what you forecasted, you won't dip into safety stock alone but also start consuming the forecast from the next month. That will result in putting less into inventory for the next month to consume and essentially telling the system that because our sales went up this month, there will be less next month. This is most likely not true (however, there are situations that might require a forward consumption) and makes the forecast planner look bad!

10.2.3 Possible Sales Interface Mental Model 3: The Make-to-Stock/ Make-to-Order Decision

A distributor or manufacturing firm can employ many planning strategies for manufacturing and selling products, but the two most common ones are MTS and MTO (if a distributor, procure-to-stock and procure-to-order are used). These strategies determine how the replenishment cycle works, how much inventory is kept, how sales communicates availability to the customer, and much more. A sloppy setup and use of these strategies in the SAP system is a major cause of inefficiencies because it will drive miscommunication, cause misunderstandings, lead to bad service levels, degrade transparency, and spoil automation. Relating back to the specific inefficiencies in the beginning of this chapter, making the wrong decision or no decision about MTO versus MTS will degrade material efficiency, process efficiency, and, most prominently, market efficiency. This is due to the fact that you're less flexible and agile in your production program, which diminishes responsiveness to the ever-changing customer demand.

To determine the strategy for a specific product, you should perform a segmentation or classification. The most common classification is an ABC analysis, and its drawbacks are explained in Chapter 5. You can only derive acceptable results if you combine the ABC analysis with an XYZ for sales volume, UVW for price, and EFG for replenishment lead time. It also doesn't hurt to classify according to lifecycle.

Don't forget to reclassify regularly as your products go through a lifecycle because what has been made to stock for years might become a good candidate for another, more effective strategy. If you get careless on your MTS/MTO decision, you'll drive a rift between your sales representatives and production schedulers, which might cause a lot of trouble for the overall performance of your company.

10.2.4 Possible Sales Order Interface Mental Model 4: Checking With or Without Replenishment Lead Time

When you look at the DISPLAY SCOPE OF CHECK screen in the availability overview in Transaction MD04, you'll see the CHECK WITHOUT RLT checkbox (see Figure 10.4).

Besides this question being a bit confusing, the decision has many (some hidden) implications. First, when checked, your availability check performs its routine *without* the total replenishment lead time (TRLT).

So what is the difference between checking with or without the replenishment lead time? Let's look at an example: Assume you have nothing in inventory today, and a customer orders 100 pieces with a desired shipment sometime in the near future. There are 50 pieces coming from the production line *before* the customer wants to pick up 100, and 50 coming in *after* the customer wants to pick up 100. Then the last 50 are coming after the end of the replenishment lead time.

If our sales availability check performs its routine *with* TRLT (the CHECK WITHOUT RLT checkbox is unchecked), the availability is checked *only* within the replenishment lead time and ignores all receipts outside of it (see Figure 10.5). It also assumes unlimited availability at the end of this lead time. Therefore, 50 pieces can be confirmed to the customer's requested delivery date, and 50 pieces are confirmed just after the end of the lead time. This also has other implications.

First, the sales order will confirm *any* quantity, no matter how crazy the request is, right after the lead time, and second, it confirms quantities that aren't on the schedule or even on the plan at that moment.

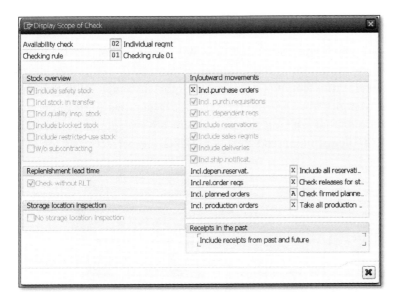

Figure 10.4 Treatment of the Replenishment Lead Time in the Availability Check

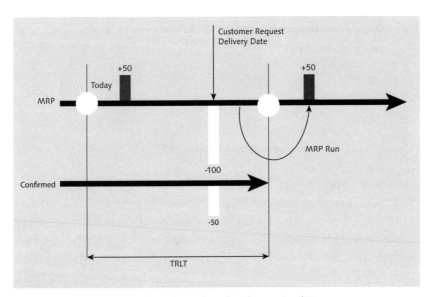

Figure 10.5 Availability Check with Total Replenishment Lead Time

There will be a planned order to meet the new demand only after MRP is run. This is a very unreliable and noisy way to do business and only makes sense if you run MRP every day or in an MTO situation where there is no stock, nor any receipts. You'll also run the danger that sales promises a very large quantity to the customer without further validation.

On the other hand, when you select the CHECK WITHOUT RLT box, availability is checked for the entire planning horizon (see Figure 10.6). This way future receipts can be taken into account and promised to the customer. With this type of check, you're basically not allowing the sales representative to promise anything to the customer that isn't on the plan (there are exceptions to this, but checking without replenishment lead time represents the correct basis for MTS processing).

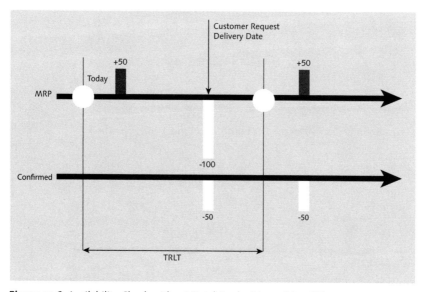

Figure 10.6 Availability Check without Total Replenishment Lead Time

Doing this right is imperative to business success. Leveling demand, reducing noise in the production program, and increasing visibility on what's demanded for the production scheduler and what's available for the customer sales representative is all driven by the decision at hand. And without making the right choice, your schedulers and sales representatives are doomed to dashing it out manually on a case-by-case basis.

10.3   A Buyer without a Cause

As we learned from reading about gate control in Chapter 3, we know that there is gate control on the demand side of the planning cycle as well as on the supply side. One of these gates controls what's coming onto the production lines, and the other one defines the interface between the materials planner and buyer. Very often, this type of gate control is nonexistent, and sometimes there is only one role executing both the materials planner's task and the buyer's task in one.

This causes purchasing to be degraded to transactional work, simply to convert the purchase requisition into a purchase order using the terms already applied. While the automated purchase order generation is a good process, it can't be effectively applied in all circumstances.

A buyer's job is to apply terms—terms of payment, terms of delivery, order lot sizes, what supplier to pick and whether to use a contract or not. The materials planner's job is to create a supply that meets given, planned demand in the most optimum way from a planning perspective. The lot size that comes out of that process isn't necessarily the same as what we can order from our supplier, but figuring that out is exactly what an effective and experienced buyer is expected to do.

The materials planner shouldn't worry too much about suppliers (more about the supply itself) when planning an effective replenishment cycle. Rather, the planner should let the buyers do their job.

10.4   Fiddling with Policy

When SAP systems are thrown at materials planners with minimal training and no standard operating procedure, they will make up their own routines and will try, to the best of their knowledge, to do a good job. In most cases, people then take flight to Excel because there are no feature limitations or configuration issues. More motivated and diligent planners will take on the challenge and try to make sense of the seemingly overcomplicated monster of a planning tool. As a result, fiddling with master data becomes the norm. We've seen planners changing a reorder point four times a day, running MRP all the time, and trying to simulate what's going to happen. With this amount of fiddling and changing, no one will ever be able to evaluate what works and what doesn't.

This is natural, human, and understandable behavior if the planner is left to his own devices to deal with something that not even seasoned, long-time consultants can figure out. Give your planners the proper education (not the transactional classes that show how to explode a bicycle), and give them strategic direction if you want them to perform with ability efficiency that holds the promise of low cost of managing change.

10.5   Capacity Planning

One of the bigger problems with MRP is that often the demand for purchased parts is coming from an unreliable, ever-changing production program. Sometimes you're getting measured by the availability you provide to the production orders that need to run on the line, but given long lead times and constant changes in the schedule, this turns out to be a moving target and hard to plan for. And as long as the schedulers don't use an effective system of periodic production planning, sequencing, leveling, and scheduling in combination with a "frozen zone", your requirements will keep on changing, and it's extremely difficult to provide high-service levels to the line while keeping inventories to a minimum. The materials planner then panics (because he's blamed for the stock-outs) and fills inventory up to the max.

Unfortunately, during most SAP implementations, the functions of capacity planning aren't even considered. Many people say it's too early in the game, often hiding the fact that they just don't know how it works in SAP. As a consequence, production scheduling is done in spreadsheets, a third-party tool is acquired, a workaround is developed, or scheduling isn't done at all. Whatever the case may be, without planning, sequencing, leveling, and scheduling orders and capacity, you're going to end up with half a process and with requirements for purchased parts or raw materials standing on the wrong dates.

This is very bad for the measure of materials efficiency as service levels degrade and inventory goes through the roof. Market efficiency doesn't stand a chance with absolutely no visibility of what's coming from the line. An agile supply chain where customer needs are flexibly fulfilled is impossible to execute.

10.6   Using Sales Orders for Intercompany Stock Transfers

If you are sourcing raw materials for production from another manufacturing plant or warehouse, if you want visibility on availability in that plant, and you'd like an automated process that ensures high service levels and minimum inventory holdings overall, SAP ERP's stock transport order (STO) process is the answer.

The STO process allows you to have an automatic purchase requisition generated to source required quantities of a raw material from another plant where you might manage its inventory. After you set the special procurement indicator correctly, the MRP run knows to request missing quantities from the delivering plant, and it performs an availability check according to rules you can define for your business.

We've seen many installations where instead of the STO process, a sales order/ purchase order procedure was set up. In this procedure, a requesting plant sends a purchase order to a delivering plant, and the delivering plant then sends the goods with a sales order delivery document. This practice has the disadvantage of not being able to plan for safety stock or generally speaking for inventories in the supplying plant. You have has to wait for the purchase order (sales order in the supplying plant) to exist before the demand shows up. Because the STO process works with forecasts, and MRP generates stock transport purchase requisitions, plannability is provided, and material and process efficiencies will go up.

For the STO process to work to your advantage, you'll have to consider a few things that might not work the way you think:

- ▸ **Checking rule**
  Set it up so it includes safety stock and available stock, and check *with* replenishment lead time. Include purchase and production orders but not planned orders or requisitions; that is, when the requesting plant's STO finds stock in the delivering plant, it confirms the shipping date after the Planned Delivery Time + GR Processing Time. When there is no available stock in the delivery plant, but there is a fixed receipt (e.g., from a production order), it will confirm the shipment date to the date the receipt is confirmed + Planned Delivery Time + GR Processing Time. When there is no stock and no receipt, it will use the TRLT in the MRP 3 screen to confirm the shipment date (but only if the Procurement Type in the MRP 2 screen is set to E).

423

▶ **Total replenishment lead time**
This is the estimated time it takes to replenish the product from scratch through the entire supply chain. Set it to a value that you feel comfortable quoting to your customer when you have no stock.

▶ **Planned delivery time (and GR processing time)**
This represents the time to transport the product from the delivering plant to the warehouse when it's freely available to transport.

▶ **Special procurement type**
This points the demand to the specific delivering plant. When MRP runs, it covers open demand by generating stock transport requisitions pointing to the plant defined in the special procurement type. These STOs are offset by the planned delivery time.

▶ **Procurement type**
Here lies the tricky part. You would think the PROCUREMENT TYPE option should be set to F for external procurement so it generates requisitions. In that case, however, the TRLT wouldn't be considered. Therefore, you need to set it to E (because you set a special procurement indicator, it will still create a requisition), and the TRLT is used in case there is no stock or fixed receipt in the delivering plant.

> **Note**
>
> MRP works with the planned delivery time to plan for transport, whereas the availability check looks for stock or uses the TRLT to meet demand. Inefficient planning and execution can occur in many places in the STO process, which is why it requires careful design. The planner needs to know all the details about STO to make the right decisions when variability shows up.

Note that there is a widely persisting perception that the STO process doesn't work when the supplying plant procures to orders from the requesting plant and doesn't keep any inventory. People rightfully claim that the TRLT in this case, should use the time it takes to deliver from the supplying to the requesting plant plus the time it takes for the supplying plant to receive the goods from the external supplier. But as soon as you use procurement indicator F, the system ignores TRLT from the MRP 3 screen and uses Planned Delivery Time + GR Processing Time from the MRP 2 screen. Because that replenishment time doesn't consider the supplying plant's replenishment time, the process fails.

This is absolutely correct, however, if the supplying plant doesn't hold or plan for stock, why use the STO process at all? Shouldn't the requesting plant then order directly from the external supplier and plan for its own inventory holdings? What's the point of going through the other plant when that plant does nothing but strictly order the same quantities from an external vendor for the same time the requesting plant is asking for it—without any planning. Aren't we artificially and inefficiently increasing the replenishment lead time as we go through another location that doesn't contribute any value to the process?

Very often, the solution to the problem (or the increase in efficiency) doesn't lie with additional functionality or a process improvement. A mental model (perceived but not necessarily accurate perception) stands in the way sometimes. Figure 10.7 shows an example of the situation just described. The mental model might have looked like the following scenario: A factory in Ohio needs a purchased part that is sourced from a supplier in China. Because the global company that the requesting plant belongs to has operations and warehouses in China, it was decided to employ an STO process where the purchase order is routed through the supplying plant in China. As shown in the figure, the shipping time from China (the intercompany transport time) takes 40 days. Because the supplying plant doesn't plan or hold any inventory of the part, it takes another 20 days to ship the part from the vendor to the supplying plant—every time the receiving plant needs the part.

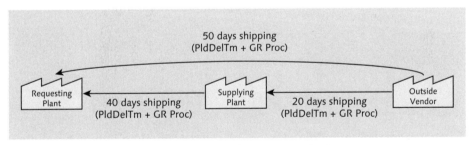

Figure 10.7 Increased Lead Times through a Stock Transport Order Process

We can't be sure if the TRLT goes down to 50 days if the requesting plant orders directly from the vendor in China, but it's obvious that the insertion of an additional plant into the process doesn't add any value.

10.7 Chasing Demand

The Beer Game, developed in the early 1960s at MIT, is an excellent simulation to demonstrate the effects of delays in supply chain management. The participating agents—consumers, retailers, wholesaler, and producer—are linked through information (orders) and material (beer) flow. The consumer buys beer at the retail stores. The store then orders beer from the wholesaler to fill inventory voids in the shelves, and the wholesaler, in turn, orders from the producer. All goes well as long as the beer consumers don't change their behavior. What's interesting to observe in the example is that because of a sudden, but not drastic, increase in demand from consumers (because of a music video featuring a certain beer brand), all hell (wide swings in inventory holdings of that brand of beer) breaks loose toward the other end of the supply chain. In the simulation, everybody simply waits until the order comes in and only then springs into action to fulfill the demand as it is at that time. Figure 10.8 illustrates the beer game and its associated swings in order quantity and stock holdings.

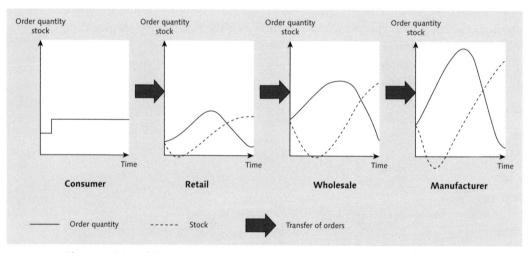

Figure 10.8 Variability in the Beer Game

You might be wondering why no one works with safety stocks or forecasts. Well, this is a situation that still enjoys widespread occurrence in SAP supply chains for a number of reasons. Sometimes the planner believes that a specific order from a specific customer will have to be tracked throughout the entire chain. This is sometimes a good thing to do (when you're making the product to the customer's order), but in so many cases it's not. And still, planners refuse to work with anonymous orders and inventory. In one noteworthy example, a maker of standard products sold through a catalogue sent a yellow slip with every order through the entire distribution *and* production process, sometimes also with the purchase order to the supplier. The forecast, which was placed on a six-month rolling forward plan, was completely ignored until a sales order came in. Then it was adjusted to match the changing actual demand, and the yellow slip was on its merry way.

Needless to say, the manufacturer in question here was bragging about its service levels of 99.9%, but for some odd reason, the numbers didn't add up. Something was terribly wrong, and the manufacturer just couldn't get understand the problem. We call the problem "order-specific production" to distinguish it from an MTO process that has its validity in many situations.

In the next part of this book, we'll use systems thinking, which is an excellent tool to describe dynamics and structures to find problems and associated solutions that relate to the problem just described.

10.8 Hiding the Buffer

There is a widespread misconception in the SAP ecosystem that the static safety stock (the SAFETY STOCK field in the MRP 2 screen of the material master) buffers demand fluctuation during the planning process. This is simply not true.

As you probably know, setting a safety stock in the MRP 2 screen of the material master will result in a subtraction of that quantity from available inventory in the Transaction MD04 stock/requirements list. Therefore, the MRP run ignores that part of the inventory and plans without it. This seems to be good practice but only from an execution point of view. In other words, you're setting aside a safety inventory so that you can dip into it and use it when you need it. However, from a planning point of view, this constitutes a different perspective. In Figure 10.9, for example, you'll see that safety stock is simply subtracted from available stock and therefore not available for planning purposes.

Now imagine there is a forecast of 50 pieces for the next month, and you've maintained a safety stock of 30 pieces in the MRP 2 screen of the material master record. The system will plan to have an inventory of 80 pieces in stock at the beginning of next month. As you're approaching the next month, and actual customer orders drop in, the forecast is replaced by actual orders. Should the actual order exceed the forecast—let's say that customers demand 60 pieces instead of

50—the MRP run will generate a new replenishment proposal for an extra 10 (instead of using the safety stock), and you end up with 90 pieces in inventory, even though you only need 60. This type of behavior creates dead stock and misses the purpose of using safety stock as a buffering strategy. The case worsens if you have a rounding value or a fixed lot size.

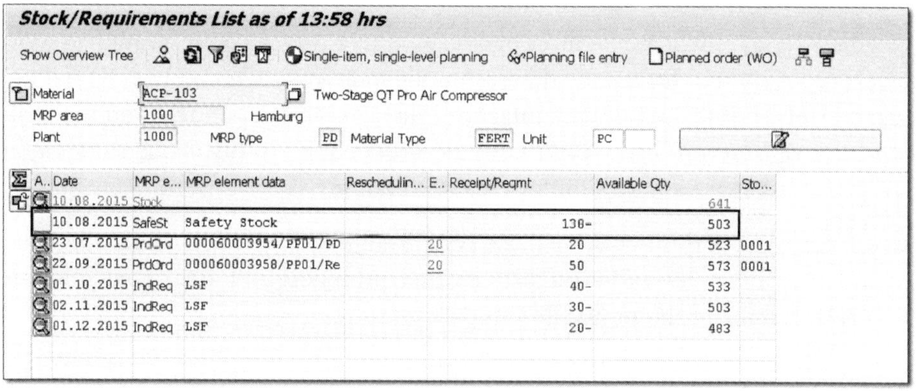

Figure 10.9 Safety Stock Reducing Free Available Quantity for Planning Purposes

To remedy this, you can use a range of coverage profile that drives a dynamic safety stock if the situation allows for it. In a range of coverage profile, you have a target safety coverage and a minimum safety coverage (in days of coverage). The MRP run can "see" the safety levels and *only* generates a replenishment order when the minimum safety coverage is broken. Therefore, you have to make sure that the minimum safety coverage is set to one day, and the target is higher. In that case, the MRP planning run uses all the days in the target coverage as a buffer to counter demand variability.

Remember that the range of coverage also has a maximum safety coverage to keep the inventory from blowing up if the forecast be too high.

10.9 The Reorder Point Dilemma When Sourcing from Another Plant

When you source materials from one of your own plants, your lead time (in the PLANNED DELIVERY TIME field in the delivering plant) should be the time it takes from the issue in the delivering plant until it arrives at the receiving plant. The only question is whether the delivering plant can issue right out of available stock. If the delivering plant doesn't keep the product in stock but has to procure it also, then the total lead time until it arrives in the receiving plant will increase dramatically. But if you put that total time into the planned delivery time, you'll ask the delivering plant to issue way too early. Unfortunately, the TLRT in the MRP 3 screen doesn't work with procurement indicator F.

To get around this, people often play around with source lists and inforecords, but if you want to use an automatic reorder point calculation (VM or V2), you need to put the TRLT into the planned delivery time because that is what the reorder point calculation uses. So you're stuck with a manual reorder procedure (VB or V1), and you'll have to include the entire TRLT in your spreadsheet calculation.

Two of the SAP add-on tools—the MRP Monitor and the Safety Stock and Reorder Point Simulator—give you added possibilities. Because the MRP Monitor also performs an EFG classification for lead time and lets you pick the TRLT from the MRP 3 screen, you can build a list of items that are feasible for an auto-reorder procedure (X–consistent consumption, C–low consumption value, E–short lead times). The Safety Stock and Reorder Point Simulator then lets you calculate and simulate various service levels for optimized reorder points and safety stock settings and allows a mass update of the policy.

10.10 The Hang-from-the-Ceiling Strategy

In many situations, reorder point planning is a very good choice of policy. Unfortunately, it's rarely used for finished products. In fact, it's often used in a way that really doesn't help with the communication, delivery service rating, or inventory holding targets that are required in an effective supply chain.

A reorder level procedure is a stochastic replenishment method where stock is held before the actual orders come in. Therefore the product is MTS! The idea is to deliver to customer orders (or other requests, e.g., from a warehouse or distribution center) from free available inventory, immediately! You should *not* wait until you have an order before you trigger the action to replenish and fulfill the order.

Every time an order comes in, the inventory level drops. A replenishment is only triggered when an order causes the inventory level to drop *below* the reorder level. And if the reorder level is set (and designed) to have enough inventory within the replenishment lead time, you won't run out of stock if you have a somewhat predictable consumption. Any variability can be covered by having a safety stock lift up the reorder level.

If you follow this simple rule, your inventory will move up and down in a seesaw type pattern, and the minimum and maximum levels depend on the lengths of the lead time and the mean average deviation from the mean. The service level — set in the MRP 2 screen of the material master — also plays an important role. The higher you set it, the more safety stock you'll hold to guarantee good availability and to only rarely run out.

However, if the rules aren't followed, you might be faced with a situation that frustrates the entire organization because frequent stock-outs become the norm. Often the planner waits until the orders come in before the replenishment is triggered. This behavior stands in stark contrast to the strategy underlying a reorder point procedure. The idea behind reorder point procedures is to hold stock in anticipation of an estimated average daily consumption so that demand can be fulfilled from stock. If you wait for the actual order, you never have anything to withdraw from and therefore you constantly run after the demand.

Combine this situation with a lot-for-lot lot sizing procedure (EX), and you'll end up bringing in exactly what you need too late — all the time.

10.11 Summary

Efficiency in the supply chain warrants good processes, clean data, appropriate tools, and most importantly a solid understanding of the underlying dynamics of the system. Sometimes, mental models, with their inherent simplification (and often falsification) of the perceived outcome, stand in the way of productivity, automation, and an effective process. Therefore, it's important to focus more on a better understanding than to make the tool do what we perceive to be better (often it isn't).

Efficiency can be measured in different ways. In this chapter, we've looked at material efficiency, which focuses on inventory and service levels; process efficiency, with its sometimes-low degree of automation; ability efficiency and the difficulty of managing change; market efficiency, including flexibility and responsiveness to the market; and efficiency in decision making regarding visibility and transparency.

As we look to improve efficiency and evaluate our processes and transactions with these categories, we can evaluate the existing setup and define improvement activities to root out problems and suboptimized states in our system. The second part of this chapter provided some examples of where some of these inefficiencies might lie so that you can cross-reference and relate these to your own business.

There is always space for improvement, no matter how long you've been in the business.
— Oscar De La Hoya

11   Improvement and Optimization Programs

In early 2013, SAP announced that its business suite would henceforth run on SAP HANA, a superfast, real-time, in-memory database technology. Up to that point SAP HANA had mainly been used for SAP Business Warehouse (SAP BW) analytics and SAP Customer Relationship Management (SAP CRM). The announcement was good news because it meant that transactions could run up to ten thousand times faster than they ran before. Batch processing would be unnecessary, and the platform opened up windows for what-if analysis, reporting, production scheduling heuristics, forecasting, and sales & operations planning. Additionally, you could start the planning run ten thousand times a day!

SAP HANA enables things for the user that are hard to predict at this time. To have free reign on transaction usage because there is no resource issue anymore will prove to be invaluable to the performance of a materials planner's daily work.

However, running a falsely configured process much faster produces chaos in a blink of an eye. This stuff is for the companies that have their foundation in order and not for the tech enthusiast who doesn't know how to operate and plan a complex supply chain. Keep your house in order, and then speed it up to achieve great results.

The following suggestions for improvements and increases for your efficiencies are all grounded in a better understanding of the dynamics a complex system such as the SAP ERP-driven supply chain is exposed to and operating under. Further developments and achievements in technology will help, but they won't provide the drastic improvements we're looking for. In the next part of this book, we'll provide some insights to using scientific modeling to develop intuition and a good understanding about the little things that can make a big difference. But before we go there, let's explore some of the basic steps you can take immediately to further the use of this great tool (SAP).

11.1 Benchmarking the Current State

Making better use of standard functionality provided by SAP ERP software to its fullest extent is hard, especially if you don't have years and years of exposure to, and practice with, the intricacies of integrated, transparent, efficient, flexible, and automated systems. It can also be difficult to find eloquent leading examples from industry.

We also need to know where to look to find the data that will help us develop benchmarks. SAP is full of information but because everything is structured in transactions you can easily get lost in the sea of transaction codes. A good understanding of how the Logistics Information System (LIS) aggregates and cumulates data, how SAP BW does the same, and how you can retrieve data from document evaluations is very helpful but not so easy to figure out.

> **Note**
>
> As we've noted previously in this book, the SAP add-on tools provide excellent cockpits and monitors where you can see a wealth of information in one place. These tools allow for slicing and dicing, filtering, sorting, and graphically displaying information; some of them then also let you update the basic data. Therefore, they provide an excellent basis for benchmarking but also deliver guidance during the improvement initiatives and progress measuring.

One way of easing into the difficult task of continuous optimization is to look for low hanging fruit first. To find those, another form of classification and segmentation (different from the one we do before policy setting) is necessary. You can use the Supply Chain Performance Index to do so and filter out opportunities and candidates for improvement that way. In the Supply Chain Performance Index, we break down the indicator into 10 major areas of measurement and rating. Each one of those success factors is built and aggregated from a detailed set of key performance indicators (KPIs), which are all evaluated by a rating based on real data and perceived value. In the following subsections, we'll explore 8 of the 10 success factors, so you can build your own system of benchmarking and evaluation.

11.1.1 Inventory Performance

As an example, we can look at inventory performance and collect the KPIs listed in Table 11.1 in regards to the current state.

KPI	Value
Average Inventory Value over the Past 12 Months	$1,250,000
Target Inventory Value	$850,000
Dead Stock Value	$415,000
Dead Stock Value as a Percentage of Average Inventory	35%
Inventory of Nonmoving Stock	$15,000
Safety Stock Value	$487,000
Safety Stock Coverage (Average)	5 days
Number of Stock-Outs over Past 12 Months	216
Number of Failed Availability Checks	225
Days of Supply over RLT (Average)	13/25

Table 11.1 Inventory KPIs and Their Values

From these values, we can now derive the rating for select performance measurements. The average inventory over the past 12 months may be related to the target inventory value, which was defined as the following:

Target Inventory Value ($) = Average Daily Consumption (/d) × Replenishment Lead Time (d) × Standard Price ($) × Safety Factor (1.2 for X items, 1.4 for Y items, 2.0 for Z items)

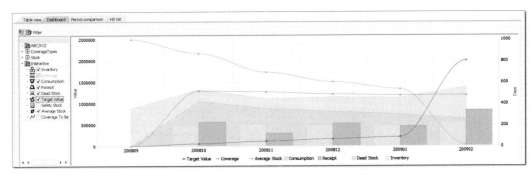

Figure 11.1 Comparing Target Inventory Levels with Average Inventory Holdings in the Inventory Cockpit

Now we can rate the performance the actual inventory delivered. Because the average inventory holdings lie at $400,000, or approximately 50% above the target inventory, this is mediocre performance at best and shouldn't be rated any higher than 40 out of 100.

Figure 11.1 shows a screenshot of the SAP add-on tool called the Inventory Controlling Cockpit. This tools helps you define a target inventory level and compare it to your actual inventory holdings.

Dead Stock

Another rating can be assigned to dead stock. Dead stock is that portion of the inventory that isn't touched during the period of investigation. A dead stock value of $415,000 doesn't tell us much; however, if we relate dead stock to average inventory and compare it to an industry standard, the KPI becomes much more meaningful and can be rated. In our case, dead stock makes up approximately 35% of the inventory we're typically holding and paying for. Industry standards say that between 20% and 25% dead stock of the average is an acceptable and good rating. With our 35%, we earn a rating of no more than 80.

Looking at $15,000 of inventory for stock that doesn't move, we can conclude near perfect performance and rate that KPI with a 97.

Safety stock makes up about 40% of average inventory and gives us five days of supplier variability buffering. To come up with relevant conclusions, you should probably also include the average safety stock holding of the past and compare it to your service level or buffering efficiency by looking at your stock-outs and failed availability checks. If your safety stock is high, and you still have lots of stock-outs, ratings for buffering efficiency degrade and provide an excellent opportunity for improvement through better policy.

Comparing stock-outs with the number of failed availability checks delivers clues about the expediting capabilities of an organization. You might want to ask questions such as the following: "Do we perform a collective availability check early enough for our buyers to be able to expedite and still cure the problem?" The answer might drive you to possible improvement activities.

Days of Supply over Replenishment Lead Time

Another great piece of information is the matrix that shows the Days of Supply over Replenishment Lead Time KPI (Figure 11.2).

In the matrix, you can see the size of the portfolio that makes up a certain segment. For example, there aren't a lot of materials with 3 days of Coverage and 5 days of lead time, compared to the many materials that need an average 7.5 days to be replenished but have only 4 days of coverage in inventory before they're depleted. Double-clicking the bubble provides you with a list of the respective material numbers and descriptions.

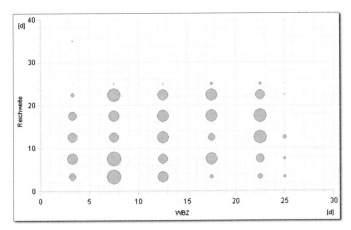

Figure 11.2 Matrix Showing Materials Categorized for the Relation between Days of Coverage and Replenishment Lead Time in the Inventory Cockpit

As we identify our ratings, we might want to aggregate our findings to the Inventory Performance success factor. The final result might look something like what appears in Figure 11.3.

Score								0% ◯ 50% ◑ 100% ●		
36%	**1 INVENTORY PERFORMANCE**									
		KPI		result				rating	weight	total
	purchased parts								1	◯ 36%
	average inventory (12m)	$1,250,000						40%	0.2	8%
	target inventory value	$850,000								
	dead stock	$415,000						0%	0	0%
	dead stock % of average	33%						80%	0.1	8%
	turns	4	Measures how many times a company's inventory has been sold (turned over) during a period of time." It equals "the cost of goods sold, divided by the average inventory level of inventory on hand.					25%	0.2	5%
	no movers inventory	$15,000	report on inventory value for parts that are moving zero to five times over the past 12 months					50%	0.1	5%
	safety stock value (total)	$487,000	from Safety Stock Simulator					0%	0	0%
	safety stock coverage	5 days						60%	0.1	6%
	days of supply over RLT	13/25						20%	0.1	2%
	number of stock-outs	216	bad performance since we were not able to expedite many items					10%	0.1	1%
	number of failed availability checks	225						10%	0.1	1%
									1	
										◯

Figure 11.3 Inventory Performance Rating

As depicted in Figure 11.3, our inventory performance is rated with 36% out of 100. This is a somewhat subjective measurement and relies heavily on the experience of the person evaluating, but it provides a solid basis for benchmarking and building improvement initiatives.

But before we get into the definition of improvement initiatives, let's take a look at the other measures.

11.1.2 Service

Service is a measure that has a huge relevancy for MRP. However, it's not the service to the customer we're primarily concerned with in this area (of course customer service is the ultimate measure for the company); instead, we're focusing on the service we're providing to the production lines. No one seems to measure the service provided to production even though it's one of the most complained about issues in manufacturing. Materials planners are made responsible for stock-outs, which make up one of the greatest contributors to chaos on the shop floor. But yet, we're not measuring this very important provider to performance and efficiency. Find a way to count stock-outs and measure how often they occur and under what circumstances. Then define some actions to reduce stock-outs and increase availability to the production lines. Performing a collective availability check right after you put together next week's production program will give you valuable insight into this situation and, in the least, give you awareness about a potentially damaging process. But be careful about simply raising the safety stock levels. That is a practice done by people who work with Excel and don't see the whole picture.

After you provide great service to the production orders that use and consume the materials you're planning, then you maintain minimum inventory to fulfill reservations from production orders to a very high degree (percentage) of requests. The other service rating a materials planner is concerned with is the degree of performance from your suppliers. Some deliver early, and some deliver late. Both are equally bad for you as you'll either face stock-outs or high inventory levels with too long of a coverage. SAP ERP has a module for supplier evaluation. Use it and discuss any issues with your partners. But be sure to clean your house first before evaluating others.

11.1.3 Automation and Integration

To measure automation, of course, is a bit subjective, especially when you're looking in an SAP transaction for the value. But nevertheless, you should make the effort and go through the evaluation. Automation and integration provides for some of the greatest potential for increases in efficiency and savings through a lower manual workload and the associated cost savings.

Look into your process for policy setting and policy review, the way you're running the MRP run, how exceptions are dealt with, and expediting is performed. Scrutinize the way your purchase requisitions are converted and how the MRP types, strategy groups, and lot-size procedures support the quality of the order proposals that are generated by the system.

Do your availability checks and subsequent transfers of demand get stuck in a faulty configuration, or does information flow accurately and in a timely manner? Some organizations lack a good interface between the sales and production scheduling departments. Make sure your situation doesn't suffer the same fate.

11.1.4   Flexibility and Responsiveness

How agile, to use a buzzword, is your materials planning? As will be discussed in Chapter 12 of this book, there is a very tight connection between responsiveness to varying demand and efficiency of process. The relationship can best be expressed with inventory (safety stock design) and process improvements. The more inventory (safety stock) you put in place, the more responsive you are, but there is a trade-off—cost of inventory. So you don't want to be quite that responsive, unless you increase your process efficiency and become more responsive to changing demand, still keeping relatively low inventories.

While this might seem self-explanatory, have you ever *measured* the status you're operating under in terms of responsiveness and agility? And have you ever designed an improvement process based on these measures so that your team knows whether to put more safety stock in place or work on a better process?

To get these measure out of your SAP system, you can use a number of KPIs available in the Supply Chain Performance Index. For example, for the Responsiveness group, you should use the Forecast Accuracy KPI. The more accurate your forecast, the more responsive you'll be because with the same amount of safety stock on a good forecast, you'll achieve a much better fill rate of your orders. In SAP ERP, you can measure forecast accuracy when you compare all demand caused by requirement types LSF, VSF, and VSE with your actual consumption within the frozen zone. Of course, if your setup doesn't support correct consumption of forecast or you're operating without a frozen zone, then you'll have some process improvements to do before you can measure forecast accuracy.

You can also use the Responsiveness to Change in Strategic Direction KPI to measure how accurately and quickly your organization will follow a manager's decision to raise a service level or shorten the lead time to customers. How is that measurable? Again, your process comes first. When a manager raises service levels, one of the direct implications is a rise in safety stock levels. If these decisions are well documented and communicated, you can look at when the decision was made and whether the implication emerged as expected.

Agility can be measured by looking at the variety in your SKU portfolio. If you do your homework, analyze the market, and establish an offering of products that customers like to buy, then chances are that you're operating much more agile with what you're making to stock than if you don't. Of course, an important agility measure is the MTS/MTO split and the supplier delivery variability, which, if it's high, restricts you in acting quickly to changing demand. With a longer freezing period, or frozen zone, you protect the production schedule, but you also limit responsiveness.

And one more important KPI for your flexibility, responsiveness, or agility is flow, as in material flow and in information flow. After information and materials freely flow through your supply chain structure, changes in demand can be applied with much more transparency and predictability of the outcome.

This brings us to the next subset of KPIs, which we'll discuss in the following section.

11.1.5 Transparency, Visibility, Communication

Without knowing how visible and transparent your process is, you can't improve on this important driver of efficiency and accuracy. To measure visibility, look at the availability checks and how they're configured in the SAP ERP system. Figure 11.4 shows an example of such a configuration for the rule Z1 when a sales order is created.

The sales availability check causes demand to be transferred in a certain way (with the determination of the material availability date) and allows you to greatly improve the way information is channeled through the supply chain. Similarly, the component availability check improves communication and visibility between the production scheduling and purchasing departments if set up correctly and efficiently.

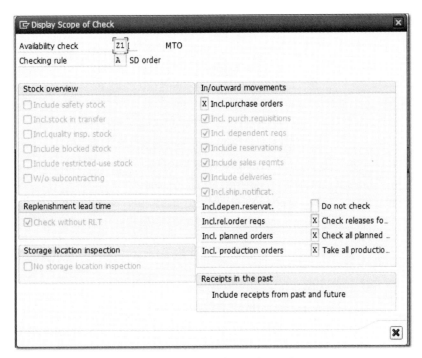

Figure 11.4 Availability Check Configuration for a Sales Order

An aspect of utmost importance is the degree of the exception-minded business in your organization. Are you managing exceptions, or do you constantly watch the rule? Watching the rule, or its outcome, every day means that you don't trust in your basic data setup to deliver the expected results automatically. If you did, all you would need to do is watch for and act on the exceptions that come out of your monitor. Lots of exceptions every day mean that your basic data setup is suboptimal. And there is only one way to get your exceptions down: improve master data and policy. The sheer number of exception messages and evaluating how meaningful they are will give you a good measurement of whether you manage exceptions or operate as a firefighter day by day.

11.1.6 Measuring Information Maturity

Mature information can be measured by the quality of basic and transactional data. While implementations are predominantly focused on getting transactions up and running, information maturity suggests that organizations need to allow technology to do the work. Allow the user to apply tribal knowledge, experience, and unique abilities to work toward the business goals leadership has set. Information maturity can be measured by an organization's ability to accurately set basic data and let the system generate accurate transactional data from it. By proactively managing data through segmentation, policy setting, and daily exception monitoring, the organization can better control the business and its associated risks.

To measure information maturity, look at the use of your policy, MRP controller groupings, bill of materials (BOM) structures and routing setup, material quantity calculations in recipes if you're a process manufacturer, and the correct provision of available capacity in the work centers. All of this has a huge impact on how the system generates order proposals with quantities and dates that the user can trust.

11.1.7 Competence

Don't drive this too far. Measuring competence is often a point of contention as users feel tested and have a fear of failure. Of course, the easiest way to measure the planner's competence is to subject him to a written test. However, if you've ever participated in one of those certifications, you know that, especially in the case of multiple choice tests, there is a lot of room for arguments, and the testers aren't always able to formulate the questions correctly or provide the correct answers. This proves to be especially bad for morale if a student fails the test because of a disputable answer he gave.

Hanging a certificate in your cubicle after you pass some sort of a test might be nice, but nothing beats the knowledge about your planner's competence in the use of the SAP system as a tool to raise efficiency, accuracy in data, transparency, and automation. And that can be evaluated without forcing the planner through high school again. Perform interviews, sit with the user while he does the job, and evaluate the way they make use of policy, manage exception messages, and use reports to gain visibility in achieving their goals.

And don't forget that if you see incompetence, its roots are most likely come from a lack of training, an inefficient setup of the configuration supporting their transactions, and bad data rather than a lack of intelligence. Their job is hard enough, considering that, in many cases, this system was thrown at them without the much-needed support in process design.

11.1.8   Organizational Support

This measure raises the question about how much responsibility management and leadership should bear for the success (or lack of success) of SAP ERP running the organization's operations. Management, in general can be blamed for inefficient use of SAP ERP software because SAP ERP is only the tool. The other two components that must be implemented for the system to operate successfully are a competent user and a sound strategy. And a sound strategy is very often missing.

People often talk about supply chain strategies, but a detailed description of it isn't commonly found. And yet, for an organization to work, a manager has to be specific about what service levels he wants to materialize, what lead times the business should promise to the customer, and which buffers (inventory, capacity, and time) can be used in what combination.

Management should be measured by the degree of clarity that is in their message and guidelines to the workforce. Their job is to be supportive in the planner's endeavor to raise efficiencies and make the customers happy. That includes providing support for the tool (purchase and make available a good one like SAP ERP), raising competence (arrange for the right education and training), and providing a sound strategy to follow.

11.2   Developing Improvement Initiatives

To improve is to make better—not just kick off an initiative. And to make better, at least in the context of our focus here, is to increase efficiency in planning and execution, to be more responsive to your customer, or both. In Chapter 12, when we explore the modeling of materials planning, we'll develop causal loop diagrams (CLDs), which provide more insight into how these two variables interact. Already we can show that responsiveness and efficiency both may be kept at a high level with either improvements in inventory levels or process.

You've likely heard of the benefits of a lean supply chain or the advantages of an agile supply chain, but both a lean *and* agile supply chain is an even better option. In other words, everybody is looking for a setup that increases efficiencies *and* flexibility or responsiveness in the supply chain. When you're efficient, the cost, and therefore waste, is low, and when you're responsive, you achieve a high degree of customer satisfaction because customers pretty much can get what they want when they want it.

In Figure 11.5, we can see that improving efficiency as well as improving responsiveness both require investments (for efficiency, this might be the investment in building better planning processes; for responsiveness, the investment in higher safety stocks). However, we can also see that achieving the desired results for either one of these improvements will also deliver a return on the investment into the improvements. On one side, this might be the right-sizing in inventory, and on the other side, it might be more product sales. In systems thinking terms, this could be interpreted as a virtuous cycle (more about systems thinking in Chapter 12, Section 12.2) where investing in improvements raises efficiency and responsiveness, whereas increases in efficiency and responsiveness reduce the cost of maintaining an optimized system. After you're in the mode of continuous improvements, all indicators will consistently and continuously progress; most organizations sadly just never get into it.

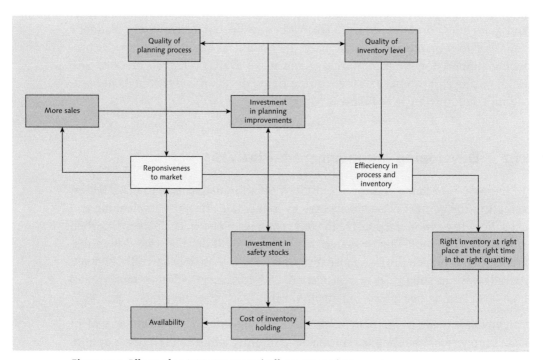

Figure 11.5 Effects of an Initiative around Efficiencies and Responsiveness

The problem with improvement initiatives is that you can't (and shouldn't) work in silos. Because of its integrated nature, the SAP supply chain rarely allows for a change in one area (no matter whether it's good or bad) without an impact in another (which is sometimes good, sometimes bad). That is why you'll have to carefully design an improvement process and anticipate possible effects in other spaces. An example of designing improvements is shown in Figure 11.6.

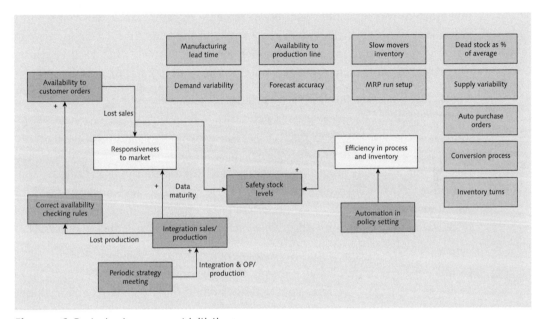

Figure 11.6 Designing Improvement Initiatives

Our two major goals for the lean and agile supply chain are improvements in responsiveness and increases in efficiencies. You can list all (or some) influencing factors that enable the achievement of these goals. This is a great exercise to compile a list of all the KPIs and get them on the same page together with the results. You can then start to draw out the causalities and therefore derive a valuable map for insights into the complex structure of a supply chain and its associated functions in MRP.

If, for example, we want to increase our flexibility and responsiveness to our customers, we could move back from our goal and initially think about how to reduce lost sales and the associated available inventory of product for the customer. Better and more accurate rules in the sales availability check would certainly improve on that KPI. One way to get together correct rules is with more integrated working between the sales and production departments, which is hopefully improved with a possible quarterly strategy meeting where performance boundaries and policy are discussed and decided upon. This, in turn, improves communication, transparency, and data maturity.

However, as you can see by making the connection, an increase of available inventory to the customer requires an increase in safety stock. To counter this potentially negative effect, you might want to, at the same time, try an increase in efficiency so you don't require too much more safety stock. That positive consequence could come from an improvement in your policy setting.

Conflicting goals are the things we'll have to deal with on a day-to-day basis if we're determined to improve our operations. When we want service levels to go up, inventory in safety stock needs to go up as well. But what inventory needs to go up, and what inventory can go down? If we don't perform a segmentation and classify our materials according to their value, predictability, lead time, or consumption volume, we can't truthfully decide how much safety stock we need for which material. However, if we do, we're in fact right-sizing our inventories and respective safety stocks and effectively increasing some but reducing others.

When engaging in continuous improvements, do your homework. Pay attention to the effects all around that KPI you want to improve, and make sure you're aware of any negative effects your activities could possibly have. Look at things holistically, and be aware of your surroundings and the impacts that come from changing things.

11.3 Measuring Progress

There are many discussions, recommendations, white papers, and even books on how to best measure progress after goals have been set and initiatives are defined. The improvement programs aren't always successful, and the cause of failure doesn't lie in the unwillingness to succeed but rather in the way we measure success. Take, for example, one of the most widespread American activities that is measured for success with a very high rate of failure: human weight-loss programs. Sometimes, subjects of this activity profusely measure every little KPI they can, such as calories of each meal, number of activity minutes, intensity of exercise, number of steps taken in a day, calories burned, and so on.

But often we forget that the one little thing we do every morning in the bathroom is the most telling measure of it all—stepping on the scale. And that little thing that gives a major indication about our progress toward the goal can be described as the General Outcome Measurement (GOM) method within the science of progress monitoring (mostly, but not nearly exclusively, used in education). Essentially the idea of GOM is a process of measuring one simple or "little" thing the same way over time to make a statement about something complex or "big."

For example, major decisions are made about the state of the economy by just looking at the development in the Dow Jones Industrial Average (DJIA) when it only measures 100 companies. Or look at how doctors evaluate your overall health (and make big decisions about it) based on a simple measure of your blood pressure. In the same or similar way, we can evaluate progress on the health of your supply chain. Sometimes, we just need to see things a bit different.

Now, let's move on to view MRP with SAP ERP in a similar manner. We've all tried the numerous functions and features available in SAP ERP, and not much has changed with the basic view we have of how it's working.

In the beginning, there was MRP, where diligent planners were exploding BOMs and handily figuring out ordering quantities and dates for purchased parts. This was pre-1960s, and nothing has basically changed since. Yes, manufacturing resource planning (MRP II) was coming to introduce capacity leveling as an additional step and doing it with computers. Then SAP ERP integrated MRP with HR, Sales, Finance, and much more. Eventually, the new big thing of Advanced Planning Systems (APSs) was trying to automate everything without human intervention. Solutions such as supply chain management, big data, in-memory computing, cloud computing, and mobility promised a better world, but none ever delivered much improvement on the problem at hand: optimizing the ordering process to hold perfect inventories for good availability and high service levels.

Do we need another point of view? For example, David Katz M.D. (director at the Yale Prevention Center) when referring to thinking from another point of view, suggests considering health like wealth and seeing obesity like drowning. All of a sudden mental models shift and break apart. If health is like wealth, it becomes something we invest in and live for. Dr. Katz says, "We care about it both for our own sake, and the sake of those we love. We recognize most get-rich-quick proposals as scams; we are sensible about money. We don't spend everything we have today; we think about the future, and save for it. We get financial guidance from genuine experts, not just anybody who had a piggy bank once." And Dr. Katz continues about seeing obesity like drowning, "If instead, we treated obesity more like drowning, we would tell the truth about food. We would not market multicolored marshmallows to children as part of a complete breakfast. We would not willfully mislead about the perilous currents in the modern food supply. We would not look on passively as an entire population of non-swimmers started wading in over their heads."

So what about materials planning? How can we get to a better place? What is the metaphor or simile? Maybe we should use the perspective of systems thinking by looking at things more holistically and considering feedback, interaction, and behavior a bit more and not being so fixated on individual process and transactions. CLDs can provide us with a new way to "see," whereas stock and flowcharts provide a useful metaphor to interpret the behavior of agents and describe the system's structure for better interpretation and decision making.

One feature of GOM certainly stands out—its simplicity. Usually the measures aren't time-consuming to collect, and they are collected the same way each time. The data, once collected, isn't difficult to organize, report, or understand. This leads to one of the major advantages of GOM, which is its feasibility. In other words, progress decisions can be made economically in terms of time, cost, and complexity.

Of course, GOM isn't a perfect solution, and it requires KPIs that meet certain criteria. The most challenging is that a general outcome measure may be validated as a predictor of proficiency in a broader domain. Something "little" or simple is related to something "big" or more complex, and here is where caution is recommended in putting too much value on such a method of progress measuring. However, GOM's usefulness stands. If you don't have an elaborate system of accurate and detailed measuring (and most organizations don't), GOM provides an easy-to-use alternative.

If, for example, you decide on an initiative to right-size inventory and improve turns for your purchased part, you may want to look at the production order's failed availability checks. If the number goes down, you know that the efforts bear fruit and bring with it the desired results.

11.4   Summary

To improve performance, things must change. But before you change, you'll have to understand the current situation. Benchmarking the current state is an activity we strongly recommend to execute at the beginning of any optimization efforts. Using KPIs, success factors allow for the measurement of your supply chain and its performance and efficiency.

Only then can you define specific activities to improve performance, work more efficiently, and drive waste out of your process. Package your activities into a sequenced program, and success will come.

Last, but certainly not least, you must quantify and measure your progress toward clearly defined goals. Sustainability, which should constitute the most desired outcome of a supply chain optimization, only comes when you meticulously pursue perfection and success—and that only comes with the availability of clarity, visibility, and transparency.

PART IV

Modeling Materials Planning

We live in a society exquisitely dependent on science and technology, in which hardly anyone knows anything about science and technology.
—Carl Sagan

12 Scientific Modeling of the SAP Supply Chain

In this chapter, we want to go above and beyond the traditional approach to SAP supply chain optimization and materials planning. Very often, SAP software is implemented using blueprints, templates, and guidelines that have little to do with methods and theories employed in the science of operations planning. Many people even believe that there is no such thing as a science for operations planning. However, there is extensive literature on the subject, and the theories have been around for a very long time. And maybe therein lies the problem: a scientific framework of operational science doesn't jive with the buzzwords in recent years describing supply chain management.

Works such as Elijah Goldratt's *The Goal*, the associated *Theory of Constraints* by the same author, Wallace and Hoop's textbook, *Factory Physics*, and John Sterman's excellent contribution to the book *Thinking in Systems* are old in supply chain terms. People still read them and discuss the subject matter, but very seldom are the resulting principles, laws, and corollaries applied to the way we use SAP ERP as a tool to manage, plan, and execute our operations.

It can be disconcerting because for most everything, from engineering to product development, we apply science to achieve predictable and desired results. However, when it comes to the management and planning of operations, we traditionally base our decisions on experience and intuition. As good intuition can be an extremely efficient guide to making good decisions because it's primarily developing out of a solid scientific framework of reference over the years. Experience also must be of the right kind. What good is experience coming from many years of making bad decisions?

Many of these decisions are made at the time when we implement SAP software to run our operations. Some are made later during the use of that software. And if you take a close look at how most SAP implementations are conducted, you may recognize that the nature of the implementation doesn't have very much to do with any scientific theory. You might argue that SAP software works in a certain way. Is that really true? Isn't SAP ERP the tool that provides options that can be customized to your specific process? Doesn't SAP software provide a very large toolbox of options from which to pick a fitting one for your operations? Who says you must transfer the forecast onto every finished product with strategy 40? What is the logic behind using the same sales availability check rules across the board? Why do people say that you *have* to use the safety stock if you want to reorder materials based on inventory levels?

These are decisions made during the implementation and beyond. They are based on rumors, hearsay, guesswork, and loose assumptions but certainly not on knowledge or a scientific basis that can guide us to better setups and subsequently better results. Take, for example, the process of planning for finished goods sold through a product catalogue. Almost all SAP-using customers we've seen would set up the product with standard strategy group 40 and then the sales representative would take orders with Transaction VA01. Sometimes the availability check produces a delivery proposal, and, if it does, the representative doesn't always fully understand the implications on the production line when confirming or fixing the date. Should he fix the date? Should the quantity and proposed delivery date be confirmed to the customer? What happens in the planning department? How is the forecast consumed (if it even is consumed)? Can we learn from the fact that we couldn't deliver on time (what was the forecast accuracy)? Where is the source of the problem that we can't deliver, and how can we improve for the next time around?

The only way these and other questions can be answered, to develop a more effective, profitable, and transparent organization, is through the application of a scientific framework of reference.

Using systems thinking, you can detect causal relationships and look across silos to see the effects. The Factory Physics principle allows for the development of predictive intuition, and design thinking can open up opportunities that might have never crossed your mind. Let's embark on some, maybe, new ideas on how to deal with the SAP supply chain.

12.1   Operations Management and Science

Materials planning is a discipline within operations management (OM). And operations management was a term being used long before computers and IT took on the task of supporting planning and execution in manufacturing and services firms. OM deals with the design and management of products, processes, services, and supply chains. It considers the acquisition, development, and utilization of resources that firms need to deliver the goods and services their clients want.

The discussion around OM ranges from strategic to tactical and operational levels. Specific strategic issues include determining the size and location of manufacturing plants, deciding the structure of service networks, and designing technology supply chains. Tactical issues include plant layout and structure, project management methods, and equipment selection and replacement. Operational issues include production scheduling and control, inventory management, quality control and inspection, traffic and materials handling, and equipment maintenance policies.

As you can deduce from the preceding characterization, OM deals with all aspects of planning from strategic to tactical and eventually operational aspects of planning and managing resources for transformation. The differentiation of strategic and tactical planning and the pointing out of the extra step of operational execution within the framework of OM is important. Very often, these distinct activities are merged into one, and the expected results blur into meaningless key performance indicators (KPIs).

Additionally, if we refer and stick to the term OM, we stay clear of any confusion resulting from a maze of buzzwords frequently used in our profession to demonstrate competence or cutting-edge thought leadership that is bordering on fraud in some cases. Throwing around new terms like they are running out of style doesn't help with the task at hand: the administration of business practices to create the highest level of efficiency possible within an organization. This task can be easily defined as OM because it's concerned with converting materials and labor into goods and services as efficiently as possible to maximize the profit of an organization.

By using OM as our framework that includes materials planning, we can now, unambiguously, talk about how we can apply some science to the disciplines of planning and execution, so that we're achieving more efficiency, automation, transparency, and profitability in the process.

But before we delve into some exciting applications from the world of operations research and learn how to apply the results to daily work, we should take a look at some organizational aspects of OM and how these can shape the performance boundaries we're operating under.

Let's consider the military, for example. Highest-level senior officers shape strategy and revise it over time, while line officers and lieutenants make tactical decisions in support of carrying out the overall strategy. The boundaries between these levels aren't always distinct because tactical information dynamically informs strategy, and people often move between levels and roles over time.

This is no different in business. C-level executives usually define financial, HR, and supply chain strategy, while demand planners, materials planners, and buyers make tactical decisions to execute on the plan (strategy). However, the strategic direction doesn't always connect well with the tactical execution. Sometimes the strategy isn't based on the real-life performance capabilities an organization historically demonstrates. And if that isn't the case, the strategy is often impossible to execute. On the other hand, the strategy might not be communicated clearly (see the mention of commander's intent in Chapter 4, Section 4.1), and the tactical execution will experience lack of information and therefore become useless.

Whatever the case may be, the integration of strategy and tactical execution within a framework of operation planning is a necessity without which good performance is very hard to achieve.

Figure 12.1 depicts a suggested organizational framework of OM from strategic through tactical planning and execution.

As shown in the illustration, decisions are made on different levels of the organization, at different points in time, and by different people. In meeting number ❶—the strategy meeting—performance boundaries are defined, and the general supply chain strategy is discussed and given. This meeting typically takes place once a year with quarterly revisions. Information from this meeting flows into the monthly demand planning meeting ❷, in which demand variability is managed, buffering strategies are conceived, and a policy playbook is developed. A major goal is to improve on the forecast accuracy before demand is placed in operational MRP.

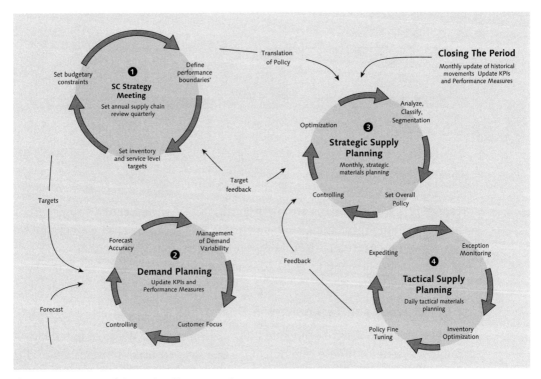

Figure 12.1 Integrated Operation Management

After the hand-off, supply planning takes over. First, the strategic supply planner sets overall policy ❸, and then the tactical materials planners will fine-tune the policy, expedite, reschedule, and manage and monitor exceptional messages ❹.

Of utmost importance here is the necessity to respect the various planning horizons we're moving in. As Figure 12.2 shows, there are distinct phases in the timing of planning and execution. There is also a point in time when planning stops and execution takes over. You can't keep on changing the plan into the future. There must be a stopping point at which a consensus is reached that planning has subsided its activities, and what we're changing now is different from the plan and not an adjustment anymore.

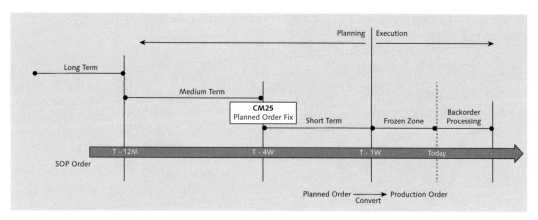

Figure 12.2 Planning and Execution Horizons

Respecting a frozen zone is an important aspect of an integrated framework of effective operations planning, and violating it with continuous adjustments of the plan disallows any comparison between the plan and actuality that could help improve plannability and forecast accuracy.

12.1.1 Science and Technology in Operations Management

So where does the science come into play in effective OM? We need to build rules around a system of predictable outcomes that help us make sense of a world of uncertainty. Like the laws of nature, there are principles in the science of OM. If we can lay out the ground rules for such a system of OM, we can use scientific methods to predict future inventory and service levels, and we can buffer variability with strategies that are based on explainable models rather than guesswork and the fear of running out of stock.

The more we apply scientific rules and watch outcomes by testing the policies we've developed before, the better intuition we'll develop to work within such a system and achieve the desired results. We gain control over the process and over the management of our operations. Everybody involved will work more analytically, will be more geared toward decision making and predictive control, and will let the system do the transactional work.

OM, however, has traditionally been based on experience and intuition. People working in the field are basing their decisions on what they personally perceive as the best way of doing business. Decisions are usually not based on standardized formulas that have been tried and tested but rather on what has worked historically and what can be remembered. When a planner sets up the basic data in the material master record, he typically uses an MRP type and lot-size procedure that he knows, hopes that inventories won't blow up too much, and, more prominently, attempts to avoid stock-outs at all cost. As humans err on the side of caution, the natural result is higher inventory than necessary.

Why not try for a more scientific basis for decision making that we can use for the creation of reusable materials planning models? With these models, we simulate future results with standardized formulas and build a policy for every possible situation. This represents a system where we use science to predict possible outcomes and technology to execute on the most probable method to achieve the best possible result.

The Difference between Science and Technology

Science can be described as knowledge, or a system of knowledge, covering general truths or the operation of laws when tested by scientific methods. In other words, when using the laws that govern a system (OM, materials planning), we can use specific methods to test and predict the outcomes of the application of a method. Using the term "policy" instead of "method," it becomes clear that when we test a policy, we attempt to predict the policy's outcome in terms of, for example, future stock levels. If the policy is developed based on the laws of the system, we can say that we employ a scientific way to manage our operations. And if science can be described as knowledge, then our scientific way uses exactly that knowledge, and we're getting better with increasing knowledge.

It's important to note here that we're not always operating with full knowledge of the underlying system because we don't have the rule framework in place that is necessary to gain the knowledge. That is even more argument for a scientific approach.

Now that we've established that science *is* the knowledge, technology then is the practical application of knowledge. It's the tool that allows us to tell the system (SAP ERP) to operate on that knowledge. We still have to feed the tool with the decision (policy) and provide it with the rule framework (knowledge), but after it's set up correctly, it can do the heavy lifting for us. Instead of carrying out transaction code after transaction code, it's time to develop the rule set and employ a system of periodic reviews and intelligent decision making. It's time we use the tool the way it was meant to be used—as a tool—and allow human beings to do what we do best: cognitively make decisions based on knowledge, experience, and well-developed intuition.

12.2 Systems Thinking

Systems thinking is a science employed by many people who want to look at things in a more holistic way. Instead of breaking a problem into its individual parts to look for a solution, the systems thinker assembles the bigger picture and looks for feedback to determine possible, highly probable outcomes. The systems thinking approach contrasts with traditional analysis, which studies systems by breaking them down into their separate elements. Here we look at complete systems instead of individual parts to find the source of the problem and to understand behavior caused by interactions.

Systems thinking can be used in any area of research and has been applied to the study of medical, environmental, political, economic, HR, and educational systems, among many others. Why not use the systems thinking approach in the supply chain? It's defined as an approach to problem solving. Specifically, it's doing so by looking at problems as parts of an overall system. This is very different from our traditional way of reacting to specific parts, outcomes, or events, and then, maybe, contributing to the appearance of unintended consequences.

Take, as an example, the way we deal with inventory levels that are perceived as too high. With the traditional approach, people just simply want to order less because they perceive the root cause to be the amount of purchase orders that were placed in the past (maybe based on a forecast that was too hopeful). As a result, if the consumption stays the same, inventory goes down. But because of the singular focus on one cause and no consideration of other possible effects, the availability of parts for production orders might go down as well, and you may be faced faced with a large increase of stock-outs as an unwanted consequence.

This kind of analysis and action can be described as event-oriented thinking as shown in Figure 12.3. In event-oriented thinking, or linear thinking, everything is explained by a chain of events. You might go backwards from the problem D and eventually arrive at the root cause: A or B. Per our example, the problem is high inventory levels, and the causes might be ordering too much and/or too little consumption. Because consumption behavior lies outside the materials planner's control, the event-oriented thinker will reduce ordering quantities and frequency to improve the situation.

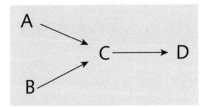

Figure 12.3 Event-Oriented Thinking

This isn't the case when we apply systems thinking, in which we can see that a system's behavior emerges from the structure of its feedback loops. When we're thinking in whole systems, we're looking to understand problems in the context of relationships with other individual component parts and with other systems, rather than in isolation. Systems thinking focuses on cyclical rather than linear cause and effect, as shown in Figure 12.4.

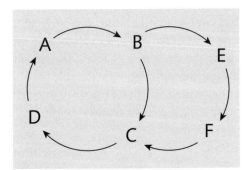

Figure 12.4 Systems Thinking

When we apply such a problem-solving technique, the system's behavior emerges from the structure of its feedback loops. Root causes aren't simply individual nodes, but rather a force that emerges from a particular feedback loop. Therefore, if A represents ordering quantities and frequency, the logical consequence is that the more you order, the higher your stock level (B) will be and with it the concerns of the executive about too much capital tied up in inventory will rise (C). When executives get concerned, improvement initiatives (D) are initiated, and one of the actions refers to the reduction of ordering quantities and frequencies. This, in turn, changes the inventory levels again and so on.

But there is another set of dynamics going on when inventory levels change. If B (inventory) goes down, availability of parts to the production lines (E) goes down with it. And if availability goes down, stock-outs (F) increase, which, of course, raises the executive's concerns (C). As you can see in Figure 12.4, we're taking a more holistic approach toward problem solving and deriving behavior from the structure of a system rather than working backwards from a problem to find one, and maybe only one, cause that we subsequently fix. This type of approach poses incredible opportunities for our world of SAP ERP supply chain optimization where, traditionally and overwhelmingly, consultants and customers (planners, buyers, schedulers) have simply looked at the problem at hand and applied a quick fix to the best of their knowledge. And that knowledge, in most cases, isn't necessarily based on feedback systems, patterns, and structures with their resulting dynamics or behaviors.

In systems thinking, we have a variety of tools and software applications at our disposal. There are computer simulations (e.g., Monte Carlo simulations) and a variety of diagrams and graphs to model, illustrate, and predict system behavior. Among the systems thinking tools are the behavior-over-time (BOT) graph, which indicates the actions of one or more variables over a period of time; the causal loop diagram (CLD), which illustrates the relationships between system elements; and the stock and flow diagram, which allows for the depiction of levels (stock) and rates (flow). The latter—stock and flow diagrams—will play a major role for the interpretation of demand and transformation, which is a basis for the extremely helpful research in the Factory Physics principle, which we'll discuss shortly.

12.2.1 Causal Loop Diagrams

To better illustrate systems thinking and CLDs, let's look at the example of a shortening of the lead time to the customer. Sometimes the materials planner is faced with a surprise. Some committee made up of representatives from finance, sales, and marketing had decided to shorten the lead time to the customer to be more competitive in the market and increase revenues.

After we depict the situation with a CLD (Figure 12.5), we can see that publishing a shorter lead time will invariably increase demand and raise the amount of orders for our products. Great stuff, but can we handle it? An increase of order volume places a huge amount of pressure on the production department, materials planning, and our suppliers. Variability will go up, along with the need for buffers. Eventually, because of reduced availability of purchased parts, production will slow down and won't be able to keep up with order volume. The order backlog increases, customers start complaining about late deliveries, and market share goes down.

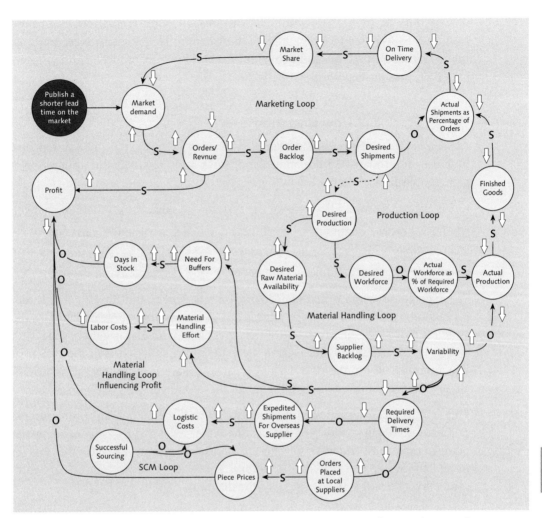

Figure 12.5 Impact on Material Planning Group When Marketing Requests a Short Lead Time and Nothing Else Changes

The CLD in Figure 12.5 and our new view on problem solving shows that an isolated decision on shortening the lead time to the customer not only misses its goal to increase market share and demand but also has the adverse effect of actually reducing revenues. There are many insights in this CLD that can't be gained with an event-oriented thinking approach as is done so often. Certain improvement activities don't deliver the desired results often because we base the perceived outcome of an activity on what we were told and what we were reading, instead of drawing the appropriate causal conclusions. In other words, we make false assumptions due to a lack of complete information, lack of a structure, and misinterpretation of patterns and behavior. We build mental models that don't necessarily represent the world correctly.

12.2.2 Stock and Flow Diagrams

As seen before, CLDs represent a simple way of showing the parts of a system and how they interrelate. On the other hand, stock and flow diagrams are more elegant and visual and do the following:

▶ Distinguish between the parts of the system and what causes them to change.

▶ Allow precise, quantitative specification of all the system's parts and their interrelation.

▶ Provide a basis for simulating the behavior of the system over time.

These diagrams contain two major components: stocks and flows. A stock represents a part of a system whose value at any given instant in time depends on the system's past behavior. The value of the stocks at a particular instant in time can't simply be determined by measuring the value of the other parts of the system at that instant in time; the only way you can calculate it is by measuring how it changes at every instant and adding up all these changes.

This sounds more complicated than it actually is. If we're looking at the example of a bathtub (Figure 12.6), you can see the water level and its value at any given point in time. How the water level is changing depends on the water that was let in and the water that was let out before. The water level is your stock, represented by a rectangle in a stock and flow diagram.

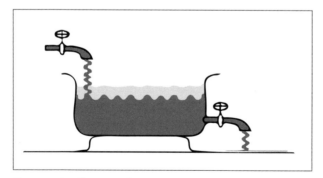

Figure 12.6 Inflows, Outflows, and Inventory of a Bathtub

A flow, on the other hand, represents the rate at which the stock is changing at any given point in time. It either flows into a stock (causing it to increase) or flows out of a stock (causing it to decrease).

Flows are represented as arrows in a stock and flow diagram, and a little valve symbol denotes the levers you have available to control the flow. Causal loops can also be depicted in this diagram so that you get a nice view of the causal relationships in combination with valuable information on how flow rates influence stock levels and how the stock levels feed information (because stocks hold information) back to other components of the system. Figure 12.7 illustrates how various parts of a system may impact the inventory level of pork at a distributor and how the inventory level of pork itself then has an influence on parts of the system (price).

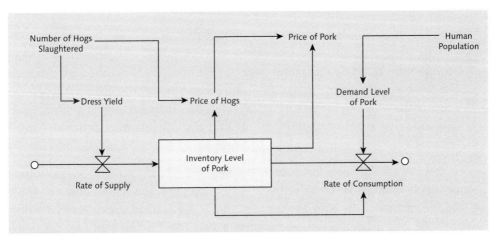

Figure 12.7 Stock and Flow Diagram for a System of Demand and Supply (of Pork)

In another illustration, we can relate back to our previous example of shortening the lead time to customers and lay out the factors that allow us to control the inventory levels for purchased parts or raw materials. We can use the stock and flow diagram in Figure 12.8 to construct the necessary model that we can use to set replenishment policies as described in Chapter 6 of this book.

Safety stock settings, replenishment type (stochastic or deterministic), and lot-size procedure (static, periodic, or optimizing) are all parts for the policy construct, whereas we'll have to consider supply and demand variability, available resources (or capacity), and many other factors for the design and balancing of service levels and capital inventory investment.

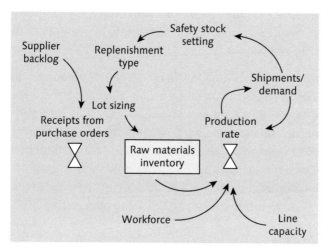

Figure 12.8 Policy Development with a Stock and Flow Diagram

From the stock and flow diagram, you can run specific stocks through a simulation (Monte Carlo simulation as an example) and plot a BOT diagram to predict future levels with varying factors or variables. BOT diagrams depict behavior over time and serve as an excellent instrument for simulative model design to control behavior emerging from your system structure.

As you can see, the tools for systems thinking provide an excellent scientific basis for supply chain and materials replenishment optimization. They allow you to see the big picture, help with the anticipation and avoidance of unwanted consequences, and deliver great insight so that you can develop intuition for better decision making to reach the goals set forth by management. However, when we try to apply the principles laid out here, we're almost always running into a more difficult obstacle that is hard to explain and difficult to overcome: the human aspects of a change effort.

12.2.3 Behavior-over-Time Diagrams

A BOT diagram is used to show what happens to something over time. In a BOT, the horizontal axis is always time, and the vertical axis is what we're concerned with and want to monitor. As an example, a BOT diagram could show share prices because these change over time or your body weight as you go on a diet. It could also display what happens to the water level in a bathtub after you pull the plug as is shown in Figure 12.9.

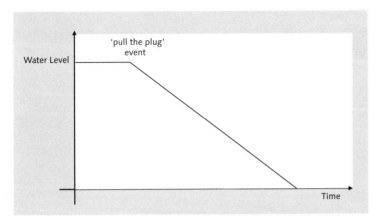

Figure 12.9 Behavior over Time Diagram for When the Bathtub Plug Is Pulled

In systems thinking, we try to understand trends over time rather than focusing attention on individual events, such as pulling the plug. With these diagrams, you can learn if the system you design and optimize is approaching a goal or limit and, if so, how quickly. The key BOT dynamics are exponential growth or decline, goal seeking, oscillation, or a combination such as S-shaped growth. Sometimes an oscillation is overlaid on top of an exponential growth pattern. It's these patterns that give us insight about what causal structures are strongest in the system we deal with. Figure 12.10 shows key BOT dynamics

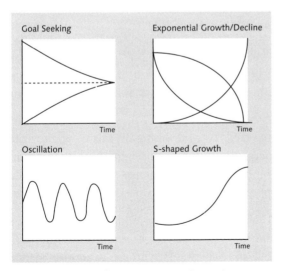

Figure 12.10 Key Behavior over Time Dynamics

Applicability of BOT diagrams to materials planning is given by an example from inventory planning. The BOT diagram in Figure 12.11 illustrates how inventory and service levels influence each other's BOT.

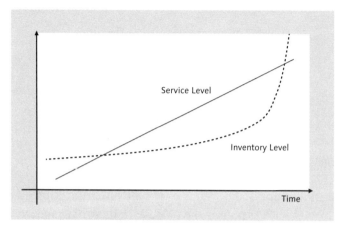

Figure 12.11 Service and Inventory Levels Graphed in a Behavior over Time Diagram

Just like systems thinking helps and strives to make you aware and bring clarity to the many implications one specific change to the system and its underlying structure has, BOT diagrams visualize the effects in a schematic way that helps us understand the dynamics of a system. It serves as another great tool to develop good intuition and experience for sound decision making in our supply chains.

12.2.4 Mental Models in Materials Planning and How to Break Them

Mental models are perceptions on how we think the world should be and are sometimes also described as someone's thought process about how something works in the real world.

In psychology, mental models are referred to as reasoning. In this view, they can be constructed from imagination, perception, and comprehension, which means that mental models have a very high likelihood of being false, deceptive, and convenient to use. They are often temporarily assumed to be true and that makes them very dangerous.

One mental model that can cause a number of problems is *order related replenishment*. Sales representatives, planners, and schedulers who are using this mental model assume that every demand (no matter whether MTO, MTS, or FTO) must be supplied with a chain of directly-related supply. Nothing in this replenishment process is done anonymously. Everything is directly related to the original demand, and the owner of the model believes that progress in the fulfillment of the demand can be monitored any time on every level of the replenishment process.

Because this is true for a pure MTO process, it's a very bad idea to apply to everything else from MTS to an inventory/order interface anywhere in the chain. If you lay out the causal relationships in CLDs and stock and flow diagrams, and you design the model's structure so that you can derive standard operating procedures for the various cases, you can break down this mental model and replace it with a more scientific and truthful representation of the process.

Another mental model that you might recognize is the widely used practice of adjusting a plan not only into the present but sometimes even into the past. Refer to Figure 12.2, and you can see that there should be a strict cut-off point in your planning horizons where planning ends and execution starts. This point is at the beginning of the *frozen zone*, T-x days. If you have a lead time to the customer and can't immediately produce to instant demand, you need to start executing on the plan before the demand is due. Otherwise, you wouldn't need planning.

These mental models and many more potentially hindering ones can be found all over industries and departments from small- and mid-sized businesses to large, global organizations. It's the supply chain optimizer's duty to recognize them and integrate remedies into the optimization initiatives. Otherwise. these projects— and we can see this everywhere—don't deliver the promised results, at least not in a sustainable manner.

Another very valuable thought process that helps make sense of supply chains and their emerging behavior is Factory Physics, which is a mindset developed by Wallace Hopp and Mark Spearman to improve intuition for better decision making.

12.3   Factory Physics

The Factory Physics theory brings science into the supply chain. In the book by the same name, which we've mentioned previously, Wallace Hopp and Mark Spearman introduce a framework for manufacturing management. According to the book's preface, Factory Physics is the following:

...a systematic description of the underlying behavior of manufacturing systems. Understanding it enables managers and engineers to work with the natural tendencies of manufacturing systems to:

– Identify opportunities for improving existing systems.
– Design effective new systems.
– Make the trade-offs needed to coordinate policies from disparate areas

The *Factory Physics* book is used both in industry and in academia for reference and teaching on OM. It describes a new approach to manufacturing management based on the laws, principles, and corollaries of Factory Physics science. Its fundamental Factory Physics framework states that the essential components of all value streams or production processes are demand and transformation, which are described by structural elements of flows and stocks. There are very specific practical, mathematical relationships that enable you to describe and control the performance of flows and stocks.

The book also states that, in the presence of variability, there are only three buffers available to synchronize demand and transformation with lowest cost and highest service level:

▶ Capacity

▶ Inventory

▶ Response time

The book states that its approach enables practical, predictive understanding of flows and stocks and how to best use the three levers to optimally synchronize demand and transformation.

Ed Pound from Factory Physics Inc. co-authored the book *Factory Physics for Managers*, in which he says that to achieve excellent cash flow and customer service using your current IT system and data (including SAP software), you should be required to execute on three things:

▶ Operations science

▶ An understanding of performance boundaries

▶ Good management control

The following subsection explains how to include these in your materials planning system.

12.3.1 Operations Science within a Framework of Demand and Transformation

Fundamentally, Factory Physics considers all values streams and processes to be made up of elements of either demand or transformation. Because transformation can be regarded as supply, it's made up of the structural elements of stocks and flows. Figure 12.12 represents a simple diagram of stocks and flows.

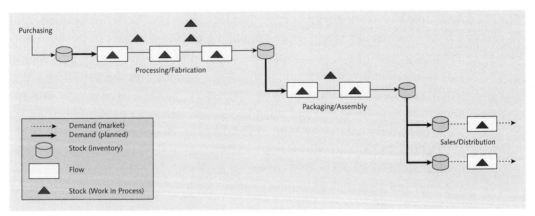

Figure 12.12 Demand and Transformation – Stock and Flow Diagram

Market demand usually pulls product out of stock while a planned demand had filled the same stock beforehand (this represents an MTS strategy). The stocks in the diagram are accumulation points where products are stored between flows. These products may be finished goods, intermediates, or raw materials but other than work in process (WIP), a stock is inventory managed by SAP ERP. There must be a material master record for the product that is stored in a stock, and transactions need to be executed (goods receipts and goods issues) to manage the levels. Flows then include resources such as machines and people (capacity) and WIP.

> **Note**
>
> It's imperative to understand that WIP isn't a managed inventory but rather an element that is part of a flow. WIP is often measured in a time unit (hours, days) and therefore can easily be related to a rate.

One of Factory Physics' main premises is the existence of the following:

> *…very specific practical, mathematical relationships that enable one to describe and control the performance of stocks and flows. In the presence of variability there are*

only three buffers available to synchronize demand and transformation with highest cash flow and service level: capacity, inventory and time.

This represents the core message from Factory Physics, which we want to carry over into our efforts to optimize materials planning with SAP ERP: when trying to find the optimal replenishment policy in the face of variability, find the best buffer combination among response time, safety stock, and extra capacity.

According to Factory Physics, rather than looking at each buffer individually, you achieve much better results when combining the three buffers in the most optimal arrangement. Take, as an example, the buffer time, which develops as soon as you have variability in your supplier lead time. Sometimes the parts arrive after five days, and sometimes they arrive after seven. As we all know, SAP ERP systems work with fixed replenishment lead times, which act as an offset from the required delivery date in the MRP run so that a purchase order's start date can be determined. In SAP ERP, this offset is maintained in the PLANNED DELIVERY TIME in the material master's MRP 2 screen. Because you can only maintain one value, and your suppliers deliver with variability, some people consider this a flaw of the SAP ERP software.

However, because we can consider time as a buffer (one out of three), we may use the value in the PLANNED DELIVERY TIME field as a parameter that works in combination with another parameter (e.g., DYNAMIC SAFETY STOCK in the range of coverage profile) to build a policy that includes a buffering strategy (combination of the time and inventory buffers).

In this example, you can see how taking a different point of view—using SAP ERP for parameter optimization rather than viewing it as forcing you to do business a certain way (which you do when you look at the PLANNED DELIVERY TIME field value as an isolated determinant of a single purchase order start date)—can suddenly transform perception (and set right the purpose) of the SAP suite of software from "business process has to change to fit the business" to "optimize parameters to resourcefully buffer variability automatically, efficiently and under constantly changing conditions." Maybe this is another mental model we just broke down.

12.3.2 Performance Boundaries

We've discussed the importance of knowing performance boundaries of your system in Chapter 11. Without knowledge of boundaries and not operating inside, you're basically shooting from the hip. Performance boundaries frame your operations with doable activities and improvement programs. Factory Physics provides thought processes with which you can easily quantify the limits you may operate under. Three steps to determine boundaries are worth mentioning:

1. Define what is best possible outcome for a given demand, demand variability, product mix, and process complexity (the maximum possible performance).

2. Define where you're performing today, compared to the best possible outcome (your actual performance to achieve a given service level with the inventory you're holding).

3. Define improvement activities, and quantify the associated dollar savings (close the gap).

When engaging in the optimization of your materials planning, go through these steps because you don't want to waste your money on unstructured, half-hearted, and short-lived inventory optimization projects that promise quick rewards on low-hanging fruit. Factory Physics provides excellent methods and systems to identify your best possible performance as well as to know your current place. It doesn't matter what tools or software you use; the corollaries are system agnostic and therefore easily adoptable to your SAP policies and planning transactions. Factory Physics distinguishes here again between stocks and flows.

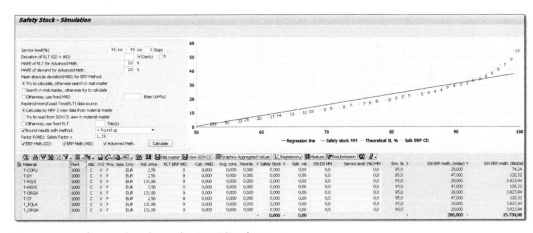

Figure 12.13 Safety Stock and Reorder Point Simulator

For stock points, Factory Physics uses the *efficient frontier curve*. Originally introduced by Harry Markowitz, efficient frontiers in portfolio management mark the border to its highest level of return for the minimum level of risk. In an efficient frontier curve, you can then plot for each expected service level the least amount of inventory needed to achieve that service level for a group of materials. The SAP add-on tool Safety Stock and Reorder Point Simulator allows for such visualization and determination of stock performance boundaries (see Figure 12.13).

For flows, we can refer to what Factory Physics calls *flow benchmarking*. For a production flow, as an example, we're concerned about having minimal cycle time with maximum throughput. A flow benchmarking diagram shows the dynamics described and formulated by Little's Law. The formula can be articulated as follows:

$$WIP \text{ (work in process)} = TH \text{ (throughput)} \times CT \text{ (cycle time)}$$

With this formula, we can measure two of the variables and calculate the third. This provides a number of opportunities as shown in Figure 12.14.

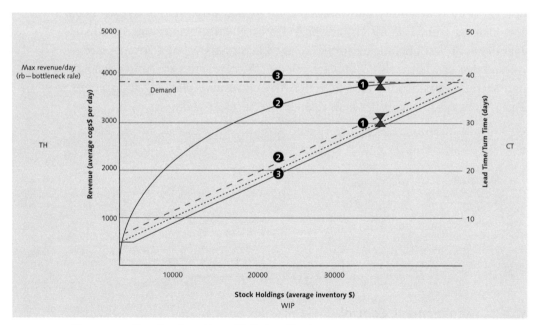

Figure 12.14 Flow Benchmarking with Factory Physics

In Figure 12.14, maximum performance is represented by the straight line going across on top of the screen. The line was determined by measuring the maximum throughput that is possible with the given capacity available and measuring the raw processing time it would take to produce a product with absolutely no variability present. Knowing the two variables maximum throughput and minimum cycle time, we were able to use Little's Law to calculate the minimum WIP necessary.

$$minWIP = maxTH \times minCT$$

Using this formula, we were able to plot the maximum performance boundary that we can never achieve because there is no real-life system without variability.

Using the same formula, but considering the presence of a fairly large amount of variability, we then plotted what Factory Physics calls the *practical worst case*. Its resulting plot can be seen as a curve somewhat far below the best case. You can now determine your own performance using Little's Law and your current measures for throughput and cycle time.

If you find yourself in the area between the practical worst case and the best possible performance, you're operating in the lean zone. However, if your performance indicates you're below the PWC (practical worst case) curve, improvement activities must be defined to move up and left in terms of WIP or stock holdings.

But beware, as shown clearly in Figure 12.14, a blind inventory reduction (moving plot point ❶ to plot point ❷) also brings with it a reduction of throughput, which might be devastating to your career. It becomes obvious that only a combination of inventory reduction and variability reduction (better scheduling methods, better policy, and/or improvement of supplier reliability) results in improved performance (moving to plot point ❸).

Generally speaking, if your improvement activities do get you from plot point 1 to plot point 3, you're effectively reducing inventories, cutting down on cycle time, meeting planned demand, and raising your throughput all at the same time. That is undoubtedly a more efficient approach to optimization than any promise to quickly save a few bucks with a shady approach to inventory reduction.

12.3.3 Management Control

If you want to evaluate the performance of different organizational units (finance, HR, planning), and your organization as a whole as to the strategies employed and agreed upon, you need to apply some sort of management control. Management control is concerned with coordination, resource allocation, motivation, and performance measurement and evaluation. The practice of management control and the design of management control systems draw upon a number of academic disciplines, including Factory Physics.

For good management control, Factory Physics considers three elements as essential and proposes to tie these together using an IT system:

- Strategy
- Policy
- Control and execution

The elements need to be linked, but very often they aren't. Many times SAP ERP systems are used to carry out transactions only, but nowhere is a translation from strategy to execution found. This represents a major problem with the use of SAP software. Strategy design is considered an activity that has no place in an IT system, and therefore planners, schedulers, and buyers aren't even aware of the strategic intent and work toward very different goals.

Following is a brief description of how strategy and execution can be connected so that the strategic goals are known and executed upon:

1. Pick a point that lies within your performance boundaries. This represents a strategic decision.
2. Generate and set the policy that follows the strategic decision.
3. Monitor the system via exception messages, and expedite when necessary.

To sum it up, good management control becomes visible in your organization when planners, buyers, schedulers, and management all work toward a given strategic direction (and not everybody in their own silo to the best of their potentially limited knowledge about the whole). Strategic direction is accomplished when the defined goal is determined by a point *within* the system's boundaries (and not somewhere out there in wishful thinking). According to that strategy, all the detailed policies are used to drive individual resources (materials, humans, suppliers) toward the achievement of those goals. And, finally, there is a monitoring system in place to ensure that variability and uncertainty don't get the best of us.

If you adhere to these guidelines and principles, you'll achieve standardization, automation visibility, and great performance and efficiency in planning *and* execution.

12.3.4 Some Basic Factory Physics Principles

Factory Physics relies primarily on three basic formulas:

▶ **Little's Law**
Relates basic plant performance measures through the formula *work in process = cycle time x throughput*. You need to know only two variables to calculate a third one. As actual cycle time is hard to measure, the formula is mostly used for calculating cycle time with a measured WIP level and known throughput.

▶ **VUT or Kingman's equation**
Quantifies queueing effects and relates variability, capacity, and time buffers. Strategists can define and determine policy to drive goals operating within a company's performance boundaries. The formula reads as $CTq = V \times U \times T$ and is mostly used for buffering strategies in Inventory Management.

▶ **Variance of lead time demand**
Drives inventory and service, and also accounts for variability in demand *and* supply. As the lead time gets longer, the chance of varying demand gets higher, but there are supply chains where a short lead time opens up for variability to creep in at a high rate, which has a devastating effect on supply chains. In particular, firms usually prefer to have a longer, more reliable lead time rather than a shorter, more variable lead time.

According to Factory Physics, appropriate use of these principles provides predictive control and optimal performance. They ought to be used as they are applicable. Just knowing that they exist will provide a huge advantage for you to take on any improvement project in your organization.

12.4 SAP Value Stream Mapping

We all know value stream maps and why they're so helpful in the visualization of material and information flow. As shown in the example in Figure 12.15, typically in a values stream map the customer of the stream is placed to the right, and the vendors are shown on the left. Information then flows from right to left, and materials flow from left to right. At the bottom, usually lead and cycle times are identified so that you get a complete picture of a product group's value chain.

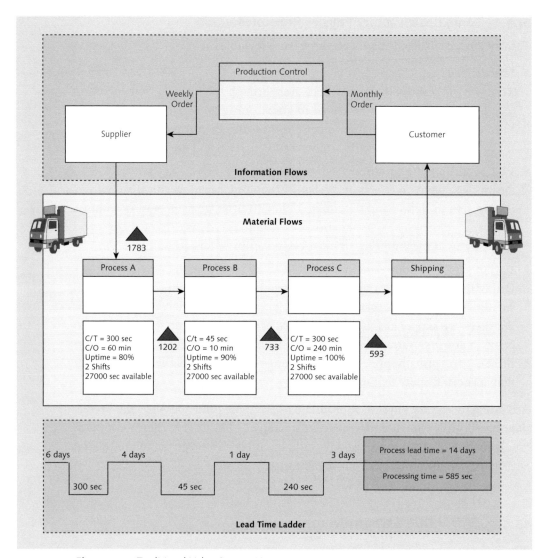

Figure 12.15 Traditional Value Stream Map

Value stream maps come from the world of lean and therefore they are meant to primarily reduce waste. However, we can also derive very valuable information about the degree of flow in the chain, WIP levels, and the functions used to control the processes that are employed in the system.

In our system of effective materials planning, we've developed a number of standard value stream maps that may be used as a template. We distinguish these according to the planning strategy (MTS versus MTO, etc.)

Figure 12.16 provides an example for a template of a standard MTS stream, where finished goods are delivered from the warehouse. The goods were manufactured to a forecast ahead of the sales order calling for it.

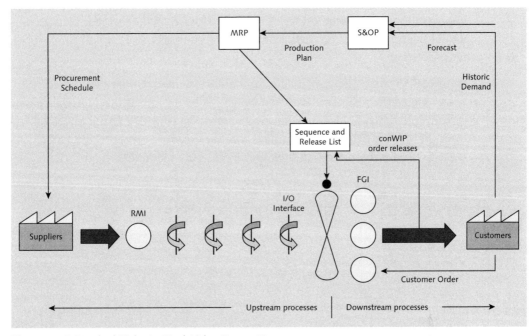

Figure 12.16 Standard Make-to-Stock Value Stream Map

Figure 12.17 shows a template for an MTO value stream. Other than in the previous example, the goods are only manufactured when a sales order is present. That is why the lead time to the customer is longer, but the finished goods inventory level is nonexistent.

Figure 12.18 depicts a mix of the two maps discussed before. The finish-to-order (FTO) process pulls the goods to be finished from an inventory/order interface and manufactures semi-finished materials into inventory so they can be made available when needed for an incoming sales order.

Next, we want to introduce the 'SAP' in SAP value stream mapping. In many of the optimization programs we execute with our clients, we create an SAP value stream map first. This has a number of advantages because you can pinpoint opportunities for improvements easily and mark them right down on the map. The flow of materials can be improved through, for example, more fitting scheduling methods, the inventory/order interface placed at its optimum point in the value chain, and inventory levels evaluated through the KPI range of coverage and the lead times from suppliers and internal production lines. Maybe the most important opportunity in SAP value stream maps lies in the fact that you can document the basic data and transactional data setup that is necessary to support better processes.

Figure 12.19 shows how such data can be documented. Under the inventory triangle, we can place a box with the policy to be set up in the material master record. Individual field values can be shown such as MRP TYPE, LOT SIZE PROCEDURE, or STRATEGY GROUP. The same is true for the work center record whose box is placed under the corresponding operation in the manufacturing process.

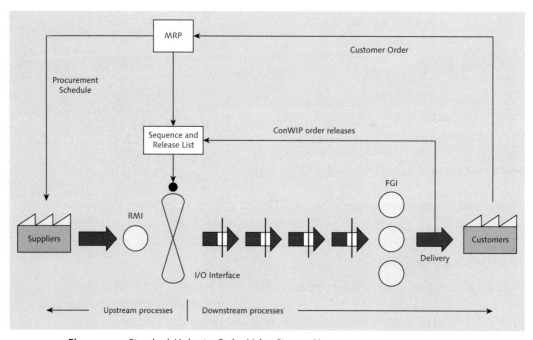

Figure 12.17 Standard Make-to-Order Value Stream Map

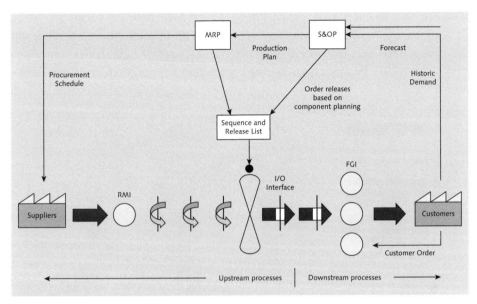

Figure 12.18 Standard Finish-to-Order Value Stream Map

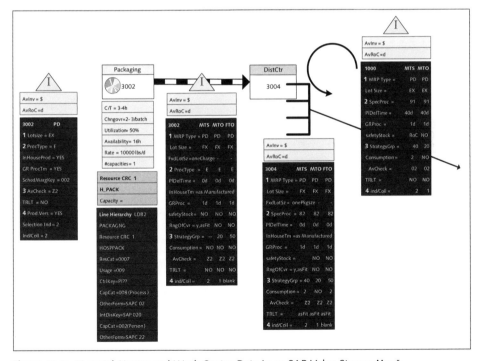

Figure 12.19 Material Master and Work Center Data in an SAP Value Stream Map*

481

You can also define and document functions and transactions on an SAP value stream map. SOP, MRP, production scheduling, and procurement are all driven by transactions and the way they're executed. Figure 12.20 shows how those transactions may be carried out by the user to follow a standard operating procedure.

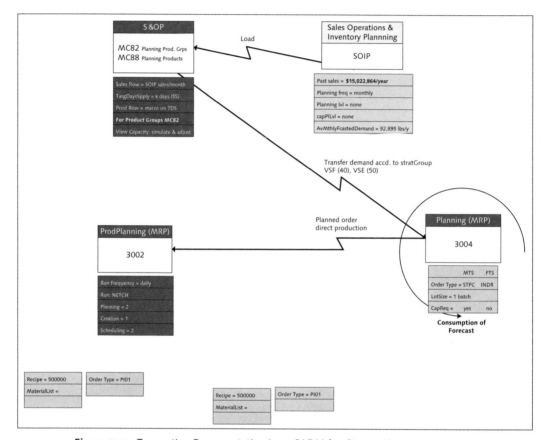

Figure 12.20 Transaction Documentation in an SAP Value Stream Map

Besides documenting data and transactions, you can also describe process and subsequently improve on the same with an SAP value stream map. Take, for example, the opportunity to introduce an FTO strategy with the goal to reduce the lead time to the customer, limit the amount of finished goods inventory required, and increase agility to changing market demands. After you identify the value chain and product group for the stream in question, the placement of the inventory/order interface (the point where MTO meets MTS) can be found by studying, evaluating, and scrutinizing the SAP value stream map.

Figure 12.21 shows an example of the placement of the inventory/order interface.

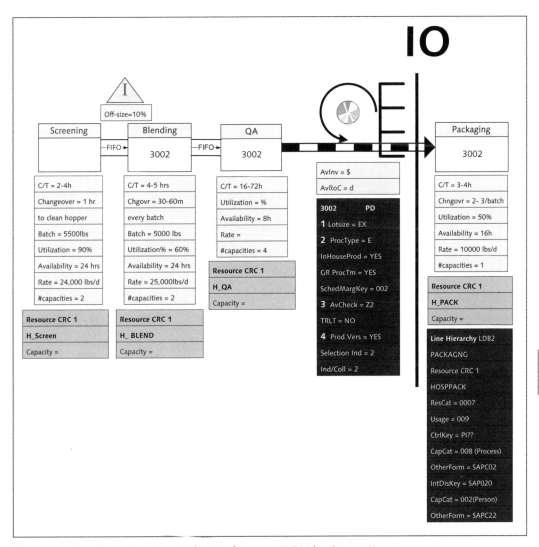

Figure 12.21 Defining an Inventory/Order Interface in an SAP Value Stream Map

SAP value stream maps can become quite comprehensive, as Figure 12.22 shows. Nevertheless it may become your documentation of choice in an otherwise widely disjointed definition of a supply chain optimization project. We usually print a poster of the map and work on it with the group. Anything can be written down on the map and later digitalized.

Don't even try to read the SAP value stream map depicted in Figure 12.22. It's for large-scale printing only and fully serves its purpose when using Visio or some other charting software.

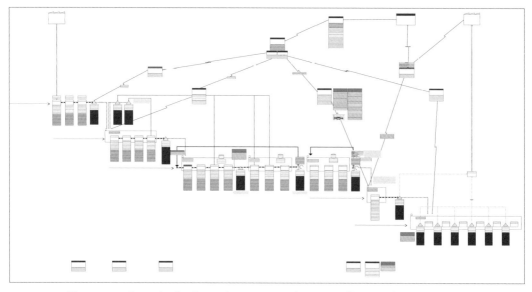

Figure 12.22 Example of a Comprehensive Map That Is Usually Printed on a Large-Scale Poster*

Because value stream mapping serves as the preferred tool of choice for lean practitioners, SAP value stream mapping may become an instrument for design, improvement, and standardization of SAP-driven supply chains. Simply add SAP data and process definitions to an existing value stream map and off you go with a central object of reference.

12.5 Summary

Science has been a bit neglected in our efforts to implement SAP software to run OM or, generally speaking, our supply chain. To put some proven theories at work to improve productivity and efficiency can't be wrong. And there is plenty to go around as some of these theories have been around for a very long time and are proven to work over and over. It's just that we need to do some thinking regarding how best to apply them in our SAP-driven supply chain.

System thinking, Factory Physics, the general principles of OM, or a new way of looking at a value stream map are just a few ideas that are worth exploring further.

With all the troubles prevailing in today's SAP-supported processes, it's certainly worth the effort to fall back on some proven theories and maybe try out something new.

Business is about being the best that you can be, and there are always glowing examples of people that we can all learn from.
—John Caudwell

13   Examples from Industry

Every company, sooner or later, will embark on an inventory optimization initiative. Very often, this comes about because leadership feels that inventory holdings will have to be reduced as they look at financial reporting and building new budgets toward the end of the year. A one-sided effort with a reduction of inventory value will never produce the desired results of increasing productivity because, in most cases, the inventory reduction will have an immediate negative impact on parts availability for the production lines. And with an increase of stock-outs comes a decrease of revenue because you don't have much inventory of finished goods to sell to your customers on time.

Therefore, it's of utmost importance to define appropriate goals and design the proper program to achieve better service and have enough inventory of the required parts and less inventory of the slow-moving or nonmoving parts.

In the following, we present some of those customers who have been very successful by implementing a system of effective materials planning. These companies have not only experienced better inventory and service levels but also achieved sustainability in the process. And sustainability in the process is probably even more important than a one-time optimization of stock turns, averages, and dead stock values.

13.1   Continuous and Sustainable Optimization at Tennant Company

The Tennant Company, a leading manufacturer of indoor and outdoor cleaning machines, is headquartered in Minneapolis, Minnesota, and has production facilities in Minnesota, Michigan, The Netherlands, Scotland, China, and Brazil. Tennant also operates a warehouse and distribution center in Louisville, Kentucky.

The process of building these machines can best be described as various value streams where fabrication turns raw materials (primarily sheets of steel) into semifinished structural components. These components are then assembled, together with thousands of purchased parts, into finished cleaning machines. Therefore, the Tennant Company may easily be compared to an automaker.

Like a car, Tennant's cleaning machines have wheels, consoles, a chassis, steering, and a seat. There are also brushes, holding tanks for water and detergents, complex electrical wiring, and motors that keep things moving. As you might imagine, many parts make up a cleaning machine, and to stay competitive and provide value to its customers, Tennant offers quite a selection of different models of all sizes and uses. Additionally, customers can pick many options and features to customize just the machine they like.

All of this, however, requires a lot of discipline, capability, and manual labor to keep inventories low and availability to the production lines high. Complexity is high and with it variability comes into play, making it difficult to efficiently plan and manage parts replenishment. Another complication in the area of planning materials comes from the customers' requests for quick delivery of spare parts. These aftermarket parts are held in a large warehouse in the United States as well as in Europe, Asia, North America, and South America locally for fast delivery. To manage the huge volumes and complexities, Tennant decided to acquire SAP software to better run its operations.

The implementation was done in the early 2000s, and rollouts took place to the various sites. Much like many SAP implementations, the project was constrained by time, budget, and specific knowledge about SAP functionality, so that it became difficult to immediately make full use of what SAP's materials planning has to offer. Time passed, processes and people changed, and it became obvious that there was more to materials planning than just the functionality the planners were taught to use many years ago. It also turned out that inventory holdings in the Louisville warehouse increased, and stock-outs still happened.

Something had to be done, and people started to wonder (rightfully so) why the expensive implementation of SAP software hadn't take care of the problems. Then the consultants came in. Promises were made, money was spent, and optimization programs came and went, but there was no tangible improvement. And worst, no one could tell why these programs, that Tennant spent so much money on, didn't produce the promised results. Some very motivated staff took matters in their own hands and went on to see what could be done to optimize the supply chain on their own. One of the most important insights was to see that a tool (such as SAP software) is just that—a tool—nothing more and nothing less. If things needed to get better, the process and some perceived mental models would have to change.

And so the Tennant staff evaluated the way business was performed repeatedly on a daily basis. Standard operating procedures providing a common approach to exception monitoring, policy setting, and inventory optimization were perceived to make things better. Rather than chasing individual orders, buffers were designed and made available for planning and consumption.

The inefficiencies were found in a lack of managing groups of parts. Before, the planners separated the items that were perceived as more important from the rest. They monitored and maintained these important items one by one and, being short of time, filled up inventories of the others so that the dreaded stock-outs didn't happen. All of this resulted in high inventory levels and lots of transactional work. The planner's day was filled with expediting, rescheduling, calling suppliers, receiving and answering email from the shop floor about missing parts, and maintaining an incredible amount of Microsoft Excel spreadsheets. Rest assured, every planner came up with his own system of "ineffective" materials planning.

Every now and then, members of staff attended a training class—mostly on SAP master data and sometimes on procurement or forecasting best practices. The Tennant planner became very competent and proficient in maintenance of the SAP material master, creating inforecords, using a forecast maintained in Transaction MD61 and most prominently in the use and interpretation of Transaction MD02 (Stock/Requirements List). The planners were confident that they did the right thing; however, the warehouse was full of parts and spares to the max. At the same time, there were plenty of failed availability checks. What was wrong? No one could tell. The planners knew so much about SAP functionality, and, yet, there were so many parts with too much stock lying around unconsumed or too little inventory when it was needed most.

What followed then was another initiative with external consultants to further deepen the knowledge and competency in planning and master data setup. The four MRP screens in the material master were dealt with one by one, and all the fields were explored, explained, and further customized with more options. New MRP types were investigated (such as V2 or VV), optimizing lot-size procedures were used, and range of coverage profiles were added so that safety stocks became more dynamic and in line with growing or shrinking demand.

So much more was taught, trained, simulated, and executed that eventually the planners complained about spending more time on trial and error than they did on planning and ordering. Frustration kicked in. Not because the learning didn't provide the desired effect, but because the workload was rising up to the impossible. Analyzing one specific material according to its value (ABC), consumption consistency (XYZ), replenishment lead time, and lifecycle took one person at least two hours. To then make a decision on a replenishment procedure and set it up in the materials master record required at list one more hour. So with one material, it took the planner half of his day to set the supporting data right for automation. The rest of the day was spent checking on how the newly updated replenishment process worked for those items that were updated last week. And many times, it didn't work out at all. There is so much variability in this world that when you try a policy on one single material and watch the result over time, chances are that something happened that makes you believe the policy didn't work. Only when you take a whole group of materials with a similar classification can tell if the policy works or if it doesn't.

To make a very long, frustrating story short, neither the individual planners nor Tennant's management was content with the results and wished they would have spent their money on something more useful. However, in retrospect and considering what happened next, everyone would probably agree that the education on master data and more automated procedures was neither a waste of money nor a waste of time. It was an absolute necessary exercise to set the stage for better things to come.

And better times did come with the SAP add-on tools. We've explained the SAP add-on tools in several chapters during the course of this book, and by now you know that they're developed by SAP for SAP mainly, but not exclusively, for SAP ERP (there are also add-on tools for SAP Advanced Planning & Optimization [SAP APO]). These tools do a number of things. For one, many of them act as a cockpit of transactions, meaning that you no longer have to toggle from one transaction to the next because you get all the information in one place. For example, the Inventory Controlling Cockpit provides a tabular view of all inventory key performance indicators (KPIs) available in the Logistics Information System (LIS) and allows for sorting, filtering, aggregation, and dis-aggregation of various objects; all kinds of period comparisons are possible. The IOC (SAP add-on tool, Inventory Controlling Cockpit) also includes powerful graphics that provide valuable insight to stock and inventory performance.

But Tennant didn't start there. They first acquired the MRP Monitor with a Lot Size Simulation Tool and the Safety Stock and Reorder Point Simulator, which calculates safety stocks and reorder points automatically. This set of SAP add-on tools added much-needed functionality (classification into six dimensions, filtering, sorting, aggregation), provided an enormous amount of automation, and, most important of all, gave Tennant a way to update policy and keep the master data straight for many, many materials with the push of a button—all with utmost control over the planner's portfolio.

The MRP Monitor classifies materials into specific buckets according to value, price, predictability, replenishment lead time, volume, and lifecycle. You can then take an entire group of materials that were similarly classified and update the entire group with a fitting policy (master data setup). Should the group be updated with a reorder policy, you can pull the entire cluster into the Safety Stock and Reorder Point Simulator to determine the optimal safety stock levels and reorder points for a subsequent automated update into the material master record.

All of a sudden, most of the frustration was gone (not all of it right away), but there were still some questions that had to be answered: How often do we run the classification? Isn't it dangerous to update many materials all at the same time? What if the policy doesn't work?

Even more questions are raised when, after years of setting up master data manually one by one with limited knowledge about specific field values, the planner is told to run a program that does it for him. The planner's hesitation here is quite understandable. However, when you have to make a choice about which 50 materials you're watching closely and which materials out of your portfolio you must leave unattended because you don't have enough time in the day, then you might wonder what harm can come from taking the hundreds of materials that were clearly classified as cheap (50 cents each), were consumed regularly (almost the exact same consumption every week), and have an order time of less than a week and updating them with a reorder point procedure where for each individual material, an optimum reorder point is calculated based on an agreed-upon service level. No human can do this as fast or with the same precision as the machine can do it for you.

Tennant now began to implement the four pillars of effective materials planning: prioritized portfolio management, automated and periodic policy setting, intelligent exception monitoring, and eventually continuous inventory optimization. In portfolio management, the bucketizing concept was adopted, and each planner had three MRP controller keys to work with. Nonmoving and very slow-moving items were filtered out with the use of the MRP Monitor and subsequently provided with a newly created policy. The policy for the slow movers was defined as plan on demand (MRP type PD) and no stock holdings—neither in safety stock nor in a reorder point procedure. This ensured that a very large portion of the materials planner's portfolio was kept in an MRP controller bucket that the planner didn't have to watch every day.

All remaining items were put into bucket number 2, and the tactical materials planner started analyzing and providing each part with a fitting policy. By using the MRP Monitor, policy setting could be done per segmentation and classification, and large groups of materials were all set up with the best possible policy. Every time a material (or group of materials) was provided with a fitting policy, these materials were also moved into the MRP controller bucket 3. So eventually bucket 3 contained all materials that were important to the success of inventory optimization, and they had to be watched very carefully. Therefore, exception monitoring was executed on that bucket every morning with a well-defined prioritized process of exception monitoring. Whenever a policy didn't produce good results, the planner was alerted through exception messages and was able to cure the situation through fine-tuning of the policy. If that didn't work, the material was placed back into bucket 2 and dealt with at some other time.

So the method was clear, it just needed to be documented to provide standardization. To that extent, Tennant drew up a chart with the frequency and sequence of the various activities to perform effective materials planning.

Figure 13.1 shows that the Material Document Analysis (MDA), the task to build consumption and receipt history for each part, had to be run initially for the past 24 months. Thereafter, a job to append the last month's history was to be run every fifth day of the new month.

Next, Tennant had to decide how often a classification or segmentation should be executed. Nobody wants to classify and reclassify a portfolio too often. A monthly look at whether a material's past consumption was regular or not proved to be sufficient, but in the end, Tennant decided that looking at classification every quarter is enough detail. However, to provide enough information for the Inventory Controlling Cockpit, a monthly MRP Monitor run was necessary.

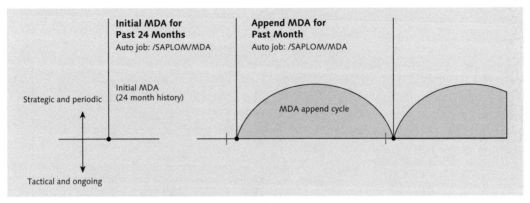

Figure 13.1 Frequency to Run Material Document Analysis

As shown in Figure 13.2 the MRP Monitor run was saved every month for the IOC, but classification and segmentation was saved in the material master record only every quarter.

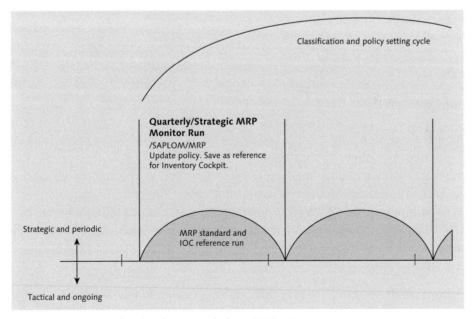

Figure 13.2 Frequency for Classification with the MRP Monitor

493

Finally, all the tasks of tactical materials planning were added to the model as shown in Figure 13.3.

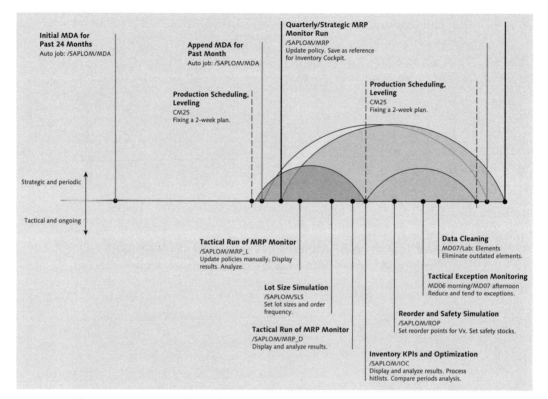

Figure 13.3 Putting It All Together

Because all the tasks, periodicity, and frequency were added to the chart, Tennant formulized, documented, and made perfectly clear how a system of effective materials planning can be rolled out to every plant in every country to ensure that the planners were all doing the same thing. Most importantly, measurements were harmonized, which clearly showed what was successful and what wasn't. Additionally, if something turned out ineffective, everybody knew what to do about it, and the addition of user guidelines, policy playbooks, and regular meetings ensured clear and effective communication and standards.

Figure 13.4 shows a summarized chart of the typical tasks executed by a strategic planner and a tactical planner in a system of effective MRP. Tennant today enjoys a standardized approach to materials planning where leadership can gain quick and true insights into the effectiveness of the supply chain, and they have a solid basis to make effective decisions that are clearly communicated to the planners. Through the use of performance boundaries, user guidelines, and control limits, the actions to continuously optimize service and inventory levels are clearly defined, and even though the planner can still enjoy creative use of the tools made available to them through the system, its boundaries are clearly defined so that standardization and comparability is given.

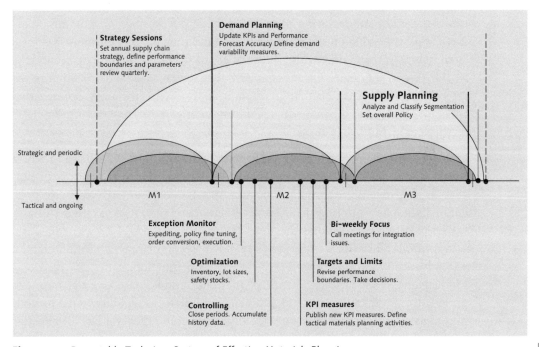

Figure 13.4 Repeatable Tasks in a System of Effective Materials Planning

Tennant and its people have been pioneers in the area of effective materials planning, the use of performance guidelines, and building policy playbooks for SAP supply chains (hard to believe when you consider how long SAP inventory optimization has been around). The company still blazes trails for other companies to follow its high achievements in terms of standardization, automation, and efficiency in materials replenishment and providing availability of spare parts using SAP ERP. The planners from Tenant Company are living and successful proof that there is much more to effective materials planning than simply buying the software (the tool) and implementing it.

13.2   Plant Transformation at ASEA Brown Boveri

ASEA Brown Boveri (ABB), headquartered in Zurich, Switzerland, is operating mainly in the power, robotics, and automation technology areas. ABB is one of the largest engineering company conglomerates in the world. ABB has operations in around 100 countries, with approximately 150,000 employees in November 2013, and reported global revenue of $40 billion for 2011.

Using SAP ERP software for, among many other things, materials planning, ABB has about 400 manufacturing plants worldwide purchasing and holding inventory for parts needed on the manufacturing lines to make transformers, gas-insulated switchgear, and many other finished goods for its customer base around the world. One of the main objectives at ABB was to achieve standardization in the replenishment process, so that a common approach to inventory optimization could be provided to the individual plants operating in different cultures with different people, but using the same SAP software.

In early 2014, I met with some ABB managers from Europe, Asia, and North America for a two-day workshop to explore some options in the area of purchased parts inventory optimization. An SAP sales representative was also present to discuss new offerings in SAP software functionality. ABB has used SAP software for a long time, and at the time of the meeting, SAP ERP was rolled out across almost all business units in pretty much all countries where ABB operates. SAP advanced planning with SAP APO was also functional, and the then-new product Integrated Business Planning (IBP), alongside SmartOps, was meant to provide the silver bullet for some problems with parts availability to the production lines, high inventory on slow-moving parts, and a general lack of effective planning procedures and policies.

It quickly became blatantly obvious that the solution to the problem could be found in the implementation of a system of standardization, scientific framework of reference, and the building of competence in the use and application of all the tools already available to the materials planner. ABB's managers wanted to capitalize on the already quite large investment they had made in all the software currently available.

So we went on to explore alternatives to the strategy of implementing new technology. What seemed to be a good idea at the time was to come up with a standard method of materials planning that could be rolled out to each plant in the same manner with education and training on the four pillars of effective materials planning. Next we worked on a definition of scope, selection of the right tools and functionality, and the design of an effective training program to transfer knowledge and then to finally start implementing the package.

A roadmap was developed as shown in Figure 13.5. The roadmap basically is a transformation with three on-site workshops, remote support, documentation, and a measuring system to determine the KPIs that would guarantee success and measure the same in the beginning, during, and after the transformation.

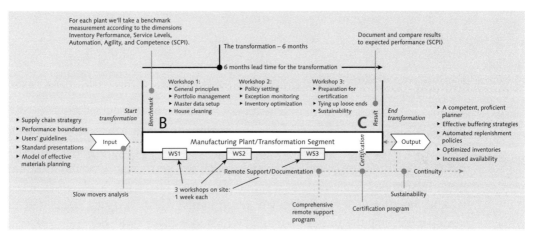

Figure 13.5 Standard Transformation Activities at ABB

As the top measure, we identified inventory turns. Because inventory turns are determined by the formula turns = consumption ÷ average inventory, the options for improvement are to either increase consumption or to lower the averages. Increasing consumption is a hard thing to do and doesn't really make sense. So we decided that bringing averages down could do a lot of good, and the best way to measure success is to look at the resulting change in inventory turns, which will hopefully increase.

So ABB went on a mission to use the principles (and four pillars) of effective materials planning in many of its production facilities so that turns go up, better tools are used, and competence in using the tools rises to a high level for sustainability and effectiveness of the model. A pilot site was chosen, and one of the first actions taken was to implement a series of meetings with a frequency that guarantees good communication of a well-designed supply chain or inventory strategy. Figure 13.6 provides an example of such a meeting series within the model of planning horizons.

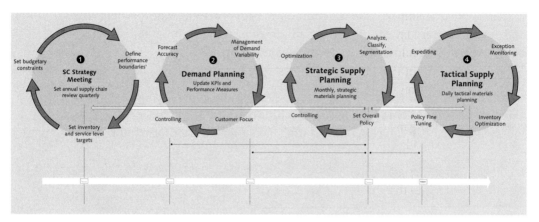

Figure 13.6 Series of Meetings and Planning Horizons to Improve the Communication of a Supply Chain Strategy

Before the supply chain strategy could be communicated, it had to be defined. ABB's pilot site for the transformation in Mount Pleasant, Pennsylvania, did so by putting together user guidelines, which contained performance boundaries and buffering options. They also put together a standard policy playbook with a set of replenishment policies and detailed descriptions. All of this was presented to leadership during the strategy meeting, which took place at the beginning of each fiscal year. Leadership could then have a look at the proposed Service Level Agreements (SLAs), customer lead times to be published, and prioritization of the buffers inventory, time, and capacity—and then sign off on their favorite version.

With leadership approval and direction in place, the materials planners now had guidance regarding how to set up sales availability checking rules, the way demand was transferred (make-to-stock [MTS] or make-to-order [MTO]), and what service level to achieve for a certain class of materials (e.g., AX). Getting such an agreement between planners and leadership has a number of great advantages, including providing clarity and easing decision making. For example, if it was agreed that AXE parts (high value, highly predictable, short replenishment lead time) are planned for a 96% service level, then it's perfectly clear that it's accepted to have stock-outs in up to 4% of the cases in which these parts are needed for the current production schedules. This is acceptable because, in turn, the company doesn't have to stock an exorbitant value of safety stock to guarantee 99% or even 100% service or availability.

Naturally if leadership wanted to know how well the planners performed (and how well inventory levels were planned), they had to look at classes of materials and compare the resulting service levels (or amount of stock-outs) to what was reasonably agreed on in the supply chain strategy. If, for example, the planner had only 3% stock-outs on materials requested with a 96% service level, the planner's evaluation should have been judged as better than expected. This is in very stark contrast to many organizations where planner performance—if measured at all—is confusing at best and doesn't provide any platform or basis for improvement.

Figure 13.7 provides an example of a service level grid in the user guidelines presented to leadership during the strategy meeting.

Service Levels for Reorder Points and Safety Stocks			
A	high consumption volume	80%	
B	medium consumption volume	15%	
C	low consumption value	5%	
X	low consumption variation in past	> 0.4	
Y	medium consumption variation in past		
Z	high consumption variation in past	< 1.5	
N	non-movers	no movements in past 12 months	
W	$	Less than 100	
V	$$		
U	$$$	From 500 to 1000	
	X	Y	Z	N
AU	94%	94%	94%	0%
AV	96%	96%	96%	0%
AW	98%	98%	98%	0%
B	98%	95%	80%	0%
C	99%	90%	85%	0%

Figure 13.7 Performance Boundaries for Service Levels to Determine Safety Stock Requirements

The planning group at Mount Pleasant also used the performance boundaries to set control limits for important parts. They established a grid that defined the upper- and lower control limits for inventory ranges. The example in Figure 13.8

shows how you can decide how much coverage should be provided as a maximum and as a minimum for classified groups of parts.

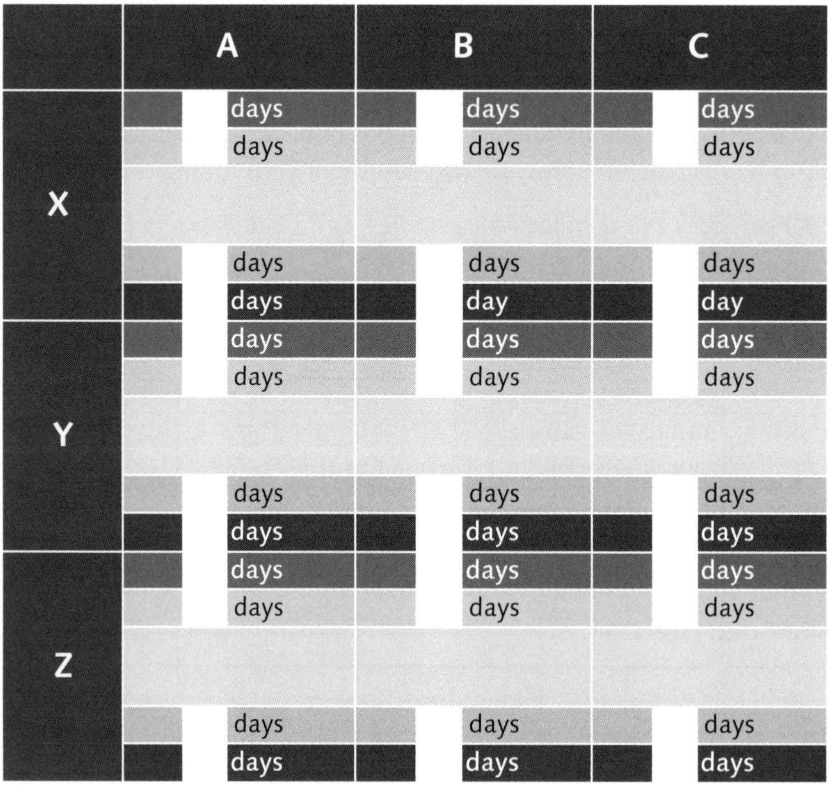

	A		B		C	
X		days		days		days
		days		days		days
Y		days		days		days
		days		day		day
		days		days		days
		days		days		days
Z		days		days		days
		days		days		days
		days		days		days
		days		days		days
		days		days		days
		days		days		days

Figure 13.8 Upper- and Lower Control Limits for Classified Parts*

You can then plot a graphic with historic inventory levels and overlay the control limits so it becomes clear how good or bad inventory performed in the past.

The control limits may also be visualized with the traffic light settings in Transaction MD07, so that the planner can see at a glance which parts are above or below the desired levels.

The story at ABB continues. What the Mount Pleasant team has achieved in a very short period of time has raised awareness, caused wonder (how did they do that?), and received praise all over the organization in many countries. The system was then packaged and is enjoying widespread application all over the board.

The planning team at Mount Pleasant has built an exceptional model for everybody else in the organization to use and they have done so with tremendous engagement, lots of experience and great detail, and, most importantly, with the greater goal of success for the entire organization in mind.

13.3   A Model for the Process Industry from Bellisio Foods

The process industry is defined by making products through a process (cooking, blending, etc.) rather than through assembly or a discrete transformation step. Typically, what a process manufacturer does can't be undone. You can't go backwards to make oranges from orange juice, and after beer has been brewed, there's no way to get the hops back. However, not every step in a process plant has to be done by a process order with a recipe. Take a food manufacturer, for example. In a cheese plant, you might have big blocks of cheddar that were processed in a container. These blocks are then cut, sliced, or grated to be packaged on a final assembly line. The cheese plant represents a hybrid of process-based and rate-based repetitive flow manufacturing.

A big differentiator of the process industry is that one deals with V-shaped bills of materials (BOMs), meaning that only few raw materials make up a large variety of finished goods.

Using a V-shaped BOM, as shown in Figure 13.9, materials planning becomes a bit less involved than it is with the A-shaped BOM that is typical for discrete manufacturing or assembly. However, in the process industry, the materials you're planning are mostly ingredients that have a shelf life and can't be stored for a long time. Planning accuracy is important, and SAP ERP and its MRP run doesn't take into account the fact that these purchased raw materials are perishable and have an expiration date for its latest, possible usage on the production line. Many third-party vendors offer solutions to this problem, and most of them integrate with standard SAP software. The actual resolving of the problem, as with most issues described in this book, lies with the definition of a good process and a subsequent implementation of the solution using the appropriate tool or functionality.

SAP software contains most (but surely not all) of the technological solutions you need, but if you pick the wrong option from the vast variety of available applications, you might break the integrational nature of the package and make it seem as if SAP software doesn't work for you. This is especially true when using discrete production orders in process manufacturing. When processing ingredients, very often a reaction happens that can only be described by a formula. When blending 50 pounds of one ingredient with 50 pounds of another ingredient using heat or some other catalyst, you might not get 100 pounds out of the container after it's processed. There are yields and outcomes from a chemical or physical reaction that are much better described in a recipe and executed with a process order.

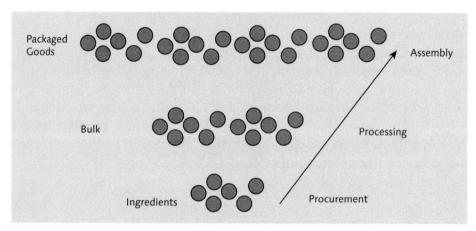

Figure 13.9 V-Shaped Bills of Materials in the Process Industry

If you're not doing this right, you'll get false and useless material requirements quantities, and planning for inventories becomes exponentially more difficult because you're also dealing with perishability and limited availability from shelf-life expirations. Additional tools are available on the market that can help you with planning for shelf life in MRP, but standard SAP ERP doesn't handle these issues.

Bellisio Foods in Minneapolis, Minnesota, is currently engaging in a transformation to use process orders where needed. This brings about tremendous improvement not only in materials planning but also with the new ability to use the "product wheel" concept for production scheduling. This will result in a more demand-driven, just-in-time production program that makes planning much more intuitive and automated and brings about the right materials (ingredients) at the right place in the right quantity at the right time. Bellisio is also using the SAP add-on tools for improved efficiency, automation, and accuracy of data and planning. The MRP Monitor will classify the materials portfolio on a monthly basis and allow a strategic materials planner to set overall policy. The Safety Stock and Reorder Point Simulator provides the ability to set appropriate service levels across the board so that optimum safety buffers can be designed. And the new SAP add-on tool Supply Chain Performance Monitor provides a customized KPI framework with which Bellisio is able to measure progress and define targeted activities for improvement in flow inventory performance and increased availability to the production lines as well as customers.

The transformation at Bellisio included not only materials planning but other activities such as planning and production scheduling, which were integrated into the overall model of SOP+. As shown in Figure 13.10, materials planning sits between the demand and supply gates in the overall model

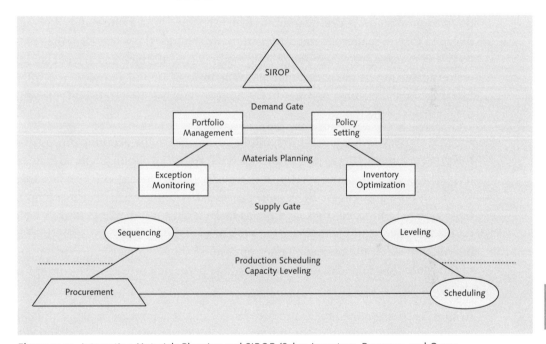

Figure 13.10 Integrating Materials Planning and SIROP (Sales, Inventory, Resource, and Operations Planning) into the Overall Model of SOP+

SOP+ can best be described as a way of thinking to join and connect planning (in phases) with the execution and manufacturing of said plan into optimum levels of inventory for great service levels to the customer.

Note

SOP+ is an extended model of sales and operations planning.

503

13.4 Lean Materials Planning with SAP at Kraft Foods

The process industry is more complex because flow isn't an optional requirement—it's mandatory. So to provide the right materials at the right place in the right quantity at the right time, a more advanced model is required. Kraft Foods had investigated a number of options to introduce more flow into the process and reduce the amount of transactional work required to plan for materials (ingredients) and execute processing on the shop floor. One of Kraft's cheese-processing plants acted as a vanguard for this initiative.

The first activity evolved around scheduling the packaging lines. Using SAP's tools for repetitive manufacturing, it was possible to schedule rates rather than discrete production order quantities, which resulted in a noise-reduced, flow-like, and easy-to-manage frozen production program for the week. Next the company had to make sure that enough bulk material (specific type and age of cheese) was available to run the packaging lines. The introduction of an inventory/order interface for an assemble-to-order (ATO) strategy was used to locate buffer inventory in front of the line.

An ATO strategy brings about tremendous advantages in the planning process for the process industry because it allows for the forecasting of bulk material instead of placing a plan on every variety of the packaged, finished good. The fact that you have only a few ingredients and processed bulk materials that make up a huge variety of finished, packaged goods make it almost impossible to plan well on the SKU level. But planning on the bulk level and placing an inventory buffer of bulk in front of the packaging lines opens up a huge number of opportunities to introduce flow and take the noise out of the packaging process. The concept is shown in Figure 13.11.

In an ATO strategy, the bulk is produced according to a forecast or plan and kept in inventory before the packaging lines. Any customer orders can now start the packaging process and pick the bulk inventory as required to finish and fulfill the actual demand.

Kraft Foods has achieved tremendous improvements in terms of flow, visibility, and plannability in its packaging lines. But the biggest advantages were realized in the ability to better process and age its bulk cheese at the right time in the right volume at the right place.

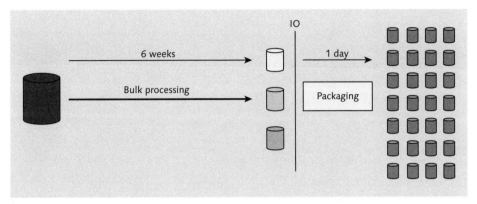

Figure 13.11 Postponement or Assemble-to-Order strategy with an Inventory/Order Interface

13.5 Summary

When looking at examples from real companies and how they advance their materials planning process, it's no surprise that an integrated approach to improvement service and inventories delivers much better results than an isolated view of how purchased parts or materials are replenished. A more thorough view of the impact of a production schedule, a finished goods forecast, or a well-defined planning strategy, outside the demand and supply gates of materials planning, provides great opportunities to generate better, more timely, and noise-reduced material requirements.

The repeating message this book delivers is that a holistic approach with standardized procedures and the use of the four pillars of effective materials planning will deliver results. As these examples provide proof· for, the magic happens when detailed and well-defined strategy is supported by efficient tools and is met by a proficient, motivated, and educated planner.

I don't believe there's anything in life you can't go back and fix. The ancient Vedas—the oldest Hindu philosophy—and modern science agree that time is an illusion. If that's true, there's no such thing as a past or future—it's all one huge now. So what you fix now affects the past and the future.
—Alan Arkin

14   Conclusion and Outlook

SAP, as a software company, will change. Materials planning will not. The basic premise will remain. Planners will continue trying to balance demand with supply in the most optimized way possible. The biggest challenge to delivering highest availability with lowest inventory holding will remain as variability in supply and demand. The world continues to become more complex and difficult to predict, which will not only increase variability but also, with the provision of more automation, technology, and faster processing of data, customers will demand faster turnarounds, more customized offerings, and cheaper prices. Can software vendors fulfill the promise of delivering more tools for better handling while working with these challenges?

Before answering this question, we should first look into whether the provision of new, faster, and more technologically advanced tools will provide the solution to the problems or if the answer possibly lies elsewhere. Think about it—what other software tools do we require to run effective materials planning? We can't think of any transaction, routine, or report that isn't already available today, which would improve the process of replenishing purchased parts inventory.

Although an XYZ analysis would be nice to have, and a cockpit with more information in one place (rather than toggling back and forth between transactions) would increase productivity, these are enhancements best provided on top of existing solutions we already own. They don't require new technology or new systems.

As SAP is continuing to develop new technology around SAP HANA, the cloud, and mobility, our future will change nevertheless. The 2015 SAPPHIRENOW conference in Orlando, Florida, made it clear that the future technology customers will buy from SAP is less functionality and more platform. The idea behind this strategy is to enable more flexibility, faster adoption, and less rigid standardization in the way we're using the tools to execute our process design today. The first customers adopting SAP S/4HANA (the new suite of software running on the superfast SAP HANA platform) will find little in the way of functionality and transactions at first. However, flexibility, technology, and guidance will abound to develop functionality and features never to be imagined before. Every company can develop its own customized solutions and, if done right, deal with every possible challenge in the most effective and efficient way. The possibilities are endless, and there is no more limit or rigidity to the way you can plan, execute, and monitor your supply chain.

But we have to get there first. What do we do until then? There will be trial and error, there will be mistakes from which we'll have to learn, and SAP S/4HANA is pretty slim in functionality at this moment. We can't just throw away what we have today to plan, transact, and move to something new, especially when we don't know exactly how it will turn out.

SAP S/4HANA will, no doubt, be the future of planning, but until it's matured and ripened to the degree that it makes our supply chain world better, we'll have to make sure we can keep on producing goods to sell to stay competitive and survive.

If new technology and its adoption are meant to drive the way we pursue "The Goal" as defined by Eliyahu Goldratt in his legendary book of the same name, than we're missing the point entirely. Technology never has, and never will, define the success of a manufacturing or service company on the market alone. However, people with the right process using the right technology have and always will.

For now, improve your process and help your people with enhanced functionality added to your existing tool. There is so much to improve and so much "low hanging fruit" to be picked up. Have a look at what the SAP add-on tools have to offer in conjunction with a better utilization of SAP ERP (the stuff you already own and paid for). There is much you can do in the area of building intuition for better decision making, and, for a long time to come, the generation of an efficient, sound, and productive supply plan will depend on good master data. SAP's promise of Integrated Business Planning (IBP) won't succeed without sound parameter optimization in SAP ERP 6.0.

Although these suggestions aren't popular with people who want to advance the world with new technology to make it faster, more flexible, and better looking, the suggestions are, at least to some degree, well received by people who continue to follow their quest of balancing supply with an ever-changing demand so that business value increases and customer service is improved. They pursue "The Goal" to generate profit now and in the future within the boundaries of ethical business practices.

A   Bibliography

Forrester, Jay Wright, *Industrial Dynamics* (Eastford, CT: Martino Fine Books, 2013).

Hopp, Wallace J., and Mark L. Spearman. *Factory Physics, 3rd Edition* (Long Grove, IL: Waveland Press, Inc., 2011).

Hopp, Wallace J., *Supply Chain Science* (Long Grove, IL: Waveland Press, Inc., 2011).

Meadows, Donella H., Diana Wright, *Thinking in Systems: A Primer* (White River Junction, VT: Chelsea Green Publishing, 2008).

Pink, Daniel, *A Whole New Mind: Why Right-Brainers Will Rule the Future* (New York City, NY: Riverhead Books, 2006).

Pound, Edward S., *Factory Physics for Managers: How Leaders Improve Performance in a Post-Lean Six Sigma World* (New York City, NY: McGraw-Hill Education, 2014).

Reynolds, Garr, Presentation Zen: *Simple Ideas on Presentation Design and Delivery, 2nd Edition* (San Francisco, CA: New Riders, 2011).

Schneider, David, "Systems Thinking and the Supply Chain." *We Are The Practitioners*. September 2013.

Senge, Peter M., *The Fifth Discipline: The Art & Practice of The Learning Organization* (New York City, NY: Doubleday, 2006).

Sterman, John D., *Business Dynamics: Systems Thinking and Modeling for a Complex World* (New York City, NY: McGraw-Hill Education, 2000).

B   The Author

Uwe Goehring is an SAP Mentor and has worked in supply chain optimization for more than 20 years. He is the founder and president of bigbyte software systems corporation, which optimizes SAP supply chains around the world by coaching planners, buyers, and schedulers in policy setting and strategic and tactical planning.

Index

T

Interested in reading more?

Please visit our website for all new book
and e-book releases from SAP PRESS.

www.sap-press.com